THE COMMON WEALTH

TREASURES FROM THE COLLECTIONS OF
THE LIBRARY OF VIRGINIA

THE COMMON WEALTH

TREASURES FROM THE COLLECTIONS OF
THE LIBRARY OF VIRGINIA

Edited by Sandra Gioia Treadway and Edward D. C. Campbell, Jr.

Library of Congress Cataloging-in-Publication Data

The common wealth : treasures from the collections of the Library
of Virginia / edited by Sandra Gioia Treadway and Edward D. C.
Campbell, Jr.
    p.   cm.
    Includes bibliographical references and index.
    ISBN 0-88490-185-8
    1. Virginia—History—Sources. 2. Library of Virginia—History.
    I. Treadway, Sandra Gioia. II. Campbell, Edward D. C., 1946–   .
    III. Title.
    F221.L53 1997   97-8430
    975.5—dc21   CIP

Standard Book Number: ISBN 0-88490-185-8

Library of Virginia, Richmond, Virginia
© 1997 by The Library of Virginia
All rights reserved.
Printed in the United States of America

This book is printed on acid-free paper meeting requirements
of the American Standard for Permanence of Paper for Printed
Library Materials.

Jacket illustration: Ca. 1920s library reading poster, by
Jon O. Brubaker, from the collections of the Library of Virginia

Jacket design: Paris Ashton-Bressler, Virginia Department of General
Services, Office of Graphic Communications

To the dedicated staff of the Library of Virginia,

past and present,

for their careful stewardship of the commonwealth's

history and heritage

CONTENTS

FOREWORD

Virginia's enduring contributions to the development of the American experience are not better understood than through the historic collections of the Library of Virginia. From the banks of the James River in 1607 to the halls of the State Capitol in Richmond today, Virginians down through the centuries have attempted to collect and preserve their history for the benefit of mankind. Since the Library's establishment in 1823, no other public or private institution in Virginia can claim closer identity with the recorded heritage of the commonwealth than can the Library of Virginia. The history of the state is reflected in the history and collections of the institution.

Today the Library of Virginia is recognized nationally and internationally as having the most comprehensive collection of the primary research materials devoted to the history of the commonwealth of Virginia in a single repository. Yet far too few Virginians are aware of the existence of this venerable institution and the treasures illustrated in this book.

On behalf of the Library Board and the staff of the Library of Virginia, it is with great pride that we issue this monumental volume heralding the priceless and irreplaceable treasures held in trust by the library and archives for the citizens of the commonwealth and nation. Through publication of this book we hope to increase awareness of the rich history of Virginia and the value of the Library's collections and services.

We also hope that this volume instills a sense of ownership and pride in the Library's collections in all who cherish the rich history of Virginia. I cordially invite you to visit the Library of Virginia and see for yourself the truly wondrous books, manuscripts, maps, and public records that document nearly four hundred years of our history.

It is my sincere hope that this book will generate a greater public interest in the ongoing need to acquire and preserve Virginia's printed and manuscript heritage for future generations to come.

NOLAN T. YELICH
State Librarian

PREFACE

In September 1993, when the commonwealth of Virginia broke ground for construction of the new Library of Virginia building at 800 East Broad Street, public curiosity about the Library and its future home began to mount. Advance publicity promised an inviting atmosphere, convenient access, large public spaces, elegant reading rooms, and the latest technological enhancements. The community watched with great interest as the imposing structure took shape and finally opened in January 1997.

While the location and handsome architectural features of the new Library building provide Virginians with a beautiful civic space in downtown Richmond, the building's true significance derives from the magnificent archival and printed collections that are housed within. A number of these collections are familiar to the thousands of researchers who use them every year, but many Virginians still know less than they should about their state library and its centuries-old holdings. The opening of the Broad Street building—the Library's fourth home since its founding in 1823—seemed a most appropriate time to tell the story of how the Library came to be and how its collections grew through the years, and to showcase some of the commonwealth's historic treasures that have been entrusted to the Library's care.

A staff committee representing all areas of the Library began work on this volume late in 1993, a few short weeks after the groundbreaking ceremony. The first and most daunting task the committee faced was selecting a manageable number of items that, together, would be representative of the variety and richness of the Library's collections. Each and every manuscript, book, map, newspaper, deed, will, court record, and photograph is precious to us, and eliminating items from consideration proved to be an excruciating experience. After months of research and discussion, however, the committee pulled together to make the difficult choices, and the photographic work and text preparation began.

From the outset, the steering committee for this volume applied an inclusive definition of a Library treasure. Many items were selected because they are truly rare, in numerous cases the only examples of their kind in existence. Others are included because they are associated with a great event in Virginia history, bear a famous signature, or have an intriguing provenance. Still others are here for their intrinsic beauty or merit, or because they are delightful curiosities. Quite a few, however, are what some might consider ordinary materials, produced for or written by Virginians whose names or accomplishments may never be famous. While perhaps they are not treasures in a monetary, collectible, or aesthetic sense, the Library considers them to be priceless parts of our collective heritage, for they provide insights into daily life in Virginia in days past that can be found nowhere else. The life experiences and struggles, successes and failures, triumphs and tragedies, and enduring faiths of generations of Virginians from all walks of life who have gone before us are thoroughly documented in the Library's collections. It is fitting that their voices and memories have a special place in this volume, too.

As with any ambitious undertaking, space, budget, and other practical considerations placed strict parameters on the project. There are hundreds of items among the Library's vast collections that could have been added to the final list of treasures or substituted for any item that the steering committee chose to include, and readers, as well as Library staff members, are sure to find many of their favorite books or documents missing. Just as it would be impossible to absorb all that the Library has to offer in a single visit, no one volume can pretend to do justice to the millions of archival items or hundreds of thousands of books, maps, photographs, newspapers, and other holdings. Our modest intent in publishing *The Common Wealth: Treasures from the Collections of the Library of Virginia* is to capture and share the essence and variety of the Library's holdings and to suggest the wonderful research opportunities that are available. Our hope is that Virginians who read this volume, and all those who cherish and study the commonwealth's past, will take ownership and pride in the library and archival repository that belongs to all the people of Virginia and will accept with the Library's staff the ongoing challenge of preserving the records and writings of the past for generations yet to come.

SANDRA GIOIA TREADWAY
EDWARD D. C. CAMPBELL, JR.

ACKNOWLEDGMENTS

This volume was truly a labor of love on the part of all who participated in its creation. The entire Library staff, particularly those who work directly with the collections, responded enthusiastically when the Treasures project was first announced and submitted hundreds of ideas and suggestions of items to be included. Several staff members graciously agreed to serve on an agencywide Treasures Steering Committee, consigning themselves to substantial work above and beyond their normal duties. The committee spent two years compiling what became a list of more than 800 proposed items, reviewing that list and making the final selections, and assisting the editors in the research and writing of the captions for each item. Committee members Nancy Brantley, Conley Edwards III, Mark Fagerburg, Stacy Moore, Carolyn Parsons, Ida Patton, Jennifer Reed, Brent Tarter, Minor Weisiger, and Phyllis Young gave unselfishly of their time and expertise and demonstrated an incomparable spirit of cooperation in the face of numerous meetings, deadlines, and last-minute requests. Every page of this volume bears witness to their sustained effort and their pride in the Library's fine collections.

The editors also enlisted the aid of many colleagues knowledgeable about the collections to prepare portions of the text. Special thanks go to Brent Tarter for the superb historical essay that opens the book, and to Nancy Brantley, Bob Clay, Daphne Gentry, Henry Grunder, Don Gunter, Lyn Hart, Kelly Hayes, Louise Jones, Chris Kolbe, Gregg Kimball, John Kneebone, Bill Lange, Jennifer McDaid, Marianne McKee, Stacy Moore, Tom Ray, Selden Richardson, Don Rhinesmith, Emily Salmon, Brent Tarter, and Minor Weisiger for preparing captions for selected materials.

A generous grant from Philip Morris Companies, Inc., supported the photographic work for this volume, allowing the Library to engage acclaimed Richmond photographer Katherine Wetzel. Katherine adjusted her busy schedule to accommodate this project and took up residence in the Rare Book Room of the old Library building two days each week for several months to complete the job. Committee members Mark Fagerburg, Stacy Moore, and Jennifer Reed (ably assisted in the final months of the project by research associate Kelly Hayes) coordinated the photography schedule, provided essential logistical support, and kept several hundred transparencies and negatives in order. Henry Grunder advised the committee on the conservation status of each item prior to the photography sessions, and Minor Weisiger, Phyllis Young, and Petie Bogen-Garrett graciously retrieved and returned materials to their proper places.

Staff photographers Mark Fagerburg and Pierre Courtois photographed the maps and numerous other materials of unusual size, as well as several additional items as they received conservation treatment. All other images of Library treasures are by Katherine Wetzel. Unless otherwise noted, the illustrations in the opening section of the book depicting the Library's history are from the Library's Picture Collection.

As always, the editorial staff of the Publications Division met the challenge of guiding the volume through the production cycle despite the stress and disruption of the Library's move. Gregg Kimball, assistant director for publications, managed the production process, identifying and solving problems, monitoring and adjusting schedules, and cracking the whip when necessary. Without his vigilance, and the advice and assistance of Stacy Moore, this volume would never have seen the light of day. Copy editor Emily Salmon worked closely with Gregg to ensure that the book met her rigorous factual, stylistic, and grammatical standards, never allowing a tight deadline to affect the quality of the final product. Daphne Gentry, Don Gunter, Jeff Looney, and Brent Tarter devoted many hours to proofreading and indexing and corrected several inadvertent errors. The editors are extremely grateful to Director of Publications and Educational Services John Kneebone as well for his constructive counsel and logistical help. Pat Kloke also assisted this project in numerous ways, particularly in keeping detailed and faithful minutes of the Treasures Steering Committee meetings.

Our wonderful designer, Paris Ashton-Bressler, head of the Virginia Office of Graphic Communications, gave her very best to this project, not only during working hours, but also on more nights and weekends than she would care to recall. The editors are profoundly grateful for her inspired design, practical advice, dogged determination, and inexhaustible patience.

State Librarian Nolan Yelich and the members of both the Library Board and the Library of Virginia Foundation Board encouraged this project from its inception. Their vision has made many dreams come true for the Library in recent years, this project foremost among them. Development Director Sandra Roger Peterkin also appreciated the significance and potential of this volume and provided unfailing assistance at every turn.

This volume is dedicated to the talented men and women who have worked through the years to acquire, preserve, describe, catalog, and provide patron access to the Library's archival, research, and special collections. They have been, and continue to be, faithful stewards of Virginia's official history and heritage.

THE COMMON WEALTH

TREASURES FROM THE COLLECTIONS OF
THE LIBRARY OF VIRGINIA

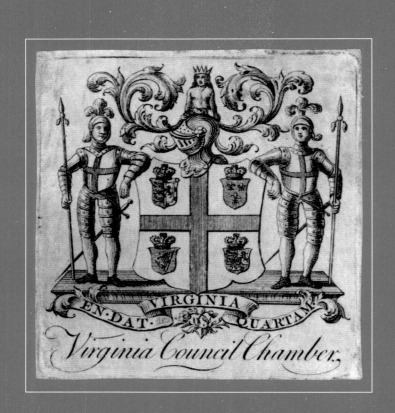

VIRGINIA
EN·DAT· QUARTAM

Virginia Council Chamber.

A RICH STOREHOUSE OF KNOWLEDGE
A History of the Library of Virginia

by Brent Tarter

The Library of Virginia—known throughout much of its history as the Virginia State Library—traces its official founding to 24 January 1823 when the General Assembly first provided public funds to purchase books for a reference library at the seat of government.[1] The origins of the Library of Virginia's impressive printed and archival collections, however, go back to the very beginning of Virginia itself, to the establishment of the first permanent English settlement in North America at Jamestown in 1607.[2]

Two hundred years ago, historian John Daly Burk remarked that the history of the United States was synonymous with the history of Virginia. His prescient observation still holds true as Virginians anticipate the four-hundredth anniversary of the founding of the colony. From the beginning, Virginians have been directly involved with creating, developing, preserving, and defending America's democratic tradition, and their triumphs and tragedies comprise the essence of the national experience. More Americans look for their roots in Virginia than in any other state, and the Old Dominion has been at the center of the two great military struggles—the American Revolution and the Civil War—that defined the United States.

Tragically, only a small portion of the historical record documenting the earliest years of Virginia and our nation survives, due in no small part to the legacy of war. Invading armies, fire, natural disaster, and years of neglect together have taken a serious toll, making ever more precious the documents, books, maps, and artifacts that have endured. The collections of the Library of Virginia abound with treasures saved from the ravages of time—treasures that document the lives and accomplishments of Virginians of every era, background, and walk of life. From its inception, the Library has been dedicated to preserving this priceless heritage while also meeting the complex and ever-changing information needs of the present and future.

◄ This distinctive bookplate is found in many of the volumes that belonged to Virginia's colonial Council. The Latin motto *En Dat Quartam Virginia* means "Lo Virginia the Fourth Quarter," referring to the colony as the fourth realm of the British Crown.

COLONIAL COUNCIL LIBRARY

The books and manuscripts gathered and preserved by Virginia's colonial governor's Council form the nucleus of the Library of Virginia. The Council normally consisted of a dozen of the most prominent male colonists who received life appointments directly from the British Crown. They advised the governor in all executive matters and sat together as the upper house of the General Assembly. Council members also served as judges of the colony's General Court and the Court of Oyer and Terminer, the highest trial courts and the only courts of appeal in Virginia. To guide them in fulfilling their extensive executive, judicial, and legislative duties, the councillors required access to the texts of British and Virginia statutes, to English lawbooks and court reports, and to learned treatises and reference works on a wide variety of subjects.

The Virginia Company of London, which founded the colony and provided for its governance until Virginia became a royal colony in 1624, purchased a number of books on law, navigation, colonization, natural history, and religion for the use of the councillors in Jamestown. There is no extant inventory of the volumes that arrived safely in the New World during the colony's first fifteen years, but the colony's leaders expressed a continuing desire for printed materials.[3] In 1621 George Thorpe wrote from Virginia to London asking that a supply of useful volumes on the law and other subjects be sent to Jamestown.[4] Little direct evidence survives to document the Council's purchases in the first forty years of royal administration. Confirmation that the Council continued to accumulate an official reference library can be found, however, in a 1666 act of assembly requiring the auditor of the colony to obtain a complete collection of the laws of England as well as several standard manuals on the practice of law.[5]

During the colonial period, the members of the Council, their clerks, and the lawyers who practiced before the General Court often recommended new books for the library. Council members usually acted through the clerk of the Council or the receiver general of the revenue to purchase books from London publishing houses. They paid for books, stationery, and other paper supplies of the government from what was known informally as the "king's fund," money arising from quitrents and other revenue sources that was used to finance the operations of the royal government.[6] The surviving official records contain only a few direct mentions of book purchases. The papers of Receiver General William Byrd reveal that on 19 July 1694 the government paid £16 9s. "for Law Bookes, paper &c for the use of the Councill Chamber," and again on 31 May 1695 the sum of £5 7s. for more purchases for the same purpose. Byrd's namesake son and successor continued to make purchases, and on 2 November 1705 he received reimbursement of £59 19s. 3d. "for Law Bookes & other things for the use of his Excellcy and the Council."[7] In the meantime, a joint General Assembly committee charged with revising the colony's laws ordered a number of standard titles from London, indicating that the Council's collection of lawbooks was still small and inadequate.[8] If the books were delivered, they may well have become part of the Council library's collection after the work of the revisors was completed in 1705. The only known record of an order for books for the Council library that names specific titles was entered in the Council's minute book on 30 May 1763: "The Receiver General was requested to write for the following Books, viz. Hayne's State Papers; Robertson's History of Scotland; Anchitel Grey's Parliamentary Proceedings; Hume's History of England; Guthrie's New British Peerage; Continuation of Acts of Parliament."[9]

Seven years after that request, Councillor Philip Ludwell Lee drew up a list of thirty titles that he believed should be added to the Council's library, virtually all of which were collections of statutes, court reports, and documentary histories of Great Britain and the colonies. That Lee's list did not include some of the most widely used lawbooks and histories suggests that the library probably already owned them. That he mentioned Sir William Blackstone's then-new *Commentaries on the Laws of England* indicates that he intended the library to be kept as up-to-date as possible. Lee also listed English translations of orations by Cicero and Demosthenes, suggesting that he wished to begin a collection of classics or to augment the library's collection of works on antiquity. Lee also did not list any of several essential documentary records such as John Rushworth's eight-volume *Historical Collections of Private Passages of State*, probably because the library already had a reasonably complete collection of historic documents.[10]

Some of the standard works were definitely present in the Council library in Williamsburg, which became the capital of Virginia in 1699, and they were used for more than courtroom reference. The most famous instance occurred in May 1774 after news arrived in

Williamsburg that Parliament had passed the Coercive Acts in retaliation for the Boston Tea Party and other colonial protests against British policies. Thomas Jefferson, Patrick Henry, Richard Henry Lee, Francis Lightfoot Lee, and a handful of other members of the House of Burgesses met to devise a plan of strategy. Jefferson later recalled that they met "in the council chamber, for the benefit of the library in that room." They searched the documentary histories of England for records of effective protests against improper official conduct and found what they wanted in the records of the English Civil Wars. "With the help therefore of Rushworth, whom we rummaged over for the revolutionary precedents & forms of the Puritans of that day," Jefferson's recollection continued, "we cooked up a resolution, somewhat modernizing their phrases, for appointing the 1st day of June . . . for a day of fasting, humiliation & prayer."[11] This resolution led directly to the first of the Virginia revolutionary conventions and to the issuance of the call to assemble the first Continental Congress in the autumn of 1774.

Council members, prominent attorneys, and other influential men were sometimes permitted to take books out of the library, but until 1772 the clerk of the Council, who had the custody of the books, kept no record of who took which books or whether the volumes were returned. To remedy this situation, the clerk published an announcement in the *Virginia Gazette* of 12 March 1772 calling on "all such Gentlemen as are in Possession of any of the Books, to return them" and stating that in the future he would keep an alphabetical list of books taken from the library. About that same time, Council member Robert Carter borrowed the first three volumes of Sir James Burrow's five-volume *Reports of Cases Adjudged in the Court of King's Bench* and all three volumes of the fifth edition of *The Works of John Locke*, and it was not until Carter's agent was closing up his Williamsburg house in 1792 that the volumes were discovered and restored to the library.[12]

The only known description of the library as it existed during the colonial period is from the pen of Josiah Quincy Jr., of Boston, Massachusetts, who viewed the books in the Capitol in Williamsburg on 9 April 1773. Quincy described the library simply as "a large, well-chosen, valuable collection of books, chiefly of law." Evidence from various other sources suggests that the library held more than two hundred volumes, and, if its collections of British and Virginia statutes and legislative proceedings were reasonably complete, the number would have been substantially larger. British and Virginia statutes and reports of cases in the English courts of King's Bench, Queen's Bench, and Common Pleas formed the bulk of the collection, but the Council library also contained a rare and valuable Vinegar Bible published in London in 1717 and a folio-sized *Book of Common Prayer* printed in 1745 that once belonged to the British royal family. Among the remarkable surviving books are several legal volumes purchased pursuant to the Council's resolution of 30 May 1763 or after Philip Ludwell Lee drew up his list of needed books in 1770. The library also contained the earl of Clarendon's celebrated three-volume *History of the Rebellion*

THE
HOLY BIBLE,

CONTAINING THE

Old TESTAMENT and the New:

Newly Translated out of the

ORIGINAL TONGUES:

And with the former TRANSLATIONS

Diligently Compared and Revised.

By His Majesty's Special Command.

Appointed to be Read in CHURCHES.

OXFORD,

Printed by JOHN BASKETT, Printer to the King's most Excellent Majesty, for
GREAT BRITAIN; and to the UNIVERSITY. M DCC XVII.

The parable of the vinegar.   **S. Luke.**

chief priests and the scribes came upon him, | scribes the fa
with the elders, | him; and th
2 And spake unto him, saying, Tell us, | perceived th
By what authority doest thou these things? | against them

▲ Title page and frontispiece of the Library of Virginia's copy of a rare
Vinegar Bible, printed by John Baskett in 1717. This edition derives
its name from a misprinting in the heading of chapter twenty in the
Gospel of Saint Luke, which reads "The parable of the vinegar"
instead of "The parable of the vineyard."

and Civil Wars in England, which the Library of Virginia still possesses; the 1751 edition of *The Works of John Locke* that Robert Carter once borrowed; and a two-volume edition of *The Complete Collection of the Historical, Political, and Miscellaneous Works of John Milton*, which is also still in the Library of Virginia. The Library no longer has its original set of John Rushworth's *Historical Collections*, but it still owns several other large, multivolume collections of state papers and statutes that were in the colonial library, and nine volumes of a ten-volume English translation of Pierre Bayle's *General Dictionary, Historical and Critical*.[13]

Written in English, French, and Latin and covering a wide variety of historical and legal subjects, the volumes in the colonial Council library ranged from the highly theoretical to the practical. Together they comprised a select but comprehensive reference library that had been carefully chosen to guide the decisions of Virginia's colonial and revolutionary statesmen.

PUBLIC RECORDS IN COLONIAL VIRGINIA

The principal keeper of the government's records during the colonial period was the secretary of the colony, but most public documents were probably stored in the offices or private residences of the various functionaries of government. The clerk of the House of Burgesses had an office for the records of the House, and the officers of the royal revenue kept their own records, as did the treasurer of the colony, the attorney general, the courts, and the governor and Council.

In Jamestown, the secretary's office was located in the statehouse, for many years in a damp ground-floor room. Its condition was the subject of numerous complaints and unsuccessful attempts to put the records in better order.[14] As early as 1664 the General Assembly passed an "Act Concerning the Regulating the Secretaryes Office" to try to bring order out of chaos, "since it appeares," in the words of the statute, "that there hath beene a great neglect in keeping the records in this country."[15] In 1692 Lieutenant Governor Francis Nicholson studied the condition of the records and found that "Severall of the Bookes of Records in the Secret[ary's] Offic[e] were much torne and defaced, and divers papers of great conceirne are very old much Worne and lye in great Confusion." He noted that "for want of more roome in the Secret[ary']s Office there could not be such Conveniences made as was requisite, and for want thereof the Records in that Office were to[o] much exposed, and in great danger of being imbesled by any evill minded person." Nicholson and the Council gave orders for repairs to the office and instructed the clerks to take "great paines Care and trouble" in arranging and preserving the documents "with as much Expedition as possible."[16] One of the clerks in the secretary's office had transcribed the colony's badly deteriorated land patent book number one in 1683; another clerk transcribed book number two in 1694 and book three sometime thereafter.[17]

The statehouse was burned to the ground in 1676 during Bacon's Rebellion, and the rebuilt statehouse burned in October 1698. It is probable, though not known for certain, that the first fire destroyed some of the colony's public records, but the 1698 fire probably did not. Some damage must have occurred, though, when, according to a description of the scene in 1698, "the Publick records & papers . . . were

forced to be hurryed Out & thrown into heaps." Two former chief clerks of the secretary's office, Peter Beverley and his brother, Robert, later sorted through and arranged the documents, which were soon transferred to the new capital city of Williamsburg.[18] The records were temporarily lodged at the College of William and Mary, where the General Assembly and the Council met while the new public buildings were under construction. Not long after government officials moved into the new Capitol, the college caught fire and burned.

The only good description of the documents in the secretary's office in the first Capitol building in Williamsburg is that left by William Stith, a minister who visited the office regularly during the 1740s while conducting research for a history of Virginia. Stith reported in 1746 that many of the old documents that he and his contemporaries had recalled seeing in the secretary's office on earlier visits had disappeared, and "those, which have survived the Flames and Injuries of Time, have been so carelessly kept, are so broken, interrupted, and deficient, have been so mangled by Moths and Worms, and lie in such a confused and jumbled State (at least the most ancient of them) being huddled together in single Leaves and Sheets in Books out of the Binding, that I foresee, it will cost me infinite Pains and Labour, to reduce and digest them into any tolerable Order." Stith complained to the House of Burgesses, which ordered that the documents in the worst condition "be reviewed and fairly transcribed."[19]

Not long after Stith recorded this description, the Capitol caught fire. The blaze began in the roof during the night of 29–30 January 1747 and spread toward the secretary's office. A fortunate change in the direction of the wind slowed the fire's progress, so that "all Papers of any Consequence" and the books in the Council's library could be removed from the building, but they "were thrown together in great Disorder" on the ground outside.[20] The colony erected a new Capitol on the founda-

▶ A detail of the brickwork beside the doorway of the Public Record Office in Williamsburg

◀ Virginia's Public Record Office in Williamsburg, completed in 1748

tion of the old one and constructed a separate brick building to house the records of the secretary's office. The new Public Record Office in Williamsburg was completed in 1748, and it is possible that by that date, if not earlier, more of the public records than just the working papers of the secretary's office had been brought under one roof for safekeeping.[21]

Colonial officials occasionally removed documents from the Capitol or from the secretary's office in order to do legal or historical research, and in a number of instances they never returned the documents. The most famous examples are the valuable collections of early colonial records that Sir John Randolph and Richard Bland had in their possessions and that Thomas Jefferson subsequently purchased from their heirs and still later sold to the Library of Congress.[22] Contemporaries, had they known of the removal of the documents from their proper places in the colonial archive, might have deplored the practice, but, as luck would have it, it was only because the documents were not where they were supposed to be that they escaped destruction during the American Revolution and the Civil War.

Virginia suffered a further loss of archival records and its first serious loss of books during the American Revolution. In April 1780, the state capital was moved from Williamsburg to Richmond. Although Governor Thomas Jefferson made careful preparations for the safe transfer of the government's holdings, it is possible that some of the books and public documents may have been lost or harmed in transit.[23] British incursions up the James River during the next year, however, caused considerable damage. During the first advance in January 1781, according to a memorandum entered into the Council journal, the "letters and other Papers of the Council" were destroyed, and the Council issued orders that "a proper person be appointed" to obtain copies of records, papers, and letters of importance associated with the conduct of the war.[24] It is very likely that this destruction included the bulk of the colonial Council's executive journals, letter books, and most of its files, which were never thereafter seen or cited. One of the letter books from the governor's office containing Governor Thomas Jefferson's correspondence was stolen and taken back to England, but most of the remainder of the eighteenth-century executive records perished.[25] As the British approached Richmond again in April 1781, Jefferson gave orders to the clerks of the various government offices to be ready at a moment's warning to move their records to places of safety.[26] Judging by the records that existed in Richmond during the nineteenth century, their efforts were largely successful.[27]

The Council's library also suffered during the move and the invasions. As the General Court prepared to transport the lawbooks into the Henrico County courthouse in 1783, Attorney General Edmund Randolph informed the chief judge that he could find from the Council's original collection (which he described as the "scattered remains of the Public Library") only about "fifty dissorted Volumes," which were then "exposed to great injury from the Want of Proper

▼ *View of Richmond*, 1817, looking across the James River from Manchester

Presses," or book shelves, "and an Apartment for their Reception."[28] That same month, the Council decided that because "many of the Books were lost & destroyed in the invasion," it was no longer worthwhile to pay the clerk of the Council an extra sum for duties as "Keeper of the Library."[29] Nevertheless, for almost fifty more years the clerk of the Council retained custody of the volumes that the Council owned. After the completion of the new Capitol late in the 1780s, the General Court and the Council both moved into the building, and the clerk of the Council again took custody of all of the books.

CREATING A STATE LIBRARY

The library acquired a small number of books during the immediate post-Revolutionary period. Most of these were copies of state and national laws and published reports of cases decided in federal courts or the courts of other states. It is probable that they were acquired by exchanges, with federal and state governments receiving copies of Virginia's statutes and court reports in return for sending their reports to Virginia. No evidence exists to indicate that the Council or the General Assembly purchased any significant number of books for the library, either to replace the books lost during the Revolution or to keep the research collection up-to-date, but not everybody was unmindful of the need to replenish the library or of the value of having a well-stocked research library at the seat of government. While Thomas Jefferson was governor he and the Council unsuccessfully sought to acquire several general reference works, and Jefferson also drafted a "Bill for Establishing a Public Library." Jefferson's bill would have provided for an annual allocation of funds to purchase books and for the appointment of a board of directors to take care of the collection, but it would not have created a lending library available to all citizens, which the term "public library" today implies. James Madison introduced the bill on Jefferson's behalf in 1785 while Jefferson was in Paris, but the assembly did not enact it into law.[30]

The next recorded attempt to create a state library began on 15 December 1819, when Delegate Joseph Lovell, of Kanawha County, proposed a bill "Providing for the Purchase of a Library for the Use of the Members of the General Assembly, and Others." The House of Delegates named him chairman of a twelve-member committee to draft the measure. The following day, the judges of the Virginia Supreme Court of Appeals and of the General Court asked the assembly for a small appropriation for the "purchase of law books for the use of the said courts, and other departments of the government, to be deposited in some chamber in the Capitol." The House referred the judges' memorial to Lovell's committee.[31] In January 1820 Lovell introduced a bill to provide an annual appropriation for the acquisition of such "Law and other Books, as shall be approved by the Governor for the time being with the advice of Council," and to empower the governor and Council to appoint a librarian. The bill went no further than its first reading before the assembly.[32]

The judges of the General Court did not let the issue drop, and on 7 December 1822 they requested that the General Assembly appropriate funds for the "procurement of a small but well selected library on criminal Law at publick expense, for the public use." The judges complained that they frequently had to visit the offices of local attorneys to search their printed collections for authoritative information before handing down rulings on important points of criminal law or procedure. The House of Delegates referred the petition to its Committee on

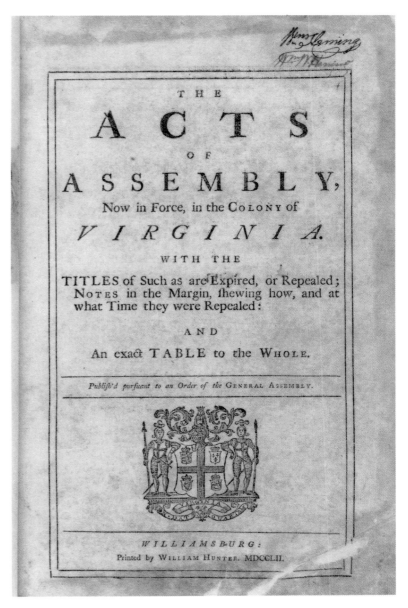

▲ Title page of the first volume of the eight-volume *Acts of Assembly, Now in Force, in the Colony of Virginia*, published in 1752, bearing the autograph of the noted legal scholar William Waller Hening.

Courts of Justice and subsequently ordered the committee to bring in a bill to meet the request.[33]

Two days before the judges presented their memorial, the General Assembly received another request that ultimately provided a solution. William Waller Hening, clerk of the chancery court for the Richmond district and a noted legal scholar, had just completed the compilation of a now-famous thirteen-volume edition of Virginia laws enacted from the early 1600s through the general revision of 1792. Hening had undertaken this project in 1808 with legislative approval, having convinced the assembly that his documentary edition would be useful not only to historians, but also to citizens whose legal and property rights dated back to early legislation that had never been published or made easily accessible. To subsidize Hening's compilation and make the laws more widely available, the assembly in 1808 directed the governor to purchase 150 copies of each published volume for the use of the officers and courts of the state. As his project was nearing its end in 1822, Hening petitioned the General Assembly to adjust the terms of this

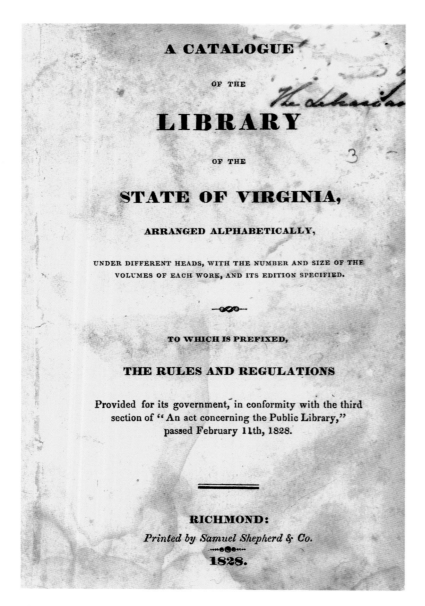

A CATALOGUE

OF THE

LIBRARY

OF THE

STATE OF VIRGINIA,

ARRANGED ALPHABETICALLY,

UNDER DIFFERENT HEADS, WITH THE NUMBER AND SIZE OF THE
VOLUMES OF EACH WORK, AND ITS EDITION SPECIFIED.

TO WHICH IS PREFIXED,

THE RULES AND REGULATIONS

Provided for its government, in conformity with the third
section of "An act concerning the Public Library,"
passed February 11th, 1828.

RICHMOND:
Printed by Samuel Shepherd & Co.
1828.

▲ Title page of the first printed catalog of the Library's collections, published
in 1828 in an edition of thirty-one pages

subsidy. The assembly referred Hening's petition to the same committee that received the judges' request. After more than a month spent
drafting, revising, and amending a bill, the House and Senate agreed to
legislation that met both Hening's and the General Court's needs.[34]

The statute adopted on 24 January 1823 substantially increased
the number of sets of Hening's *Statutes at Large* that the government
promised to purchase and provided that the government could sell any
surplus copies of the *Statutes* and use the proceeds "for the purchase of
a library, under the superintendence of the executive, for the use of the
court of appeals and general court, and of the General Assembly during the sessions thereof," thereby officially creating what is now the
Library of Virginia.[35]

The General Assembly made further provisions in 1826 and 1827
to regulate sales of Hening's *Statutes at Large* and of a newly produced
map of Virginia. This legislation allocated additional funds for the purchase of books for the state's library.[36] A three-member subcommittee
of the governor's executive Council headed by William Branch Giles
oversaw the purchases and spent $1,779.04 before issuing its final

report on 24 October 1827. The committee stated that the money had
been expended "principally in the purchase of Law-Books—because, at
this time, they are most wanted."[37]

Giles was elected governor in the spring of 1827, and in his first
annual message to the General Assembly in December 1827 he
requested clarification on access to the book collection.[38] In response,
the General Assembly passed "An Act Concerning the Public Library,"
the first legislation that provided for the library's administration. It
required the governor and Council to set aside a room in the Capitol to
house the books, authorized payment of an additional salary to the clerk
of the Council "who shall for the present act ex officio as public librarian," and required the librarian to promulgate rules for the use of the
books and to give the state's appellate judges free access to the collection.[39] The Council designated a southeast corner room where the
Committee on Propositions and Grievances of the House of Delegates
customarily met, and that "very agreeable apartment, from its light, air,
and fine prospects," became the library.[40]

William Harvie Richardson, clerk of the Council and librarian ex
officio, quickly compiled and published a list of the library's holdings.
The *Catalogue of the Library of the State of Virginia, Arranged
Alphabetically, Under Different Heads, with the Number and Size of the
Volumes of Each Work, and Its Edition Specified* listed 659 titles, encom-
passing a total of 1,582 volumes, plus several maps.[41] Richardson
divided the collection into several classes: law, political economy, history and biography, agriculture and horticulture, miscellaneous subjects, and maps. Of the 659 titles, 555 were works printed after 1776.
Virtually all of the pre-1776 imprints appear to have come from the
colonial Council's library.

COLLECTIONS OF THE STATE LIBRARY, 1800–1860

In February 1829 the General Assembly enabled the state librarian
to buy new books by arranging a loan of $6,000 from the state's Literary
Fund at 6 percent interest. The law directed the librarian to purchase
such titles as the General Assembly's Joint Committee on the Library
should thereafter recommend.[42] The joint committee maintained close
oversight of the library for the next seventy-five years. In 1830 the
assembly authorized the librarian to borrow an additional $4,000 from
the Literary Fund and increased the authority of the Joint Committee
on the Library. The assembly also gave the librarian the right to sell the
annually published journals of the two houses of the General Assembly
and the session laws as well as the published reports of the Supreme
Court of Appeals. The money obtained from the sales was then set
aside to pay back the loan to the Literary Fund and to become a permanent source of revenue for the continued acquisition of books.[43]

Following adoption of the Virginia Constitution of 1830 and the
consequent reorganization of the executive branch of government,
the assembly provided that the "secretary of the commonwealth, or
clerk of the executive department," also be "librarian of the state."[44]
From then until 1903, the books and most of the archival records generated by the executive departments were under the custody of the
secretary of the commonwealth.

The growth of the library during the remainder of the antebellum
period was steady and substantial. Conclusive evidence for this is found
in the series of printed catalogs that the secretary of the commonwealth
published between 1831 and 1856, by which time the library included
approximately seventeen thousand five hundred volumes.

While many volumes were added to the collection in this period, some were removed as well. In 1831 the General Assembly required the Supreme Court of Appeals to begin holding an annual western session at Lewisburg in Greenbrier County (now in West Virginia). Between that date and 1845 the assembly appropriated $4,150 for the acquisition of books for the Lewisburg courthouse, but the state's librarian also transferred about three dozen old lawbooks to Lewisburg, mostly duplicate copies that could be spared.[45] The Virginia Supreme Court of Appeals issued orders on 26 April 1864 to have its western records and books moved eastward to Botetourt County, but most or all of the books remained in Lewisburg and became the property of the new state of West Virginia.[46] Five lawbooks from the colonial Council's library that were in Lewisburg when the Civil War broke out eventually found their way into the collection of West Virginia's library. They are now back in the Library of Virginia's collections, having been purchased from a book dealer in 1988. One of the books bears the distinctive bookplate of the Council library; the other four have a stamping on the cover that reads "VIRGINIA COUNCIL OFFICE 1742."[47]

Several other volumes were also removed during these years. An act of 1841 creating a library for the new Virginia Military Institute, for example, authorized the librarian to send appropriate titles to Lexington if the state's library had one or more duplicates that could be spared.[48] Evidence also suggests that other books that had been in the colonial Council's library were removed before the Civil War, but extant records do not disclose why or what became of them.

Acquisitions far outnumbered removals, however, and the rapid growth of the library's collection was one of many factors contributing to the overcrowding of the Capitol and the resulting decision to build a new state courthouse in Capitol Square in the mid-1840s. Although the judges of the Supreme Court of Appeals wanted to transfer all the lawbooks into the new courthouse, the Joint Committee on the Library unanimously objected, and it is unlikely that any significant number of books, other than a set of Virginia statutes and the court's own published reports, was ever moved into the courthouse.[49]

▼ A view of the Virginia Capitol, a primitive-style, oil-on-canvas painting, ca. 1860, attributed to Howard W. Montague, of Essex County. The State Library, established in 1823, occupied rooms in the Capitol until the 1890s.

▲ William Harvie Richardson, state librarian from 1821 to 1852 in his capacity as clerk of the Council and, later, secretary of the commonwealth. (Courtesy of the Virginia Military Institute, Lexington)

In 1849 the assembly directed the library to occupy the rooms previously used by the courts and the Council because "the apartment which has been fitted up for the state library is filled with books, and does not afford sufficient space for the purposes of that institution," and "the room occupied by the secretary of the commonwealth is too small to contain the records and papers of the executive department."[50] In 1856 the assembly authorized the secretary of the commonwealth to have "the three rooms now containing the state library to be thrown into one, and such alterations made therein, and such additional fixtures constructed as may be necessary and fit for the proper arrangement of the library."[51]

A brief description of the State Library, as it had come to be called by the 1850s, appeared in the *Southern Literary Messenger* in March 1852. John Peyton Little, a Richmond physician and local historian, recounted his visit to the library: "Ascending a broad flight of stairs you reach the upper story, and enter a gallery running round the open space, through which light is admitted from the roof to the floor below; into this gallery open the doors of the State Library, the Governor's office, and other offices. The Library is a well selected and well kept one; it contains on its well arranged shelves 14,000 volumes, consisting chiefly of lawbooks, historical works, and political records for the use of the Legislature. The librarian I have found a courteous and obliging gentleman; through his kindness I have spent many pleasant hours in this rich storehouse of knowledge."[52]

The librarian Little met was William H. Richardson, who had become state librarian in 1821 in his capacity as clerk of the Council. He became secretary of the commonwealth in 1830 and thus continued as state librarian. In December 1852 the General Assembly replaced

Richardson, a Whig, with George Wythe Munford, a Democrat.[53] During Richardson's long tenure at the library, he oversaw the expenditure of about $40,000 for the acquisition of books.[54] Through the sale of government publications, he repaid the $10,000 loan from the Literary Fund by the end of 1846 and built up a moderate account from which he and his successors continued to enlarge the library's book collection.[55]

No similar source of funding existed to ensure the preservation of the state's archival records during the first half of the nineteenth century. Officials' greatest interest was for the preservation of the surviving colonial statutes. Some of the earliest laws had never been published in authoritative editions and those that had were extremely scarce after the Revolution. Because many of the laws concerned land titles, attorneys and magistrates were constantly in doubt about how to settle disputes. Thomas Jefferson expressed his concern in a 1795 letter to his friend and former law teacher, George Wythe, in which he told Wythe that he possessed a large collection of manuscript copies of early Virginia statutes, some of which he correctly surmised no longer existed in any other form.[56] Wythe agreed with Jefferson about the value of the statutes, and together they influenced the General Assembly in December 1795 to appoint a committee to collect and publish "all the acts of the legislature which in any manner relate to the landed property within the commonwealth." The following year, however, for reasons that the assembly did not record, it suspended the project.[57]

In December 1800, Governor James Monroe sent the legislature a copy of Jefferson's 1795 letter and endorsed the proposal to collect and publish the early laws. Monroe also called the assembly's attention "to the situation of the antient records of our country" generally. Jefferson's collection, Monroe wrote, "shews that many such documents have been rescued from the ordinary waste of time by the provident zeal and patriotism of one of our citizens, who wishes to transfer the valuable deposit to his Country." The governor asked the assembly to take notice of the "decaying" state of the public records and adopt a plan for their preservation.[58] Monroe's recommendation went beyond the 1795 scheme to publish only the laws relating to land, and on 21 January 1801 the House of Delegates passed a bill "for collecting and publishing acts passed by the legislature of Virginia prior to the year one thousand seven hundred and eighty-two." Two days later the Senate returned the bill to the House with two amendments, one of which the House accepted and one of which caused the delegates to postpone further consideration of the measure, in effect killing the bill.[59]

The General Assembly took the first effective step toward preserving its legislative history with the law it passed on 5 February 1808 supporting the publication of William Waller Hening's compilation of Virginia laws.[60] It was for the completion of that project that the assembly passed the landmark library law of January 1823.

In 1827 the assembly commissioned the publication of a new edition of the journals of the General Assembly for the years 1777 through 1790, the original printed editions of which had "in a great degree been lost or destroyed." The statute authorizing the publication also included a provision stating that "whensoever in the opinion of any court of record in this Commonwealth, it shall become necessary for the security and preservation of any of the records of such court, that the books should be re-bound, such court may order such re-binding accordingly."[61] On several occasions during the nineteenth century the General Assembly authorized clerks of courts to have damaged record books transcribed or to reconstruct from their minute books and loose papers the contents of any bound volumes of public documents that had been damaged, lost, or destroyed. There was nothing the assembly could do, though, to replace records ruined by floods, wars, or courthouse fires, and several counties suffered irreparable losses during the antebellum period. The assembly did not authorize local clerks to transfer records to Richmond for safekeeping, nor did it appropriate funds for any serious preservation of the state's own archival records.

The state's records in Richmond did not suffer any serious damage from accidents early in the nineteenth century, although some documents were removed from the archives on purpose. Shortly after Kentucky became a state in 1792, Virginia, without making certified copies, gave Kentucky many landbooks and other valuable records relating to the western counties that had become part of the new state. A century later, in 1892, the General Assembly enacted legislation to transfer to West Virginia many of the archival records in Richmond that pertained to the region prior to 1863, again without making copies for Virginians' reference.[62]

In spite of such occasional removals of records, the amount of official documentation that accumulated annually in the Capitol in Richmond posed storage problems and impeded the operation of the state offices. While Hening was compiling his edition of the Virginia laws early in the century, he spent many hours in the Capitol, as he had also done while a practicing attorney, as a member of the Council of State, and as adjutant general of the Virginia militia. The lack of a coherent organization of the documents often frustrated his research, as he revealed in an angry footnote in volume two of his *Statutes at Large*. He attributed the disorder in part to the practices of the secretaries of the colony in the old days rather than to the more recent custodianship of his contemporaries. Echoing William Stith's comments made three-quarters of a century earlier, Hening wrote early in the 1810s that he had been forced "to wade thro' an immense mass of crude indigested matter,

▲ Bust of Thomas Jefferson by Attilio Piccirilli after the original by Jean-Antoine Houdon. Jefferson recognized early in his public career the importance of preserving Virginia's and the nation's official records.

▲ Plaster bust of James Monroe by Attilio Piccirilli. As governor, Monroe promoted the collection and preservation of Virginia's valuable public records.

▶ John Floyd, governor of Virginia from 1830 to 1834, by William Garl Brown.

thrown together without regard to method or chronological order. Perhaps in no civilized country whatever, were the records so badly arranged and kept as in the former *Secretary's* office of Virginia."[63]

In 1832 Governor John Floyd initiated a thorough investigation of the condition of the state's archives. His investigator reported that the job was very difficult. Not only were the papers in disarray, but also a large and "useless mass of private and professional papers belonging to individuals" (probably lawyers and land agents who often worked in the Capitol) was indiscriminately intermixed with the public papers. The archival records, he reported, were in wretched condition: "there are some very dirty and decayed books in the upper part of the capitol, which are in such a condition that they cannot be examined, and will never be of value." He bundled up some documents that he thought might be of use and delivered them to the secretary of the common-wealth and to the offices of other government departments. Not long thereafter, in order to settle a number of pending claims by Revolutionary War veterans and their descendants, the General Assembly ordered a detailed inventory to be made of records pertain-ing to the services of officers, soldiers, and sailors in the American Revolution.[64]

As a result of these investigations, the secretary of the common-wealth had several series of documents sorted and tied up in bundles and labeled, but that systematic arrangement broke down in time as the clerks continued to consult and make copies of the old records without always returning them to their proper places. Lawyers and land agents probably broke into the bundles, too, and frequent handling undoubt-edly accelerated deterioration.[65] The General Assembly made an

attempt at preservation when in 1833 the Joint Committee on the Library adopted a resolution asking that $400 be set aside to purchase valuable historical documents or have transcripts of those in private hands made for deposit in the library before these records might be lost through "the wasting and consuming process of time."[66] It does not appear, however, that the State Library acquired any substantial body of documents following this resolution.

Hundreds of large and heavy volumes of tax records and other papers continued to accumulate in the Capitol, and by 1847, when the state completed construction of its new courthouse, the records belong-ing to the state's courts and various other offices were stacked in heaps in the Capitol's corridors and passageways, in the hot attic, and in the damp and dark basement.[67] Some idea of the quantity, variety, and value of the court records that were moved from the Capitol to the courthouse in 1847 can be gleaned from long and tantalizing descrip-tions compiled by attorney Conway Robinson in 1829 and by historian George Bancroft in 1836.[68] While the transfer of court records tem-porarily relieved some of the crowding in the Capitol, it did not pro-vide a long-term solution for the State Library.

DISASTER AND NEW BEGINNINGS

The Civil War had a devastating effect on the Library's collec-tions. By the eve of that conflict, the Library had become an estab-lished institution with printed holdings numbering between eighteen and twenty thousand volumes. "The Library is visited daily," the *Richmond Examiner* reported in May 1860, "by professional gentlemen and others, by whom we believe, any book can be obtained for purposes of reference and use in the room itself."[69] Following the outbreak of war in 1861, librarian George Wythe Munford permitted the members of the Confederate Congress and other Confederate officials access to the collections, but in October 1862 he had to close the Library for several days to rearrange the books because the congressmen, legislators, and visitors had left the reading room in complete disarray.[70] Munford also had to contend with two burglaries. Early in the morning of 24 July 1863 someone broke into the Library and stole more than $2,800 from the library fund.[71] In November of that same year a former inmate of the State Penitentiary was arrested for stealing valuable books on medical subjects from the Library and selling them to Confederate army doctors.[72] Several other acts of vandalism occurred during the war, too, and according to one newspaper report, some of "the most valuable volumes disappeared and the rarest engravings and documents were irreparably mutilated."[73]

The worst damage to both the archival records and the book collection took place on 2 and 3 April 1865, following the Confederate and state governments' hasty abandonment of Richmond in the face of the advancing Union army. A fire that began during the evacuation on the night of 2 April destroyed much of the city's commercial district, including the state's courthouse in Capitol Square. A large number of judicial records were lost at that time, including many of the records of the colonial General Court, the Supreme Court of Appeals, the courts of chancery, and other courts of the commonwealth. Lost, too, were the records of several of the state's district courts that, ironically, had been sent to Richmond for safekeeping after the first Union army invasions of Virginia early in the war. More of Virginia's documentary heritage was destroyed during the evacuation fire than at any other time in Virginia's history.[74]

The catastrophic fire did not reach the Capitol, but during the chaos in the days that followed, there were no responsible state officials present to care for the books and papers in the Library. Soldiers, souvenir hunters, and curious visitors carried off a large number of books and many valuable documents. Years later, a Union army officer described what he called "the sacking of the Virginia State Library." Entering the Library after the "vandalism" had begun, he found "the floor covered with the colonial and other records in which it was so rich," which "had been wantonly taken from their cases and thrown around." A guard was immediately posted outside the door, "with imperative orders to let no person pass without written permission from headquarters."[75] According to a report that appeared in the *Richmond Whig* at the end of April, "Searchers about the public buildings have been fortunate enough to get hold of great bundles of public documents, 'of no use to any one but the owner,' but of incalculable value to autograph hunters, who pay fabulous prices for them."[76] Not only state documents, but also a great many Confederate records disappeared at the war's end. Because of their value for military history, the United States Army opened an archive room in Richmond and issued an appeal for the return of official Confederate documents.[77]

Late in the spring of 1865, Francis H. Pierpont, governor of Virginia under the Restored government in Alexandria, moved to

Richmond to take charge of the state's affairs. Secretary of the Commonwealth Charles H. Lewis was astonished when he first examined his offices. The Library's books were "in great confusion, many valuable works mutilated and ruined, and many volumes belonging to important and valuable sets of works missing from the alcoves, as well as many valuable single volumes." He found the same was true for the archives, which was "also much abused, and pillaged of valuable old letters and records."[78] On 30 June 1865, Lewis published an announcement in the *Richmond Whig*, requesting that all books belonging to the State Library be returned so that the catalog could be revised and the library reopened to the public.[79]

The task of reassembling the Library and assessing its finances seemed impossible to Lewis, who reported to the General Assembly that the "account books and other papers relating to the business and financial condition of the library were removed upon the evacuation of the city, and have not yet been recovered." Lewis went on to inform the assembly that his other duties as secretary of the commonwealth required so much time that he could not personally attend to the business of sorting through the archival records, arranging the books, and replacing the lost volumes. "Considerable experience in the publication and knowledge of books will be necessary," he accurately predicted, "to restore the library to its original usefulness." He recommended that the General Assembly consider "the appointment of a librarian, separate and distinct from the office of secretary of the commonwealth, to take charge of and conduct the business of the library." At the same time, he suggested that a "great quantity of useless and worthless documents and other publications, which have been accumulating for years, lumbering up the rooms, and to some extent impairing the stability of the upper portion of the house," be sold "as waste paper."[80] The documents to which he referred were probably the unbound volumes of old statutes and printed government reports that were still taking up space in the Capitol's attic near the end of the nineteenth century.

In 1866 the Joint Committee on the Library made its first postwar report to the full assembly. The report confirmed the Library's "serious and, in some cases, irreparable" wartime losses and decried the lack of money available for rebuilding the collection. The committee supported an increase in the Library's budget, finding the prewar fund it

▲ *The Fall of Richmond, Va. On the night of April 2nd, 1865,* published in 1865 by Currier and Ives, of New York

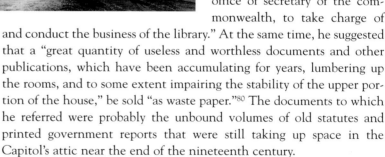

► Richmond in April 1865. Although the Capitol was spared from the evacuation fire, the general destruction of the city left many books and documents in the library vulnerable to theft and vandalism. (National Archives, Washington, D.C.)

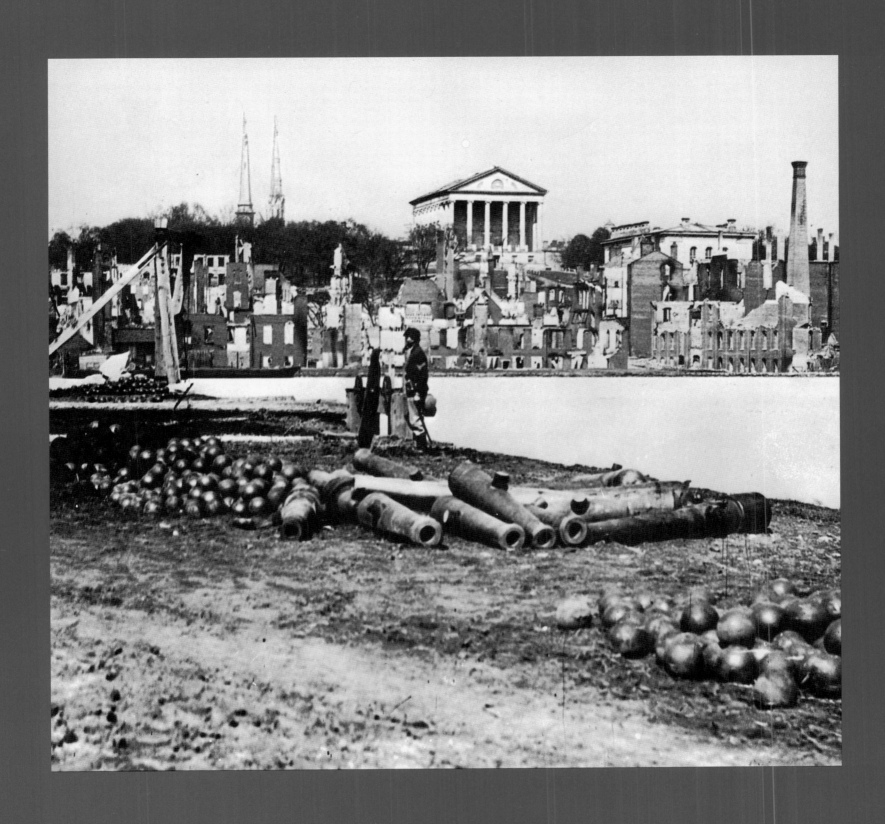

had once boasted about to be "entirely inadequate," but it was unable to remedy this situation or to convince the assembly to appoint a full-time librarian.[81] Nothing significant was done to replenish the book collection and no more than rudimentary steps were taken to safeguard the archives during Reconstruction, in large measure because of the state's severe financial crisis and the frequent changes in the office of secretary of the commonwealth while Virginia was under military rule.[82]

Nonetheless, the character of the State Library's book collection slowly began to change after the Civil War, receding in some areas and expanding in others as the Library responded to a growing mission. Early in 1867 the assembly authorized the Supreme Court of Appeals to take possession of all of the State Library's lawbooks that it needed, and three years later it permitted the court to take such "law books belonging to the state library" as it deemed necessary for stocking new law libraries at Wytheville and Staunton, where the Supreme Court of Appeals held regular western sessions.[83]

With the end of Reconstruction in Virginia and the restructuring of state government under the Constitution of 1869, the State Library began once more to acquire new books and to replace those that had been damaged or lost during the war. In 1873 the General Assembly authorized the librarian and the Joint Committee to purchase not only standard reference material, but also copies of "any book, pamphlet, or manuscript, work of art, or relic relating to the history of Virginia, not

now in the general library, which can be obtained on reasonable terms, and they may cause to be printed any manuscript relating to the history of Virginia, which has not been published," provided that publication costs not exceed $1,000 for any given year.[84] The annual reports of the Joint Committee on the Library, beginning with that of 1874, reveal that the state librarian acted promptly on this new charge. In March 1875, the library acquired a portrait of Revolutionary War hero Peter Francisco. Four months later, the son of a member of the Senate of Virginia presented the Library with a collection of forty or more "Indian relics" that he had found in the vicinity of Richmond.[85]

In 1872 the state librarian purchased two fine incunabula, or books printed before 1501. One was the first Italian edition of the *Historia Naturale* by Pliny the Elder, printed in Venice in 1476, less than twenty-five years after Johann Gutenberg's invention of moveable type. It still belongs to the Library of Virginia and is one of the oldest items in the collection. In 1872 the librarian also acquired an original copy of the so-called *Nuremberg Chronicle*, the first printed history of the world, which was published in the city of Nuremberg on 12 July 1493, a few days before news of Christopher Columbus's return from his first voyage of discovery reached northern Europe.[86] The volume was bound

▼ The Library's collection of portraits of notable Virginians grew quickly into a handsome gallery in the Capitol rotunda, pictured here ca. 1890.

with several blank leaves in the back so that readers could, if so inclined, continue and complete the written history of the world. In 1877, following several years of work by the assistant librarian, Sherwin McRae, the State Library published the first catalog of its holdings since 1856.[87]

The General Assembly also turned its attention in the 1870s to Virginia's languishing archival records. Under prodding from officers of the Virginia Historical Society, the assembly in 1872 passed "An Act to Secure the Preservation of Historical Papers in the Capitol Building." The statute directed William P. Palmer, a local historian and member of the Virginia Historical Society's executive committee, "to take charge of the manuscripts in the state library, under the direction of the librarian; to assort, index, and prepare the same for preservation in such form as to them may seem best, with authority to publish such of the same . . . provided, that said manuscripts shall not be removed from the capitol."[88]

Palmer went to work the very next day after the statute was passed. His description of the archives on 8 February 1872 reveals how little had been done since April 1865: "the documentary matter in the upper rooms of the capitol was found to be a confused mass of papers, maps and bound records of early date, scattered about in alternate bundles and heaps." Palmer saw traces of former state librarian William H. Richardson's earlier attempt to arrange the state's papers, but easy access by the public as well as the wartime treatment had wreaked havoc with Richardson's organizational scheme. Palmer discovered that the carefully bundled and labeled packets of papers "had been opened, inspected and robbed." "When not thus mutilated," he reported to the assembly, "their chronological sequence had been so entirely destroyed, that a large majority of the packages were found to contain documents separated from each other in date, by centuries. In addition to this, the frequent handling, the untying and tying up again of papers so arranged has well nigh worn out a great number of those most ancient and valuable." Palmer described "quantities of empty wrappers" from which the contents had entirely disappeared. Although he placed some of the blame on those responsible for government during the post–Civil War years, both Union army officers and Virginia's secretaries of the commonwealth, he also noted his belief that "valuable and rare records of the Colonial period of our history have gone to add to the collections of amateur antiquarians, or to enrich the show-cases of foreign historical societies. The progging industry of relic hunters, autograph collectors and others has not been idle in adding to these depredations." To protect against further loss of vital historical information, Palmer enthusiastically endorsed the idea of printing a calendar of the surviving papers similar to the series of calendars of state papers that the British government had begun to issue.[89]

The resulting *Calendar of Virginia State Papers and Other Manuscripts* ran to eleven large volumes published between 1875 and 1892. During that time Palmer, Secretary of the Commonwealth Henry W. Flournoy, and several assistants copied and prepared for publication thousands of documents from the 1640s through the 1860s, with the vast majority falling in the eighteenth century. Given the magnitude of the losses of state and local records from the colonial period, the *Calendar of Virginia State Papers* represented a remarkable achievement and ever since has been an indispensable resource for the study of Virginia's colonial and early national history.

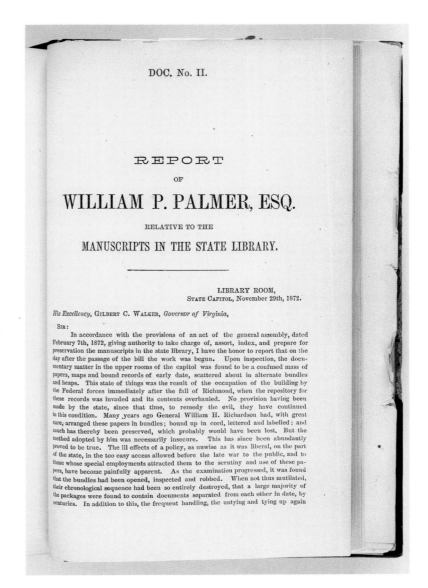

▲ William Palmer published his report, composed in the "Library Room" of the Capitol in 1872, describing the condition of the Library's archival records.

During the 1870s, the State Library also began to take steps to identify and recover early documentary evidence preserved in other locations. In 1873 the state librarian asked all of the county clerks in Virginia to report on public documents, seals, maps, and other valuable records found in their offices, and in 1892 the General Assembly appropriated $5,000 to purchase copies of early county records.[90] Recognizing that royal officials and British bureaucrats in the seventeenth and eighteenth centuries had kept many original documents relating to Virginia as well as copies of executive, legislative, and judicial records, the Joint Committee on the Library in 1872 commissioned William Noel Sainsbury to compile abstracts of Virginia documents in the newly opened British Public Record Office.[91] Sainsbury eventually submitted twenty large volumes of abstracts of more than five thousand documents, most from the seventeenth century but some as late as 1730.

Shortly before that project began, the State Library acquired two volumes of transcripts of seventeenth-century documents pertaining to the establishment of the boundary line between Virginia and North

▲ The Governor's Office in the Capitol, ca. 1890s, captured by the camera of noted Richmond photographer Huestis Pratt Cook. The Victorian neatness in this office constrasted sharply with the overcrowding and disorder in the Library's rooms in the Capitol in the early 1890s. (Valentine Museum, Richmond, Virginia)

Carolina and five volumes of transcripts on the same subject that had been compiled in 1860. Under an agreement reached in 1889, the Library also acquired two volumes of transcripts of seventeenth-century records, the second volume being entirely devoted to the records of Bacon's Rebellion. To these were added another volume concerning Bacon's Rebellion compiled in 1886 from material held by the British Museum. In 1890 the Library purchased a volume of transcriptions relating to treaties between the American colonies and the Cherokee nation of Indians during the mid-eighteenth century. The state librarian also arranged to have copies made of Harvard College's collection of documents bearing principally on the French and Indian War and the American Revolution. By the end of the nineteenth century, the State Library had thus acquired transcripts or abstracts of 6,383 documents not previously accessible to Virginians.[92] Although these did not replicate the whole, or even a large part, of the lost colonial archive, they added substantially to the available body of information about early Virginia.

One of the first significant recoveries of original documents occurred in 1897. Several years earlier, the widow of the Massachusetts collector and historian Benson J. Lossing offered some manuscripts from her late husband's collection for sale through a Boston dealer. William Wallace Scott, the secretary of the commonwealth's assistant who managed the day-to-day operations of the State Library, engaged a Boston attorney to recover the documents in that collection that he believed had been removed from the Virginia archives in the spring of 1865. Scott identified them as stolen property, since they had all been addressed to various officers of the government of Virginia. In 1897 the attorney dispatched to Virginia thirty-five documents, among which were papers bearing the signatures of King William III, Queen Anne, King George II, William Byrd I, Richard Henry Lee, General George Washington, the Marquis de Lafayette, and the Comte de Rochambeau.[93]

FIRST STATE LIBRARY BUILDING

The Library's book collection grew steadily after 1870, as its scope widened from a focus on law and public policy to encompass literature, poetry, history, art, and other cultural subjects. In 1872 the Joint Committee on the Library estimated that the collection contained about twenty-seven thousand volumes, 35 percent of which were law-books and the remainder "embracing almost every variety of subject on which books have been published in the English language."[94] By 1890 the collection had grown to about thirty-five thousand volumes, which Secretary of the Commonwealth Henry W. Flournoy considered to be "as valuable as any library of its size in the United States." "In addition to books, it contains many valuable historical manuscripts," he wrote in his annual report in that year, and boasted as well a "portrait gallery, embracing the portraits of many of the great men of the State."[95]

The Library also became a popular place to visit in the late nineteenth century. Local citizens as well as tourists went to the Library to consult the books and to view exhibits, which included a collection of Confederate flags. Early in 1875 a writer for the *Richmond Enquirer* had remarked on how much visitation to the State Library had increased since the purchase of portraits and artwork had begun to transform the Library from a "cheerless" spot into "one of the most attractive places in the city."[96] Richmond writer and humorist George William Bagby, who served for several years during the 1870s as the state librarian, complained privately (half humorously and half seriously) in March 1875 that he was "in a state of frenzy about the torrent of hummers, children, fools, idlers, gigglers &c that pour into the Library daily."[97] In 1886 the number of visitors was estimated at about five thousand per year, including one person in August of that year who assumed that the State Library must have everything and asked to see the hatchet that the young George Washington supposedly used to chop down his father's cherry tree.[98]

In 1884 and 1885 the state spent almost $6,000 enlarging, refurnishing, and repainting the Library rooms, but within ten years the collection had outgrown its cramped quarters and "hundreds of volumes" were stacked "on the floor for want of shelf-room."[99] The thousands of volumes of out-of-date statute books and paperbound government reports that Charles Lewis had wanted to get rid of in 1865 were still stored in the Capitol attic and in rented space elsewhere in Richmond.[100] At some time during the 1880s or early in the 1890s, one of the secretaries of the commonwealth disposed of a large quantity of old documents, an action that a future state librarian later described as "the most inexcusable disaster of them all." The librarian sold the documents to a local junk dealer as waste paper, and the purchaser erected long chutes from the upper windows of the Capitol to convey the papers into his waiting wagons. The dealer was said to have complained later that he lost money on the transaction because his workmen had to take time to remove all of the wax seals from the old documents before the papers could be disposed of. More than half a bushel of old seals was said to have been found in the junk dealer's yard, each of which must have been removed from an original historical document.[101] Reports also circulated sometime later that some state employees had sold old documents to paper dealers, almost certainly without authorization.[102]

The General Assembly took the first steps toward providing a separate building for the Library in 1884 by directing that revenue obtained from the sale of certain state lands be invested in bonds and held until the investment had yielded enough profit to begin con-

▲ Henry W. Flournoy served as secretary of the commonwealth and state librarian from 1884 to 1894.

struction of "a public building to be used as a library, and for public offices."[103] In March 1892, the assembly passed "An Act to Provide for the Erection of a Fire-proof State Library Building." The preamble to the legislation gave ample justification of the need: "Whereas the capital [*sic*] building is overloaded with a library, making it necessary to rent rooms in the city for the storage of books and public documents, and with archives of incalculable value to Virginia, whose loss nothing could replace; and Whereas the said building may collapse from this extraordinary weight and is in daily danger of destruction by fire, which, when once under way could not be extinguished; and Whereas the public wants have largely outgrown the capacity of the said building to meet them, and a building supplemental to the capitol is imperatively demanded by the above circumstances." The assembly directed the governor and a committee of state officials to seek bids for the design and construction of a new building.[104] On 22 October 1892 they accepted a bid of $161,246.40 from a local contractor, stipulating that the "building shall be completed by April 22, 1894, unless unavoidably obstructed."[105]

In the spring of 1894 the assembly appropriated $20,000 to furnish the new library building and to move the Library's books and archival records as well as the offices of the auditor of public accounts, the state treasurer, the adjutant general, and several other departments from the Capitol into the new building. The assembly also authorized the state librarian to hire an additional temporary clerk to assist with the transition. The move took almost three months in the summer of 1895, during which the Library was closed to the public. Convicts from the State Penitentiary furnished the labor for transporting the books across the street and down the hill from the Capitol to the new building.[106] The assembly also concluded an agreement with the city of Richmond to have the secretary of the commonwealth hire at Richmond's expense someone to staff the Library "during such hours" as the secretary directed.[107] The city agreed to pay the salary of a "night clerk" so that the Library could be open for business to the general public from 7:00 P.M. to midnight, in addition to its normal hours from 9:00 A.M. until 3:00 P.M. Once the librarian had arranged the books on the new stack shelves, he began preparation of a catalog of the Library's volumes by "the method of cataloguing known as the card system."[108]

▼ At the century's close, books and manuscripts so crowded the Capitol rooms and offices that the need for a separate library building became immediate. (Valentine Museum, Richmond Virginia)

The state librarian and the Joint Committee on the Library stirred up a controversy at the same time by offering to sell "the contents of the second gallery," that is, the "surplus annual reports of the State of Virginia, similar reports of other States, many volumes of old United States statutes at large, in paper back, and various government publications of like character, none of which had ever been deemed of sufficient value to be placed on the catalogue of the library." The librarian obtained the advice of a respected Richmond authority on Virginiana, William G. Stanard, on which volumes to sell, but former assistant state librarian Charles Poindexter protested to the governor and eventually filed suit in a Richmond court in an attempt to halt the sale. Intervention by the state's attorney general produced a ruling in favor of the librarian, and the books were sold as surplus paper at the rate of sixty-five cents per hundred pounds, the total value at that rate being two hundred and fifty dollars.[109]

Soon after the move into the new building, the secretary of the commonwealth directed one of his assistants, Thomas E. Nimmo, to prepare an inventory of the archival records. In 1902 the Joint Committee on the Library authorized the hiring of "some suitable and expert person to arrange the Manuscripts in the Library, known generally as the State Archives, with a view not only to their preservation but also to render them more accessible to students of the history of the State." Two years later, William G. Stanard published a preliminary edition of that inventory as part of an American Historical Association series on state archival collections. The published inventory, while general and imprecise, nonetheless indicated that a new beginning had been made in caring for Virginia's archives. Stanard prefaced this edition with a short history of the state's archives and included references to a number of letter books, book lists, and checkbook stubs documenting the nineteenth-century history of the Library.[110]

CREATION OF A STATE LIBRARY BOARD

The convention that met in Richmond in 1901 and 1902 to revise Virginia's 1869 constitution appointed a committee to consider the status of the State Library and its holdings of books, archival records, and artwork. The committee toured the Library and interviewed the state librarian. Its report to the convention was not flattering: "Whilst the State Library is one of the most valuable up to a certain point of time in the United States or in the world, it is in very bad condition. We are told by the Librarian that there are works there worth their weight in gold and that there are manuscripts there that are worth far more than their weight in gold; that if they were lost or damaged they could not be replaced; and that they are in such condition, unassorted, oftentimes unapproachable, that you could not find them without great labor and without doing damage to some of the documents with which they are unassorted." The report concluded "that the Library is at present, except the department of law, doing almost no service to the State; and that it is absolutely necessary that this vastly important and valuable set of books owned by the State should be brought into the condition of utility." To remedy this, the committee unanimously recommended that the Library be made a separate state agency under the direction of a board of directors composed of "the leading men in the State" and proposed that the board be empowered to hire a librarian and to make rules for the governance of the Library in order to make it "an honor and a blessing to the State of Virginia."[111]

As a result, paragraph five of section 132 of the Constitution of 1902 empowered the State Board of Education to create a five-member

▲ This building, just down the hill from the Executive Mansion on the eastern side of Capitol Square, housed the Library from 1895 through 1940. The first State Library building also contained the offices of the auditor of public accounts, the state treasurer, the adjutant general, and several other departments of government.

board of directors, who would serve without compensation, to oversee the management of the State Library and to appoint the state librarian. The new constitution transferred the law library and the appointment of a law librarian to the Supreme Court of Appeals. In 1903 and 1904, the General Assembly passed enabling legislation to carry out these constitutional changes.[112]

The first meeting of the new Library Board took place on 1 July 1903. The board designated William Wallace Scott, who had been the assistant to the secretary of the commonwealth in charge of the books, as acting state librarian. Scott soon accepted an appointment as the librarian for the new and separate State Law Library, however, and on 3 October 1903 John Pendleton Kennedy, a librarian at the Library of Congress, became the first state librarian under the authority of the board.[113] Kennedy went to work almost immediately, even before his official starting date of 2 November 1903, and initiated a general overhauling of the Library's facilities and collections.[114] The staff, including Kennedy and a janitor, numbered only five people. Kennedy revived the preparation of a proper card catalog and increased purchases of books, periodicals, and newspapers for the general readership. By the time the Library Board issued its first annual report for the fiscal year ending 30 June 1904, the State Library contained an estimated 47,640 bound volumes, about 8,500 pamphlets, and some 1,800 periodicals. The collection included 1,376 volumes of fiction and a small number of books for the blind that the librarian had selected in consultation with the principal of the Virginia School for the Deaf and Blind at Staunton. The Library Board also began developing procedures to regulate the lending of books to persons who lived outside of Richmond to ensure that the

library would be "in effect a State Library, and not merely as heretofore available for the most part to local users."[115]

The changes in the State Library attracted attention, and the state librarian made good use of the opportunity to promote the Library and increase its reputation. He announced to the press that he planned to keep the Library open evenings between October and May and told a reporter in April 1904 "that he especially wanted the attention of workingmen called to [the] opportunity now placed before them and that he would do everything in his power to advocate their interests." The reporter quoted Kennedy as saying, "We have 100,000 books, among them being works of fiction, which are at the disposal of the public, and we have all the magazines, periodicals, State and daily papers, etc."[116] A month later the newspaper characterized the Virginia State Library as "one of the most delightful places in the city these warm days. Electric fans are in motion, the windows are open, awnings keep out the sun, and the elevation makes the room comfortable at all times."[117] Early in June the same year Kennedy unveiled a display of Virginia maps in the Library's new map cases. Among the maps on display were a copy

▲ John Pendleton Kennedy, the first state librarian appointed after the Library became a state agency under the authority of a five-member Library Board. Kennedy served as state librarian from 1903 to 1907.

▼ *The Little Story Book*, a raised-print volume published in 1851 by the "Virginia Institution for the Education of the Deaf and Dumb and of the Blind," in Staunton, is a treasured reminder of the Library's historical role in developing reading programs for the visually impaired.

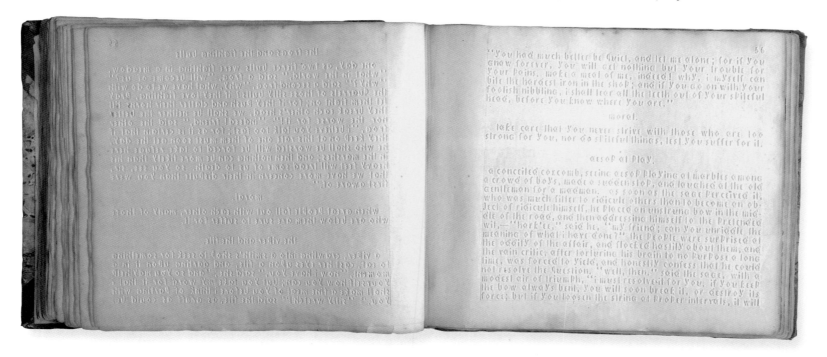

▲ The reading room and reference areas in the first State Library building were spacious and fitted with the modern conveniences of the day. Researchers could work comfortably at large library tables with oversized manuscripts as well as consult reference books shelved handily nearby. The new Library also provided space for the display of maps, portraits, and statuary from the Library's collections.

of John White's 1585 map and the 1775 printing of the famous Joshua Fry and Peter Jefferson map of Virginia. Kennedy took special pride in the display cases and in the interest shown by the public, and he pledged "to have the library co-operate with the other educational institutions in the city."[118]

The first personal contact that many Virginians who lived outside Richmond probably had with the rich and varied collections of the Virginia State Library was at the 1907 Jamestown Ter-Centennial Exposition celebrating the three-hundredth anniversary of the first permanent English settlement in North America. The exposition took place between April and November on fairgrounds located just outside the city of Norfolk. The Virginia Historical Society and the Virginia State Library jointly mounted an impressive exhibit of books, historic documents, and works of art in the exposition's large Palace of History. The State Library contributed dozens of original documents from the seventeenth, eighteenth, and nineteenth centuries as well as paintings, sculpture, and a display "of the title pages of all the important books bearing on the early history of Virginia."[119] The exhibition received one of the gold medals awarded in the division of history.[120]

The Virginia State Library had begun to develop into more than the "rich storehouse of knowledge" that John Peyton Little had described in 1852. As an independent state agency, the Library after 1903 not only stored and preserved information in the forms of documents, books, and artwork, but also it actively acquired, created, and disseminated information in a number of new ways. This became evident at the end of October 1904 when State Librarian Kennedy issued his initial annual report, to which he appended the first of what was to become a long and valuable series of publications of historic documents, bibliographies, and other compilations of information about Virginia. Fittingly, the first report contained the texts of the earliest statutes governing the Library and a tabulation of the expenses of the Library between 1 January 1829 and 30 June 1904, showing that the state had spent $334,242.64 during those years, mostly on books. The report contained information about the Library's collection of books for the blind and about the beginnings of an interlibrary loan system with other lending libraries in Virginia. The state librarian also appended the first of what later became a regular publication of statis-

tics about Virginia's libraries, a three-page list of all the libraries in Virginia with the names of their librarians, the dates of their foundings, and the sizes of their collections. In addition, Kennedy included the first of several other lists that the Library from time to time issued and updated: a description of the records in the archives, then estimated to number about two hundred thousand pieces; a list of government publications in the Library; a list of sheet music from the Confederate period that had been acquired during the preceding year; a list of periodicals currently on file; a list of the portraits "exhibited in the lower portrait gallery" and another list of portraits of Virginia governors "exhibited in the upper portrait gallery"; a list of "engravings, photographs, broadsides, manuscripts, etc.," that had also been on exhibit during the year; and a list of books acquired since the organization of the State Library's governing board.

The report contained, too, a description of the beginnings of a traveling-libraries project, through which the state librarian hoped eventually to provide three boxed sets of books to each county in Virginia to serve as local lending libraries. The General Assembly's act of March 1904 had authorized the project, but the legislature failed to appropriate any money to fund it. Kennedy persuaded the railroads to transport the boxed sets of books free of charge and solicited assistance in assembling books from women's clubs and community groups. As a result, the program went into operation almost immediately.[121] The program for lending books to the blind and sight impaired also depended on a cost-free transportation program created by the United States government. By 1907 the State Library had more than two hundred volumes regularly in circulation for the visually impaired, mostly to patrons who lived outside of Richmond and to some who lived outside the state.[122] The Library administered this program until it was transferred to the Virginia Commission for the Blind early in 1942.[123]

▲ Many Virginians saw items from the collections of the Virginia State Library for the first time at the Jamestown Ter-Centennial Exposition of 1907.

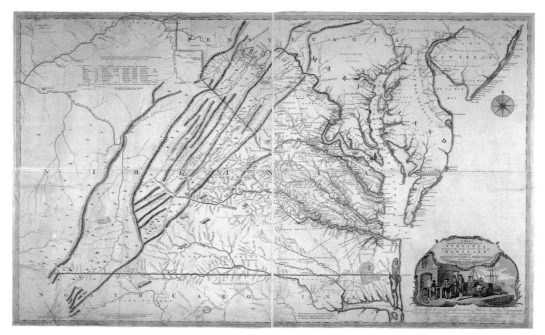

▲ One of the first maps displayed in special cases ordered for the first State Library building was the Library's hand-colored, copperplate engraving of the famous *Map of the most Inhabited part of Virginia*, by Joshua Fry and Peter Jefferson.

Initial attempts, both before and after the establishment of the Library Board, to prepare a full catalog of the Library's printed book collection failed because the Library had too small a staff to prepare catalog cards while simultaneously carrying on all the other necessary work. Oral tradition, supported by some documentary evidence, indicates that early in the twentieth century many of the State Library's books "were on shelves without any attempt at classification." A student who served as an apprentice in the Library at that time later recalled that the janitor, John Snyder, "was the only person who could locate a volume easily."[124] Two preliminary attempts at cataloging had been done partly in the Dewey Decimal system and partly in the Cutter system. During 1907, however, the Library staff, which was finally enlarged to include a full-time cataloger, adopted the then-new Library of Congress cataloging system, making the Virginia State Library one of the first large public libraries in the country to do so.[125]

ENLARGING THE COLLECTIONS

John Pendleton Kennedy served as state librarian from 2 November 1903 to 6 July 1907, when the Library Board requested and accepted his resignation following two inconclusive public investigations of his book-purchasing practices and because of reported personality conflicts between Kennedy and the members of the staff and of the Library Board.[126] At the same night meeting at which Kennedy resigned, the board appointed Henry Read McIlwaine to take his place.[127] A Farmville, Virginia, native, McIlwaine had earned a doctorate degree in history in 1893 from the Johns Hopkins University. At the time of his appointment, he was a professor of history and English and the head librarian at Hampden-Sydney College.[128] He immediately moved to Richmond and began work.[129] Although trained as a historian and not as a librarian, McIlwaine continued his predecessor's innovative policies and emphasis on professionalism during his ad-

ministration of the Library, which lasted until McIlwaine's death on 16 March 1934. One of his first tasks was to appoint a new assistant state librarian to succeed Edward S. Evans who resigned following Kennedy's departure. In August 1907, McIlwaine selected Earl Gregg Swem, then chief of the cataloging division of the Copyright Office at the Library of Congress.[130]

Henry Read McIlwaine was particularly intent on continuing his predecessor's attempt to create a modern archival program. In 1904 State Librarian Kennedy had taken an important step toward preserving Virginia's documentary heritage by creating the Department of Archives and History. He charged the new department with caring for and cataloging the state's archival records, printing those that warranted publication, and acquiring, whenever possible, new manuscripts and replacing lost ones with transcripts or photocopies. Kennedy had acknowledged his doubts that the Library would ever recover much lost original material. "Innumerable persons traffic in these papers," he wrote in 1905, "disposing of many valuable collections that lose their identity as distinct historical values the moment they become the property of collectors throughout the North and Middle West. This is largely due to the determination on the part of those who come into possession of such papers to dispose of them only when fabulous offers are made."[131]

A large portion of the public records of Virginia were not in the care of the State Library when it became a state agency in 1903. Officials in charge of the various offices of state government had operated without any guidance with respect to the retention of their records. Some departments may have deposited their noncurrent records with the secretary of the commonwealth, but others kept them in their offices or stashed them away in hidden corners of the Capitol, and still others probably threw out records that were in the way. As a result, the task of retrieving archival materials and of assembling an efficiently run archive was difficult. In his annual report in 1911, McIlwaine reported in exasperation that "in the care taken in the preservation of records Virginia is not only years,

▶ Historian Henry Read McIlwaine became state librarian in 1907 and served until his death in 1934. Foremost among his many accomplishments was the establishment of a modern and professional archival program in Virginia.

but decades and even centuries behind the enlightened countries of the world."[132] In 1918 and again in 1926 the assembly authorized local clerks of court to deposit pre-1790 records in the state archives, but it was not until the 1940s that significant numbers of original local records were transferred to the State Library. It was in part through the agency of the Work Projects Administration that the first inventories of local government records were made and the first attempts to care for them properly were undertaken.[133]

The state librarian and the Library's archivists began lobbying the General Assembly in 1921 to have the state adopt uniform standards for paper, ink, and typewriter ribbons to ensure that the public records being created during the twentieth century would be usable for later generations.[134] Preservation of records already in the archives and in

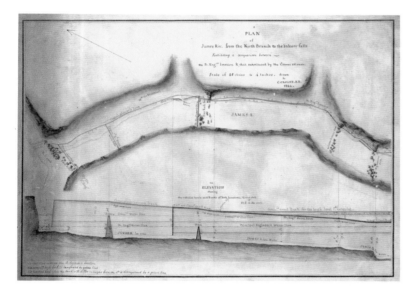

▲ "Plan of the James Riv[er] from the North Branch to the balcony falls," one of the more than 500 maps that comprise the Library's Board of Public Works Collection, accessioned in 1924.

the various state and local government offices also became a matter of concern. In 1912 a delegation from the Sons of the American Revolution had testified before a committee of the General Assembly on behalf of an appropriation to be employed for records preservation. "Though much enthusiasm on the subject of the passage of the bill was manifested," State Librarian McIlwaine laconically remarked, "the bill failed."[135] By the 1930s several patriotic societies in Virginia, among them the Daughters of the American Revolution, began contributing money for the restoration and rebinding of original documents, and thereafter the annual reports of the state librarian regularly listed dozens of volumes of records that had been stabilized or preserved with their financial aid. Martha Woodroof Hiden, a member of the Library Board from 1932 through 1952, took a leadership role in rescuing and preserving local government records and in pressing for public and private funding toward that end.[136]

During the second and third decades of the twentieth century, the State Library's staff retrieved from government offices and processed several large and valuable archival collections, including twenty-one thousand original petitions submitted to the General Assembly between 1776 and 1865 and more than seven hundred thousand documents from the auditors' offices.[137] The latter group of records included manuscripts relating to the financial history of the commonwealth as

well as records pertaining to military pension applications, trial records and materials concerning criminal prosecutions of slaves, a large collection of the papers of frontiersman and explorer George Rogers Clark, and records relevant to a wide variety of other subjects that historians had not previously studied because primary sources had not been available.[138] When Virginia abolished the Department of Confederate Records in 1918, the State Library received all of the department's service records and related documents and began the preparation of more than a hundred thousand index cards to facilitate access to the files.[139] In 1924 the Library accessioned the records of the Board of Public Works, which had overseen the commonwealth's interests in internal improvements projects during the nineteenth century. This collection included 400 maps and 142 boxes of manuscripts containing about one hundred thousand documents. The assistant state librarian described the acquisition as one of "the most important and valuable collections" the Library had ever received.[140] The voluminous records of the Virginia War History Commission, documenting Virginians' participation in World War I, were also transferred to the State Library and made available in 1932.[141]

During this period, the Library acquired several valuable collections of personal, family, and other historical papers, including the Nathaniel Francis Cabell Collection on colonial and nineteenth-century Virginia agriculture and the inventory of the contents of the Governor's Palace in Williamsburg taken in 1770 following the death of Governor Botetourt.[142] The Library also began to acquire what in time became a large collection of family Bible records, cemetery records, church records, and genealogical notes and charts. By the end of the 1930s, the Virginia State Library was regarded as one of the prime family-history research libraries in the United States. During the late 1940s, the State Library entered a cooperative program with Virginia's localities and the Church of Jesus Christ of Latter Day Saints (the Mormons), to microfilm all the known deed, order, and will books in Virginia from the colonial period through 1865. When the project was completed in 1963, the State Library had acquired more than four thousand reels of microfilm of about fifty thousand volumes of local records.[143]

Business and organizational records also became integral parts of the research collection. The largest of these was the mammoth collection of more than seven hundred volumes and more than one hundred thousand papers belonging to the Tredegar Iron Works of Richmond, the premier iron foundry in Virginia during the nineteenth century and the principal source of cannons, ironclad plates, and other ironwork for the Confederacy.[144]

The volume of new acquisitions was overwhelming, and the Library's archivists enlisted the aid of college students in the Richmond area to assist with arrangement and description.[145] Unfortunately, the Library lacked sufficient financial and human resources to prepare detailed guides and finding aids for the use of these records and many of the new acquisitions. In 1929 a researcher from North Carolina was so frustrated at the lack of indexes and finding aids that he complained to a local newspaper. "Everything seems to be down there," he told a reporter, "and perhaps somebody is able to find what they want, but not I. . . . Virginia ought to index and publish more of that material—all of it, in fact."[146]

During Henry Read McIlwaine's tenure, the State Library also began systematic purchases of histories and documentary materials of British (chiefly English) history, which were much in demand for genealogical and family history research. Acquisitions in this field

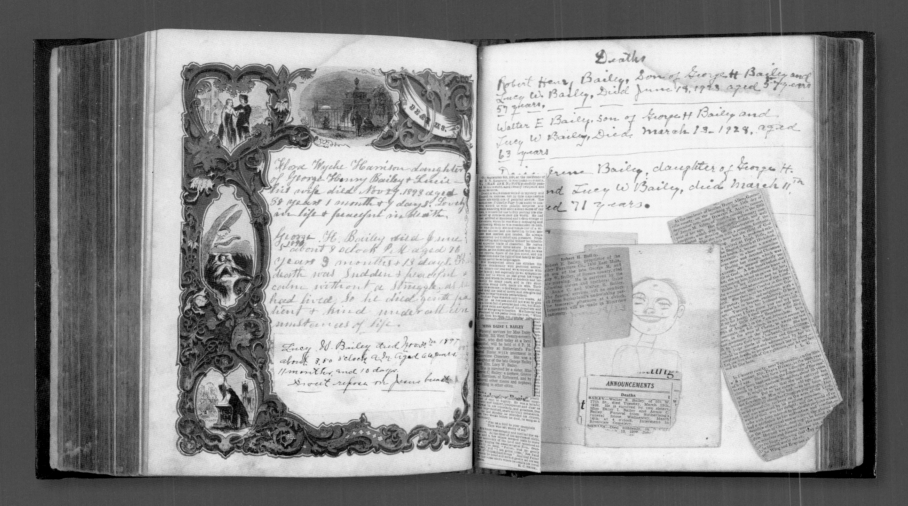

The Bailey family, of Sussex County, Virginia, faithfully recorded the births and deaths of kin from 1820 to 1941, including newspaper obituaries, in the family Bible. The Library's collection of Bible records, numbering more than four thousand, provides invaluable information particularly for genealogical research.

▲ The letter books, journals, and financial records of the Tredegar Iron Works document the everyday labors and activities of workers and managers in the sprawling ironworks. Pictured here are James Wade and an unidentified black worker posing in the Tredegar rolling mill in the early twentieth century. Wade's father, Edward Wade, supervised the rolling of the plates for the ironclad CSS *Virginia* (the former USS *Merrimack*). (Valentine Museum, Richmond, Virginia)

included genealogical works and local histories as well as parish registers containing records of births, marriages, and deaths. In 1949 the Library acquired ninety-one volumes (described as "nearly a complete set") of the mammoth *Victoria History of the Counties of England*.[147] The Library also sought to acquire two copies of every book written about Virginia or by a Virginian, which further enlarged the scope of the book collection. Biographies, travel accounts, books about the American Revolution and the Civil War, and works of southern and Virginia history comprised the most important body of literature in the State Library. Confederate imprints—books and documents printed in the Confederate States of America—were also of special interest. In 1911, the State Library published a seventy-two page *List*

of the Official Publications of the Confederate States Government in the Virginia State Library and the Library of the Confederate Memorial Literary Society, to which was appended the report of the Confederate superintendent of public printing issued in 1864.[148] The Library continued to make regular and systematic purchases of books, pamphlets, newspapers, and other ephemera printed in the South during the Civil War.

The Library's collection of Confederate imprints became one of the most notable in the United States, and in 1957 the State Library published Richard Barksdale Harwell's two-volume bibliography, *More Confederate Imprints*, as a supplement to Marjorie Lyle Crandall's pioneering two-volume *Confederate Imprints* published two years earlier. The printed-book collection surpassed a quarter-million volumes for the first time in 1932.[149]

◄ The Library of Virginia has a comprehensive collection of books, newspapers, maps, and other imprints published between 1861 and 1865. Among these Confederate items is the sheet music for "Pray, Maiden, Pray! A Ballad for the Times to the Patriotic Women of the South," written by A. W. Kercheval and A. J. Turner and published in 1864 by George Dunn and Company, of Richmond.

Unfortunately, the largest and most valuable private collection of books and manuscripts relating to Virginia failed to find its way into the State Library. Following the death of Richmond resident Robert Alonzo Brock in 1914, Brock's heirs offered his lifelong collection of Virginiana for sale. The collection included approximately fifty thousand manuscripts, seventeen thousand books, and sixty-five thousand pamphlets and small printed items. Most observers anticipated that the Virginia Historical Society or the Virginia State Library would purchase it, but neither institution had enough money to conclude the transaction. The state librarian declined to acquire the collection as well because it included many volumes that the Library already owned. Had McIlwaine realized that the Brock Collection contained a number of original public documents, his decision might have been different. In 1922 collector Henry E. Huntington purchased the entire collection and shipped it to his home in San Marino, California, which in time became the Henry E. Huntington Library and Art Gallery.[150]

In addition to purchasing books, manuscripts, works of art, and other Virginiana, the Virginia State Library also received donations of items that substantially enlarged and enhanced the collections. The earliest-known donation was of a copy of *The Natural History of the Island of Barbadoes*, by Griffith Hughes, which was published in the 1750s and contains an inscription reading, "Presented to the Library of Virginia by Addison Hansford Esq., 1833." One of the most unusual donations was a Chinese-language copy of the *Peking Gazette*, which John Lewis Shuck, of Virginia, one of the first Protestant missionaries allowed into China, "Presented to the Virginia Library" on an unrecorded date prior to his death on 20 August 1863. Another volume that was probably donated to the State Library was a copy of Henry Ainsworth's *Annotations Upon the Book of Psalmes*, which traveled to the New World in 1620 on the famous voyage of the *Mayflower*.[151] The date on which the State Library acquired the volume and the precise circumstances of the acquisition are not recorded, but it is most likely that a Virginian or someone interested in Virginiana purchased the book in England during the 1890s and gave it to the Library. This apparently was one of Henry Read McIlwaine's favorite items for he wrote about the book in a 1930 article on the Library's treasures published in the Richmond Chamber of Commerce's *Richmond Magazine*, and it was featured again in 1938 in a piece in the *Richmond Times-Dispatch*.[152]

On numerous occasions historians, poets, novelists, playwrights, and other authors have presented copies of their works to the State Library. Collectors have also often contributed works that they have acquired. In 1945 Lydia Purcell, of Richmond, donated a collection of nineteen autographed volumes of novels and plays by Virginia author Amélie Louise Rives Troubetzkoy.[153] Eight years later, Eudora Ramsay

Richardson and Cornelia S. Adair presented a check in the amount of $1,164.75 to the Library to create a fund in honor of Geline M. Bowman, founder of the Virginia Federation of Business and Professional Women's Clubs, "to build up a collection of books about women."[154] In 1967, Richmonder John J. Wicker Jr. gave the Library his collection of intercollegiate football rule- and record-books dating from 1900 through 1966. The collection was believed to contain the only complete set in existence. Five years later he added the volumes published through the 1971 season.[155]

On several occasions the State Library received large numbers of books bequeathed by friends of learning. Among the largest contributions were those from such donors as John Dunlop, of Richmond, who left the Library a valuable and varied collection of almost three thousand books that arrived in 1909; Robert L. Parrish, of Covington, from whose estate the Library received about a thousand volumes in the

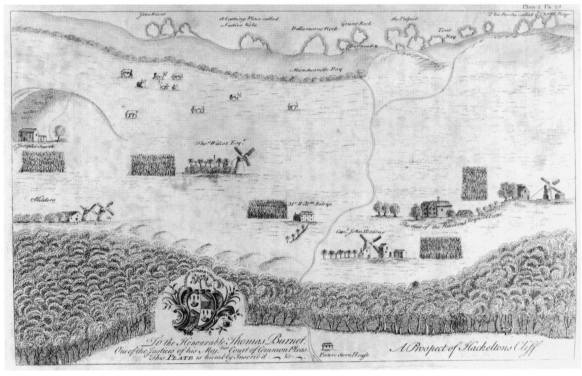

▲ This view of Hackleton's Cliff from Griffith Hughes's *Natural History of the Island of Barbadoes, In Ten Books* is one of several engravings executed for publication of the volume in the 1750s. Addison Hansford, clerk of the Senate of Virginia, presented the volume to the Library of Virginia in 1833. It is the earliest-known donation to the Library's collections.

spring of 1917; suffragist Lila Meade Valentine, whose 1,005 volumes were accessioned in 1921; and College of William and Mary president John Stewart Bryan, whose family gave the Library several thousand volumes from his library in 1952.[156] One of the largest and most valuable collections belonged to John E. Roller, of Harrisonburg, a noted collector of Virginiana, southern history, and literature. The Virginia State Library received approximately seventeen hundred volumes from Roller's huge library, among them a 1714 English edition of Baltasar Gracián y Morales, *The Art of Prudence*, that is believed to have belonged to George Washington. Other notable Virginians who contributed significant numbers of books to the Library include Richmond editor and historian Douglas Southall Freeman and State Library Board

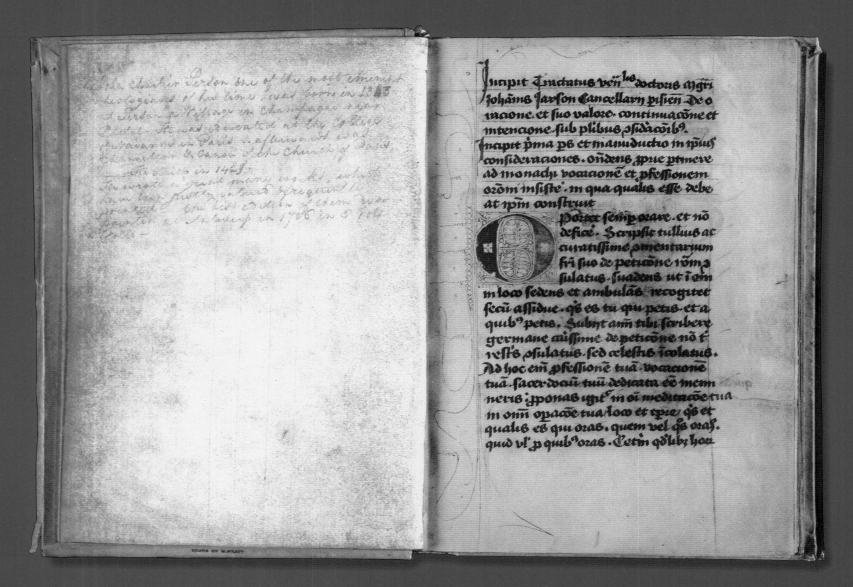

△ The oldest item among the Library's holdings is this handsome hand-written copy of Jean Gerson's *De Oratione et Valore Eius: De Arte Audiendi Confessiones; De Remediis Contra Recidivium Peccandi,* prepared by an unknown scribe in England late in the fifteenth century.

▲ In 1924, Governor E. Lee Trinkle gave the Library a commemorative slice of the so-called Washington Elm, the tree under which General George Washington took command of the Continental army in Boston. The fragment had been presented to the state of Virginia by the governor of Massachusetts.

chairman Robert B. Tunstall, who presented the Library with about seven hundred volumes when he retired in 1949.[157]

Not all the special items donated to the State Library have been books or manuscripts. In May 1923 Lawrence Groner, of Norfolk, presented a collection of Virginia paper money, "denominations ranging from $1 to $100 and date of issuance from 1775 to 1780."[158] The Library continued to add to the collection, supplementing it with currency dating from the antebellum and Civil War periods. In April 1924 Governor E. Lee Trinkle accepted on behalf of the commonwealth of Virginia and deposited in the State Library a slice of what was known as the Washington Elm, the tree under which General George Washington took command of the Continental army in Boston, Massachusetts, on 3 July 1775. The tree had blown down in a storm, and the governor of Massachusetts sent pieces of it to the governors of all the other states.[159] A collection of items that had once belonged to the first governor of the commonwealth of Virginia, Patrick Henry, including a portrait of him, was turned over to the State Library by Henry's great-granddaughter in 1902.[160] The collection of glass-plate negatives of Norfolk photographer Harry C. Mann, originally donated to the Virginia State Chamber of Commerce, were transferred to the State Library, along with many other photographs that the chamber owned, together with hundreds of Virginia scenes that had been exhibited at the 1939 World's Fair in New York.[161]

The Library's rare books and artifacts have often been the subjects of speeches or articles prepared by staff members and occasionally some have been placed on display. In May 1934 the State Library and the Valentine Museum jointly exhibited some of their oldest books. The Library's contribution on that occasion was a bound volume containing two incunabula: Saint Bonaventura's *Opuscula* (Cologne, 1484), and Johannes Nider's *Formicarius* (Cologne?, 1470).[162] The oldest item in the State Library's collections is a beautiful handwritten book copied in England sometime late in the fifteenth century: *De Oratione et Valore Eius: De Arte Audiendi Confessiones; De Remediis Contra Recidivium Peccandi*, by Jean Gerson. Henry Read McIlwaine lent it to the Library of Congress for exhibition in 1933.

RETRIEVING LOST PROPERTY

During the first half of the twentieth century, the Library was fortunate to recover a number of books and documents that had been lost during the previous century. In May 1911, Calvin G. Hutcheson, of Dorchester, Massachusetts, walked into the Library and returned a book he had "borrowed" on 7 April 1865, when he had been serving as acting assistant paymaster on a U.S. Navy gunboat. He had taken a copy of the second edition of George B. Cheever's *The Journal of the Pilgrims at Plymouth, in New England, in 1620* (New York, 1848), which contained information about his Pilgrim ancestor.[163] Late in 1916 another book stolen from the Library in April 1865 was returned. A copy of the 1856 edition of Francis Quarles's *Enchiridion* (London, 1856) taken by Union army chaplain Philos G. Cook, of Buffalo, New York, was returned in 1916 by a friend to whom Cook had given the volume.[164] At the end of November 1941 the State Library received by mail another book that had been taken in 1865, the first volume of the 1731 two-volume English translation of the memoirs of French commodore Claude, comte de Forbin (1656–1733). The book came wrapped in a package with a paperweight that had been confiscated from a Confederate government office.[165] One of the most memorable documents recovered through private generosity was the original signed parchment of the Virginia Ordinance of Secession, which Union soldier Charles W. Bullis purloined from the Capitol in 1865. In 1887 his widow sold the document to a New York collector. In December 1929,

▼ A page from the manuscript journal of the Virginia Convention of 1776; the journal was taken from the State Library in 1865 by a Union officer and restored to the Library in 1940.

following the deaths of the collector and his son, the document was returned to the Library, where it was authenticated and placed in the collection.[166]

In other instances the Library took a more active role in identifying and recovering lost property. In 1912, a second large collection of manuscripts relating to Virginia from the estate of Benson J. Lossing went on the market for sale. The state librarian and an assistant attorney general inspected the papers in New York and worked out an arrangement with the dealer handling the sale that enabled the commonwealth of Virginia to obtain 117 historic documents that had once been in the possession of officers of Virginia's colonial or state government. The collection included documents signed by Queen Anne, George Washington, and the Marquis de Lafayette. The state paid the dealer $750, "which amount," the librarian reported, "was to be looked on, not as payment for the manuscripts, but as payment for the services of Mr. Lossing and his heirs in preserving the papers, for the expense incurred in advertising them, and for other expenses incidental to the case."[167]

The precedent established in the second Lossing recovery was employed on many subsequent occasions to retrieve books or archival records taken from the State Library as well as to recover on behalf of the commonwealth missing city and county records. Several of the recoveries were of especially important documents. In 1940 a Philadelphia dealer in rare books and manuscripts acquired for $100 the original manuscript journal of the Virginia Convention of 1776, the convention that had instructed the Virginia delegates to the Continental Congress to propose a declaration of independence, that had unanimously adopted the Virginia Declaration of Rights and the Virginia Constitution of 1776, and that had overwhelmingly elected Patrick Henry the first governor of the commonwealth of Virginia. The dealer had obtained the journal from the family of a Union officer who had taken it from the Capitol in 1865, and he offered to sell it to the Colonial Williamsburg Foundation for $25,000. Officers of the foundation brought the journal to State Archivist William J. Van Schreeven for authentication and to ascertain whether the state retained the legal right of ownership. Van Schreeven pronounced the document genuine and further declared it an official public record that belonged in the state archives. The Library and the attorneys for the dealer quickly worked out a mutually satisfactory arrangement by which the State Library kept the journal and paid the dealer the original purchase price of $100 for his having "preserved the document and for his care and custody of it."[168]

In none of the instances did the purchasers have to admit that they were knowingly in possession of stolen property, and in none of the instances did the State Library admit to purchasing back its lost books or manuscripts. The agreements simply enabled the Library to recover estrayed public property and to compensate the holders of the property in such a way that others in possession of public books and manuscripts would not be tempted to destroy or dispose of them to avoid prosecution or, as the state librarian explained it in 1928, "to drive such things to cover and thus add to the improbability of their ever being heard of by the State Library authorities."[169]

Following World War II the State Library entered into cooperative agreements with a number of academic libraries and research institutions to recover originals or copies of official Virginia public records that, through no fault of the repositories, had become part of their collections through the acquisition of the papers of collectors or histori-

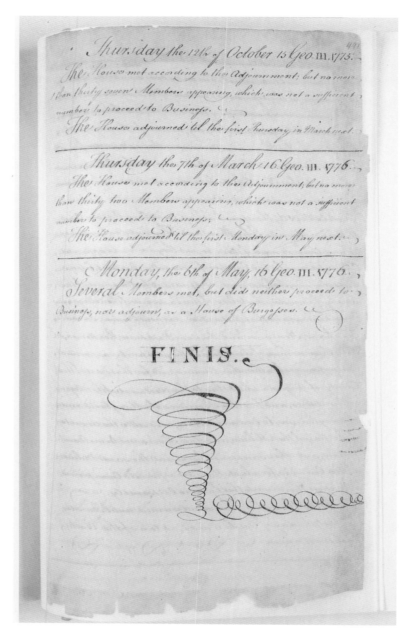

▲ The final page of the last manuscript journal of the Virginia House of Burgesses, in the hand of Jacob Bruce, assistant to the clerk of the House, George Wythe. Meeting on 6 May 1776, the burgesses refrained from conducting business or from formal adjournment and agreed thereby to bring Virginia's colonial assembly to an end forever.

cally significant persons or families. One of the first fruits of that endeavor was the return to the State Library in 1949 of a number of valuable Civil War–era manuscripts and books from the National Archives. Among them was the original journal of the advisory council that the General Assembly had established in the spring of 1861 to assist Governor John Letcher in arming the state following the secession of Virginia. The first action of the council on 21 April 1861 had been to recommend that Letcher appoint Robert E. Lee to "the office of Commander of the Military and Naval forces of Virginia."[170]

BEGINNINGS OF A PUBLICATION PROGRAM

When John Pendleton Kennedy left the Library of Congress to become state librarian in 1903, the Library of Congress had just begun to publish some of the most important national documents in its collection, among them the journals of the Continental Congress and the records of the Virginia Company of London. Kennedy quickly arranged for the State Library to publish, almost simultaneously, the journals of the Virginia House of Burgesses. Only a few of the original journals were in the state's archives, but Kennedy obtained additional texts in London and Washington. Beginning in 1905 and concluding in 1915, Kennedy and his successor, Henry Read McIlwaine, published a thirteen-volume edition of all the then-known journals of the House of Burgesses. McIlwaine almost immediately followed with three volumes of the legislative journals of the colonial Council. Publication of these journals marked a major milestone in historical editing and placed the State Library in the forefront of a new national movement for the preservation and publication of the most important public records of American history. Noted historian Clarence W. Alvord proclaimed in the *Mississippi Valley Historical Review* in 1921 that the State Library's edition of the journals of the two houses of the Virginia colonial assembly was "one of the most important contributions to our national history that has ever been published."[171]

McIlwaine soon initiated multivolume editions of the executive journals of the colonial Council and the journals of the Council of State during the American Revolution, and he edited and published three volumes of the surviving letters of the governors of Virginia during the Revolution. In addition, the State Library issued several valuable bibliographies, monographs, checklists, and other scholarly works prepared by staff members, and it also printed several colonial parish vestry books and registers edited by well-known students of the colonial period. One of the largest early publications was Edward S. Evans's *Calendar of Transcripts*, a detailed bibliography of the transcripts of documents from British repositories that the State Library had acquired during the nineteenth century. The *Calendar* was appended to the *Second Annual Report of the State Librarian* (1905). In 1908 McIlwaine began the *Bulletin of the Virginia State Library*, in which he and his successors published more bibliographies, short monographs, descriptions of archival collections, and other documentary records. By 1955 the *Bulletin* had reached twenty-five volumes.

The documentary editions, the *Bulletin*, and the bibliographies and reference lists that Kennedy and McIlwaine appended to many of their annual reports covered a wide range of scholarship and helped researchers to become aware of the variety and depth of the Library's book and archival collections. The State Library issued four comprehensive bibliographies of Virginia history,[172] as well as numerous others on specialized topics such as geography, anthropology, hydrography, fiction, science, medicine, agriculture, technology, military science, music, fine arts, photography, maps, and even Shakespeare and Shakespeariana.[173] Library publications also included scholarly monographs by Edward S. Evans on *The Seals of Virginia*, appended to the *Seventh Annual Report*, and by Hamilton J. Eckenrode on *The Separation of Church and*

State in Virginia: A Study in the Development of the Revolution (1910). Eckenrode also published two volumes of indexes to archival records in Richmond and in Washington that documented the services of Virginians in the American Revolution.[174]

No other institution in Virginia prior to 1940 did as much as the State Library to advance the study of Virginia's history and culture. In summing up the contributions to Virginia and southern history that the universities, libraries, and historical societies had made during the 1920s and 1930s, renowned scholar Lester J. Cappon singled out the Virginia State Library for special commendation for "pointing the way" and setting the example for all the others.[175]

THE STATE LIBRARY AND VIRGINIA'S LIBRARIES

The inauguration in 1904 of the traveling-libraries project and the acquisition and management of the collection of books for the blind were the first of many actions that the Virginia State Library took to extend library services into areas of Virginia that had no circulating libraries. The State Library assumed the lead in this statewide effort, and every state librarian campaigned for more and better libraries. When John Pendleton Kennedy became state librarian, the Richmond City Council was debating whether to accept the offer of a public library building from philanthropist Andrew Carnegie. Kennedy heartily endorsed the establishment of public libraries throughout the commonwealth, and, in a long article published in the *Richmond Times-Dispatch* in December 1904, he linked the establishment of public libraries to the effort to improve public education. "Education means higher wages, better citizens, perfect contentment, continued prosperity, culture and refinement," Kennedy wrote. "The public library is the banking institution, paying the largest interest on money invested in public schools." He carefully defined the complementary roles that the Virginia State Library and the public and school libraries of the state

▼ One of the early traveling libraries was stationed in the store of E. G. McGehee, in Abilene, Charlotte County, a central gathering spot for the community.

The State Library cooperated with the New Deal's Work Projects Administration in the 1930s to establish demonstration libraries in Virginia counties that did not have public library service, and the Library's Extension Division sent a fleet of ten trucks filled with books in the 1930s and 1940s to rural areas across the state. Young and old, male and female, black and white Virginians looked forward with great anticipation to the arrival of the bookmobile, as these photographs attest. Pictured here from left to right are avid readers in Orange, Charlotte, Appomattox, and Prince William Counties.

ought to fill. "A State library is primarily a library for reference, and its position is distinctly advisory. Its creed urges the formation of public libraries, and as a path-finder to education its duty is to promote all literary byways leading to the homes of the people. A public library contains books of general literature and is never designed to include other than ordinary books of reference. It reaches the homes of the people through its department of circulation."[176] The city of Richmond did not then accept Carnegie's offer and did not create its own public lending library, but the State Library and the state librarian had contributed conspicuously and constructively to setting the parameters of the public debate on the interrelated subjects of education, libraries, and literacy.[177]

As part of that campaign, the State Library issued the call for the meeting of twenty-one librarians and educators who then founded the Virginia Library Association on 6 December 1905. Kennedy presided at the meeting held in the State Library building and was elected the association's first president. He probably also drafted the constitution that the assembled librarians and educators adopted. Its preamble affirmed the group's view that library facilities were "necessary for the education and culture of the people and that libraries are as important as any branch in the great system of public education" and declared the purpose of the new organization to be "the promotion of a close intercourse among librarians and all interested in library work in Virginia and to further library interests in general." The charter members of VLA further recognized "the State Library as preeminent in the library field of Virginia."[178]

For many years the State Library's principal contribution to the reading public of Virginia was the traveling library program, which served as a substitute for a statewide system of public libraries. The State Library created a separate Division of Traveling Libraries in 1906.

In 1922 the state librarian hired a "library organizer" to assist communities in establishing their own circulating libraries, and he renamed the program the Extension Division.[179] From modest beginnings in 1904 the traveling libraries program rapidly grew into a large and influential one. By 1907 the State Library had assembled and circulated sixty-five boxed sets of books for a general readership and another forty-four boxed sets for school libraries.[180] By 1912 the number was 87 general libraries, 138 school libraries, and 7 special libraries.[181] The citizens of Virginia made such eager use of the books that in 1916 and 1917 several of the boxed sets had to be temporarily withdrawn from circulation so that they could be repaired and rebound.[182] The demand for traveling libraries increased steadily, and in 1934 the state librarian reported that traveling libraries were available in 97 of Virginia's 100 counties and also in some of the new Civilian Conservation Corps camps in Virginia.[183]

In 1936 the General Assembly enacted the first comprehensive general library law for the state and declared it "the policy of the Commonwealth, as a part of its provision for public education, to promote the establishment and development of public library service throughout its various political subdivisions."[184] In 1938 the State Library began a cooperative venture with the New Deal's Works Progress Administration to establish demonstration libraries in the many Virginia counties that did not yet have public library facilities. The program was discontinued early in World War II, by which time the number of traveling libraries had far surpassed five hundred. By then, too, the joint State Library–WPA State-wide Public Library Project had also circulated thirty-four traveling libraries to "Negro readers" who, in then-segregated Virginia, had little or no access to library books.[185]

The Extension Division kept ten converted trucks—early bookmobiles—on the road during World War II, each capable of carrying from four hundred to five hundred books into rural parts of the state. Immediately after the war, the division commissioned the first of several conversions of larger trucks into mobile libraries, each able to transport more than a thousand volumes. Within two years, eleven bookmobiles were plying the roads in fourteen counties, in addition to the approximately four hundred fifty traveling libraries also in circulation.[186] The books continued to be heavily used. On 19 July 1941 the *Richmond Times-Dispatch* published an illustrated article on the traveling libraries and quoted a member of the staff as saying that when the books were returned to the State Library they sometimes contained such peculiar bookmarks as "love letters, hairnets, bobby-pins, and of all things—bacon rind." In another instance, the librarians noticed "evidence that some busy country housewife was snatching paragraphs of literature in between cooking duties . . . by the splotches of meat and dough grease found in some books." A Library staff member assured the reporter, perhaps in order not to discourage fastidious potential borrowers, that "we fumigate those returned books."

The state librarian and the members of the Traveling Libraries and Extension Divisions tirelessly promoted the traveling-libraries program and recommended the creation of publicly supported lending libraries. They often spoke to gatherings of educators, municipal officials, and community leaders and frequently wrote articles for popular and professional journals on the benefits of libraries and on the availability of books from the State Library.[187] They also joined with other librarians and educators to press for increased public funding for local libraries.[188] In spite of the repeated efforts of librarians and educators to found city and county libraries, Virginia lagged far behind the nation in providing public library service. In 1922 Virginia still had only six cities and no counties with publicly financed lending libraries, and data that the Extension Division compiled in 1945 showed that Virginia then ranked thirty-second among the forty-eight states in the number of urban dwellers with access to a public library, fortieth in the number of rural dwellers with such access, and forty-fourth in the number of counties with a public library.[189]

The demand for books in localities without public libraries placed heavy burdens on the State Library's limited resources. In order to stimulate the formation of more community libraries and to bring a greater degree of professionalism to the delivery of library services in Virginia, the Extension Division launched a quarterly journal, *Virginia Libraries*, in April 1928. The journal was discontinued after almost four years because of the budget cuts that occurred during the Great Depression, but while it was published *Virginia Libraries* served as an unofficial organ of the Virginia Library Association and as an additional forum from which librarians and educators could push for improved library service. One of the first successes to be announced in the pages of *Virginia Libraries* was the resolution that the Virginia Federation of Women's Clubs adopted in May 1928 promising to work toward the establishment of a public library in every county in Virginia.[190] The first substantial accomplishment in the campaign came in 1942, when the Virginia General Assembly appropriated money for grants-in-aid to localities to establish public libraries. The Virginia State Library, the Virginia Library Association, the Virginia Federation of Women's Clubs, and the Virginia Women's Council of Legislative Chairmen of State Organizations had joined forces to lobby the legislators on behalf of the bill. Even though the first appropriation was only $50,000, it marked an important beginning.[191] To keep librarians informed of the administration of the grant funds, and in part to replace the lapsed *Virginia Libraries*, the Extension Division began publishing a new journal in April 1943, the *Virginia Library Bulletin*, which was "issued occasionally in the interest of Virginia libraries." The twentieth and last issue was published on 1 June 1953.

In addition to its primary responsibility of serving as a reference library and archival agency for state government, the Virginia State Library continued to act as a lending library in the city of Richmond until the city established a publicly funded circulating library in the

▲ The first State Library building, including the large wing added to the structure in 1908, as it appeared shortly after the Library's move to a new facility in December 1940. This stucture was renamed the Finance Building to reflect its new function.

1920s. Because there was no other public library in the city, the State Library became for a short time the custodian of the John Banister Tabb Memorial collection of books for children. The collection was named for Tabb, a Virginia native and Catholic priest, who became a distinguished poet and educator. In 1922 and 1923, the State Library housed and served more than a thousand children's titles.[192] After Richmond established its own public library in 1923, the State Library transferred the Tabb collection to the city.[193]

SECOND STATE LIBRARY BUILDING

The State Library, which had to share its first new building with a variety of other state government agencies, quickly outgrew its quarters. Even though a wing was added to the building in 1908, overcrowding became a serious problem again, and for thirty years the state librarian's annual reports contained constant pleas for more space. In 1906 Kennedy lamented that "thousands of books are piled on the tops of cases and on the floors, many of them being inaccessible for want of proper facilities to classify and arrange them." He had closed one of the portrait galleries to make more space for books, but even then there were "many classes of books at present that we have been compelled to box and store in the basement, and all future Government and State accessions will have to be dealt with in this way."[194] In 1911 McIlwaine reported that the "library's collections of manuscripts, books, periodicals, and maps are even now so large that the shelving at our disposal is inadequate to accommodate them, so that many of our newspapers (both bound and unbound) are piled on the floor in various parts of the building and on the top of the newspaper cases in what is called the 'archives' room, which should contain manuscripts and nothing else. This archives room is the most fearfully congested part of the building." He informed the governor and General Assembly that the State Library contained "already probably the most valuable manuscript collection in the United States outside of the Library of Congress, and its value could be very greatly increased by the addition of material in the various executive departments of the State."[195]

In the *Richmond Times-Dispatch* of 23 April 1912 (the same issue that reported the sinking of the British luxury liner, *Titanic*), the editors deplored the General Assembly's repeated failure to appropriate funds to enlarge the building and render it fireproof. "One of the most flagrant instances of the unlocked stable door within our knowledge is the present inflammable housing of the precious collection of historical manuscripts in the Virginia State Library," the paper proclaimed. "That these documents, so valuable that no real price can be set upon them, could be left at the mercy of any chance fire that might break out in the building in which they are kept can only be explained by pure stark ignorance of their worth. Neither the legislators of Virginia nor the citizens seem to have the remotest idea of the heritage of historical material left during their current generation in their careless keeping."

The anticipated accident eventually occurred. Around noon on 21 February 1916, after the staff had completed moving about forty thousand pounds of books from the stack shelves on the upper floors into the basement to reduce the strain on the floor, a fire broke out in another part of the basement among old papers in the auditor's office. The fire, which may have been started by a dropped cigarette, spread into the records of the attorney general's office, but the Richmond fire department quickly extinguished the blaze before any further harm occurred. Water damage to the books and records was slight, but dense dark smoke spread throughout the structure and hindered the evacuation of the office workers, librarians, and patrons who were in the building.[196] Members of the General Assembly watched from the Capitol across the street, and the day after the fire, the editors of the *Richmond News Leader* castigated them for inadequately protecting the archives and the library: "Until the general assembly can provide a new and absolutely fire-proof building for our archives and library, we are gambling with fire, when the stake is the history of our commonwealth. How can the state afford to delay the construction of a new building?"[197]

The General Assembly appropriated $40,000 to construct a small annex on the south side of the State Library building to enlarge the archival storage space, and the state librarian later replaced the wooden shelving in the old stacks with metal shelves. When the archival records were placed in the new "fireproof" annex, the archivists estimated that the new rooms contained 1,268,000 documents.[198] The state librarian had high hopes that a new Library building would soon be erected adjacent to Capitol Square. Following the end of World War I, the Richmond city government and the new American Legion had advocated a new Library building to serve as a city lending library, as the home for the archives, and as a memorial to the Richmond men who had lost their lives in the war. The city donated a lot at the edge of Capitol Square between Eleventh and Twelfth Streets, the former site of Ford's Hotel, to the state for this purpose. The economic recession that began early in the 1920s, the lack of support in the General Assembly, and the founding of a separate Richmond Public Library together resulted in the abandonment of the project, and early in 1925 the state returned the Ford lot to the city.[199]

The campaign for a new facility did not die. The state librarian and Library Board members were eager to keep public attention focused on the Library's needs. They welcomed a reporter for the *Richmond News Leader* who visited the State Library in March 1923 and published an illustrated article on the crowded conditions. The reporter informed the public that many valuable portraits and other artworks were unavailable for public viewing because of a lack of space; that "duplicate copies of library books and other volumes which may be sold as a

▲ Richmond youngsters enjoying the John Banister Tabb collection, housed temporarily at the State Library, in January 1923

▲ Wilmer L. Hall, state librarian from 1934 to 1946

nial period through the losses that occurred at the times of the Revolution and the Civil War, to the consequences of the inadequate resources that the state had made available for preserving them. "Thus it has come about," he bluntly wrote, "that a state whose origin and career should entitle her to the greatest of historical resources finds her documentary material, great as it is, small in amount compared with what she should possess."[204]

Hall's article was dramatic and persuasive, and his conclusion inescapable: without a proper facility for preserving the documents, more inexcusable losses were inevitable. As the building's problems worsened, Hall continued to inform the public. In November 1936, he called reporters to the State Library to announce that rats were nibbling at the priceless and irreplaceable archival records. "Frequently," he told the press, "when you go down in the basement to look up old records you find rats as big as squirrels running around."[205] Virginius Dabney, editor of the *Richmond Times-Dispatch*, took Hall's warnings to heart. Throughout the 1930s, Dabney often lent his support in print on behalf of a new building for the State Library.[206]

In 1936, the General Assembly responded to the mounting pressure and created a State Library Building Commission to prepare for the construction of a new building. On 1 December 1936 the state librarian and the chairman of the Library Board appeared at a meeting of the commission together with representatives of twenty-nine civic, professional, and patriotic organizations to argue for erection of a new facility on the Ford lot adjacent to Capitol Square.[207]

Protracted negotiations between the state and city governments broke down on several occasions, but eventually the city agreed to restore the lot to the state for the Library.[208] Once the state gained access to the lot, planning moved forward rapidly. The state librarian, his assistant, and the members of the building commission inspected the facilities of the Library of Congress, the new National Archives building, the Folger Shakespeare Library, and library and archival structures in Illinois, Indiana, Maryland, New Jersey, and Pennsylvania. The new building was designed to accommodate the State Library and all its foreseeable needs as well as to contain offices for the attorney general

source of income for the library are piled on the floor or on tops of stack shelves"; that the books for the blind were scattered about the building in "any available space, separated and easily misplaced"; and that periodicals "waiting to be bound range for yards around the wall, different publications crossed on top of each other through lack of stack space." State Librarian Henry Read McIlwaine stated that the Library had been forced "to reject valuable offers of books because we have not space to handle them." Assistant State Librarian Wilmer Lee Hall told the reporter bluntly, "We are stifled for lack of space. . . . If the library ceases to acquire new material it will die."[200] McIlwaine characterized the condition of the State Library and its collections in his 1926 report as "desperate."[201] This view was clearly shared by others in state government, for in 1933 the Library's portraits of Virginia's governors were removed from the State Library to the Capitol for permanent exhibition there.[202]

Wilmer Hall took the lead in the campaign for a new facility even before he succeeded McIlwaine as state librarian following McIlwaine's death on 16 March 1934. Hall was a professional librarian, educated at the University of Chicago. He had worked at the Virginia State Library from 1912 to 1915 and in the New York State Library from 1916 to 1920. In 1920 he returned to the Virginia State Library as the successor to Assistant State Librarian Earl Gregg Swem.[203] Hall's most influential contribution to the campaign for a new building was a long scholarly article entitled "The Public Records of Virginia: Their Destruction and Preservation" published in *Virginia Libraries*. Hall carefully chronicled the long and often sad history of the public records of Virginia, from their careless and neglectful treatment during the colo-

▼ The second State Library building under construction, photographed in November 1939

▲ The interior entrance stairway of the second Library building. Distinctive, ornamental bronze gates and grillwork separate the stairs from the oak-paneled entrance hall. The grillwork depicts stylized papyrus leaves.

▲ The information desk and oak paneling in the entrance hall, or lobby, of the second Library building. Space was reserved above the desk for a mural, which was commissioned in 1950 and unveiled in June 1951. The mural, executed in egg tempera and oil on canvas by Richmond artist Julien Binford, portrayed the founding fathers George Mason, Patrick Henry, Edmund Pendleton, and other members of the General Assembly enacting the Virginia Declaration of Rights in 1776.

of Virginia and a courtroom, library, and offices for the Supreme Court of Appeals.[209] Ground was broken at the site on 7 December 1938, and the cornerstone was put in place on Washington's Birthday in 1940.[210] During the second week of September 1940 the rooms to be occupied by the Supreme Court of Appeals were ready, and prisoners brought from the State Penitentiary moved the books of the State Law Library.[211] The State Library moved its books and archival records between the beginning of September and the middle of December 1940, with staff members and WPA workers trundling some 350 thousand volumes and between 2 and 3 million documents through the tunnel under Capitol Square from the old building to the new. Some library services were maintained in the old building during the first weeks of the move, but the Library closed completely for the first three weeks in December. The Virginia State Library opened for business in its new quarters on 24 December 1940.[212]

Formal dedication ceremonies took place nearly ten months later, on 16 October 1941. Francis Pendleton Gaines, president of Washington and Lee University, delivered the dedicatory address. With war spreading over Europe and threatening to involve the United States, Gaines contrasted Americans' attitudes toward books and learning and freedom with the intolerant attitudes of dictators in Germany, Italy, Japan, and the Soviet Union. Gaines characterized the library as the "ultimate citadel of freedom."[213]

The second State Library building contained almost five times the amount of floor space as the first.[214] It featured a monumental entrance hall flanked by two large public reading rooms, one for the general

library and reference collection and the other for the archival and manuscript records. There was also a small public lecture hall in the basement. Almost all the offices and work space for the staff were concealed behind the scenes or on the second floor. The building contained a climate-controlled room two floors underground for housing the rarest books and manuscripts as well as separate facilities for photoduplication and other technical services. The remainder of the building was fully air-conditioned in 1959.[215] The building had been designed with future expansion in mind, and in 1971 four additional floors of stack space were added to the roof, increasing storage for archival records and enabling the facility to handle most of the state's archival needs for another twenty-five years.[216]

The opening of the new building and the dedication ceremony were major events, and the Virginia State Chamber of Commerce devoted most of the October 1941 issue of its monthly magazine, Commonwealth, to the State Library and its programs. The issue contained a history of the institution by State Librarian Wilmer L. Hall, a description of the archival programs by State Archivist William J. Van Schreeven, two detailed descriptions of the facility, an article on the quotations used on the exterior frieze of the building, and brief biographical sketches of the Library Board chairman and key Library administrators.

▲ The second Library building stood squarely between Broad Street and Capitol Square, an interesting architectural contrast to its High Victorian Gothic neighbor, Old City Hall.

▲ The Rare Book Room, shortly before the Library's move in 1940. The research carrels and balcony above were furnished, as were several other areas in the building, with tubular alumninum furniture created by New York designer Warren McArthur for the Library and a number of other office and public buildings during the 1930s and early 1940s.

Planning for an administrative restructuring of the Library to make the most efficient use of the agency's thirty-two professionals and thirty-one support staff-members coincided with the construction of the new building. A new organizational plan, adopted in 1939, created four divisions. The General Library Division, under the immediate supervision of the assistant state librarian, contained an order section, a cataloging section, a reference and circulation section, and a serials section. The Archives Division, under the direction of the state archivist, included all of the archivists who arranged and described archival and manuscript records, served them to the public, and prepared them for publication, as well as the Library's photographic laboratory. The Extension Division sent out traveling libraries, worked with the WPA on demonstration projects, kept the bookmobiles on the road, advised localities on the establishment of public libraries, and, after the passage of the grants-in-aid law in 1942, assisted in the administration of state grants to local libraries. The Administration Division, under the personal direction of the state librarian, took care of the management of the physical plant and the fiscal programs of the Library. The organizational plan also called for the creation of a separate publications unit to oversee the publication of historic documents, bibliographies, and other works, but, at the time of the move into the new building, funds did not permit the hiring of additional professional staff to fulfill this function. Wilmer Hall explained that the divisions "do not and should not stand as self-sufficient units; each supplements and depends on the others because demands overlap and services are interrelated."[217] The new building and organizational structure were well publicized in professional library and archival circles and served to enhance the Library's national reputation.[218]

A PERIOD OF RAPID GROWTH

The United States entered World War II less than a year after the Virginia State Library moved into its new home. Before the end of December 1941, the state librarian, in cooperation with the National Resources Planning Board, convened a meeting of representatives from fifty of Virginia's libraries, museums, and historical repositories to make plans for preserving records, books, and other materials of cultural and historical importance in the event of enemy attack. In January 1942 the State Library began an intensive program of microfilming vital public documents. By the end of June 1942 the Library had photographed approximately 112,000 pages from 230 record books of lower tidewater counties and cities, and during the next fiscal year it copied an additional 200,000 pages of records.[219] Most members of the staff took on additional responsibilities during the war, and, as they had during the First World War, they helped to collect thousands of books and magazines for distribution to military bases in the United States and abroad. The Library placed a special collection of books on world affairs in the main reading room for those who wanted background information about the dramatic events reported in the newspaper and on the radio.[220] The Library also acquired a large collection of war-related brochures and public relations materials.[221] With several staff members called to active duty following United States entry into the war in December 1941, the Library suffered a staff shortage, but fortunately there was an accompanying reduction in the number of requests for genealogical information, which required substantial research and reference time.[222] One former employee of the State Library, Corporal Claude King, an assistant in the stacks before the war, was killed in action in Germany in April 1945.[223]

▼ The Virginia Supreme Court of Appeals convened in its formal, paneled room in the Library building for the first time on 7 October 1940. Its last meeting in the Supreme Court Room was on 16 October 1981.

By far the greatest increase in the Library's holdings after 1940 occurred in the archives. The surveys and analyses of local government records conducted by the WPA Historical Records Survey in the depression years were deposited in the archives in 1941, and the assembly passed a statute in 1940 that authorized most state agencies to deposit their noncurrent records in the archives for safekeeping. By 1971, the number of manuscripts in the State Library had risen to almost 15 million, more than five times the number that had been moved into the building in 1940, necessitating the addition of four stack floors to the top of the building.[226] Following World War II, and increasingly after the 1970s, the number of local governments that chose to deposit their noncurrent records in the State Library also rose markedly.

The two oldest archival records owned by the Library were acquired during these years: a 31 May 1630 letter from Governor Sir John Harvey to the attorney general in England, and an 11 January 1639 commission issued by Charles I appointing Sir Francis Wyatt royal governor of Virginia.[227] The Library continued to acquire collections of personal and family papers, business records, genealogical notes and charts, Bible records, and organizational records, all of which were in great demand by genealogical and family-history researchers who traveled to the State Library in larger numbers than to any other research

▼ Randolph Warner Church, fourth state librarian, actively promoted the institution's place in the larger library community.

▲ The Library of Virginia holds a sizable collection of World War II posters, printed from 1941 through 1945 and displayed at that time on store windows, library bulletin boards, and post office walls across the state.

A year and a half after the end of World War II, Wilmer Hall resigned as state librarian in order to launch the Library's long-planned Publications Division, and Randolph W. Church succeeded him as the fourth state librarian. Church, who had been the assistant state librarian since the summer of 1934, held master's degrees in English from the University of Virginia and in library science from Emory University.[224] In his first annual report as state librarian in 1947, Church reflected on the recent history of the institution and expressed his hope that the Library would soon "assume its proper place among the libraries of the nation." "Rich in older research materials," he wrote, "and fortunate in its modern equipment, the institution now faces a turning point in its development. A complacent policy may easily result in stagnation. Even now the library is rapidly slipping backward in the size and importance of its collections. In 1917 it was the third library in size in the South; in 1944 it had dropped to eighth. As long as appropriations for the purchase of material remain a fraction of what is spent elsewhere, the library will continue to decline in this field."[225]

The book collection of the State Library grew steadily in the second State Library building and reached half a million volumes by 1971.[231] The primary focus of the collection continued to remain on Virginiana of all descriptions, with special concentrations in colonial, Revolutionary, southern, and Civil War history and in American and British genealogical resources. The Library also acquired a wide array of rare and valuable books and periodicals to complement the core collection. In addition, the Library's holdings of official state and federal publications grew rapidly, in part because of the growth in the sizes of both the state and the federal governments during and after World War II. Small city and county libraries also sought to borrow books of interest to their patrons to supplement their collections, and the State Library met the demand by adding volumes on literature, history, and the fine arts. The collections of the Virginia State Library became the largest and most varied in central Virginia. The acquisitions reports published each year during the 1950s and 1960s show that the librarians were consciously broadening and deepening the quality of the printed collections. In recognition of the numerous and varied educational and reference services to the commonwealth of Virginia provided by the State Library, the General Assembly in 1984 designated the Library as an institution of higher education.[232]

ADDITIONAL RESPONSIBILITIES

In 1944 the General Assembly transferred the appointment of Library Board members from the State Board of Education to the governor and enlarged the number of board members to six.[233] The Reorganization Act in 1948 transferred the Land Office and the World War II History Commission, with its voluminous records, to the State Library.[234] The World War II History Commission continued to function after its transfer to the State Library and completed the publication of several previously planned volumes. In 1950 the World War II

▼ Land Office records were moved from the Capitol to the State Library as a result of the Reorganization Act of 1948.

▲ Commission of Charles I appointing Sir Francis Wyatt royal governor of Virginia, 11 January 1639. The vellum document, though faded by time, still has a portion of its original wax seal attached.

library in the United States. To deal with the growing collections and increasing visitation, the archives staff was enlarged to twenty by the mid-1960s. The facilities, staff, and operations of the state archives, under the direction from 1939 to 1969 of William J. Van Schreeven, were widely regarded as among the best in the United States.[228]

During the 1970s and 1980s, the State Library's archival staff began to prepare and publish formal finding aids to some of the larger and frequently used collections. These included guides to business records, family Bible records, genealogical notes and charts, church records, and such state and local records as those of the Virginia Land Office, the first and second auditors of public accounts, the Board of Public Works, the treasury office, and pre-1904 county and municipal records. This volume of publication was impressive given the ever-increasing number of patrons, accessioned documents, and reference requests.

The State Library had been a depository for United States government publications since the end of the nineteenth century, although it ceased receiving some classifications of documents in 1950.[229] It was also the official depository for Virginia state government documents. In 1981 the General Assembly established a depository system for state documents and gave the State Library the responsibility for its administration. Since then, the Library has tracked and published a list of all state publications and has distributed two copies of each to the designated depository libraries in Virginia.[230]

History Division was reconstituted as a new History Division, parallel to the Publications Division. On 12 June 1951 the History Division launched an exciting new venture, a quarterly illustrated magazine of Virginia history and culture titled *Virginia Cavalcade*, which quickly won praise for presenting well-written and -researched history to a broad reading audience.[235] In 1959 the History Division and the Publications Division were combined into a Division of Historical Publications. From 1954 to 1966 the division administered the state historical highway marker program, and from 1963 to 1976 it also operated an archaeological program, both of which were transferred to the Virginia Historic Landmarks Commission (now the Department of Historic Resources), which had been established in 1966.[236]

In October 1956 the State Library launched a new series, the *Publications of the Virginia State Library*.[237] The first publication in the series, *The Committees of Safety of Westmoreland and Fincastle: Proceedings of the County Committees, 1774–1776*, complemented the editions of the records of the Revolutionary committees of Cumberland and Isle of Wight Counties that Henry Read McIlwaine had appended to his *Fifteenth Annual Report* in 1919, and of Caroline and Southampton Counties that he had published in 1929. From 1956 through 1976, forty-two volumes of the *Publications* appeared. Many of them consisted of the annual checklists of state government publications in print, but the series also included reference works and bibli-

▼ The first issue of the Library's quarterly magazine, *Virginia Cavalcade*, featured on the cover the Julien Binford mural, which hangs in the main lobby of the second Library building.

▲ At work in his Library shop, William J. Barrow advanced the study of restoration and conservation through his research and treatment of many library books and documents.

ographies, such as Ray O. Hummel Jr.'s *Southeastern Broadsides Before 1877: A Bibliography* (1971) and his *More Virginia Broadsides Before 1877* (1975). The publications program gradually grew into a large and varied one. To coincide with the centennial of the Civil War, the Library in 1965 and 1966 issued seven volumes containing the journals and the speeches delivered in the Virginia Secession Convention of 1861, and in 1969 it published William H. Gaines Jr.'s *Biographical Register of Members, Virginia State Convention of 1861, First Session*. The most ambitious and important of the many bibliographies issued during those years was Donald Haynes's two-volume *Virginiana in the Printed Book Collections of the Virginia State Library* (1975).

During the 1970s and 1980s the State Library's publications program expanded into other new fields. In 1977 and 1979 the Library issued volumes two and three of Nell Marion Nugent's *Cavaliers and Pioneers: Abstracts of Virginia Land Patents and Grants*, to complete a project begun under the auspices of the Land Office in the 1930s. The Library also published Cynthia Miller Leonard's *The General Assembly of Virginia, July 30, 1619–January 11, 1978: A Bicentennial Register of Members* in 1978, and several book-length documentary volumes. In 1965, 1983, and 1994 the State Library issued revised editions of the valuable reference work, *A Hornbook of Virginia History*, first issued in 1949, and in 1986 an ambitious bibliographical work *Theses and Dissertations on Virginia History*, by Richard R. Duncan. The Library published its first book-length monograph in 1981, Michael B. Chesson's *Richmond After the War, 1865–1890*, and its second in 1985, Mary H. Mitchell's *Hollywood Cemetery: The History of a Southern*

Shrine. To commemorate the bicentennial of the ratification of the Bill of Rights, the Library commissioned a series of articles for *Virginia Cavalcade*, which were issued in a collected edition in 1987, *The Bill of Rights: A Lively Heritage*, edited by Jon Kukla.

For many years the State Library provided space in its building to the busy book- and document-restoration shop operated by William J. Barrow. From 1932 to 1935 Barrow had operated a small restoration shop in the first State Library building under an agreement that gave the State Library a reduced rate on restoration work.[238] Barrow moved his business into the new Library building shortly after it opened in 1940, where it remained for more than forty-five years. Barrow became an internationally renowned authority on restoration and on inks, papers, and bindings. In 1957 he received the first of several research grants from the Council on Library Resources, and in the Virginia State Library he conducted research into the causes of paper deterioration. The State Library published three of Barrow's research reports in the *Publications of the Virginia State Library* series.[239] Barrow's work under the State Library's sponsorship contributed significantly to the development of permanent acid-free printing papers during the 1960s and for the subsequent nationwide adoption of uniform standards for permanent book papers.[240] The experimentation continued after Barrow's death. In 1976 and 1977 a deacidification chamber developed in Barrow's laboratory was tested on more than 35,000 older books in the State Library. The volumes were treated with morpholine gas in a vacuum chamber in order to remove acid residues from the paper and binding so that the volumes would last

longer.[241] A restoration process developed by Barrow involving deacidification and heat-generated lamination between two sheets of cellulose acetate film was also used to preserve many manuscripts in the Library's collection. The Barrow processes have been superseded in recent years by more sophisticated techniques, but in their day they represented an important breakthrough in conservation research.

In 1959 the state's records-management program, which had begun ten years earlier, was transferred into the State Library from the Records Management Section of the Division of the Budget. The Library created the new Records Management Division to advise state agencies on proper filing and retention procedures for documents, on the disposal of noncurrent and nonessential records, and on the preservation of records of permanent value. The Virginia program was one of the first systematic state records-management programs in the United States.[242] In 1972, following a fire in the Botetourt County courthouse, the General Assembly enabled the State Library to create a Local Records Branch to begin systematically microfilming the archival records in Virginia's cities and counties.[243] The increasing needs of government agencies in Virginia for a comprehensive program of records management and preservation led to the passage in 1976 of the Virginia Public Records Act, which added substantially to the State Library's administrative responsibilities.[244] In 1990 the General Assembly levied a small fee on the recordation of deeds and dedicated the revenue to pay for processing Virginia's archival circuit court records, many of which were by then deposited in the State Library.[245]

In the mid-1950s, the State Library's longtime interest in copying records relating to early Virginia history in foreign repositories was revived in connection with the 350th anniversary of the settlement of Jamestown, and the Library helped to create the monumental Virginia Colonial Records Project. In 1955 the VCRP, under the joint sponsorship of the Virginia State Library, the Virginia Historical Society, the University of Virginia, and the Colonial Williamsburg Foundation, hired an agent who began systematic surveys and ordered microfilm copies of essential seventeenth- and eighteenth-century records in European (principally British) repositories. Copies of the microfilm and of the reports of the agents were deposited with the sponsoring institutions. By the 1980s the project had acquired 963 reels of microfilm of public and private documents described in 14,704 survey reports filling more than 28,000 typed pages.[246] Surveying and filming were suspended at that time in order to devise computer programs that would generate easy-to-use finding aids to the documents. In 1990, the Library published a two-volume guide to the VCRP materials, *A Key to Survey Reports and Microfilm of the Virginia Colonial Records Project*. Six years later, the VCRP database was made available to researchers around the world through the Internet's World Wide Web technology.[247]

The work of the Library's Extension Division accelerated and broadened during the years after World War II as governments at all levels placed additional emphasis on education and made available increased public funding for libraries. The division continued to assist local and regional authorities in the acquisition and operation of bookmobiles and in establishing and enlarging their libraries. In 1956 Congress passed the Library Services Act, which provided funds to expand library services to counties and towns with small populations.

▲ Three of the original founders of the Virginia Colonial Records Project, Edward M. Riley of the Colonial Williamsburg Foundation, William J. Van Schreeven of the Virginia State Library, and Francis L. Berkeley Jr. of the University of Virginia, gathered around a microfilm reader in the Library's Rare Book Room.

▲ The Extension Division took an active role in establishing many of Virginia's public libraries. The Becker Library of Grayson County, which opened in 1937, began two years earlier as a book-lending project between the State Library and a local lawyer, Pauline Bourne. Bourne circulated the books from her own office until it grew so crowded that she organized the construction of a separate facility. She also conceived of the log cabin design and named it for geologist and physicist George Ferdinand Becker, whose widow, Florence, had contributed greatly to the library's creation.

The Extension Division administered the distribution of federal funds as well as state appropriations for the same purpose. When Congress passed the Library Services and Construction Act in 1964, followed by amendments to facilitate interlibrary cooperation the following year, the State Library's administrative role expanded further. Between 1957 and 1969 the annual allocation of federal funds for libraries in Virginia rose from $40,000 to $747,000. By the end of the 1960s, more than half of Virginia's ninety-six counties and thirty-seven of its thirty-eight independent cities had access to public library services.[248] By the 1980s Virginia had more than ninety public library systems (city, county, and regional) serving all cities and all but three of Virginia's counties. The Extension Division also began a fellowship program in 1957 to provide financial aid for students in graduate programs in library science. The students who benefited from the program were required to work in the sponsoring library for one or two years after completing the degree program or repay the money with interest. During the program's first dozen years, fifty-nine Virginians received assistance toward the master's degree in library science.[249]

Increased government interest in public libraries was reflected in the first Governor's Conference on Public Library Service, which Governor J. Lindsay Almond Jr. convened in Richmond on 21 April 1961 under the auspices of the Virginia Library Association. The State Library published the proceedings of the daylong meeting in number 18 of the *Publications of the Virginia State Library*. On 10 April 1962 Governor Albertis Harrison visited the State Library to dedicate the new circulating collection of educational films.[250] This program made educational films available to public and school libraries and became so

popular that by 1973 the number of people who annually viewed the films had grown to more than half a million.[251] The Library's film program continued until 1992.

NEW INITIATIVES AND A NEW BUILDING

The steady growth in the number and size of the State Library's programs prompted the Library Board in the 1960s to commission a study of the organizational structure of the institution, the first in thirty years. As a result, the board adopted a new organizational system in the summer of 1968, assigning all of the Library's functions to one of three consolidated divisions. The Library Board and successive state librarians periodically reexamined and revised this structure during the next twenty-five years to ensure the efficient use of limited staff and fiscal resources and to keep pace with technological innovations in the library and information field.

Randolph W. Church retired as state librarian on 30 June 1972, but he remained at the Library on a part-time basis to complete work on *Virginia Legislative Petitions: Bibliography, Calendar, and Abstracts from Original Sources, 6 May 1776–21 June 1782*, a guide to the Revolutionary War legislative petitions in the state archives, which the Library published in 1984. Following a nationwide search for the fifth state librarian, the Library Board in September 1972 hired Donald Haynes, who had served as director of the State Library's Library Services Division for the previous three years. The third consecutive librarian to be selected from the State Library's staff, Haynes was a graduate of the University of Virginia and of the University of North Carolina Library School. He had prior experience working in academic libraries and was a keen student of Virginiana.

Communication and information-sharing among Virginia libraries increased dramatically during the 1970s and continued at an ever-accelerating rate during the subsequent decades. A pilot program to

▼ The Rockingham County reading public was no less eager. The library there enjoyed an enthusiastic turnout when it moved into new, larger facilities in March 1952.

▲ The Library's reading room, ca. 1970

△ The library, ca. 1940 with the new hospital building of the Medical
College of Virginia in the background

△ The library in 1971, during construction of several new floors for archival storage

▲ Donald Rucker Haynes (1934–1988), became the fifth state librarian in 1972. He served for fourteen years.

▼ Ella Gaines Yates, state librarian from 1986 to 1990

create an electronic network for communications among all the libraries in Virginia was begun in 1974, and in August 1975 the State Library's Information Office, inaugurated in 1971, began publication of a monthly newsletter that contained timely information about Virginia libraries and librarians and the services available to them.[252]   In 1975 the State Library joined the Southeastern Library Network (SOLINET) and began computerized cataloging by use of the electronic resources of the Ohio College Library Center (OCLC). Beginning in July 1976, the State Library and the other Virginia members of SOLINET used the computerized catalogs to generate a microfiche edition of the first union catalog of library holdings in Virginia.[253] The Catalog of Virginia Libraries (CAVALIR) union list grew rapidly as more Virginia libraries joined SOLINET and contributed information about their holdings. By October 1984, seventy-nine libraries had contributed 1.75 million records listing more than 5 million holdings.[254]

In 1982 the State Library installed a large mainframe computer and began the process of converting its main card catalog into electronic form using the computer program of the Virginia Tech Library System (VTLS). The Publications Branch installed the Library's first word-processing computer network in 1982, and before the end of the decade almost all routine textual work in the Library was done on computers. In 1990, the Library Development Division created the state's first computer link for public libraries, the Virginia Library Information Network (VLIN). During its first five years, VLIN connected more than five hundred Virginia libraries to each other and to the rapidly increasing resources of the Internet. Through VLIN, the Library in April 1995 also launched a pioneering Digital Library Project, making

▼ John C. Tyson (1951–1995), was appointed by Governor L. Douglas Wilder and served from 1990 to 1994.

selected Library finding aids, collections, and databases available to researchers through World Wide Web technology, which the Library had begun using in August 1994.[255]

In 1972 the General Assembly reorganized the executive branch of state government and created a cabinet system, placing the Virginia State Library in the Department of Education. In 1977 the General Assembly transferred the power of appointing a number of agency directors, including the state librarian, from the public advisory boards to the governor.[256] Following Donald Haynes's resignation in 1986 to become director of the Virginia Historical Society, Governor Gerald L. Baliles appointed Ella Gaines Yates, of Atlanta, Georgia, the sixth state librarian. The first African American and the first woman to hold the office, Yates had spent much of her career in the Atlanta public library system.[257] In September 1990 Governor L. Douglas Wilder replaced Yates with John C. Tyson, who was then the director of library services at the University of Richmond.[258] Tyson served until June 1994. In March 1995, Governor George F. Allen appointed Nolan T. Yelich, director of the Administrative Services Division from 1973 to 1986 and assistant state librarian from 1986 to 1994, to be the Library's eighth state librarian under the authority of the Library Board. Many Virginians became concerned about the rapid turnover in state librarians following the position's linkage to the political process, and in July 1996 the General Assembly restored the appointing authority to the Library Board. In 1986 the General Assembly had enlarged the State Library Board to fifteen members, and in 1987 it changed the name of the institution to the Virginia State Library and Archives.[259]

Among the most important of the Library's initiatives in the 1980s was the creation of the Virginia State Library Foundation, a private, nonprofit corporation charged with raising private funds to meet the Library's needs beyond its regular operating budget. The Foundation was established on 5 December 1984 with a $1.25 million bequest from Annabelle Cox McAllister, a Texas genealogist and family historian, who had left her estate to the Library in memory of her husband, Edward Nevill McAllister. Since then the Foundation has provided

▲ The conversion from the standard card catalog to a computerized system occurred in the early 1980s. To ease the transition for library patrons, both catalogs were available for a brief period; however, researchers were instructed that "Books received after 1983 are NOT listed in the CARD CATALOG. ALL BOOKS APPEAR IN THE COMPUTER SYSTEM."

▼ Nolan T. Yelich, appointed eighth state librarian in 1995

▲ The Virginia Center for the Book sponsored author James Dickey's appearance in Richmond in 1993, which included a public lecture and book signings.

financial assistance to several Library programs and publications and has purchased valuable research resources to augment the Library's collections.[260]

In 1990 and 1991, the Library joined with Philip Morris Companies, Inc., in a major venture to commemorate the two hundredth anniversary of the ratification of the United States Bill of Rights. The Library lent Virginia's original manuscript copy of the Bill of Rights to Philip Morris for an impressive traveling exhibition that focused on the history of the document and its enduring meaning in American life. After a 26,000-mile tour that began in Vermont in October 1990 and eventually extended to all fifty states, the Bill of Rights exhibition returned to Richmond in December 1991 for a grand finale that included a parade along Broad Street, special receptions and tours of the exhibition for Virginians, and a glittering benefit ball.

Another dynamic program recently added to the Library is the Virginia Center for the Book, which was started in 1987 as a state affiliate of the national Center for the Book at the Library of Congress. The Virginia Center for the Book has sponsored a traveling exhibition, public lectures, teleconferences, book signings, and symposia featuring such noted authors as Ellen Gilchrist, Virginia Hamilton, Edward L. Ayers, John Casey, Paule Marshall, Lewis B. Puller Jr., James Dickey, and the poet laureate of the United States, Rita Dove. In December 1994 the Center and the Foundation hosted a gala black-tie reception to mark the Center's publication of a *Twentieth-Century Virginia Authors* literary map.[261]

The Library's responsibilities increased greatly during the 1980s and 1990s, far outpacing its staff and operational budget. Like all other state agencies, the Library experienced difficulties in carrying out its traditional programs and services when a statewide budget

crisis forced the governor and the General Assembly to order permanent spending reductions, seriously hampering the Library's ability to buy new materials and to preserve its rarest and oldest items. Patrons, nevertheless, continued to cross the threshold in ever-increasing numbers. During fiscal year 1993–1994, more than forty-seven thousand people visited the Library; the public service staff responded to almost ninety thousand reference questions while the interlibrary loan department filled more than fourteen thousand requests.[262] As with most other educational and cultural institutions, the Library actively sought outside funding to underwrite new programs. A grant from the National Endowment for the Humanities in 1993, for example, allowed the State Library to participate in the Virginia Newspaper Project, a cooperative program to identify and catalog all extant copies of newspapers published in Virginia since the eighteenth century.[263]

In the late 1980s, space considerations as well as environmental and technological concerns led Library officials to begin planning for a modern new facility. In 1981 the offices of the attorney general, the Supreme Court of Virginia, and the Law Library had vacated their space in the Library building for more convenient quarters provided by the General Assembly. Early in 1982 the State Library occupied their two floors of offices and the former Law Library stack area, and now had exclusive use of an entire building for the first time in its history. This additional space helped temporarily, but in August 1987 a serious problem surfaced, creating a major crisis for the State Library. The introduction into the building of many computers and other electrically powered office equipment caused a dangerous electrical overload in the forty-seven-year-old structure, and the

▼ Virginia authors Rita Dove and John Casey sign a copy of the *Twentieth-Century Virginia Authors* literary map during a gala reception held at the Library in December 1994.

▲ The groundbreaking for the new Library building took place in September 1993 on a then-empty lot of downtown Richmond's Broad Street.

▲ The new Library of Virginia, a facility ten acres in size with fifty-five miles of shelving, boasts a handsome exterior of granite, limestone, metal, and glass.

Library was forced to close for almost three months while the electrical service in the building was upgraded.[264] The crisis led the Library Board and state leaders to seek approval for a new Library building, not only because the second State Library building could no longer meet the demands of the agency's increasingly automated services but also because storage space for both printed material and archival records had run out.

After a protracted planning process, the state's Department of General Services secured the award-winning, San Francisco–based, architectural firm of Skidmore, Owens, and Merrill to design a new facility. Site selection, a study of staffing and space needs, approval of final architectural drawings and a financial plan, and selection of a contractor took several years to accomplish. Finally, on 8 September 1993 the state librarian, members of the Library Board, and invited dignitaries broke ground for the third Library building. Situated on the north side of Broad between Eighth and Ninth Streets on land generously donated by the city, the site was only a five-minute walk from the second Library building. The special guest for the groundbreaking ceremony was Poet Laureate of the United States Rita Dove, who read an eloquent poem on the importance of libraries that she had composed especially for the occasion.[265] During its 1994 session, the General Assembly changed the Library's name from the Virginia State Library and Archives to the Library of Virginia to enhance its visibility and stature as an educational and cultural institution within the state.[266]

As the Library prepared to move its staff and collections across Broad Street, State Librarian Nolan Yelich created an internal task force to develop a comprehensive plan for the restructuring of the agency to maximize service in the new building to the Library's varied constituencies. Comprising 316,500 square feet plus two underground parking decks, the third Library building boasted many exciting new features. The lobby level, with an impressive atriumlike ceiling and handsome wood finishes, contained a 257-seat lecture hall, three large meeting or conference rooms, six large display vitrines and a 1,200-square-foot exhibition room, a library shop, and a multimedia orientation room. The main second-floor reading room, designed to contain more than 70,000 reference volumes, extended along three of the building's exterior walls, with specially appointed areas for researchers interested in the Library's manuscript, map, public document, microfilm, and Virginia authors collections. The building also had two floors of closed stacks for the storage of printed and archival materials, each floor measuring 65,000 square feet and equal in size to two football fields placed side by side. As final preparations for the move began in mid-1996, the Library's collections included 695,744 printed volumes and serials; 238,641 photographs, negatives, films, and videotapes; 587,293 federal government documents; 622,161 reels of microfilm and other microforms; 66,287 maps; and 54,404 cubic feet of archival records, the equivalent of 83.1 million manuscript items.

As had been the case when the Library moved in 1940, the transition to the new Library building attracted widespread public attention. Not only would the new facility enable the Library to fulfill the needs of its patrons better than it ever had before, but it also positioned the Library to join with city and state officials and other cultural institutions in promoting tourism and economic development in central Virginia. Wired and equipped to handle the latest technology, the new building allowed the Library to adopt innovative new applications for automated library service and to expand the number of its collections available through the Internet to citizens of Virginia, the nation, and the world. Virginia's "rich storehouse of knowledge" entered its 175th year in impressive new quarters, steadfastly dedicated to its longstanding mission to provide ready access to information about Virginia today while preserving the commonwealth's rich documentary and printed heritage for future generations.

▲ Entering the three-story atrium lobby of the Library of Virginia with its view of reading rooms above, the visitor understands immediately the institution's mission as a library and archival agency for the commonwealth.

▲ In the Library's Virginia Authors Room visitors can comfortably peruse the more than 5,400 books by Virginia writers published since 1950. The room is sponsored by the Virginia Center for the Book, an affiliate of the Library of Congress, whose goal is to foster a greater awareness and appreciation of books, reading, and the literary heritage of Virginia.

NOTES

1. *Acts Passed at a General Assembly of the Commonwealth of Virginia, Begun and Held at the Capitol, in the City of Richmond, on Monday, the Second Day of December, in the Year of Our Lord One Thousand Eight Hundred and Twenty-Two, and of the Commonwealth the Forty-Seventh* (Richmond, 1823), 15. (Hereafter cited as *Acts of Assembly* with the inclusive years.) Between 1987 and 1995, the Library was known as the Virginia State Library and Archives. In 1994, wishing to enhance the Library's stature as an educational and cultural institution, the General Assembly changed the agency's name again, this time to the Library of Virginia.

2. The best historical accounts of the Library of Virginia are William G. Stanard, "The Virginia Archives," *Annual Report of the American Historical Association for the Year 1903*, 2 vols. (Washington, D.C., 1904), 1:645–651; Henry R. McIlwaine, "Turning the Pages of the Past," *Richmond* 16, no. 8 (February 1930): 17–18, 42; no. 9 (March 1930): 35–36, 41; Wilmer L. Hall, "The Public Records of Virginia: Their Destruction and Preservation," *Virginia Libraries* 4 (April, July 1931): 2–22; Wilmer L. Hall, "The Virginia State Library: History, Homes, Work," *Commonwealth* 8 (October 1941): 9–16, 40; William J. Van Schreeven, "A Public Record Office for Virginia," *Commonwealth* 8 (October 1941): 17–18.

3. William S. Powell, "Books in the Virginia Colony Before 1624," *William and Mary Quarterly*, 3d ser., 5 (1948): 177–184; David B. Quinn, "A List of Books Purchased for the Virginia Company," *Virginia Magazine of History and Biography* 77 (1969): 347–360.

4. George Thorpe to Sir Edwin Sandys, 15 May 1621, in *The Records of the Virginia Company of London*, ed. Susan Myra Kingsbury, 4 vols. (Washington, D.C., 1906–1933), 3:447.

5. William Waller Hening, comp., *The Statutes at Large: Being a Collection of All the Laws of Virginia, from the First Session of the Legislature, in the Year 1619 . . .* , 13 vols. (Richmond, New York, and Philadelphia, 1809–1823), 2:246. The law also required the county courts to obtain lawbooks and manuals for the use of the local justices of the peace and sheriffs.

6. Robert Carter to John J. Maund, 10 December 1792, Letter Book of Robert Carter, 12 July 1792–March 1793, Robert Carter Papers, Vol. 10, Manuscripts Department, William R. Perkins Library, Duke University, Durham, N.C. (hereafter cited as Duke).

7. "Council Papers, 1698–1702 (From the Originals in the Virginia State Library), Account of William Byrd, Auditor, 1702 (Continued)," *Virginia Magazine of History and Biography* 24 (1916): 400; H. R. McIlwaine, Wilmer L. Hall, and Benjamin H. Hillman, eds., *Executive Journals of the Council of Colonial Virginia*, 6 vols. (Richmond, 1925–1966), 3:47.

8. H. R. McIlwaine, ed., *Legislative Journals of the Council of Colonial Virginia*, 3 vols. (Richmond, 1918–1919), 3:1520.

9. McIlwaine, Hall, and Hillman, *Executive Journals of the Council*, 6:259 n. The titles are: Samuel Haynes, ed., *A Collection of State Papers Left by William Cecill Lord Burghley*, 2 vols. (London, 1740–1759), the first volume of which (*Papers Relating to Affairs in the Reigns of King Henry VIII., King Edward VI., Queen Mary, and Queen Elizabeth, from the Year 1542 to 1570*) still belongs to the Library of Virginia; William Robertson, *History of Scotland During the Reigns of Queen Mary and of King James VI*, 2 vols. (London, 1759); Anchitell Grey, ed., *Debates in the House of Commons, from the Year 1667 to 1694*, 10 vols. (London, 1763); David Hume, *The History of England, from the Invasion of Julius Caesar to the Revolution in 1688*, 6 vols. (London, 1762); and William Guthrie, *A Complete History of the English Peerage*, 2 vols. (London, 1763). "Continuation of Acts of Parliament" is too vague to permit identification, but may have referred to one of the editions of parliamentary proceedings that the library already contained but which the councillors wished to be brought up-to-date.

10. "List of Books Necessary for the Council Chamber made out by Phil: L: Lee, June 18, 1770," Edmund Jennings Lee Papers, Virginia Historical Society, Richmond (hereafter cited as VHS); Sir William Blackstone, *Commentaries on the Laws of England*, 4 vols. (Oxford, 1765–1769); John Rushworth, *Historical Collections of Private Passages of State, Weighty Matters in Law, Remarkable Proceedings in Five Parliaments, Beginning the Sixteenth Year of King James, Anno 1618*, 8 vols. (London, 1659–1701).

11. Paul Leicester Ford, ed., *The Works of Thomas Jefferson*, 12 vols. (New York, 1904–1905), 1:11–12.

12. John Blair, Clerk to the Council, 12 March 1772, *Virginia Gazette* (Purdie and Dixon), 19 March 1772; Robert Carter to John J. Maund, 10 December 1792, Letter Book of Robert Carter, Robert Carter Papers, Duke; Sir James Burrow, *Reports of Cases Adjudged in the Court of King's Bench, Since the Death of Lord Raymond*, 5 vols. (London, 1766–1780); John Locke, *The Works of John Locke . . . With Alphabetical Tables*, 5th ed., 3 vols. (London, 1751).

13. Mark Antony De Wolfe Howe, ed., "Journal of Josiah Quincy, Junior, 1773," *Proceedings of the Massachusetts Historical Society*, 3d ser., 49 (1916): 465; *The Holy Bible, Containing the Old Testament and the New: Newly Translated Out of the Original Tongues* (Oxford, 1717); *The Book of Common Prayer, and Administration of the Sacraments . . .* (Cambridge, 1745); Edward Hyde Clarendon, *The History of the Rebellion and Civil Wars in England Begun in the Year 1641*, 3 vols. (Oxford, 1707); John Locke, *The Works of John Locke, Esq.*, 5th ed., 3 vols. (London, 1751); John Milton, *A Complete Collection of the Historical, Political, and Miscellaneous Works of John Milton*, 2 vols. (London, 1738); Pierre Bayle, *A General Dictionary, Historical and Critical*, 10 vols. (London, 1734–1741).

14. McIlwaine, *Legislative Journals of the Council*, 1:86, 90–91, 92–93.

15. Hening, *Statutes at Large*, 2:210–211.

16. McIlwaine, Hall, and Hillman, *Executive Journals of the Council*, 1:251, 252.

17. Nell Marion Nugent, *Cavaliers and Pioneers: Abstracts of Virginia Land Patents and Grants, 1623–1732*, 3 vols. and supp. (Richmond, 1934–1980), 1:152, 226, 320.

18. McIlwaine, Hall, and Hillman, *Executive Journals of the Council*, 1:392–393, 406.

19. William Stith, *The History of the First Discovery and Settlement of Virginia* (Williamsburg, 1747), viii.

20. McIlwaine, Hall, and Hillman, *Executive Journals of the Council*, 5:278, 488–489; John Pendleton Kennedy and H. R. McIlwaine, *Journals of the House of Burgesses of Virginia, 1619–1776*, 13 vols. (Richmond, 1905–1915), *1742–1749*, 235, 319.

21. Louis H. Manarin, "A Building for the Preservation of the Public Records," *Virginia Cavalcade* 24 (1974): 27.

22. E. Millicent Sowerby, comp., *Catalogue of the Library of Thomas Jefferson*, 5 vols. (Washington, D.C., 1952–1959), 2:236–244.

23. Julian P. Boyd et al., eds., *The Papers of Thomas Jefferson*, 26 vols. to date (Princeton, 1950–), 3:333–334.

24. H. R. McIlwaine et al., eds., *Journals of the Council of the State of Virginia*, 5 vols. (Richmond, 1931–1982), 2:344–345.

25. H. R. McIlwaine, ed., *Official Letters of the Governors of the State of Virginia*, 3 vols. (Richmond, 1926–1929), 2:iii.

26. McIlwaine, *Journals of the Council of the State of Virginia*, 2:337–338.

27. One general list of records is in John H. Smith to Governor John Floyd, printed with the *Journal of the House of Delegates of the Commonwealth of Virginia, Begun and Held at the Capitol, in the City of Richmond, on Monday, the Third Day of December, One Thousand Eight Hundred and Thirty-Two* (Richmond, 1832), as part of House Document No. 1, pp. 34–36 (hereafter cited as *Journal of the House of Delegates* with the inclusive years); a second general list of records is Conway Robinson's list dated 3 June 1829, printed in H. R. McIlwaine, *Minutes of the Council and General Court of Colonial Virginia*, 2d ed. (Richmond, 1979), 537–544.

28. Edmund Randolph to Edmund Pendleton, 29 April 1783, together with an order of the Virginia Supreme Court of Appeals, 30 April 1783, in Office of the Governor, Letters Received, Benjamin Harrison, 1 December 1781–30 November 1784, Record Group 3, Library of Virginia (hereafter cited as LVA), printed in William P. Palmer, ed., *Calendar of Virginia State Papers and Other Manuscripts*, 11 vols. (Richmond, 1875–1893), 3:475 (hereafter cited as Palmer, *Calendar of State Papers*).

29. McIlwaine, *Journals of the Council of the State of Virginia*, 3:240.

30. Boyd, *Papers of Thomas Jefferson*, 2:544–545.

31. *Journal of the House of Delegates, 1819–1820*, 35, 39.

32. The reasons for the defeat of the measure are not recorded. *Journal of the House of Delegates, 1819–1820*, 114, 133; MS draft bill, docketed 21 January 1820, Rough Bills, 1776–1865, Records of the House of Delegates, Record Group 79, LVA.

33. Petition of the judges of the General Court, dated 23 November 1822, Legislative Petitions, Richmond City, Records of the General Assembly, Record Group 78, LVA; presented to the House 7 December 1822, *Journal of the House of Delegates, 1822–1823*, 22, 27.

34. *Acts of Assembly, 1807–1808*, 24; Hening, *Statutes at Large*, 1:xi; petition of William W. Hening, presented 5 December 1822, Legislative Petitions, Richmond City, Record of the General Assembly, LVA; *Journal of the House of Delegates, 1822–1823*, 18, 30–31, 35, 37, 46, 48, 149; *Journal of the Senate, of the Commonwealth of Virginia, Begun and Held at the Capitol, in the City of Richmond, on Monday the Second Day of December, in the Year One Thousand Eight Hundred and Twenty-Two* (Richmond, [1823]), 27, 31–32, 44, 55–56, 60, 70 (hereafter cited as *Journal of the Senate of Virginia* with the inclusive years).

35. *Acts of Assembly, 1822–1823*, 15.

36. Ibid., *1825–1826*, 8–9; *1826–1827*, 12.

37. Report of the Committee on the Library, 24 October 1827, Office of the Governor, Letters Received, John Tyler Jr., 11 December 1825–4 March 1827, LVA, printed in Palmer, *Calendar of State Papers*, 10:558–561.

38. William Branch Giles to the General Assembly, 3 December 1827, with enclosures, printed and bound at the end of the *Journal of the House of Delegates, 1827–1828*, 3, 19.

39. *Acts of Assembly, 1827–1828*, 12.

40. Journal of the Council of State, 13 December 1827–9 December 1828, pp. 69–70, 96, Records of the Council of State, Record Group 75, LVA; the characterization of the library room is from J. S. Buckingham, *The Slave States of America*, 2 vols. (London, 1842), 2:420.

41. *A Catalogue of the Library of the State of Virginia, Arranged Alphabetically, Under Different Heads, with the Number and Size of the Volumes of Each Work, and Its Edition Specified. To Which is Prefixed, The Rules and Regulations Provided for its Government, in Conformity with the Third Section of "An Act Concerning the Public Library," Passed February 11th, 1828* (Richmond, 1828).

42. *Acts of Assembly, 1828–1829*, 9–10. The Joint Committee on the Library usually consisted of a small and select membership of both houses of the assembly who were knowledgeable in the law and interested in education and a broad range of public policies.

43. Ibid., *1829–1830*, 11–12.

44. Ibid., *1831–1832*, 11–13.

45. A Catalogue of Law Books in the State Library at Lewisburg Taken in July 1860 (listed as vol. 11 of the Virginia State Library records in John P. Kennedy, *Virginia State Library Calendar of Transcripts* [Richmond, 1905], 106), Records of the Virginia State Library, Record Group 35, LVA. This catalog contains marginal notations indicating which volumes had been sent to Lewisburg from the collection in the Capitol.

46. Virginia Supreme Court of Appeals, Richmond Session, Order Book No. 21, 1861–1868, p. 309, Records of the Supreme Court of Virginia, Record Group 100, LVA.

47.   The books include volume two of John Tracy Atkyns's three-volume *Reports of Cases Argued and Determined in the High Court of Chancery, in the Time of Lord Chancellor Hardwicke. . . . With Notes and References . . .*, 3 vols. (London, 1765–1768); two volumes, one each from the first and second editions, of William Salkeld's *Reports of Cases Adjudg'd in the Court of King's Bench; with Some Special Cases in the Courts of Chancery, Common Pleas and Exchequer, from the First Year of K. William and Q. Mary, to the Tenth Year of Queen Anne* (London, 1717–1718 and 1721); a copy of volume one of *Modern Reports; Or, Select Cases Adjudged in the Courts of King's Bench, Chancery, Common Pleas, and Exchequer, Since the Restoration of His Majesty King Charles II*, 3d ed., rev., 5 vols. (London, 1720–1725); and a black letter volume entitled *The Third Part of Modern Reports; Being a Collection of Several Special Cases in the Court of Kings-Bench: in the Last Years of the Reign of K. Charles II, in the Reign of K. James II. and in the Two First Years of K. William and Q. Mary, Together with the Resolutions and Judgments Thereupon*, 2d ed. (London, 1712).

48.   *Acts of Assembly, 1840–1841*, 55.

49.   Order of 10 December 1847, Virginia Supreme Court of Appeals, Richmond Session, Order Book No. 18, 1847–1850, p. 135, Records of the Supreme Court of Virginia; resolution of the Joint Committee on the Library, 1 February 1848, and the annual report of the librarian for the year ending 31 December 1853, indicating that the lawbooks were still in the State Library in the Capitol, both in Proceedings of the Library Committee, 1829–1861, Records of the Virginia State Library, LVA.

50.   *Acts of Assembly, 1848–1849*, 9–10.

51.   Ibid., *1855–1856*, 79.

52.   John Peyton Little, "History of Richmond," *Southern Literary Messenger* 18 (1852): 157.

53.   Richardson's appointment as clerk of the Council is recorded in the Journal of the Council of State, 19 December 1820–6 December 1821, p. 47, Records of the Council of State, LVA. George Wythe Munford was elected secretary of the commonwealth on 4 December 1852 to replace Richardson as of 1 January 1853. *Journal of the House of Delegates, 1852–1853*, 46–47.

54.   "Report of the Joint Committee on the Library," n.d., printed with the *Journal of the House of Delegates, 1852–1853*, as House Document No. 45.

55.   Librarian's annual report, 31 December 1846, in Proceedings of the Library Committee, 1829–1861, Records of the Virginia State Library, LVA.

56.   Jefferson's letter is printed in the preface to volume one of Hening's *Statutes at Large*, viii–xi, although Hening was mistaken in the chronology he gave there for the letter and the first act authorizing publication of the land laws.

57.   *Acts of Assembly, 1795–1796*, 13–14; *1796–1797*, 12.

58.   James Monroe to the Speaker of the House of Delegates, 12 December 1800, Legislative Department, Executive Communications, 1799–1802, Records of the General Assembly, LVA.

59.   *Journal of the House of Delegates, 1800–1801*, 51, 76, 79. The first manuscript draft of the bill is in the state's archives, but the version that the House of Delegates adopted and the amendments that the Senate proposed do not survive, so the reason for the failure of the proposal is not known. Rough Bills, January 1801, Records of the House of Delegates, LVA.

60.   *Acts of Assembly, 1807–1808*, 24.

61.   Ibid., *1826–1827*, 16–17.

62.   Hall, "The Public Records of Virginia," 9, 15.

63.   Hening, *Statutes at Large*, 2:509 n.

64.   Governor John Floyd to the Speaker of the House of Delegates, 3 December 1832, in the *Journal of the House of Delegates, 1832–1833*, 9, and the report of John H. Smith to Governor John Floyd printed with the *Journal of the House of Delegates, 1832–1833*, as part of House Document No. 1, pp. 34–36; John H. Smith, to Governor John Floyd, 22 November 1833, printed with the *Journal of the House of Delegates, 1833–1834*, as Document No. 1, pp. 122–124.

65.   "Report of William P. Palmer, Esq. Relative to the Manuscripts in the State Library," 29 November 1872, printed with the *Journal of the House of Delegates, 1872–1873*, as Document No. 2, pp. 1–4.

66.   Report and Resolutions of 25 January 1833, Proceedings of the Library Committee, 1829–1861, Records of the Virginia State Library, LVA.

67.   James E. Heath, J. Brown, Jr., and L. Burfoot to Governor Littleton W. Tazewell, 8 November 1834, printed with the *Journal of the House of Delegates, 1834–1835*, as House Document No. 1, pp. 45–46; Hall, "The Public Records of Virginia," 12.

68.   McIlwaine, *Minutes of the Council and General Court*, 537–544; Herbert R. Paschal, ed., "George Bancroft's 'Lost Notes' on the General Court Records of Seventeenth-Century Virginia," *Virginia Magazine of History and Biography* 91 (1983): 348–362.

69.   *Richmond Daily Examiner*, 3 May 1860.

70.   "Report of the Joint Committee on the Public Library," 3 October 1863, together with the "Report of the Secretary of the Commonwealth on the Joint Library Committee," n.d., printed with the *Journal of the Senate of Virginia, 1863*, as Senate Document No. 5, pp. 3–6; *Richmond Enquirer*, 30 October 1862.

71.   "Report of the Secretary of the Commonwealth on the Joint Library Committee," n.d., together with the affidavit of John R. Thompson, one of the library's clerks, to the Joint Committee on the Library, printed with the "Report of the Joint Committee on the Public Library," 3 October 1863, in the *Journal of the Senate of Virginia, 1863*, as part of Senate Document No. 5.

72.   *Richmond Examiner*, 6 November 1863.

73.   *Richmond Semi-Weekly Enquirer*, 26 August 1864.

74.   Palmer, *Calendar of State Papers*, 1:xv–xvii.

75. Edward H. Ripley, *The Capture and Occupation of Richmond April 3rd, 1865* (New York, 1907), 20.

76. *Richmond Semi-Weekly Whig*, 28 April 1865.

77. *Daily Richmond Whig*, 6 May 1865.

78. "Report of the Secretary of the Commonwealth to the General Assembly," December 1865, printed with the *Journal of the House of Delegates, 1865–1866*, as House Document No. 3, pp. 3–4.

79. *Richmond Semi-Weekly Whig*, 30 June 1865. The only other sizable collection of books in Richmond available to the public belonged to the Richmond Library Association and was broken up and partially destroyed during and after the war. Palmer, *Calendar of Virginia State Papers*, 1:xv–xvii.

80. "Report of the Secretary of the Commonwealth to the General Assembly," December 1865, printed with the *Journal of the House of Delegates, 1865–1866*, as House Document No. 3, pp. 3–4.

81. "Report of the Joint Committee on the Library," 4 February 1867, printed with the *Journal of the House of Delegates, 1866–1867*, as House Document No. 2, pp. 3–4.

82. "Report of the Joint Library Committee," n.d. (ca. February 1870), printed with the *Journal of the House of Delegates, 1869–1870*, as House Document No. 15, pp. [1]–3; *Richmond Daily Enquirer*, 22 April 1870.

83. *Acts of Assembly, 1866–1867*, 551; order of 14 February 1867, Virginia Supreme Court of Appeals, Richmond Session, Order Book No. 21, 1861–1868, p. 446, Records of the Supreme Court of Virginia, LVA; *Acts of Assembly, 1869–1870*, 219–220.

84. *Acts of Assembly, 1872–1873*, 36.

85. *Richmond Enquirer*, 20 March, 20 May 1875.

86. "Annual Report of the Joint Committee on the State Library," n.d. (ca. February 1873), printed with the *Journal of the Senate of Virginia, 1872–1873*, as Senate Document No.13, pp. 4–5.

87. *Catalogue of the Virginia State Library, 1877, Arranged Alphabetically* (Richmond, 1877). The annual reports of the Joint Committee on the Library during the last twenty years of the nineteenth century seldom contain details about the purchases of books, but the report issued for the year 1883 does include a full list (though by short titles only) of the purchases made during the period 1882–1883. See "Report of the Joint Committee on the Library," ca. January 1884, printed with the *Journal of the Senate of Virginia, 1883–1884*, as Senate Document No. 36, pp. 8–23.

88. The memorial of the Virginia Historical Society was printed with the *Journal of the Senate of Virginia, 1871–1872*, as Senate Document No. 10, pp. 13–14; *Acts of Assembly, 1871–1872*, 55–56.

89. "Report of William P. Palmer," 29 November 1872, printed with the *Journal of the House of Delegates, 1872–1873*, as House Document No. 2, pp. 1–4. A long excerpt from Palmer's report was printed in the *Richmond Enquirer* of 9 December 1872.

90. "Report of Librarian," 1 January 1874, printed with the "Annual Report of the Joint Committee of the State Library," 10 February 1874, in the *Journal of the Senate of Virginia, 1873–1874*, as Senate Document No. 9, pp. 9–16; Stanard, "The Virginia Archives," 651.

91. "Annual Report of the Joint Committee on the State Library," n.d. (ca. February 1873), printed with the *Journal of the Senate of Virginia, 1872–1873*, as Senate Document No.13, pp. 5–6.

92. A list of the several series of transcripts and abstracts is included in the *Calendar of Transcripts*, published with the 1904–1905 annual report of State Librarian John P. Kennedy, 118–119.

93. Governor Charles T. O'Ferrall to the General Assembly, 1 December 1897, with enclosures, including a list of the documents, printed in *Journal of the House of Delegates, 1897–1898*, 42–43, 54–56. The episode was written up at length when a second recovery of documents from the Lossing estate was made fifteen years later. *New York Evening Post*, 7 May 1912; *Richmond Virginian*, 7 May 1912; *Richmond Evening Journal*, 12 June 1912: clippings in Virginia State Library Publicity Scrapbooks, 1905–1981, Records of the Virginia State Library, LVA.

94. "Report of the Joint Committee on the Library," n.d., printed with the *Journal of the Senate of Virginia, 1871–1872*, as Senate Document No. 15, pp. [1]–3.

95. "Communication from H. W. Flournoy, Secretary of the Commonwealth, to Hon. Conway R. Sands, Chairman of the Joint Library Committee," n.d., in the "Report of the Joint Library Committee" (ca. February 1890), printed with the *Journal of the Senate of Virginia, 1889–1890*, as Senate Document No. 22, p. 4.

96. *Richmond Enquirer*, 17 February 1875.

97. George William Bagby to John Hampden Chamberlayne, 17 March 1875, Bagby Family Papers, VHS.

98. *Richmond Dispatch*, 22 August 1886.

99. "Report of [the] Joint Library Committee," 20 February 1886, printed with the *Journal of the Senate of Virginia, 1885–1886*, as Senate Document No. 39, pp. 1–12; "Report of the Joint Library Committee," 27 February 1896, printed with the *Journal of the Senate of Virginia, 1895–1896*, as Senate Document No. 15, pp. 1–6.

100. "Report of the Joint Library Committee," 27 February 1896, printed with the *Journal of the Senate of Virginia, 1895–1896*, as Senate Document No. 15, pp. 1–6.

101. Hall, "The Public Records of Virginia," 16–17.

102. Stanard, "The Virginia Archives," 650.

103. *Acts of Assembly, 1883–1884*, 465–467.

104. Ibid., *1891–1892*, 980–983.

105. "Communication from the State Board of Building Commissioners," 8 December 1893, printed with the *Journal of the Senate of Virginia, 1893–1894*, as Senate Document No. 3, p. [1].

106. For a long account of the construction of the building, the arrangement of offices within it, and the plans that had been made for moving the contents of the Library, see the *Richmond Times*, 17 March 1895.

107. *Acts of Assembly, 1893–1894*, 934–935.

108. "Report of the Joint Library Committee," 27 February 1896, printed with the *Journal of the Senate of Virginia, 1895–1896*, as Senate Document No. 15, pp. 1–6.

109. Ibid.; a number of Poindexter's letters to the librarian and to the governor are in the Library of Virginia. The $250 sum is found in an article about the sale of the books that appeared in the *Fredericksburg Free Lance*, 15 October 1895.

110. Journal of the Proceedings of the Joint Committee on the Library, 1894–1902, Records of the Virginia State Library, LVA; Stanard, "The Virginia Archives," 645–664.

111. *Report of the Proceedings and Debates of the Constitutional Convention, State of Virginia*, 2 vols. (Richmond, 1906), 1:1053.

112. *Acts of Assembly, 1904*, 93–95.

113. Minute Book of the Virginia State Library Board, 1 July, 3 October 1903, Records of the Virginia State Library, LVA. A contemporary biographical sketch of Kennedy (with a portrait engraving) is in Lyon G. Tyler, ed., *Men of Mark in Virginia*, 5 vols. (Washington, D.C., 1906), 1:197–198.

114. *Richmond Times-Dispatch*, 31 October 1903.

115. *First Annual Report of the Library Board of the Virginia State Library for the Year Ended June 30, 1904* (Richmond, 1904), 5–8 (hereafter cited as *Annual Report of the Virginia State Library* with the date of the fiscal year).

116. *Richmond News Leader*, 29 April 1904.

117. Ibid., 27 May 1904.

118. Ibid., 10 June 1904.

119. A full list of all State Library items exhibited at the exposition is in the *Annual Report of the Virginia State Library, 1906–1907*, 66–101.

120. *The Official Blue Book of the Jamestown Ter-Centennial Exposition A.D. 1907. The Only Authorized History of the Celebration, Illustrated* (Norfolk, 1909), 463, 525–526.

121. *First Annual Report of the State Librarian of Virginia for the Year Ended October 31, 1904* (Richmond, 1904), 68–69; *Richmond News Leader*, 27 May 1904; Sandra Gioia Treadway, *Women of Mark: A History of The Woman's Club of Richmond, Virginia, 1894–1994* (Richmond, 1995), 45–46.

122. *Goodson Gazette* (the publication of the Virginia School for the Deaf and the Blind at Staunton), 1 February 1908; *Annual Report of the Virginia State Library, 1907–1908*, 44.

123. *Annual Report of the Virginia State Library, 1941–1942*, 9–10. In 1942, the collection for the blind contained approximately eighteen hundred volumes.

124. Gaston Lichtenstein to the editor, *Richmond Times-Dispatch*, 15 September 1945.

125. *Annual Report of the Virginia State Library, 1906–1907*, 8–9; *1907–1908*, 14–17; *1909–1910*, 16–19.

126. Minute Book of the State Library Board, 1903–1924, pp. 71–98. In addition, a carbon copy of a typescript of the investigation begun on 5 February 1907 and other records of the investigations, including a six-page typescript dated 22 February 1907 in which Kennedy described his actions, are also in the Records of the Virginia State Library, LVA; *Richmond Times-Dispatch*, 30 June, 2, 3, 6, and 7 July 1907.

127. Minute Book of the State Library Board, 1903–1924, pp. 98–99, Records of the Virginia State Library; some of McIlwaine's correspondence respecting his appointment is in the Henry Read McIlwaine Papers, Acc. 20124 and 24641, Personal Papers Collection, LVA.

128. A contemporary biographical sketch is in Philip Alexander Bruce, Lyon G. Tyler, and Richard L. Morton, *History of Virginia, Volume IV, Virginia Biography* (Chicago, 1924), 132–133.

129. *Richmond News Leader*, 8 July 1907.

130. Minute Book of the State Library Board, 1903–1924, pp. 101, 102, Records of the Virginia State Library, LVA.

131. *Annual Report of the Virginia State Library, 1904–1905*, 23–25.

132. Ibid., *1910–1911*, 24.

133. *Annual Report of the Virginia State Library, 1917–1918*, 14; *Acts of Assembly, 1918*, 409–410; *1926*, 654–655; *Richmond News Leader*, 30 August 1940.

134. *Annual Report of the Virginia State Library, 1920–1921*, 17; Morgan P. Robinson, "Suitable Materials for Public Records of Virginia," *Virginia Libraries* 3 (1930): 8–11.

135. *Annual Report of the Virginia State Library, 1915–1916*, 20.

136. "Citations," *Commonwealth* 4 (June 1937): 17; *Annual Report of the Virginia State Library, 1958–1959*, 10–11; *Newport News Daily Press*, 1 and 3 March 1959; *Richmond Times-Dispatch*, 1 and 21 March 1959.

137. *Annual Report of the Virginia State Library, 1916–1917*, 29.

138. Ibid., *1912–1913*, 11–14; Earl G. Swem, comp., "A List of Manuscripts Recently Deposited in the Virginia State Library by the State Auditor," *Bulletin of the Virginia State Library* 7 (April, July 1914).

139. *Annual Report of the Virginia State Library, 1917–1918*, 14.

140. Ibid., *1924–1925*, 6–7.

141. Ibid., *1931–1932*, 7.

142. Earl G. Swem, comp., "A List of Manuscripts Relating to the History of Agriculture in Virginia, Collected by N. F. Cabell, and Now in the Virginia State Library," *Bulletin of the Virginia State Library* 6 (January 1913); *Annual Report of the Virginia State Library, 1920–1921*, 12.

143. *Richmond News Leader*, 17 March 1950; *Annual Report of the Virginia State Library, 1955–1956*, 8; *1962–1963*, 9.

144. *Annual Report of the Virginia State Library, 1952–1953*, 8.

145. Morgan P. Robinson, "Virginia's Historical Laboratory," *Virginia Journal of Education* 14 (1921): 392–395, reprinted from the February 1920 issue of *Historical Outlook*.

146. *Richmond News Leader*, 10 September 1929.

147. *Annual Report of the Virginia State Library, 1948–1949*, 6.

148. Hall, "The Virginia State Library," 14–15; "A List of the Official Publications of the Confederate States Government in the Virginia State Library and the Library of the Confederate Memorial Literary Society," *Bulletin of the Virginia State Library* 4 (January 1911).

149. Richard Barksdale Harwell, *More Confederate Imprints*, 2 vols. (Richmond, 1957); Marjorie Lyle Crandall, *Confederate Imprints*, 2 vols. (Boston, 1955); *Annual Report of the Virginia State Library, 1931–1932*, 5.

150. Descriptions of the Brock Collection and accounts of how it found its way to California are contained in an editorial (probably written by Douglas Southall Freeman) in the *Richmond News Leader*, 1 November 1922; in the *Huntington Library Bulletin* 1 (May 1931): 66–67; in Louis B. Wright, "For the Study of the American Cultural Heritage," *William and Mary Quarterly*, 3d ser., 1 (1944): 207–209; and in Beverley Fleet, ed., *Virginia Colonial Abstracts*, 34 vols. (Richmond, 1937–1949), 30:88–89.

151. Henry Ainsworth, *Annotations upon the Book of Psalmes* ([Amsterdam?], 1618).

152. Henry R. McIlwaine, "Turning Pages of the Past," *Richmond* 16 (March 1930): 36, 41; *Richmond Times-Dispatch*, 18 December 1938.

153. *Richmond Times-Dispatch*, 11 July 1945.

154. *Richmond News Leader*, 18 June 1953.

155. *Richmond Times-Dispatch*, 21 September 1967.

156. *Annual Report of the Virginia State Library, 1909–1910*, 11–12, 104–140; *1916–1917*, 8, 13–26; *1920–1921*, 4; *1951–1952*, 6.

157. Ibid., *1948–1949*, 6; *Richmond News Leader*, 21 January 1946.

158. *Richmond News Leader*, 5 May 1923.

159. "Pieces of Famous Washington Elm in State Library," *Richmond* 10 (May 1924): 14.

160. *Richmond Dispatch*, 3 June 1902.

161. *Richmond Times-Dispatch*, 18 April 1943; *Norfolk Ledger-Dispatch*, 21 March 1939.

162. *Richmond News Leader*, 8 May 1943.

163. Unidentified newspaper clipping dated 19 May 1911 in Virginia State Library Publicity Scrapbooks, 1905–1981, Records of the Virginia State Library, LVA.

164. Jon Kukla, "Touches of Sentiment in the Affairs of Old Books," *Virginia Cavalcade* 28 (1978): 78–80.

165. *Richmond Times-Dispatch*, 28 November 1941.

166. *Richmond News Leader*, 1 January 1930. In the Library of Virginia's archives is a large folder of correspondence and memorandums concerning two 1860s lithographs of the Ordinance of Secession. Those lithographs had been so skillfully executed that many historical repositories, including the National Archives, had erroneously believed they possessed the original.

167. Portions of the narrative of the negotiations, which were not concluded until 1914, are contained in the *Annual Report of the Virginia State Library, 1911–1912*, 24; *1912–1913*, 25; and *1913–1914*, 6, 20–27, which includes a list of the documents. The initial attempt of Virginia to take possession of the documents and to establish ownership received wide publicity: *Richmond Times-Dispatch*, 7 May 1912; *Richmond Evening Journal*, 7 May 1912; *Richmond Virginian*, 7 and 8 May 1912; *Richmond News Leader*, 9 May 1912; *New York Evening Post*, 7 May 1912; *New York Herald*, 8 and 9 May 1912; and *New York Times*, 9 May 1912, all in Virginia State Library Publicity Scrapbooks, 1905–1981, Records of the Virginia State Library, LVA.

168. William J. Van Schreeven, Robert L. Scribner, and Brent Tarter, eds., *Revolutionary Virginia, The Road to Independence; A Documentary Record*, 7 vols. in 8 (Charlottesville, Va., 1973–1983), 7:25–26.

169. *Annual Report of the Virginia State Library, 1927–1928*, 11.

170. Ibid., *1949–1950*, 7; *Richmond News Leader*, 6 December 1949; *American Archivist* 13 (1950): 190. In 1977, the State Library published the journal: *Proceedings of the Advisory Council of the State of Virginia, April 21–June 19, 1861*, ed. James I. Robertson, Jr. (Richmond, 1977).

171. *Mississippi Valley Historical Review* 7 (1921): 383–385.

172. William Clayton-Torrence, *A Trial Bibliography of Colonial Virginia (1754–1776)* (Richmond, 1910); Earl G. Swem, "A Bibliography of Virginia, Part I: Containing the Titles of Books in the Virginia State Library Which Relate to Virginia and Virginians, the Titles of Those Books Written by Virginians, and of Those Printed in Virginia," *Bulletin of the Virginia State Library* 8 (April, July, October 1915); Swem, "A Bibliography of Virginia, Part II: Containing the Titles of the Printed Official Documents of the Commonwealth, 1776–1916," *Bulletin of the Virginia State Library* 10 (January, April, July, October 1917); Swem, "A Bibliography of Virginia, Part III: The Acts and the Journals of the General Assembly of the Colony, 1619–1776," *Bulletin of the Virginia State Library* 12 (January, April 1919); Wilmer L. Hall, "A Bibliography of Virginia, Part IV: Three Series of Sessional Documents of the House of Delegates," *Bulletin of the Virginia State Library* 18 (June 1932).

173. See *Bulletin of the Virginia State Library*, vols. 1 (October 1908), 2 (July 1909), 5 (July 1912), and 7 (April, July 1914).

174. H. J. Eckenrode, *List of the Revolutionary Soldiers of Virginia* (Richmond, 1912), and Eckenrode, *List of the Revolutionary Soldiers of Virginia (Supplement)* (Richmond, 1913).

175. Lester J. Cappon, "Two Decades of Historical Activity in Virginia," *Journal of Southern History* 6 (1940): 192–193.

176. *Richmond Times-Dispatch*, 28 December 1904.

177. Carolyn H. Leatherman, "Richmond Rejects a Library: The Carnegie Library Movement in Richmond, Virginia, in the Early Twentieth Century" (Ph.D. diss., Virginia Commonwealth University, 1992), especially chapters 5 and 6.

178. *Richmond Times-Dispatch*, 7 December 1905; Minutes of the First Meeting, 6 December 1905, Minute Book (1905–1924), Virginia Library Association Records, Organization Records, Acc. 32434, LVA.

179. *Annual Report of the Virginia State Library, 1922–1923*, 14–15.

180. Ibid., *1906–1907*, 28–29.

181. Ibid., *1911–1912*, 7.

182. Ibid., *1915–1916*, 17; *1916–1917*, 11.

183. Ibid., *1933–1934*, 8.

184. *Acts of Assembly, 1936*, 107.

185. *Annual Report of the Virginia State Library, 1942–1943*, 12–13.

186. *Richmond News Leader*, 6 May 1943, 23 November 1946; *Annual Report of the Virginia State Library, 1945–1946*, 12; *1946–1947*, 9.

187. G. Carrington Moseley, "Field and Future of Traveling Libraries in Virginia," *Virginia Journal of Education* 3 (January 1910): 250–252; Moseley, "Free Traveling Libraries in Virginia," *Virginia Journal of Education* 4 (January 1911): 213–215; W. A. Moon, "Books for Rural Virginia," *Commonwealth* 9 (August 1942): 13–17; also *Richmond News Leader*, 5 October 1923.

188. See John S. Patton, "Why We Must Have a State Library Commission in Virginia," *Virginia Journal of Education* 4 (June 1911): 553–554, and "A Correction" 4 (July 1911): 614; H. R. McIlwaine, "Campaign of the American Library Association," *Virginia Journal of Education* 14 (September 1920): 16–17; McIlwaine, "How the Virginia State Library Can Serve the People of Virginia," *Virginia Journal of Education* 23 (September 1929): 9–10; McIlwaine, "The County Free Public Library," *Virginia Libraries* 3 (July, October 1930): 37–43; Wilmer L. Hall, "How the Municipalities Can Use the State Library to Advantage," *Virginia Municipal Review* 18 (December 1941): 287–288, 297; Christine Coffey, "Bringing Books to the People by County Library and Bookmobile Service," *Virginia County* 1 (November–December 1947): 18–19, 20.

189. Ernestine Grafton and Christine Coffey, "Public Library Service in Virginia," *University of Virginia News Letter*, 1 February 1946.

190. "Virginia Federation of Women's Clubs Supports County Library Movement," *Virginia Libraries* 1 (July 1928): 32.

191. *Annual Report of the Virginia State Library, 1941–1942*, 6–8.

192. Ibid., *1922–1923*, 10–11; *Richmond News Leader*, 4 May 1922; Robert L. Scribner, "Father John B. Tabb," *Virginia Cavalcade* 6 (Summer 1956): 5–9; Howard Merewether Lovett, "Father Tabb's Memorial," *Commonweal* 14 (20 May 1931): 65.

193. *Annual Report of the Virginia State Library, 1922–1923*, 10–11.

194. Ibid., *1905–1906*, 7, 14.

195. Ibid., *1910–1911*, 23–25.

196. Ibid., *1915–1916*, 21–22.

197. *Richmond Times-Dispatch* and *Richmond News Leader*, both 22 February 1916.

198. "Historic State Archives Transferred to New Building," *Richmond* 7 (February 1921): 4; *Annual Report of the Virginia State Library, 1928–1929*, 5.

199. *Annual Report of the Virginia State Library, 1922–1923*, 4–5. See also articles in *Richmond*: "Community Building Urged as Memorial For Richmond Dead" 6 (December 1919): 8, 15; "$2,000,000 Memorial in Richmond for Virginia's War Heroes" 6 (March 1920): 7; "Action to Expedite Memorial Library Building Urged" 6 (April 1920): 2; "Richmond's Chance to Get Library and Auditorium" and "Priceless Virginia Records in Fire-Proof Building" 6 (June 1920): cover photograph, 3, and 6; "Permit for State Archives Building Issued" 7 (October 1920): 16; "Historic State Archives Transferred to New Building" 7 (February 1921): 4; "Conference on $2,000,000 War Memorial Library" (April 1921): 13; "Archives in State Library Exceeded Only by Those in Library of Congress" 9 (December 1922): 3; "Return of Ford Lot to City to Follow Selection of Site for War Memorial" 10 (June 1924): 16; "Ford Lot Returned to City" 12 (August 1925): 13; "Ford Lot Back to City" 12 (September 1925): 8.

200. *Richmond News Leader*, 24 March 1923.

201. *Annual Report of the Virginia State Library, 1925–1926*, 4.

202. Ibid., *1932–1933*, 6.

203. Harry Clemons, "Hearty Good Wishes to Wilmer L. Hall," *Virginia Library Bulletin* 9 (1 July 1947): 1–2.

204. Hall, "The Public Records of Virginia," 3.

205. *Richmond Times-Dispatch*, 8 November 1936.

206. See, for example, *Richmond Times-Dispatch*, 28 June 1931.

207. *Annual Report of the Virginia State Library, 1936–1937*, 5; *Richmond Times-Dispatch*, 1 December 1936.

208. *Annual Report of the Virginia State Library, 1937–1938*, 5–7; *Richmond News Leader*, 10, 15, 16, 24, and 25 February 1938; *Richmond Times-Dispatch*, 15, 16, and 25 February 1938.

209. *Annual Report of the Virginia State Library, 1937–1938*, 6–7; Alfred Morton Githens and Francis Keally, "An Example in Library Design," *Commonwealth* 8 (October 1941): 7–8.

210. *Richmond Times-Dispatch* and *Richmond News Leader*, 8 December 1938, 22 and 23 February 1940.

211. *Richmond News Leader*, 11 and 23 September, 7 October 1940; *Richmond Times-Dispatch*, 12 September, 8 October 1940.

212. *Annual Report of the Virginia State Library, 1939–1940*, 5; *Richmond Times-Dispatch*, 4 September 1940; *Richmond News Leader*, 24 December 1940, with numerous other stories and photographs in both newspapers between those dates.

213. *Richmond Times-Dispatch* and *Richmond News Leader*, both 17 October 1941.

214. Randolph W. Church, "A Library Reorganizes through Building," *College and Research Libraries* 5 (1944): 318.

215. *Annual Report of the Virginia State Library, 1958–1959*, 7.

216. A photograph of the work in progress was printed in the *Richmond News Leader*, 8 July 1971.

217. Hall, "The Virginia State Library," 14.

218. Randolph W. Church, "The Relationship Between Archival Agencies and Libraries," *American Archivist* 6 (1943): 145–150; and Church, "A Library Reorganizes through Building," 315–321, 334.

219. Francis Howard Heller, *Virginia's State Government During the Second World War: Its Constitutional, Legislative, and Administrative Adaptations, 1942–1945* (Richmond, 1949), 155–157.

220. *Annual Report of the Virginia State Library, 1941–1942*, 15; *Richmond Times-Dispatch*, 14 February 1942.

221. *Richmond News Leader*, 14 May 1941.

222. *Richmond Times-Dispatch*, 10 January 1944.

223. *Annual Report of the Virginia State Library, 1944–1945*, 6.

224. Ibid., *1946–1947*, 10; *Richmond Times-Dispatch*, 22 February 1947; a contemporary biographical sketch of Church is in *Virginia Librarian* 18 (Spring 1972): 1, 10.

225. *Annual Report of the Virginia State Library, 1946–1947*, 5.

226. Ibid., *1971–1972*, 9, 14, 15.

227. The Harvey letter was purchased in 1949 and the Wyatt commission in 1958. Ibid., *1948–1949*, 7; *1957–1958*, 9.

228. Ernst Posner, *American State Archives* (Chicago, 1964), 278–285; Morris L. Radoff, "Reports of State Archivists," *American Archivist* 17 (1954): 336; biographical sketch of Van Schreeven in *American Archivist* 34 (1971): 412.

229. The library was receiving United States government publications in quantity before the publication of the *First Annual Report of the State Librarian of Virginia for the Year Ended October 31, 1904*, 70–90; *Annual Report of the Virginia State Library, 1969–1970*, 9.

230. *Acts of Assembly, 1981*, 1:259.

231. *Annual Report of the Virginia State Library, 1970–1971*, 23.

232. *Acts of Assembly, 1984*, 1:609.

233. *Annual Report of the Virginia State Library, 1944–1945*, 5–6.

234. Ibid., *1948–1949*, 5.

235. Ibid., *1950–1951*, 5; W. Edwin Hemphill, "Facsimiles in a Popular Historical Magazine," *American Archivist* 20 (1957): 111–117.

236. *Annual Report of the Virginia State Library, 1958–1959*, 7, 13; *1953–1954*, 7, 11; *1965–1966*, 8; *1963–1964*, 17–18; *1975–1976*, 15.

237. Ibid., *1956–1957*, 12.

238. *Richmond Times-Dispatch*, 23 October 1932; *Annual Report of the Virginia State Library, 1931–1932*, 7.

239. Randolph W. Church, ed., *Deterioration of Book Stock, Causes and Remedies: Two Studies on the Permanence of Book Paper Conducted by W. J. Barrow* (Richmond, 1959); *The Manufacture and Testing of Durable Book Papers, Based on the Investigations of W. J. Barrow* (Richmond, 1960); and *Permanent/Durable Book Paper: Summary of a Conference Held in Washington, D.C., September 16, 1960, Sponsored by the American Library Association and the Virginia State Library* (Richmond, 1960).

240. Ken Munden, "In Memoriam: William J. Barrow, 1904–1967," *American Archivist* 30 (1967): 635–637.

241. *Report of the Virginia State Library, 1976–1977*, 5, 8.

242. Ibid., *1958–1959*, 7; review of *Records Management Program Manual of Procedures* (Richmond, 1949) in *American Archivist* 13 (1950): 161–162; Posner, *American State Archives*, 284–285.

243. *Annual Report of the Virginia State Library, 1971–1972*, 14.

244. *Acts of Assembly, 1976*, 2:1169–1172.

245. *Acts of Assembly, 1990*, 1:145–147.

246. Julian P. Boyd, "A New Guide to the Indispensable Sources of Virginia History," *William and Mary Quarterly*, 3d ser., 15 (1958): 3–13; John T. Kneebone and Jon Kukla, eds., *A Key to Survey Reports and Microfilm of the Virginia Colonial Records Project*, 2 vols. (Richmond, 1990), 1:xv–xxiv.

247. John T. Kneebone, "The Virginia Colonial Records Project," *Perspectives* 30 (December 1992): 15–20.

248. Florence B. Yoder, "Federal Library Aid in Virginia: Effects and Prospects," *University of Virginia News Letter* 46 (15 September 1969): 1, 3.

249. Ibid., 2.

250. *Annual Report of the Virginia State Library, 1961–1962*, 8; *Richmond News Leader*, 10 and 11 April 1962; *Richmond Times-Dispatch*, 11 April 1962.

251. *Annual Report of the Virginia State Library, 1972–1973*, 2.

252. Ibid., *1974–1975*, 8; *1975–1976*, 16.

253. Ibid., *1974–1975*, 8; *Virginia State Library News* (June 1979), 1–2.

254. *Virginia State Library News* (October 1984), 2.

255. *Virginia State Library and Archives Biennial Report, July 1, 1990–June 30, 1992*, 17; *July 1, 1992–June 30, 1994*, 15; *The Library of Virginia Annual Report, July 1, 1994–June 30, 1995*, 12–13; John T. Kneebone and Elizabeth Roderick, "Advancing Your Library through High Technology: He Who Hesitates Is Lost; or Fools Rush in Where Angels Fear to Tread," *Information Technology and Libraries* 15 (March 1996): 35–37.

256. *Acts of Assembly, 1977*, 1:819.

257. *Virginia State Library News* (May 1986), 1.

258. *Richmond Times-Dispatch*, 11 September 1990.

259. *Acts of Assembly, 1986*, 2:1408–1409; *1987*, 1:609–610; *1996*, 2:1482.

260. *Virginia State Library and Archives Biennial Report, July 1, 1990–June 30, 1992*, 15–16; *July 1, 1992–June 30, 1994*, 17.

261. Ibid., *1992–1994*, 9; *The Library of Virginia Annual Report, July 1, 1994–June 30, 1995*, 14.

262. *Virginia State Library and Archives Biennial Report, July 1, 1992–June 30, 1994*, 19.

263. Ibid., 18.

264. *Richmond Times-Dispatch*, 19 August 1987.

265. Ibid., 9 September 1993; *Virginia Librarian* 39 (October–December 1993): 19–20.

266. *Acts of Assembly, 1994*, 1:137–156.

TREASURES

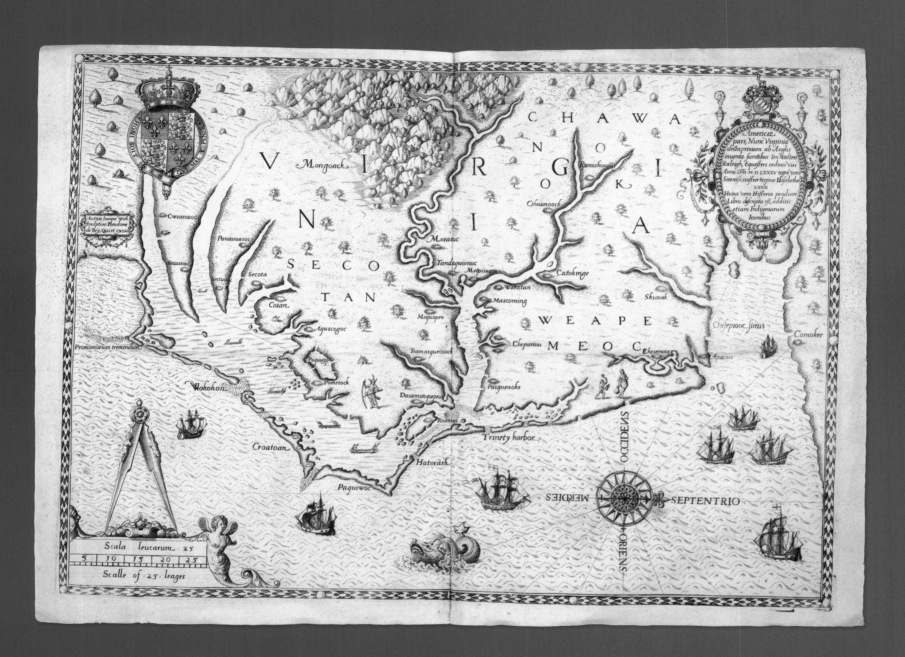

V I R G I N I A

SECO TAN

CHAWANOOK

WEAPE MEOC

Mongoack

Cwarnuoc

Panauuaioc

Neuuisoc

Sectuoc

Secota

Cotan

Aguscogoc

Mequopen

Tramarquecooc

Paquype

Pomerock

Dasamonqueperic

Roanoac

Wokokon

Croatoan

Hatorask

Paquwoc

Trinety harbor

Moratuc

Tandaquomuc

Metocanien

Waratan

Mascoming

Chepanum

Pasquenoke

Ohanooch

Catokinge

Skicoak

Ramushouuog

Chesepiooc sinus

Ehesepiooc

Apaus

Comokee

Americæ pars, Nunc Virginia dicta primum ab Anglis inuenta sumtibus Dni Walteri Ralegh, Equestris ordinis Viri Anno Dni M D LXXXV regni vero Serenissimæ nostræ Reginæ Elisabethæ XXVII Huius Vero Historia peculiari Libro descripta est, additis etiam Indigenarum Iconibus

Autore Ioanne With Sculptore Theodoro de Bry. Qui et excud

Promontorium tremendum

Scala leucarum. 25
5 10 15 20 25
Scalle of 25 leages

OCCIDENS

MERIDIES

ORIENS

SEPTENTRIO

MAPS

Cartography has played an integral part in the history of Virginia since its beginning. Charts, maps, and other geographical reference works accompanied the earliest English ships on their voyages of discovery, even before the settlement of Jamestown in 1607. Maps were also an essential part of the first histories of the Chesapeake and Atlantic coasts: Captain John Smith's maps of the newfound land were included in several volumes, among them his own *Generall Historie of Virginia, New-England, and the Summer Isles*, printed in London in 1624. Moreover, maps—whether as separate documents or as illustrations accompanying the first published accounts of exploration—were mentioned in some of the oldest-surviving records of private libraries in Virginia. During the seventeenth and eighteenth centuries, for example, the colonial governor's advisory Council maintained a reference library with maps as a necessary and much-used component. From simple, rough plats of private landholdings to elaborate and detailed renderings of counties and regions, maps and charts were ubiquitous reminders to colonial Virginians of how much their personal well-being and prosperity increasingly depended on an exact knowledge of their region's geography.

◄ John White (fl. 1585–1593). *Americae pars, Nunc Virginia dicta . . .* , 1590. Scale: 25 leagues = 1 inch. Orientation: north is to the right. Theodore de Bry (1528–1598), *Admiranda narratio, fida tamen, de commodis et incolarum, ritibus Virginiae*. Frankfort, 1590.

The engraver Theodore de Bry based his 1590 map on a 1585 watercolor by John White. White's drawing was the first to depict Virginia as the principal focus of a map and the first to include the printed use of the name "Chesepiooc Sinus" for the Chesapeake Bay. Oriented with north to the right, the map features an area extending from the Chesapeake Bay to Cape Lookout. Elegant in its simplicity and replete with ships and sea monsters, the map remained an important and basic source of information about the mouth of the Chesapeake Bay until John Smith made more extensive explorations in 1608.

White was part of the first group of colonists brought to Roanoke Island, North Carolina, by Sir Walter Ralegh. One of several individuals recruited by Ralegh to document the new country, White illustrated flora and fauna and the lives of the indigenous people. MM

During the nineteenth century, maps became an even more important component of economic growth. The remarkable age of canal, railroad, and turnpike construction required a great many extremely detailed topographic maps. At the same time, as mining and other extractive industries increased, maps depicting the variety of mineral and other natural resources scattered throughout the Old Dominion became equally important. Of special interest are the more than five hundred maps, drawings, and plans—primarily manuscript renderings and totaling approximately nine hundred sheets—commissioned and collected by the commonwealth's Board of Public Works between 1816 and 1859. The earliest series of county maps completed by John Wood and Herman Böÿe between 1819 and 1825 as well as detailed state maps completed in 1827 and 1859 are also found in the Board of Public Works collection.

Today, the Library of Virginia's cartograph collection consists of more than sixty-six thousand maps, primarily of the state and its political subdivisions. Although the collection includes numerous maps drawn or printed as single items, many others were produced as part of state, county, or local records and reports or as enclosures to letters and legislative petitions. Included within the collection are copies of sixteenth- and seventeenth-century maps created to promote and regulate settlement in the colony, surveys and plats of both small and large landholdings, and maps drawn during the American Revolution and the Civil War. A collection of nearly three hundred maps from the Chesapeake and Ohio Railroad Company contains approximately eighteen hundred sheets created between 1836 and 1943, primarily tracing rail routes along the towpaths of the James River and Kanawha Canal. Other commercial maps include original and microfilm copies of the Sanborn Map Company's fire-insurance maps of Virginia communities, highlighting businesses, construction materials for individual buildings, and overall neighborhoods in exact detail. Early topographic maps of the United States Geological Survey are also available for Virginia and most other states.

▶ Jodocus Hondius (1594–1629) and Wilhelm Blaeu (1571–1638). *Nova Virginiae Tabula*, 1650, first derivative, second state. Scale: Militaria Germanica Communia 12 = 3⅛ inches. Orientation: north is to the right. Copperplate engraving, hand-colored, 13⅞ x 18 1/16 inches. Map 755/1650.

The Dutch engraver and printer Jodocus Hondius based his map, first published in 1618, on Captain John Smith's early map of Virginia. Smith's map, however, when completed in 1608 and published in 1612, had lacked any designations for longitude as well as many of the place-names added in later editions, or states, of the early drawing. Acquired by Wilhelm Blaeu after Hondius's death in 1629, the imprint was changed to reflect the transfer of the plate. The map appeared in a variety of atlases from 1630 until circa 1761. This particular map was published in a 1650 atlas with Latin text.

Many early explorers and publishers oriented their maps to demonstrate just how a particular landfall appeared from the deck or lookout of a ship approaching the New World from western Europe. The Hondius-Blaeu map reflects the common practice, with its compass rose (*lower left*) thereby showing north to the right. The map includes images of the Native American chief Powhatan in his hut, the royal arms, and an Indian, based on the extraordinary drawings of John White that he completed in 1585 on a voyage to the North Carolina coast. Various elements of topography are represented by simple sketches of mountains and trees. MM

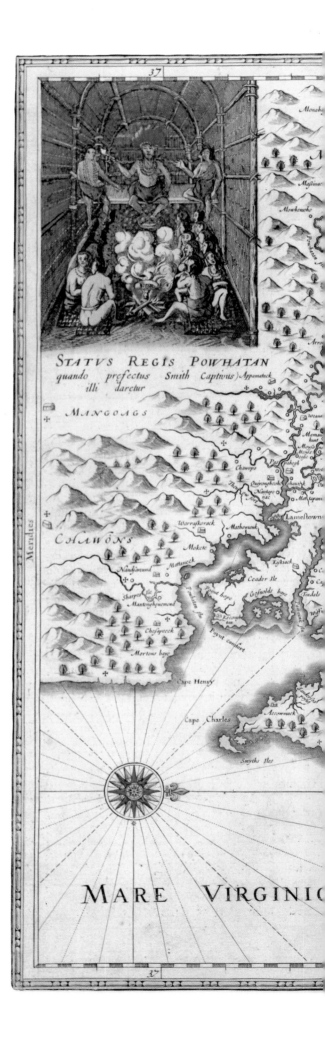

◀ Arnoldus Montanus (1625?–1683) and John Ogilby (1600–1676). *Nova Virginiae Tabula*, 1671. Scale: Militaria Germanica Communia 12 = 2½ inches. Orientation: north is to the right. Copperplate engraving, hand-colored, 11 x 13½ inches. Map 755/1671.

Prepared for the "first encyclopedia of the Americas" written by Arnoldus Montanus and published in Amsterdam in 1671, the highly decorative map is a derivative of Captain John Smith's 1608 map of Virginia. By the terms of an agreement with the publisher, Jacob Meurs, to issue Montanus's "encyclopedia" in an English edition, John Ogilby utilized the same plates and maps as in the Dutch volume. The English edition also appeared in 1671.

John Ogilby, born in Edinburgh, is remembered primarily as a geographer, historian, and publisher. He compiled the first book of road maps in 1675 and before his death held the title of "king's cosmographer and geographic printer." As a young man, he had made his first money through a lottery "for the advancement of the plantation in Virginia"; he had then worked as a dancing-master in London and later as a theater director in Ireland. After losing much of his property in the early 1640s during the English Civil War, he eagerly awaited the restoration of the monarchy and contributed a poem to the coronation ceremony of Charles II. Ogilby received an appointment as a city surveyor after the Great Fire of London in 1666. His last enterprise was as a prosperous publisher and owner of a large printing company, through which he published atlases and geography books. MM

▶ Herman Moll (d. 1732). *A New and Exact Map of the Dominions of the King of Great Britain on ye Continent of North America. Containing Newfoundland, New Scotland, New England, New York, New Jersey, Pensilvania, Maryland, Virginia and Carolina*, 1715. Scale: 240 British miles = approximately 4¹³⁄₁₆ inches. Copperplate engraving, hand-colored, 39 x 23¼ inches. Map 700/1715/1st State.

This lovely map, with its five insets, depicts the Atlantic coast from Louisiana to Labrador and reflects British claims in North America following Queen Anne's War (1702–1713). The striking insets are dominated by *The Cataract of Niagara* with its prominent illustration of beavers, from which this map received its popular nickname, "the Beaver map." The lower insets provide considerable detail on the geography of the southeastern United States, particularly South Carolina.

The engraver Herman Moll was a naturalized Englishman who moved to London from Germany in the 1670s. Moll frequently borrowed illustrative elements from other sources: the famous beaver inset, for example, is a reverse copy from an earlier map by the Frenchman Nicolas de Fer, and the lower insets are modifications adapted from a 1711 map of the Carolinas by Edward Crisp. Moll also scattered his personal theories and opinions throughout his maps and especially directed his energies toward discrediting the work of Guillaume Delisle, the French royal geographer whose maps exaggerated French claims in the New World. MM

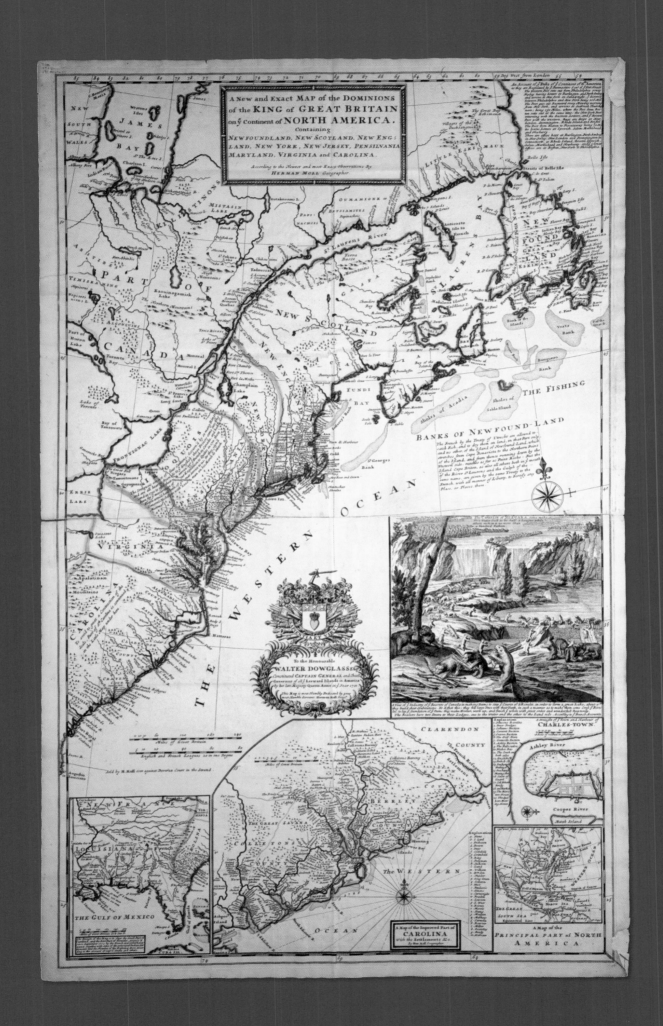

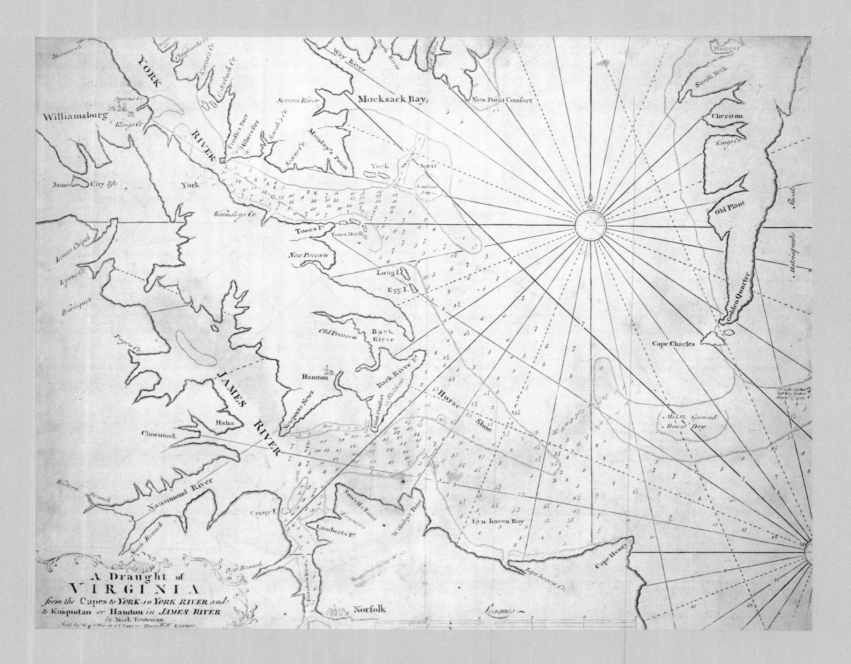

▲ Mark Tiddeman (fl. 1724–1728). *A Draught of Virginia from the Capes to York in York River and to Kuiquotan or Hamton in James River*, [1737/1773]. Scale: 1 mile = ½ inch. Copperplate engraving, 17¾ x 22⅝ inches. Map 755.1 [1737/1773].

This chart was included as an illustration in *The English Pilot: The Fourth Book. Describing the West-India Navigation, from Hudson's Bay to the River Amazones*, published in London by J. Mount and T. Page in 1764. John Seller (d. 1697), hydrographer to Charles II and James II as well as a publisher and maker and seller of nautical instruments, had originated the idea for a series of chart books such as the subsequent sixty-six-page *English Pilot*.

Intended as a working-pilot's navigational guide through the Virginia capes into Hampton Roads and the York River, the chart has little ornamentation. The Virginia chart is based on the work of Mark Tiddeman, master of the Royal Navy ship *Tarter* from 8 February 1724 to 2 August 1728. According to the vessel's logbook, now in the British Public Record Office in London, the *Tarter* sailed from Plymouth, England, with 155 men on board on 17 May 1725 to monitor the American coastal waters. The ship made several trips between Virginia and New York. While off the coast of each colony, Tiddeman took detailed and frequent soundings of water depths for his chart and recorded place-names of particular interest to navigators. After the *Tarter* returned to Plymouth on 11 July 1728, Tiddeman probably sold his maps of Virginia and New York to the publishers of *The English Pilot*. The charts appeared in several editions of the volume from 1729 to 1794. MM

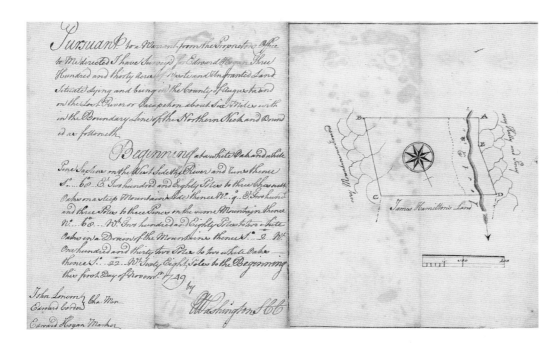

◀ George Washington (1732–1799). *Survey of 330 Acres in Augusta County for Edward Hogan,* 1 November 1749. Scale: 100 poles (550 yards) = 1 inch. Manuscript, 7⅞ x 12¾ inches. Northern Neck Surveys, Land Office Records, Record Group 4.

George Washington received an appointment as surveyor for Culpeper County on 20 July 1749. Washington signed his surveys "S.C.C.," indicating that he was the official and duly commissioned Surveyor of Culpeper County. It appears that he served in the position for only about a year, after which he may have assisted Henry Lee, the new surveyor appointed on 3 November 1750. Washington completed more than 190 surveys in his three years of work as a surveyor, most of them beyond the boundaries of Culpeper County in Lord Fairfax's Northern Neck Proprietary.

The attractive survey is bordered with topographic notations: Washington recorded that a portion of the land included "very Mountainous Ground" while another sector was "very Hilly and Piney." In the center of the survey is a handsome compass rose, with north pointing to the bottom of the document. Note that Edward Hogan, for whom the survey was done, served as marker, one of the surveying team. Whereas the surveyor laid out land boundaries with a compass, and the chainmen measured distances, the marker notched trees to indicate the line of property. MM

▲ William Anderson (fl. 1794). *Survey of 2100 Acres in Botetourt County for George Chambers,* 26 October 1794. Scale: 100 poles (550 yards) = 1 inch. Manuscript, hand-colored, 9⅞ x 15¾ inches. Map 755.814/S8/1794.

Each angle of this simple yet detailed 1794 survey by William Anderson is illustrated by the appropriate tree or trees. In the eighteenth century, it was customary for surveyors outside the Northern Neck area to add initials following their names, indicating the Virginia county in which they had been appointed. "S.B.C." indicates that Anderson was the commissioned surveyor for Botetourt County. Anderson undertook the survey in behalf of George Chambers on the presentation of a land warrant, number 612, for ten thousand acres. The warrant had originally been issued on 6 August 1794 to Robert Douthat. George Chambers, of Franklin County, Pennsylvania, was an assignee for a portion of the warrant and with his brother, Benjamin Joseph Chambers, had contracted with several Philadelphia merchants to locate and patent Virginia lands for one-half interest in the enterprise. Most of the lands acquired were in Botetourt County. The October 1794 survey was among a collection of Chambers family papers purchased by the Library of Virginia in 1923; the papers also included notarized copies of land grants, powers of attorney, receipts, and opinions on the validity of land titles and on the value of the various tracts of land in question. MM

▶ Joshua Fry (1700–1754) and Peter Jefferson (1708–1757). *Map of the most Inhabited part of Virginia, containing the whole province of Maryland with Part of Pensilvania, New Jersey and North Carolina*, 1755. Scale: 30 miles = 2 ¹⁵⁄₁₆ inches. Copperplate engraving, hand-colored, 30 ⅞ x 48 ⅞ inches. Map 755/1751/[1755?b].

The map of Virginia produced by Joshua Fry and Peter Jefferson was a much-needed one. Their collaborative work brought up to date in one cartographic resource the considerable geographical information about Virginia gathered in the eighty-two years since the much-relied-on Augustine Herrman map of 1673. The product of the Fry-Jefferson partnership thus quickly served as the primary map of the colony. Complete with its ornamental and neatly drawn cartouche, highlighting the title, the map also greatly influenced European mapmakers, including a few French printers who published several maps of Virginia based on Fry and Jefferson's work.

It was in 1738 that Joshua Fry had first proposed to the House of Burgesses that it finance a survey and map of the colony. The proposal failed to attract the necessary support but was referred to each subsequent biennial meeting of the Virginia assembly until 1744, when it was finally rejected. In 1750, however, the royal Board of Trade directed Virginia's acting governor, Lewis Burwell, to commission a map of the inhabited part of Virginia. Fry and Peter Jefferson were chosen to perform the work, largely on the strength of their earlier surveys of Lord Fairfax's lands between the headsprings of the Rappahannock and Potomac Rivers and of lands west of the Blue Ridge and along the border between Virginia and North Carolina.

Born in England and educated at Oxford University, Joshua Fry had taught mathematics at the College of William and Mary in Williamsburg. He settled in an area south of Charlottesville in about 1740 and when Albemarle County was established in 1744 received an appointment with Peter Jefferson as a county justice. When Fry died in 1754, he bequeathed his surveying instruments to his fellow mapmaker. Peter Jefferson, of Welsh descent and one of the first residents of Albemarle County, was a self-educated man who by hard work became an expert surveyor and mapmaker. He served in various county offices and was also a member of the House of Burgesses. On his own death in 1757, he in turn left his surveying instruments to his son Thomas Jefferson. MM

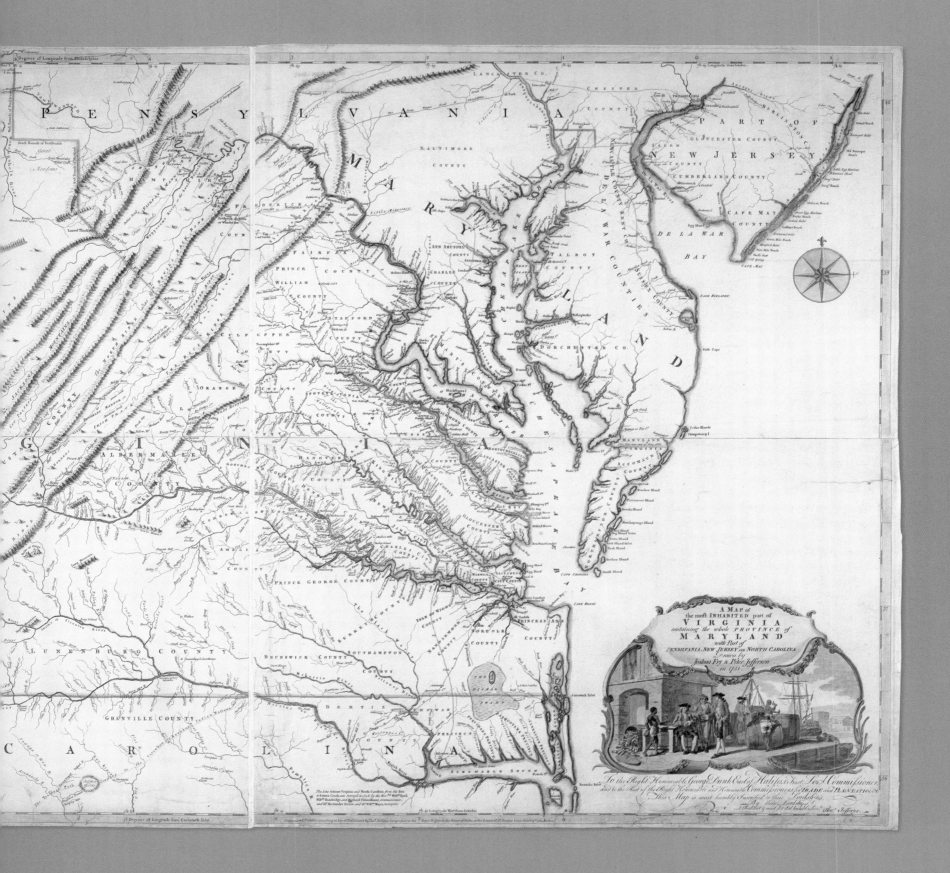

A Map of
the most INHABITED part of
VIRGINIA
containing the whole PROVINCE of
MARYLAND
with Part of
PENSILVANIA, NEW JERSEY and NORTH CAROLINA.
Drawn by
Joshua Fry & Peter Jefferson
in 1751

▼ Claudius Crozet (1790–1864). *A Plan of James Riv[er] from the North Branch to the balcony falls Exhibiting a comparison between the Pr. Engrs location & that substituted by the Commissioner,* 1824. Scale: 25 chains (1,650 feet) = 4 inches. Manuscript, hand-colored, 13 x 18 ¼ inches. Board of Public Works, Entry 495(23), Record Group 57.

Among the many public works Virginia considered during the early 1800s was a canal to permit safe navigation through the Blue Ridge Mountains from the North Branch to Irish Falls in Rockbridge County. An act of the General Assembly on 8 March 1824 called on the "civil engineer of this State" to locate the canal "in such a manner as he may think best." In practice, the state's engineer worked with private companies on projects approved by the commonwealth's Board of Public Works. In this case, the board's principal engineer, Claudius Crozet, was to work with the commissioner of the Kanawha Road

and Navigation Company. After the commissioner revised several of Crozet's plans for the location of a dam, the type of locks to be used, and the depth of the first section of the canal, Crozet outlined his objections in a 24 June 1824 report to the president and directors of the Board of Public Works. In particular, Crozet cited the greater expense and risk to canal traffic posed by the alternative proposals.

Six months later, on 15 January 1825, Crozet submitted a second report regarding the Blue Ridge Canal. With it, he included this delicately drawn and colored map as well as diagrams prepared "with great care" from his own field book, "shewing the relative position and dimensions of both lines of canal." On the map, Crozet's plan is marked in red, the company commissioner's in yellow. Crozet included the diagrams to "present a comparative view of the quantity of excavation, walling, paving, etc. at each successive station." "I have the honor," he added, "to lay them before you; they will elucidate this report." The dispute led to a ruling by the Virginia attorney

general on the respective duties of the engineer and the commissioner. The compromise was sufficient for work on the canal to commence.

Born in France, Claudius Crozet had been educated as an engineer and had served in the army of Napoleon Bonaparte before immigrating to the United States in 1816. After teaching at the United States Military Academy at West Point for seven years, Crozet from 1823 to 1831 and from 1837 to 1843 served as principal engineer for Virginia's Board of Public Works, directing internal improvement projects throughout the state. He also prepared Virginia's internal improvement maps for 1838, 1848, and 1855. From 1837 to 1845, he was a member of Virginia Military Institute's board of visitors. And from 1849 to 1857, as chief engineer for the Blue Ridge Railroad, Crozet supervised the complex construction of a tunnel through the mountains. He died in Midlothian, Virginia, in 1864 and is now buried in Lexington at Virginia Military Institute. MM

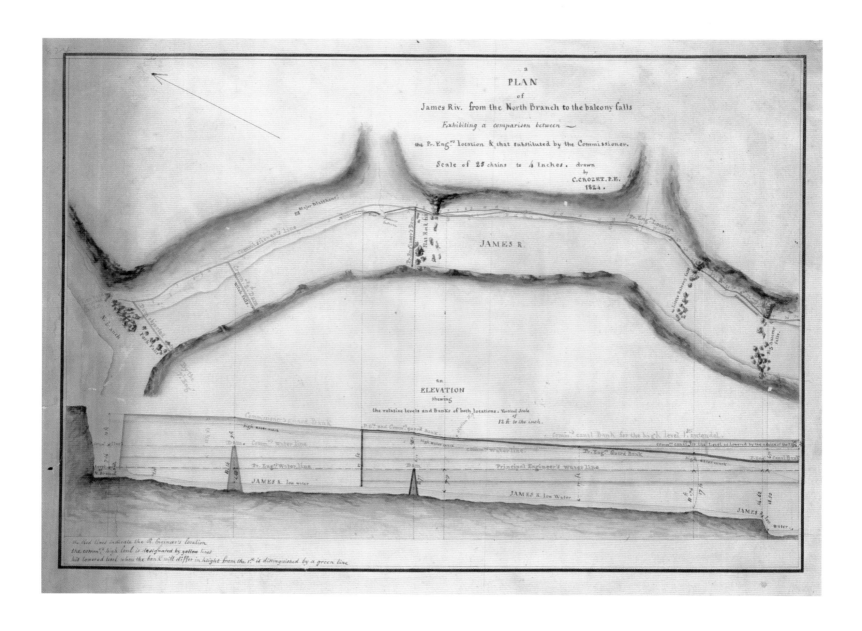

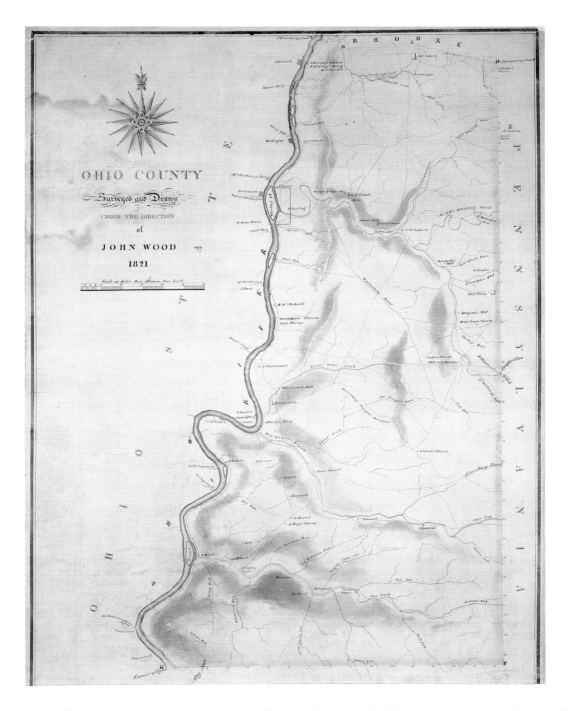

▲ John Wood (ca. 1775–1822). *Ohio County*, 1821. Scale: 1 mile = 1 inch. Manuscript, hand-colored, 33 ⅛ x 25 ½ inches. Map 754.14/ 1821/ part 1. Board of Public Works, Entry 711(24), Record Group 57.

Born in Scotland, John Wood came to the United States about 1800. After residing in Richmond, Virginia, he moved to Kentucky, then to the District of Columbia, next to Williamsburg (as a professor of mathematics at the College of William and Mary), and finally to Petersburg, where he established the Petersburg Academy. An editor and publisher of political pamphlets, Wood became most noted for his series of Virginia county maps intended as the basis for a single, detailed map of the commonwealth. At his death in 1822, he had finished

ninety-six maps in addition to draft maps for all 102 counties. Herman Bőÿe, who had immigrated to the United States from Denmark in 1816, was charged with completing the few remaining county maps and, from them, at last constructing an updated map of the state. The new map was distributed in 1827, five years after Wood's death, and revised in 1859.

Forty-eight Wood-Bőÿe county maps are known to have survived. The Library of Virginia contains thirty-eight of these. Although the maps' drafting styles sometimes vary, they are easily recognizable. Many bear the name of John Wood or Herman Bőÿe near the title. Many, too, include distinctive features such as a blue wash indicating topographical features and waterways; roads usually appear in red. Other maps in the series, perhaps preliminary copies, bear only the

respective county's name. All of the maps, however, are quite large and usually include stations and distances, probably referring to field-book entries.

It is hoped that perhaps other Wood-Bőÿe maps survive and will be recognized, acknowledged, and preserved. A general standardization of format and the numerous place-names included on each of the maps, as required by the 1816 General Assembly act authorizing the project, make them invaluable for researchers today. Although Wood and Bőÿe had to employ several sheets to complete most of the oversize county maps, the entire map of Ohio County (now part of West Virginia) appears on a single sheet; a second sheet includes statistics for the area. MM

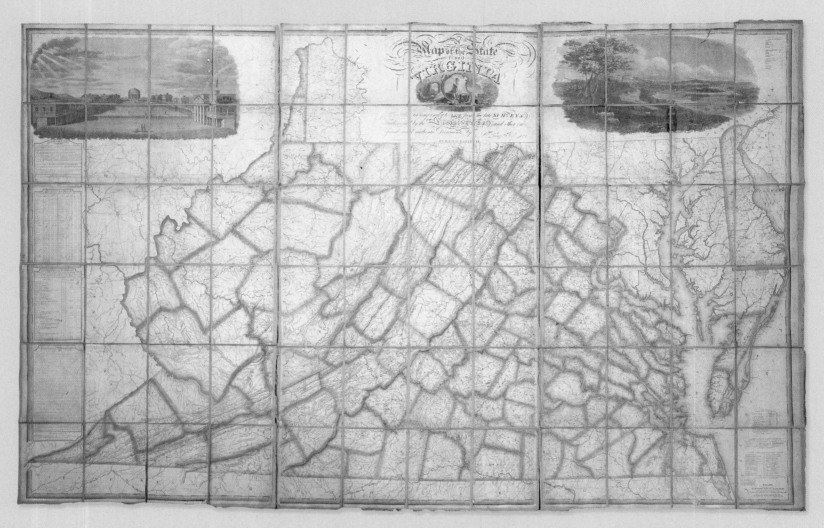

▲ Herman Bőÿe (1792–1830). *A Map of the State of Virginia, Constructed in Conformity to Law . . .* , 1827. Scale: 20 American miles (1,760 yards each mile) = approximately 4 inches. Copperplate engraving, hand-colored, 62 x 93 inches. Board of Public Works, Entry 712(1), Record Group 57.

By the late eighteenth century, many Virginians recognized that the commonwealth needed an updated, accurate map to reflect the rapid increase in settlements, the numerous new roads, and the many changes in county boundaries. On 27 February 1816, the General Assembly passed an act "to provide an accurate account of each county and a general map of the territory of the Commonwealth." Thomas Jefferson, whose father, Peter Jefferson, had helped complete the influential Fry-Jefferson map, had been a prominent supporter of the legislation.

An editor and publisher and sometime schoolmaster, John Wood was appointed to the task and by his death in 1822 had completed maps of nearly all of Virginia's counties. In November 1822, Herman Bőÿe began the work of completing the few remaining county maps— while also laboring nearly three years to reduce his predecessor's maps to a uniform scale—and then constructing a state map from his own and Wood's cartographic work.

Once Bőÿe was finished, the Philadelphia engraver Henry S. Tanner was awarded the contract for engraving the state map onto nine separate copperplates. Finally distributed in 1827, the finished map measured 62 by 93 inches. Special presentation copies were hand-mounted and -tinted and then sent by the commonwealth of Virginia to important dignitaries and institutions throughout the country. Tanner also printed a reduced-size, four-plate version, including everything but the larger map's central cartouche and pictorial insets.

Soon after the map's publication, it became apparent that Bőÿe had resorted to considerable guesswork when reconciling John Wood's data with his own, juggling county boundaries until, correct or not, they appeared to coincide. The incorrect boundaries, together with the subsequent creation of new counties in the western part of the state, quickly made the Bőÿe map obsolete. Despite the efforts of Claudius Crozet, former principal engineer of the Board of Public Works, to produce a more accurate map, the state's unwillingness to fund such an expensive project led the General Assembly to require that corrections be made directly onto the original 1827 copperplates. Lewis von Buchholtz, a young German engineer, was given the task. Counties created before 1827 received a copy of the

applicable portion of the Wood-Bőÿe map so that local surveyors could reconcile discrepancies; counties created after 1827 submitted new surveys. The Buchholtz revision contained significant improvements, particularly in the more precise delineation of coastal areas based on recent U.S. Coast Survey charts and on astronomical observations.

Despite its persistent errors, the Bőÿe-Buchholtz map of 1859 is nevertheless important as a manifestation of the state's early recognition that an accurate map was essential for the political and economic development of Virginia. Furthermore, the map's impressive size and pictorial embellishments make it one of the last great Virginia examples of the tradition of decorative cartography inherited from Europe. MM

▲ Herman Bŏÿe (1792–1830) and Lewis von Buchholtz (fl. 1825). *A Map of the State of Virginia . . . By Herman Bŏÿe. Corrected by Order of the Executive By L. V. Buchholtz*, 1825. Engraved copperplate, corrected in 1859, section two of nine sections, 22 x 33 inches. Board of Public Works, Entry 712, Record Group 57.

So large is the map of Virginia by Herman Bŏÿe and Lewis von Buchholtz that it required nine different printing plates, each one engraved in 1825 by Henry S. Tanner, of Philadelphia. Tanner was assisted in the project by Benjamin Tanner, his brother, who engraved the inset view of the University of Virginia; by James W. Steel, who completed the Richmond scene; and by Joseph Perkins, a lettering expert, who fashioned the title section with views of Natural Bridge and Harper's Ferry. The map was issued in 1827; it was not until thirty-two years later, during the winter of 1859–1860, that the plates were corrected and republished by Selmar Seibert, of Washington, D.C. On the second of the nine copperplates, Seibert removed the original nota-tion, "Engraved by H. S. Tanner," but retained the original 1825 date and added the year 1859; he also noted that the revision was "Corrected by order of the Executive." Eight of the original nine copperplates survive and are part of the records of the Library's Virginia Board of Public Works.

Copperplate engraving, such as that used for the Bŏÿe-Buchholtz map, had become the pre-ferred graphic medium for most printing, includ-ing mapmaking, as early as the late fifteenth century. As opposed to woodcuts, for example, copperplate engraving allowed for much larger printing plates as well as a finer incise line for greater precision and ease in making corrections or revisions. Moreover, the durability of copper-plates resulted in considerably reduced costs. As copperplate engraving soon became a special-ized profession, separate from book printing, it alleviated the requirement that all printing craftsmen be literate. Copperplate engraving remained the preferred method of map printing until the lithographic process, developed about 1800, was improved and widely accepted later in the century. MM

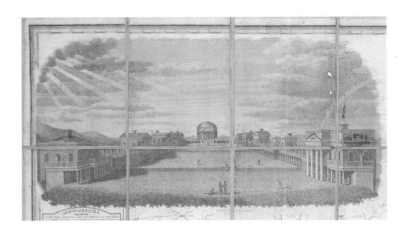

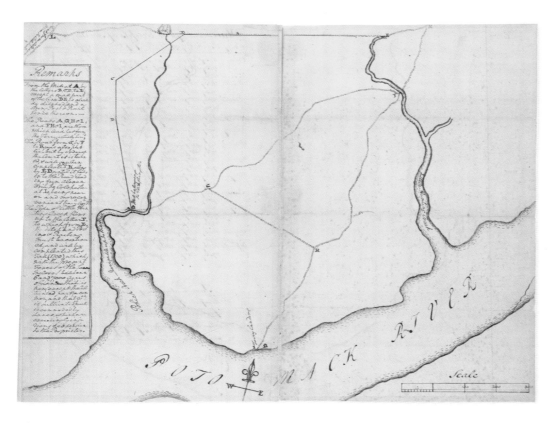

▲ George Washington (1732–1799). Petition to the General Assembly, with survey, 21 October 1790. Scale: 100 poles (550 yards) = 1 inch. Manuscript, 12½ x 16¼. Records of the General Assembly, Legislative Petitions, Fairfax County, Record Group 78.

On 21 October 1790, George Augustine Washington presented to the Virginia General Assembly on behalf of his uncle George Washington a legislative petition concerning a Potomac River ferry. The younger Washington, after service as a major and as an aide to the Marquis de Lafayette during the American Revolution, had married in 1785 and soon thereafter taken up residence at Mount Vernon. It was in April 1789, when George Washington journeyed to New York to take the oath of office as president of the United States, that the general's nephew assumed the day-to-day management of the Mount Vernon estate. One year later, he submitted the legislative petition.

The ferry had been established in 1783 on the land of John Posey, of Fairfax County, and crossed to a landing on the Maryland property of Thomas Marshall. George Washington had since purchased Posey's property and, if the General Assembly agreed, wished to discontinue the crossing service. It was not an easy issue; the right and obligation to operate ferries and other modes of public transportation were not granted idly, nor were they withdrawn without considerable thought given to the impact on the local populace. Washington, however, reasoned that the ferry had been hampered by a decrease in income, unfavorable weather, and "especially by the lately adopted mode of travelling in State Carriages none of which pass this way." Accompanying the petition as supporting documentation were a list of receipts for the last year and the neatly drawn survey of the ferry route, landings, and roads. The remarks included on the survey are in George Washington's hand and refer to the lettered areas on the drawing. Perhaps not surprisingly, the General Assembly found Washington's request to be a reasonable one and granted permission. MM

▶ Charles Murray (fl. 1839). Petition to the General Assembly, 7 December 1839, with a map (dated 12 November 1839). Scale not indicated. Manuscript, hand-colored, 10¾ x 15⅞ inches. Records of the General Assembly, Legislative Petitions, Fairfax County, Record Group 78.

In 1839, Charles Murray submitted a petition to the Virginia General Assembly, requesting that the legislature prohibit the location of a graveyard within a given distance of an inhabited dwelling or improved property. Murray included a map to illustrate his dilemma. Four lots, outlined in red, had been sold by one Robert Taylor to a Methodist congregation of free African Americans and slaves from the town of Alexandria, at that time within the District of Columbia. The congregation wished to use the lots as a graveyard, but Murray feared that the cemetery would contaminate three nearby wells, indicated by small, bright red circles. Murray's petition resulted in the draft of a bill, but there is no evidence that the General Assembly enacted it into law. MM

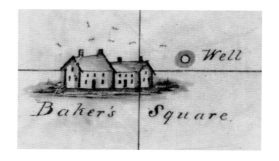

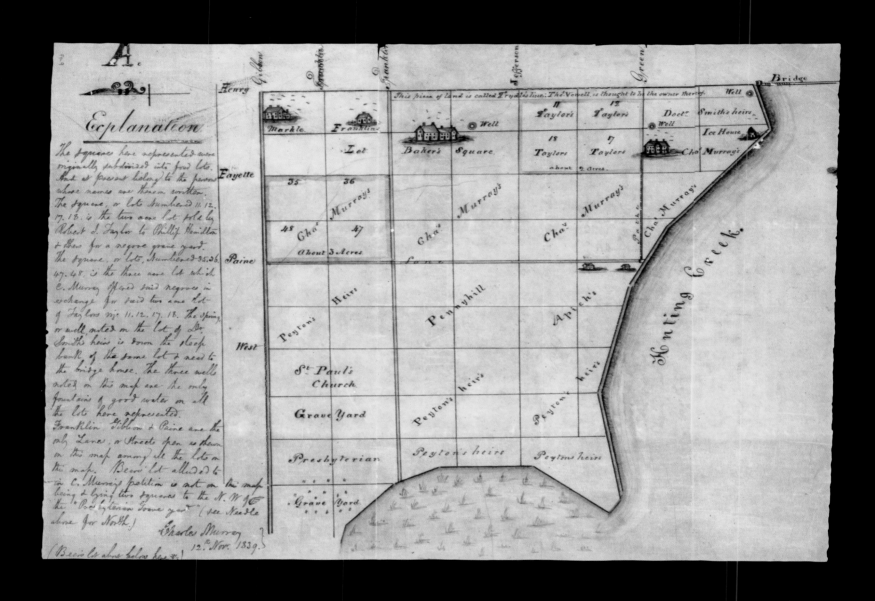

A.º

Explanation

The squares here represented were originally subdivided into four lots. And at present belong to the persons whose names are therein written. The square, or lots Numbered 11. 12. 17. 18. is the two acre lot sold by Robert S. Taylor to Phillip Hamilton & others for a negroe grave yard. The square, or lots, Numbered 35. 36. 47. 48. is the three acre lot which C. Murray offered said negroes in exchange for said two acre lot of Taylors viz 11. 12. 17. 18. The spring or well noted on the lot of Dr. Smiths heirs is down the steep bank of the same lot & next to the bridge house. The three wells noted on this map are the only fountains of good water on all the lots here represented. Franklin, Gibbon & Paine are the only Lanes, or Streets open as shewn on this map among all the lots on this map. Bews lot alluded to in C. Murrays petition is not on this map being & lying two squares to the N. W of the "Presbyterian grave yard" (see Needle above for North.)

Charles Murray
12.º Nov. 1839.

(Bews lot abve below here #.)

Henry

Fayette

Paine

West

Markle

Franklins
Lot

35   36

48   Cha.ˢ Murrays 47
About 3 Acres

Peytons
Heirs

St. Paul's
Church

Grave Yard

Presbyterian

Grave Yard

This piece of land is called Fryolles line: Tho.ˢ Vowell is thought to be the owner thereof.

Bakers Square.
Well

Cha.ˢ   Murrays

Cha.ˢ

Lane

Pennyhill

Peyton's heirs

Peyton's heirs

Peytons heirs

Taylors   Taylors   Doct.ʳ Smiths heirs
11   12   Well
18   7   Ice House
Taylors   Taylors   Cha.ˢ Murrays
about 2 Acres

Cha.ˢ   Murrays

Cha.

Cha.ˢ Murrays

Apichs

Peyton's heirs

Well

Bridge
Well

Hunting Creek.

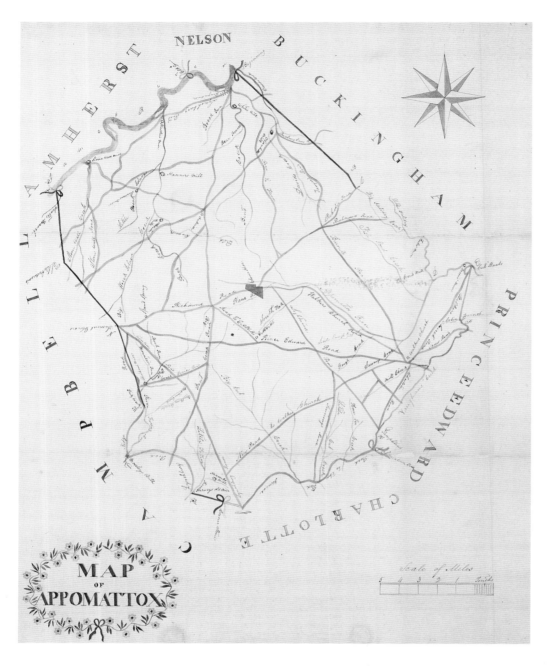

◀ John Patteson (fl. 1846), Alexander Austin (fl. 1846), and E. Cheatham (fl. 1846). *Map of Appomattox*, 1846. Scale: 1 mile = ⅝ inch. Manuscript, hand-colored, 23 x 18 ¾ inches. Map 755.58/1846.

The map of Appomattox County was at one time folded into a small bundle and lost in the midst of countless similar bundles in the extensive local records of Prince Edward County. Accompanied by a clearly written report, the map was submitted to the Prince Edward County Court and signed by the surveyors of Buckingham and Campbell Counties as well as by the surveyor of the newly formed Appomattox County. This is thought to be the oldest map of Appomattox County, established in 1845 from parts of Buckingham, Prince Edward, Charlotte, and Campbell Counties. Yet another portion of Campbell County would be added in 1848. The new county was named for the Appomattox River, which in turn had been named for an Indian tribe that had lived near the mouth of the stream. Initial surveys of individual counties such as this retain considerable value today in verifying long-established land boundaries. MM

▶ A. T. McRae (fl. 1861). *Map of the Battle Ground of Greenbrier River, Drawn and Published by A. T. McRae, C.S.A. Quitman Guards, First Reg't Ga. Vols*, 1861. Scale: 100 yards = ⁵⁄₁₆ inches. Wood engraving, 12 ⅛ x 18 inches. Map 754.87/M6/1861–1865/[1861].

Engraved by J. Baumgarten and printed in Richmond in 1861, the map by A. T. McRae depicts a minor engagement that occurred in the northwestern part of Virginia early in the Civil War. On the morning of 3 October 1861, a brigade under Union brigadier general Joseph J. Reynolds drove Confederate pickets back across the Greenbrier River. The Federals quickly followed with a direct, frontal assault but were repulsed by approximately eighteen hundred Confederates under the command of Henry R.

Jackson. After a second attack, this time against the defenders' flank, the Union force gave up and withdrew. The Federals lost eight killed and thirty-three wounded; the Confederates had six killed, thirty-three wounded, and thirteen missing. The engraving is a good example of the simple yet clear unofficial map published only infrequently in the Confederacy and is particularly interesting for the desire of McRae to publish his overview of such a small engagement. The war was still young, printing materials still generally available, and the thirst for news from the front unabated. The woodcut map's simple illustrations depict several Confederate camps, houses, roads, Jackson's headquarters, the position of the "Yankee artillery," and the Greenbrier River flowing through the middle of the encampment. MM

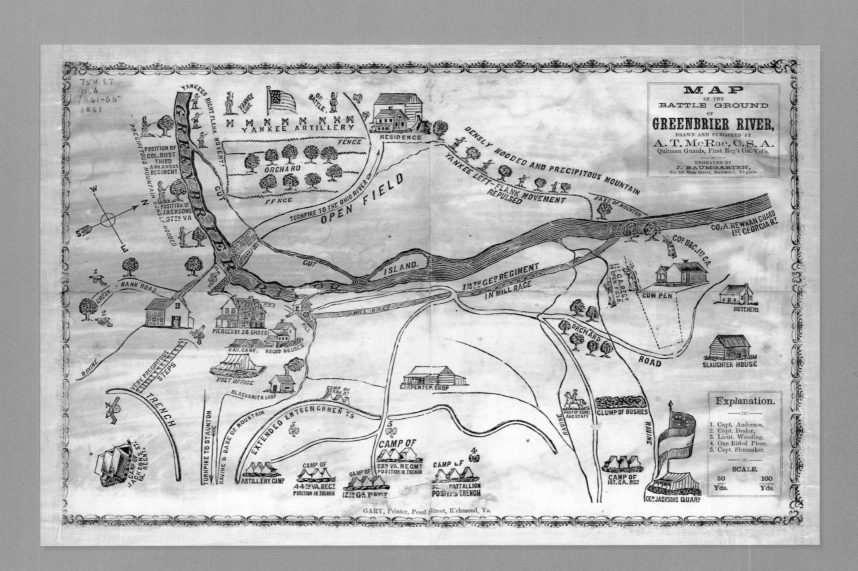

MAP
OF THE
BATTLE GROUND
OF
GREENBRIER RIVER,
DRAWN AND PUBLISHED BY
A. T. McRae, C.S.A.
Quitman Guards, First Reg't Ga. Vol's.
ENGRAVED BY
J. BAUMGARTEN,
No. 161 Main Street, Richmond, Virginia.

Explanation.
1. Capt. Anderson.
2. Capt. Desler.
3. Lieut. Wooding.
4. One Rifled Piece.
5. Capt. Shumaker.

SCALE
50   100
Yds.   Yds.

GARY, Printer, Pearl Street, Richmond, Va.

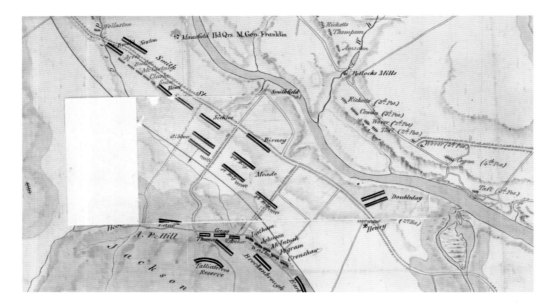

▲ Denis Callahan (fl. 1863). *Passages of the Rappahannock and Battle of Fredericksburg, December 10th to 16th, 1862 . . . compiled from the Surveys of the Topographical Dept, . . . and a survey of the rebel position by Lt. Jed. Hotchkiss, T. E., to Lt. Gen. Jackson, C.S.A. [signed] by Alexander Doule, Major, 2D N.Y. AY., Insp. of Arty. Copied from the Original belonging to Gen'l Burnside/Topographical Bureau, April 8th 1863/D. Callahan.* Scale: 1 mile = 3⅛ inches. Manuscript, hand-colored, 24½ x 31 inches, with attached overlay. Map 755.36/M6/1861– 1865/1862(2).

This unique manuscript map accompanied a battle report submitted by Brigadier General Henry Hunt, chief of artillery for the Army of the Potomac. The map shows not only the several stationary positions held by Federal and Confederate forces on 13 December 1862, but also the various maneuvers carried out by Union troops under General Ambrose Burnside as they attempted to break through the Confederate defenses at Fredericksburg, Virginia.

The map illustrates the positions held by Union troops after crossing the Rappahannock River. The battle began southeast of Fredericksburg when General William B. Franklin's Left Grand Division attacked Confederate forces commanded by General T. J. "Stonewall" Jackson. A featured map overlay shows the initial attack positions held by the Union divisions commanded by Generals George G. Meade and John Gibbon (*detail, above*). Beneath the overlay (*detail, below*), the Federal lines are depicted both in their initial positions (uncolored) and in their subsequent attacking positions (colored black and red). Although the Union divisions penetrated a gap in the Confederate line, Jackson's veterans repulsed the assault.

The Union army recrossed the Rappahannock on the night of 15 December. Of the approximately one hundred thousand Union soldiers engaged, more than twelve thousand were killed, wounded, or listed as missing—far more than twice the number of Confederate casualties. MM

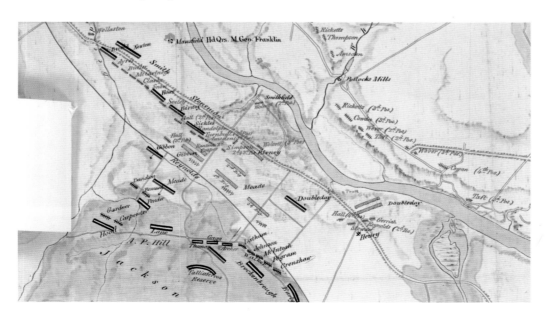

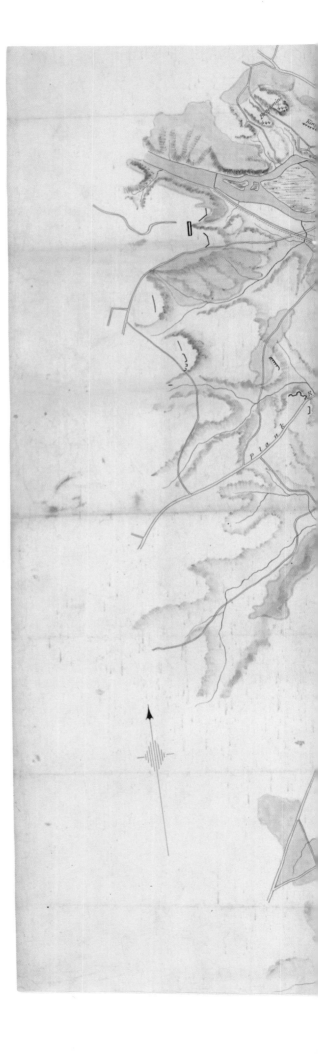

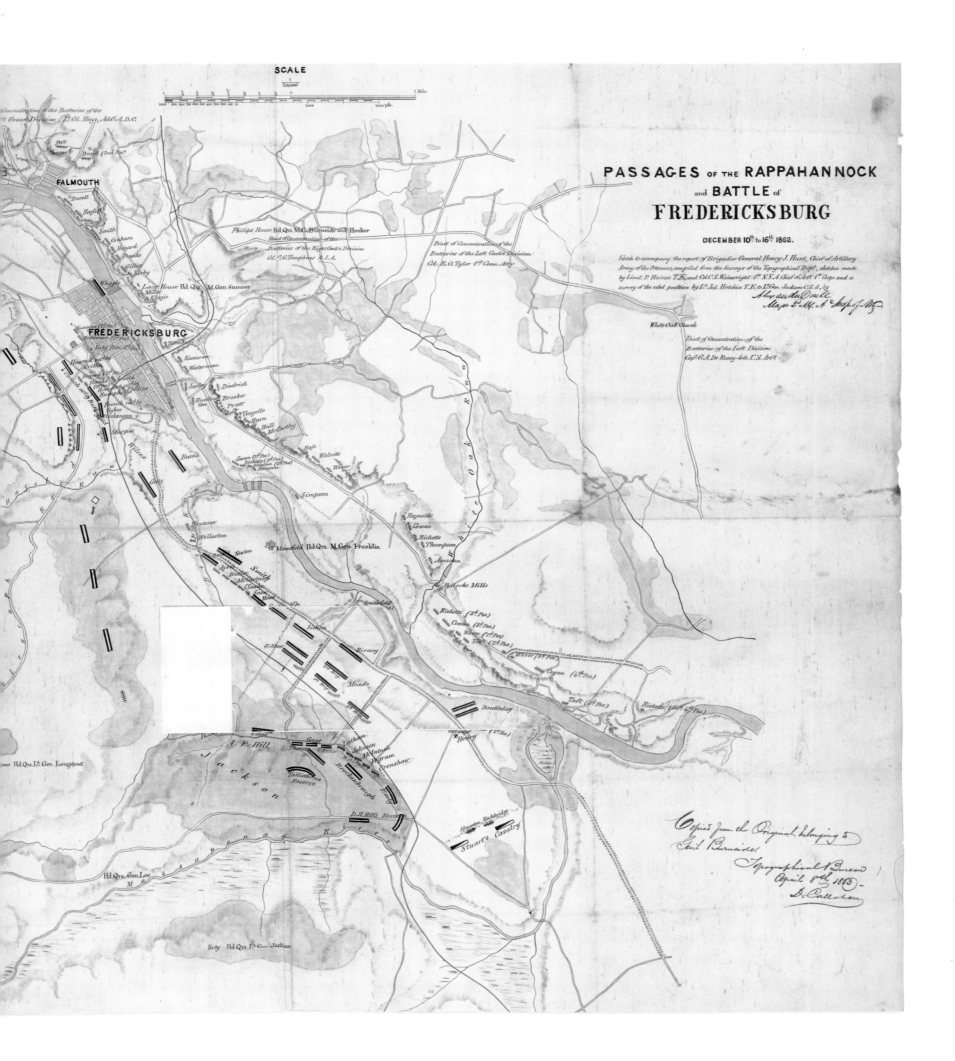

PASSAGES OF THE RAPPAHANNOCK
and BATTLE of
FREDERICKSBURG
DECEMBER 10th to 16th 1862.

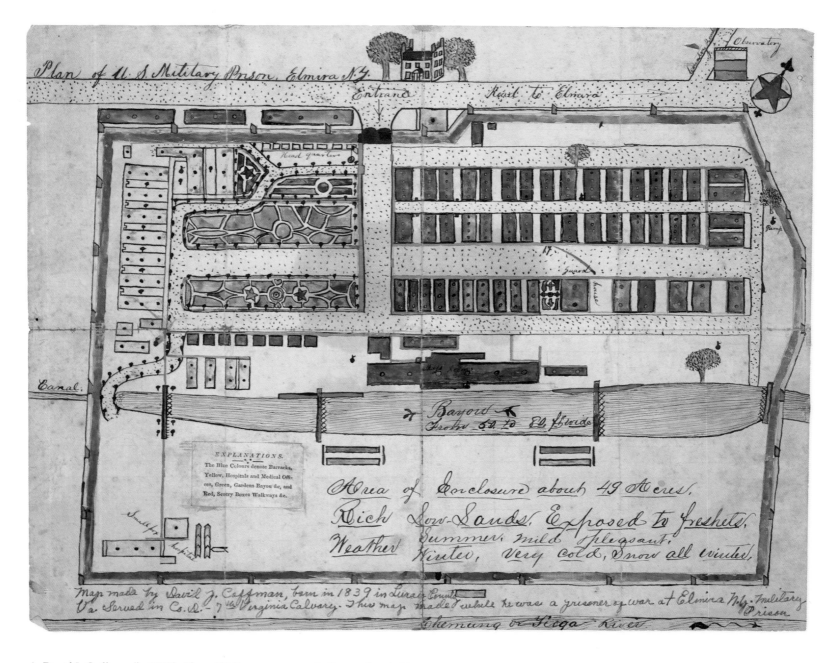

▲ David J. Coffman (b. 1839). *Plan of U.S. Military Prison, Elmira, N.Y.*, n.d. Scale not indicated. Manuscript, hand-colored, 12 ½ x 15 ½ inches. Map 747/M6/1861–1865/n.d.

David J. Coffman, of Page County, Virginia, was a twenty-three-year-old farmer when he enlisted on 1 April 1862 as a private in Company D of the Seventh Virginia Cavalry. In May 1864, Coffman was captured near Bowling Green, Virginia, taken to Port Royal, Virginia, and subsequently transferred to the new U.S. Military Prison at Elmira, New York. Established to handle the huge increase of enlisted Confederate captives after the Union government suspended the long-standing policy of exchanging prisoners, Elmira Prison was badly overcrowded. Food and blankets were scarce, and half of the ten thousand prisoners of war held there were forced to live in tents, even during the harsh winter months.

Coffman's detailed but untrained drawing, complete with an identification key, provides an interesting and unique personal perspective on prison facilities during the Civil War. The notation at the bottom indicates that the drawing was made during the year that he was confined. However, the use of watercolors and his printed explanation of the color code suggest that he added these embellishments after he had taken the oath of allegiance and gained his release on 27 June 1865. MM

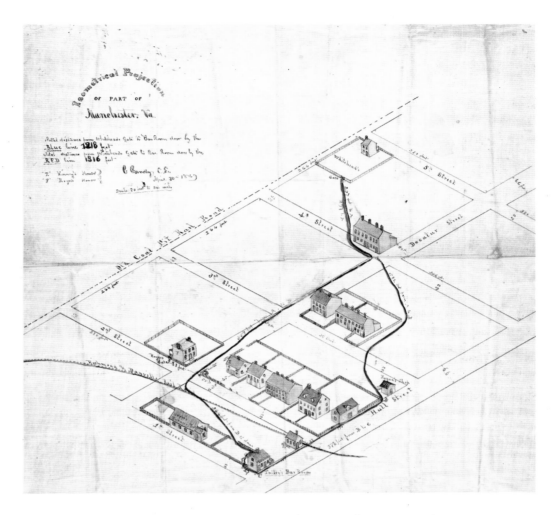

▲ C. Bradley (fl. 1869). *Isometrical Projection of Part of Manchester, Va.*, 1869. Scale: 70 feet = 1 inch. Manuscript, on tracing linen, 18 ⅛ x 19 inches. Chesterfield County, County Court, Criminal Causes and Grand Jury Presentments, *Commonwealth* v. *Willis and Whitehead*, 1870.

This interesting scale drawing of a portion of Manchester, Virginia, illustrates a 21 February 1869 murder scene—specifically two different routes from a local tavern to the home of Richard H. Whitehead, later convicted of the murder of James Rogers, forty, a stonemason and the father of four children. Whitehead, twenty-four, worked for the Manchester Cotton and Wool Mills; his accomplice, Thomas Willis, twenty-eight, worked for the Tredegar Iron Works. While drinking with Willis at Talley's Bar Room, Whitehead had been unable to suppress his considerable ill will toward Rogers. Whitehead's dark mood erupted into a shooting later that evening. The Chesterfield County Court convicted both Whitehead and Willis of murder in the second degree and sentenced the former to eighteen years in the penitentiary, Willis to seven. Whitehead appealed the verdict, but died of consumption in May 1870 before any action could be taken. Both Rogers, the victim, and Whitehead, his assailant, are buried at Richmond's Hollywood Cemetery.

Besides the part it played in the murder trial, the map is equally interesting for its depiction of particular buildings and residences of the time, revealing considerable information about how the area actually looked. The Library of Virginia's archival staff discovered the map in the records of the Chesterfield County Court on deposit at the Library during the processing of the collection. MM

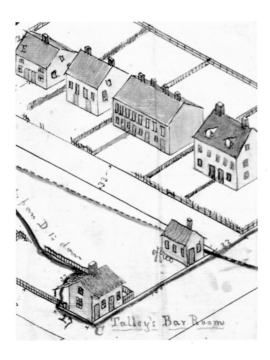

▶ Octave Jacob, Jr. (fl. 1892). *Tangier Sound/ Public Oyster Grounds State of Virginia. Survey under the direction of J. B. Baylor Assistant U.S. Coast & Geodetic Survey, 1892.* 1000 yards = ⅞ inch. Manuscript, with red ink, 25⅛ x 14½ inches. Map 755/09/[15].

The manuscript chart, prepared for printing under the direction of Captain James Bowen Baylor (1848–1924), shows the natural rocks in Tangier Sound through which the Maryland-Virginia boundary line runs. Baylor, a member of a prominent Albemarle County family, conducted the survey while detached from duty with the U.S. Coast and Geodetic Survey. The Tangier Sound oyster grounds were the subject of frequent disputes and spirited turmoil between Virginia and Maryland, especially since their own oyster supply was depleted, and Maryland watermen too often openly pirated Virginia oysters.

To help define the public oyster beds—those areas available to independent watermen who harvested oysters commercially for a small annual licensing fee—the Virginia General Assembly on 29 February 1892 established what became known as the Baylor Oyster Survey. Confusion over the boundaries between the natural rocks and the barren and as yet unproductive grounds were often contested. The survey, in essence, was meant to define those barren grounds that could for a fee be leased to oyster planters and thus raise income for the state. The public oyster grounds and land stations are marked in red on Baylor's 1892 survey. The General Assembly act required a written report, charts for the surveyed areas, and the placement of these charts in the state archives in Richmond, with a copy also in the office of the county clerk for the particular area surveyed. The survey resulted in printed reports for each of the sixteen affected counties as well as the publication of thirty charts, issued by the Norris Peters Company, of Washington, D.C. The maps remain a valuable resource and are still consulted as part of the management of Virginia's fragile oyster industry. MM

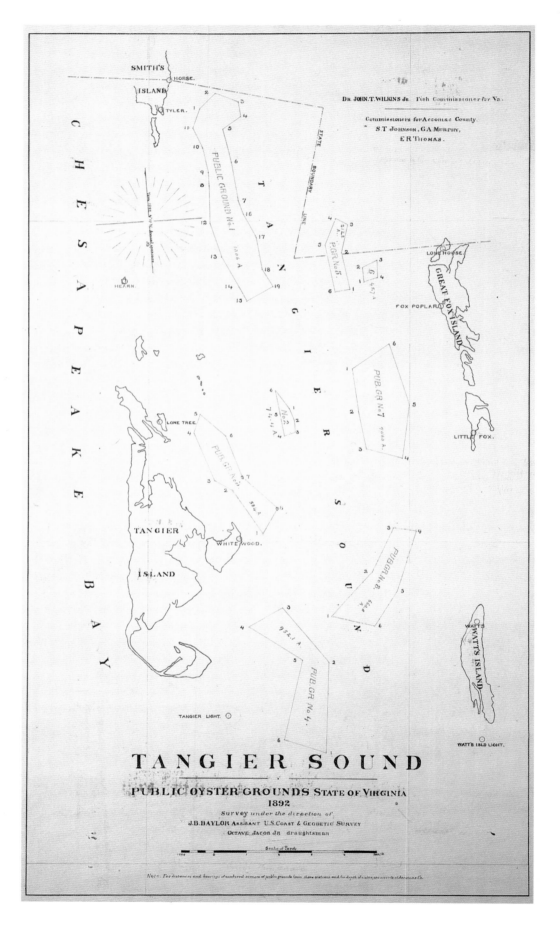

Item	Sort	Size	Qty	Price	Value	Total
						£1062.14.11½
× Worsted Stock[ings]	Mens	3	4 pair	28/.	9.4	
		7	10	26/.	1.1.8	
		8	6	32/.	16.–	
	Womens	2	7	23/.	13.5	
		6	8	25/.	16.8	
× Thread Stock[ings]	Youths	35	1	19/6	1.7½	
	Mens	8	4	26/.	8.–	
		2	3	22/.	5.6	
		4	7	26/.	15.2	
		39	5	24/.	10.–	
	Womens		1	24/.	2.–	
× Thread Buttons	Jacket		3 Gro:	2/.	6.–	
	Shirt		10	2/.	1.–.–	
× Looking Glasses	Painted	1	4 [illegible]	11/.	3.8	
		2	4	13/.	4.4	
		3	3	15/.	3.9	
		4	4	17/.	5.8	
	Walnut	5	5	21/.	8.9	
		6	6	26/.	13.–	
		7	5	3/6	16.8	
		8	2	4/9	9.6	
		9	2	6/.	12.–	
		10	2	7/3	14.6	
		11	3	10/6	1.11.6	
		12	4	12/6	2.10.–	
	Pocket		5	4/.	1.8	16.0.4½
× Bibles	Quarto		2	8/.	16.–	
	Common		34	1/8½	2.18.1	
× Prayer Books	Gilt		7	28/.	16.4	
	Common		21	15/6	1.7.1½	
× Testaments			57	7/6	1.11.10½	
× Spelling Books			46	8/.	1.10.8	
× Psalters			31	5/6	14.2½	
× Primmers			43	2/6	8.11½	
× Battledores			21	1/2	2.0½	
× Horn Books			12	1/.	1.–	
× Watts	Hymns		82	18/.	6.3.–	
	Psalms		13	18/.	19.6	
	Prayers		9	15/.	11.3	
× Willison's on	Sabbath		16	12/.	16.–	
	Sacrament		6	12/.	6.–	
	Catechism		11	12/.	11.–	
	Balm Gilead		21	12/.	1.1.–	
	Afflicted man's Com:		24	12/.	1.4.–	
× Marshall on Sanctification			20	12/.	1.–.–	
× Grays works	Large		2	30/.	5.–	
	Small		2	30/.	5.–	
× Duty of Man			11	20/.	18.6	
× Bostons 4fold Estate			11	18/.	16.6	
× Harveys Meditations			5	30/.	12.6	
× Crawfords dying Thoughts			2	12/.	2.–	
× Pilgrims Progress			28	5/.	11.8	
× Col. Garners Life			55	12/.	2.15.–	
× Allans Alarm			26	5/.	10.10	
× Dyers Golden Chain			9	5/6	4.1½	
× Elizabeth West			3	9/.	2.3	
× Russells 7 Sermons			13	5/6	5.11½	
× Grace abounding			19	4/.	6.4	
× Gospell Sonnetts			21	12/.	1.1.–	
× Harwoods Chearfull Thoughts			15	3/.	2.5.–	
× Addisons Evidences			2	2/.	4.–	
× Sherlock on Death			3	2/.	6.–	
× Evans Sermons in 2 Vol.			2	10/.	1.–.–	
Carried forward					£35.9.6½	£1078.15.4

Item	Sort	Vols	Qty	Price	Value	Total
Brought forward					£35.9.6½	£1078.15.4
× Fordyce Sermons			7	3/.	1.1.–	
× Welch's Sermons			1	1/6	1.6	
× Senecas Morals			1	3/.	3.–	
× Gentleman	Instructed	in 2 Vo.	2	6/.	12.–	
	Library		8	3/.	1.4.–	
× Ladies Library		in 3 Vol.	1	9/.	9.–	
× Song Books	Compleat		1	2/.	2.–	
	Ramsays			3/.		
	Bull Finch		1	3/.	3.–	
	Mocque		1	3/.	3.–	
	Linnett		1	2/.	2.–	
× Gentle Shepherd			1	18/.	1.6	
× Royal Kellander			1	2/.	2.–	
× Kimbers Peerage			1	4/.	4.–	
× Spy's	Turkish	in 8 Vol.	2		1.4.–	
	Jewish			15/.		
× Rochesters Poems			1	4/.	4.–	
× Harriot Stuart		in 2 Vol.	1		6.–	
× Spectators		in 8 do.	10	14/.	7.–.–	
× Smollets History of England		in 16	1	96/.	4.16.–	
× Robertson do. Scotland			1	12/.	12.–	
× Sterns Sermons		in 5	2	15/.	1.10.–	
× Tillotson's ditto		in 10	1		1.10.–	
× Youngs works		in 4		10/.		
× Companion to Alter			1	5/6	5½	
× Satans invisible World				5/6		
× Campbells Trial			1		3.6	
× Scotch Magazines		say 20			10.–	
× Fool of Quality		in 5 Vol.			15.–	
Virginia Laws in folio 1 Copy in Currency						
× Dictionaries	Postlewhite's in folio		1		3.5.–	
	Bayleys		7	6/.	2.2.–	
	Dyches		5	6/.	1.10.–	
× Sir George Ellison		in 2	1		6.–	
× Mellwoods Glimpse of Glory			5	10/.	4.2	
× Haliburtons Memoirs			2	12/.	2.–	
× Night Thoughts			1		2.–	
× Sherlock on Death			3	2/.	6.–	
× Craigs Poems			2	1/6	3.–	
× Crawfords Memoirs			1	3/.	3.–	
× Baxters Call to Unconverted			3	5/.	1.3	
× Wilsons Preparation			9	5/6	4.1½	
× Communicants Catechism			12		1.–	
× Mystery of Faith			3	4/.	1.–	
× Rutherford on Faith			3	14/.	3.6	
× Crawford Zion Traveller			4	10/.	3.4	
× Buchaneers of America			5	5/6	2.3½	
× Esops Fables			3	5/6	1.4½	
× Gill Blase			3	5/6	1.4½	
× Jests Johnson's do.			6	5/6	2.9	
× Cynthia			4	5/6	1.10	
× Songs			5	5/6	2.3½	
× Tatchies Master Piece			1	5/6	5½	
× Wise Masters & Mistresses			6	5/6	2.9	
× Reynard the Fox			4	5/6	1.10	
× Nine worthies			1	5/6	5½	
× Robbers History			2	5/6	11	
× Fairy Tales			4	5/6	1.10	68.6.0½
Carried forward						£1147.1.4½

BUSINESS RECORDS

In 1911 State Librarian Henry Read McIlwaine announced the acquisition of the business records of William and David Allason, of King George, Stafford, and Frederick Counties. In assessing the papers' significance, McIlwaine commented that the collection was, "so far as Virginia is concerned, probably unique. Its value is beyond cavil. From this source by itself it would be possible . . . to reconstruct accurately the business methods obtaining in Virginia in the latter half of the eighteenth century—in fact, to set forth the whole economic condition of the people." The acquisition marked the inception of the Library of Virginia's Business Records Collection.

◀ William Allason (ca. 1720–1800) and David Allason (fl. 1761–1815). Ledger Book, 1769–1774. Bound manuscript volume. Acc. 13.

During the eighteenth century, the strength of Virginia's economy was dependent primarily on two modes of commerce. One was restricted to closely knit, local communities in which farmers, small merchants, tradesmen, and laborers carried on an exchange of foodstuffs, goods, and basic manufactures. On this everyday activity rested the fate of towns, parishes, and counties. The second mode of commerce involved a complex trade over great distances, whether from the tidewater to the Shenandoah Valley, or to the ports of the British Isles. On this activity rested the fate of the colony and the betterment of Great Britain. One merchant who developed his business relationships and his wealth based on both methods was William Allason.

Born in Glasgow, and perhaps no older than seventeen when he first arrived in Virginia in 1737, Allason for a brief time served in the colony as a supercargo, or importer and exporter of goods. After returning to Scotland, he evidently followed his trade throughout the Caribbean but eventually returned to Virginia in 1757 as an agent for the well-known Glasgow firm of Baird and Walker. It was on his own initiative, though, that his success depended. The Scottish firm had agreed that he could conduct some trade of his own, and, by the time the firm failed in the 1760s, Allason had established an effective mercantile network throughout the Old Dominion.

From his store at Falmouth in King George, later Stafford, County, Allason had acquired numerous acquaintances and a broad knowledge of Virginia. He traded with both the tidewater and the lower Shenandoah Valley and kept careful notes of the financial standing and business character of most of his clients. With the help of his brother, David Allason, he opened a store in Winchester in 1761 and extended his trading

network even farther. The Allasons regularly shipped goods to and from London, Glasgow, Liverpool, Whitehaven, Leeds, Bristol, and the West Indies. After William's death in 1800, David Allason continued to operate the family business until 1815.

The Allason collection includes eighty-seven volumes of ledgers, memorandums, and various sales, invoice, and inventory books. It also includes more than three thousand items of correspondence. William Allason communicated with John Murray, earl of Dunmore, before and after the royal governor fled Virginia, and maintained a close association with Lord Fairfax, acting as his factor, buying and selling his slaves, and engaging people to collect quitrents for his Northern Neck Proprietary. Other prominent correspondents include members of the Beverley, Burwell, Carter, Nelson, Page, Washington, and Wythe families. KH

The collection now includes the records of more than three hundred businesses, ranging from those of the Carter family's Shirley plantation in Charles City County to a single daybook kept by a tailor in New Kent County. Many of the collections mark the day-to-day fortunes of the smallest entrepreneurial efforts: the daily ledgers and business-entry books, to cite but several, of an Alexandria grocer, an Augusta County apothecary, a Bath County hatter, a Caroline County physician, a Dinwiddie County blacksmith, an Essex County miller, a Gloucester County coach maker, a Montgomery County bookseller, a Petersburg commission merchant, and a Richmond tavern owner. The collection, moreover, includes the 1783–1795 account book and law notes of Richmond attorney John Marshall, who served as chief justice of the United States Supreme Court from 1801 to 1835, and account books of attorney Patrick Henry, with entries for the period 1758–1798.

This extremely diverse collection includes ledgers, letter books, journals, and other records of merchants, banks and bankers, canal and railroad builders, real estate agents, ironmakers, manufacturers, and insurance companies. Included, too, are the records of Richmond resident Silas Omohundro, who engaged in the buying and selling of slaves and whose records for the years 1851 to 1864 offer valuable insights into this aspect of Virginia's slave economy. For the most part, the Business Records Collection preserves valuable information about Virginia's entrepreneurs and about how they interacted with other Virginians who rode on their railroads, shipped merchandise on their canals, bought dry goods and medicines in their shops, or worked in their mills, factories, and stores.

Among the many valuable business records are the papers of J. Henry Brown Monuments, Inc., which contain an enormous amount of detailed information concerning the many gravestones and inscriptions this Richmond company produced between 1899 and 1920. The records of the Mutual Assurance Society contain some of the earliest extant descriptions and drawings of a number of important Virginia commercial buildings as well as residences both large and small, including grand houses such as Monticello and Mount Vernon and the ordinary homes of shopkeepers. The Mutual Assurance Society materials also contain valuable information about tobacco factories and other structures in Richmond that were familiar sights to ordinary working people. Plantation management records are included in the collection as well, as are registers of hotels and boardinghouses, canal and railroad companies, distillers, paper manufacturers, lumber companies, and many other businesses. When studied closely, few records are as rich in the particulars of everyday life as are the business records of Virginia.

► Allen & Ginter Tobacco Company, Richmond. Cigarette Advertising Cards, ca. 1875–1890. Chromolithographs on paper. Acc. 27354.

The Virginia tobacco industry resorted to whatever means it could to recover from the destruction, and loss of market, caused by the Civil War. One way was through innovative advertising —bold, colorful advertising made easier by the improvement of lithographic printing techniques. And as advertising changed, so, too, did tobacco products.

It was Lewis Ginter, a Richmond business leader, who realized that the coming of the cigarette was "the final triumph for tobacco." A New York native, he had come to Richmond in the 1840s and opened a dry goods shop that succeeded in part because of the innovative way in which he packaged his merchandise. The postwar years were difficult, however, and by the

mid-1870s he had joined the Richmond tobacco firm of John F. Allen and Company. Ginter and Allen became partners in what would become known as the firm of Allen and Ginter, with offices in London, Paris, and Berlin. The company sold its first commercial cigarettes in 1875 and by 1880 was producing more than a million cigarettes every week.

Competition was nevertheless fierce, and advertising and promotion became an ever-more-necessary component of the tobacco business. Manufacturers, for example, developed series of lavishly illustrated giveaways to attract and retain their customers. Trade cards proved particularly popular. Sometime between 1875 and 1890, the Allen and Ginter Company first offered the "American Indian Chiefs" and "Birds of the Tropics" series in packages of the company's most popular brands, including Richmond Straight Cut No. 1. The cards were lithographed

by George S. Harris and Sons, of Philadelphia, and by the New York firm of Linder, Eddy, and Clauss. Besides their value as an advertising medium, the cards also served a more utilitarian function by adding a degree of stiffness and shape to the soft cigarette packages.

In 1890, the Allen and Ginter Company and three other tobacco firms merged with and became known as the American Tobacco Company. The newly formed conglomerate manufactured 90 percent of all the cigarettes made in the United States. Because the General Assembly of Virginia refused to issue a charter for the new tobacco giant, the American Tobacco Company located its headquarters in New York. Allen and Ginter continued, however, to operate as its Richmond subsidiary, and at its peak produced 800 million cigarettes per year in its Cary Street plant. KH

CHIEF JOSEPH,
NEZ PERCES.

SITTING BULL,
DAKOTA SIOUX.

IRON BULL,
CROW.

GREY EAGLE,
APACHE.

KEOKUK'S SON,
SAC & FOX.

TRUE EAGLE,
MISSOURIA.

RUSHING BEAR,
PAWNEE.

RICHMOND

The Banded Araçari Toucan.

Straight Cut No. 1.

CIGARETTES

ARE THE BEST.

BIRDS of the TROPICS,

ONE PACKED IN EACH BOX OF 20

Richmond Straight Cut No. 1 Cigarettes.

Java Peacock.

African Flamingo,	Jungle Fowl,	Satin Bower Bird,
Alexandrine Ring Parakeet	King Bird of Paradise,	Schreiber's Humming Bird,
Apteryx,	Lyre Bird,	Shoe-Bill,
Banded Araçari Toucan,	Magnificent Bird of Paradise,	Sun Bittern,
Black Swan,	New Zealand Parrot,	Swindern's Love Bird,
Black-throated Golden Pheasant,	Notornis,	Swinhoe Pheasant,
Cassowary,	Owl Parrot,	Toco Toucan,
Cock-of-the-Rock,	Paradise Tanager,	Top Knot Pigeon,
Concave-casque Hornbill,	Pitta,	Torquata,
Crimson Topaz,	Quezal,	Tri-colored Cockatoo,
Festive Green Parrot,	Rainbow Pitta,	Tropic Bird,
Fiery-tailed Sun Bird,	Red and Blue Macaw,	Violaceous,
Great Bird of Paradise,	Red Bird of Paradise,	White-throated Shag,
Horned Screamer,	Rhea,	Yellow-breasted Sun Bird,
Impeyan Pheasant,	Sacred Ibis,	Yellow-casque Black Hornbill,
India Peacock.	Sacred Kingfisher,	Yellow-crested Cockatoo.
	Saddle-billed Stork.	

Allen & Ginter

Richmond, Virginia.

27354 (28)

GEO. S. HARRIS & SONS, LITH. PHILA.

LIPE, RICHMOND

WALSH, NORFOLK

RYAN, ROANOKE

SMITH, PORTSMOUTH

◀ ▲ American Tobacco Company, Richmond. Cigarette Advertising Cards, ca. 1910. Photographic reproductions on paper. Acc. 29187.

Throughout the early 1900s, tobacco companies experimented with several themes and designs to heighten the advertising impact of the colorful cards inserted in cigarette packages. Some companies offered detailed illustrations of butterflies, birds, or flowers in an effort to attract more women to cigarette smoking. But it was not until the 1920s that women in any significant numbers became regular customers. As a result, advertisers had to rely on more masculine subjects to ensure effective marketing. It was not surprising then that baseball and other sports proved to be an early and enormously effective tobacco-advertising theme. The American Tobacco Company, for example, began including baseball cards in two of its brands, Contentnea and Old Mill cigarettes, between 1909 and 1911. The cards featured well-known Norfolk, Portsmouth, Richmond, and Roanoke players from the Eastern Carolina and the Virginia and Southern Leagues. Today, collectors consider the cards to be among the most valuable baseball sets ever issued. With the dissolution of the tobacco monopoly in 1911, the Contentnea and Old Mill brands became part of the Liggett and Meyers Tobacco Company. KH, WL

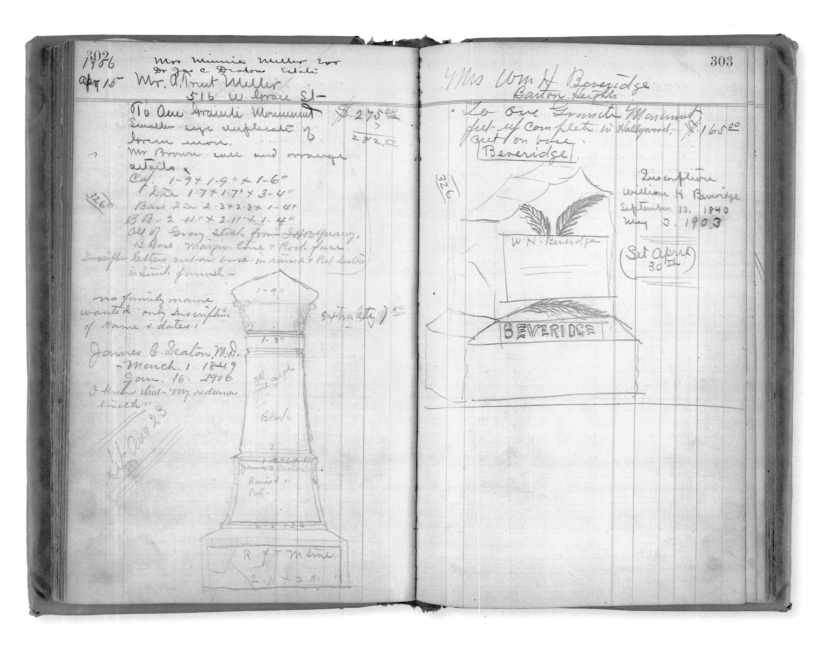

▲ J. Henry Brown Monuments, Incorporated, Richmond. Order Book, ca. 1906. Bound manuscript volume. Acc. 23985.

J. Henry Brown (1859–1921) was a Richmond stonemason and monument designer whose artistry can be found in cemeteries and on buildings throughout Virginia. Because Brown was working during the period between 1897 and 1911 when Virginia's Bureau of Vital Statistics recorded neither births nor deaths, the inscriptions for gravestones and cemetery monuments contained in his records are particularly valuable as a resource for family and local history research.

After a brief partnership with Walter R. Harwood, Brown managed a succession of businesses. He served as president or general manager of the Virginia Granite Company, the Capitol Granite and Monument Works, and J. Henry Brown and Son. Twelve order books, kept from 1899 to 1920, contain detailed design sketches of each commission he received—with dimensions, specifications, and inscriptions—as well as information regarding the individual or organization commemorated in the work. Among the sketches are designs for the monuments of James C. Deaton (1849–1906), a physician, and William H. Beveridge (1840–1903), attorney-at-law. Brown's account books also include the name and address of the individual commissioning each monument as well as the price of the work. KH

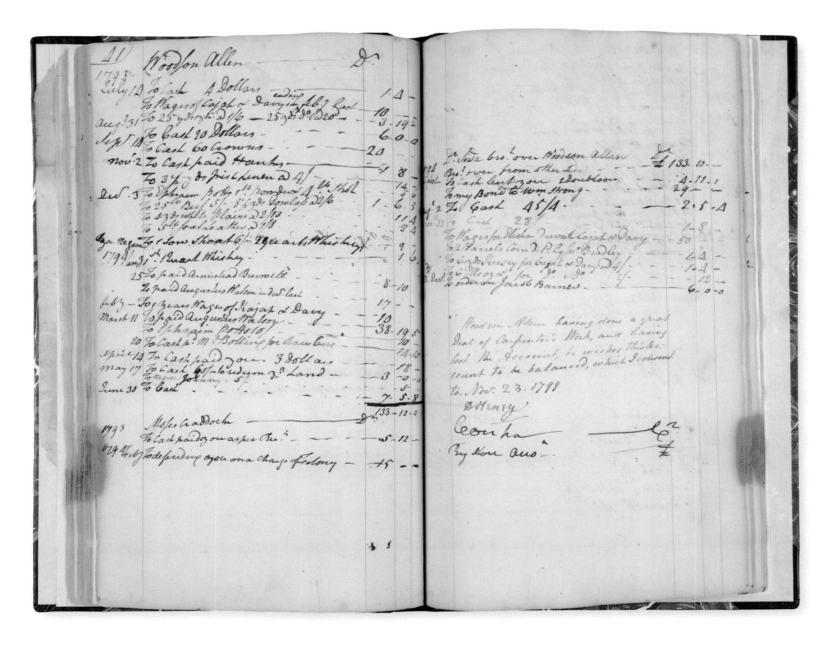

▲ Patrick Henry (1736–1799). Ledger Book, 1764–1798. Bound manuscript volume. Acc. 22408b.

Patrick Henry, orator, statesman, and first governor of the independent commonwealth of Virginia, was born in Hanover County. As a young man he was unsuccessful at both farming and storekeeping and finally turned to the profession of law. He received his license to practice in 1760 and was elected to the House of Burgesses in 1765. He was a delegate to the First Continental Congress in 1774 and the next year attended the revolutionary convention held in Saint John's Church in Richmond. It was here that Henry delivered the best known of his many speeches in which he urged the colony to adopt a posture of military preparedness against Great Britain. He served as governor of the commonwealth from 1776 to 1779 and from 1784 to 1786 and in the Virginia General Assembly from 1786 to 1790. He retired from public service to Charlotte County in 1794.

The Library's collections include three ledger books kept by Henry from 1758 to 1798. Besides containing entries relating to his brief career as a storekeeper, the volumes provide considerable detail about his long and distinguished legal career. There are thousands of entries listing the names of his clients, their places of residence, and the fees charged for his legal services. From this record, it is possible to reconstruct the nature and history of Henry's law practice and to identify the Virginians he represented. All three volumes have been indexed. The ledgers also contain entries relating to Henry's expenditures, such as the purchase of a thousand acres of land in Kentucky and "Beds, &c. . . . to furnish the palace when I was first app'd Gov'r." KH

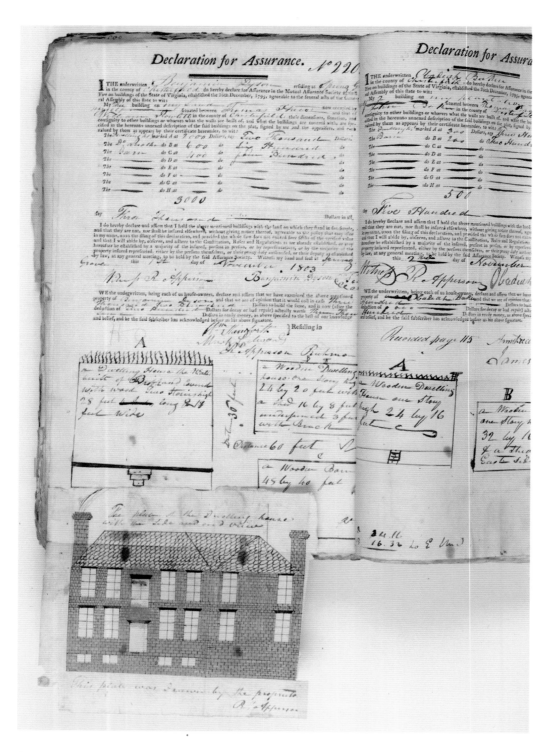

◀ Mutual Assurance Society, Richmond. Declaration for Assurance Book, Volume 24, Policy No. 2205, 1 November 1803. Bound printed volume with manuscript notations. Acc. 30177.

The Mutual Assurance Society, against Fire on Buildings, of the State of Virginia was incorporated by the General Assembly on 22 December 1794. William Frederick Ast, a Prussian then residing in Richmond, suggested the plan of the society, which is alleged to have been modeled after a system of mutual guarantee introduced by Frederick the Great. The company offered insurance against "all losses and damages occasioned accidentally by fire" and determined its rates according to the material composition of each building, what purpose the structure served, and its contents. Grain mills and stables with highly combustible straw, playhouses utilizing large numbers of candles, and buildings housing steam-powered machinery, for example, could be insured only under special contract. As a further protection, the society conducted revaluations of all its insured properties every seven years or whenever additions were made to a policy.

The Mutual Assurance collection includes 257 volumes of individual applications—called declarations and revaluations of assurance—dating from 1796 through 1966. The applications give the name of the insured, the place of residence, the location of the particular property to be insured, the name of the occupant, and a description and estimated value of each structure included in the policy. At the bottom of each policy is a sketch of the specific property—in most instances, a rough outline giving the dimensions of the building but, for others, a more elaborate and detailed drawing, some so large that they required folding. Benjamin Dyson's declaration for Spring Grove in Chesterfield County included coverage for two dwelling houses, one brick and one wood, and a barn. Attached is a color drawing of the brick "Dwelling House with the side and end view," in this case "Drawn by the proprietor."

The records of the Mutual Assurance Society hold invaluable information for many areas of research, but in the field of architectural history their meticulous descriptions and pen-and-ink and pencil drawings have no equal. During the re-creation of Colonial Williamsburg in the 1930s, in fact, few sources provided as much crucial information about original buildings as the Mutual Assurance Society's fire insurance records. SM

▶ Mutual Assurance Society, Richmond. Declaration for Assurance Book, Volume 26, Policy No. 2049, 13 March 1803. Bound printed volume with manuscript notations. Acc. 30177.

Among the thousands of applications submitted to the Mutual Assurance Society, perhaps the one for Mount Vernon features the most elaborate drawing. The oversize, folded illustration accompanied the 1803 application of Bushrod Washington, a member of the society's original board of directors and nephew of the president. While serving as a colonel in the French and Indian War, George Washington had left the care of Mount Vernon to his favorite brother, John Augustine Washington, Bushrod's father. Colonel Washington had also agreed—"while we were both bachelors"—that if he failed to return from the fighting his brother should have the estate he had so carefully tended. At his death in 1799, George Washington bequeathed a life-interest in the property to his wife, adding that at her death Mount Vernon was to be divided into three parcels, with the Mansion House and its adjoining acres to pass to his brother's son. Martha Washington died in the spring of 1802, and Bushrod Washington applied for a policy in his own name the following year. SM

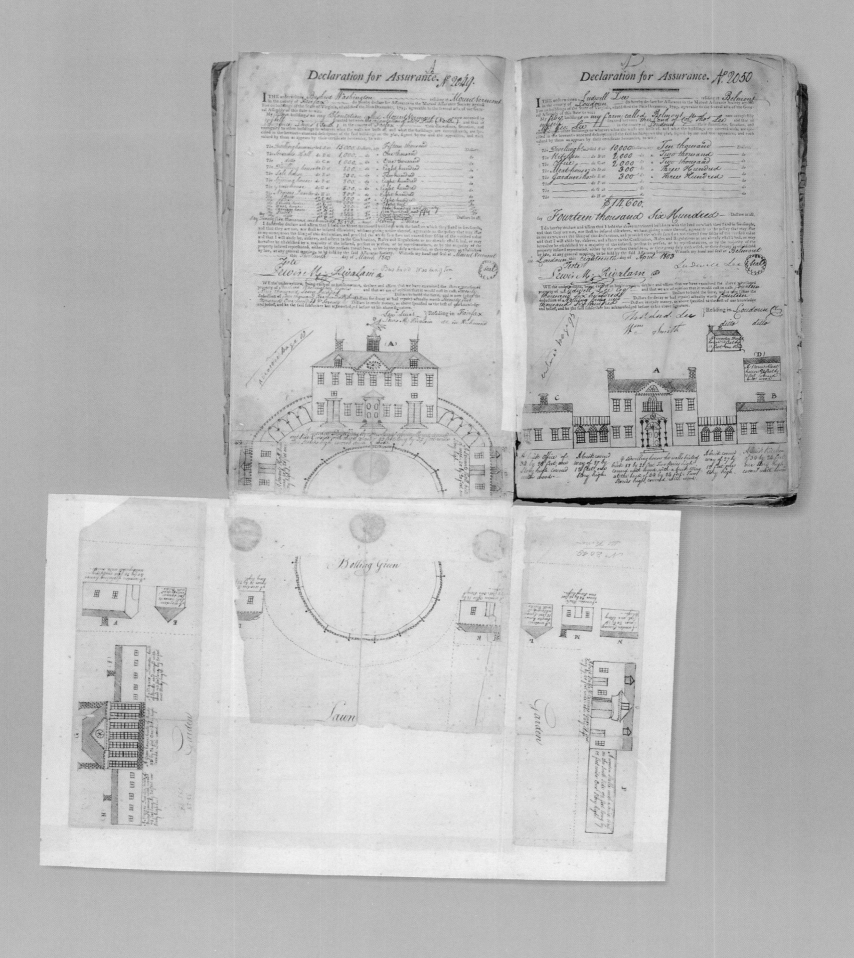

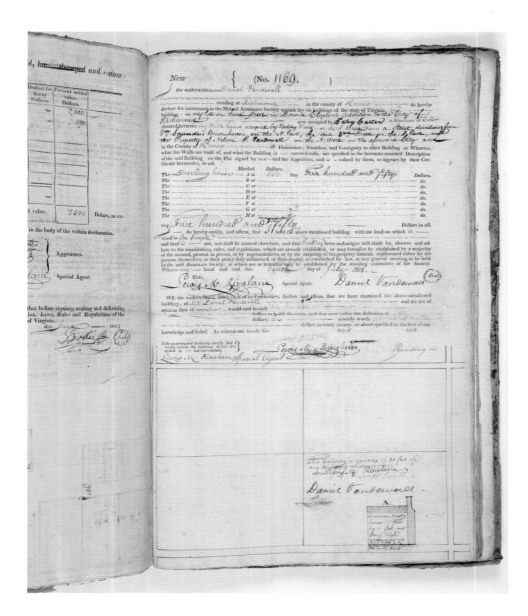

▲ Mutual Assurance Society, Richmond. Declaration for Assurance Book, Volume 55, Policy No. 1169, 10 July 1818. Bound printed volume with manuscript notations. Acc. 30177.

The agents of the Mutual Assurance Society sketched and compiled structural details about many of the great houses owned by Virginia's well-to-do planters and entrepreneurs, but they also documented the humble cottages of laborers and artisans as well as the urban slave-quarters and outbuildings that dominated the landscape of the Old Dominion's cities and towns in the post-Revolutionary era. Patsy Carter, "a Wooman [sic] of Color," lived in a one-room house owned by Daniel Vanderwall, located on Third Street in Richmond. The structure, with an exterior chimney, measured only eighteen by eighteen feet. Although such houses were typical of the modest dwellings of the lower- and middle-class residents in the early years of the capital, they have virtually disappeared from Richmond's streets, making the Mutual Assurance Society records even more important to an understanding of the town's social and architectural fabric. GK

▶ Silas Omohundro (1807–1864). Ledger Book, 1851–1877. Bound printed volume with manuscript notations. Acc. 29642.

Silas Omohundro operated as one of Richmond's largest slave traders, with offices at Seventeenth and Broad Streets and between Main and Franklin Streets on Wall Street. Omohundro also ran a private jail located in the alley on the west side of Wall Street. Within a block of some of the city's most fashionable hotels, Omohundro fed and housed fellow slave dealers, masters in search of a purchase or sale, and the human chattel in which he dealt. His business extended to every southern state. The unique and extensive collection of Omohundro's records offers a rare opportunity to examine the daily business of slave trading and is the Library's only example of primary documentation for this profession. Omohundro's ledgers include various charges for boarding slaves, records of sales, and newspaper notices for runaways. At his death in 1864, Omohundro emancipated "my woman Corinna Omohundro" and her five children, "who are also my children." SM

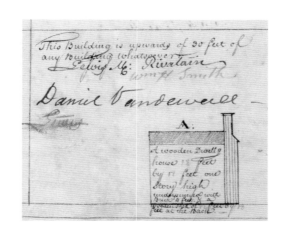

1857   Transient Custom

Feb 14   Bennet Robinson to Breakfast off 19, 4 day   Pd   7 50
"   20   J. A. Jones 1 Man Edmund off 25   Pd   2 02
"   "   do 1 Man Reuben off 21 March 29 day   Pd   11 60
"   21   do 1 Man Charles off 23   Pd   0 80
"   26   M. Rice 1 Man Ellick   off 27   Pd   80
"   "   do 1 Man Edmund   off 27   Pd   57
"   "   do 1 Man John   off 27   Pd   50
"   "   do 1 Boy Erasties   off 27   Pd   50
March 1st R. F. Omohundro 1 Boy John off 7, 8 days   Pd   3 20
"   "   do 1 Boy Jim   off 11,   Pd   4 40
March 2d Mr J. G. Murphy   off 12, 14 days b/f Pd   12 00
"   9   J. W. Omohundro to Breakfast off no change   Pd   00
March 18 J. A. Jones 1 Girl Judy off 19   Pd   50
"   "   do 1 Boy Ben   off 19   Pd   50
"   "   do 1 Boy Larry   off 19   Pd   50
"   "   do 1 Boy Littleton   off 19   Pd   50
March 18 Edmund Ruffin 1 Girl Ella   Pd   29 50
June 12 J. A. Jones 1 Man Alfred off 13   Pd   50
"   "   do 1 Woman Eliza & 3 Children off 13   Pd   1 00
June 22 Henry Wilson 1 Girl Susan Frances off no charge   00
"   "   do 1 Girl Louisa   off no charge   00
"   "   do 1 Girl Catherine   off no charge   00
"   25   W. H. Betts 1 Boy George   off 18 July   Pd   9 20
"   26   F. G. Murphy 1 Boy William off 14 July 18 Pd   7 20
"   27   Cook to do   Pd
"   27   do 1 Boy John Henry   off 14 July 17   Pd   6 80
"   "   do 1 Boy Joe   off 14 " 17   Pd   6 80
"   "   do 1 Girl Susan Jane   off 14 " 17   Pd   6 80
"   30   do 1 Boy John London   off 14 " 15   Pd   6 00
July 1st do 1 Man John   off 14 " 14 day   Pd   5 60
"   "   do 1 Girl Clavity   off 14 " 14 day   Pd   5 60
"   "   do 1 Man Price   off 14 " 14 day   Pd   5 60
"   "   do 1 Girl Agnes   off 14 " 14 day   Pd   5 60
                              forward $ 141 50

1857   117

March 12 H. R. H. Dickinson 1 Girl Jinny off 30 May   27 60
"   "   Doct R. G. Cabells Bill   8 00
"   "   Medicine for Jinny   1 50
"   "   1 Shine 3/-   0 50

                                            Payment $ 37 60
May 19th   Received Payment $
                              Silas Omohundro
                                   forward

July 2   Murphy Griffin & Co 1 Girl Lilly off 14, 12 day   4 80
"   6   do 1 Boy Isaac   off 14, 8 day   ,   3 20
"   7   do 1 Man Albert   off 14, 7 day   ,   2 80
"   "   do 1 Girl Amanda   off 14, 7 day   ,   2 80
"   "   do 1 Girl Bartholy   off 14, 7 day   ,   2 80
"   7   do 1 Man Charles Roberts off 14, 7 day   ,   2 80
"   8   do 1 Man Peter   off 14, 6   ,   2 40
"   "   do 1 Boy Nathan   off 14, 6   ,   2 40
"   "   do 1 Girl May   off 14, 6   ,   2 40
"   "   do 1 Girl Betsey   off 14, 6   ,   2 40
"   9   do 1 Girl Sicy   off 14, 5   ,   2 00
"   "   do 1 Girl Marcella   off 14, 5   ,   2 00
"   10   do 1 Man Henry   off 14 4   ,   1 60
"   "   do 1 Man Joe   off 14, 4   ,   1 60
"   "   do 1 Man Moses   off 14, 4   ,   1 60
"   "   do 1 Girl Rebecca   off 14, 4   ,   1 60
"   "   do 1 Girl Mahaly   off 14, 4   ,   1 60
"   "   do 1 Man Robert   off 14, 4,   ,   1 60
"   11   do 1 Girl Hannah   off 14, #3,   ,   1 20
"   13   do 1 Man   off 14, 1 day   ,   0 40
"   13   do 1 Man   off 14, 1 "   ,   0 40
July 14 do 1 Girl the above Negros all off 14   ,   0 25
"   14   do 3 Negros   off 14   ,   75
"   "   2 Flour Barrels 1/6   ,   50
"   14   Waggon hire 3/   ,   50

July 24   Received Payment $ - 36 40
                            Silas Omohundro
                                forward

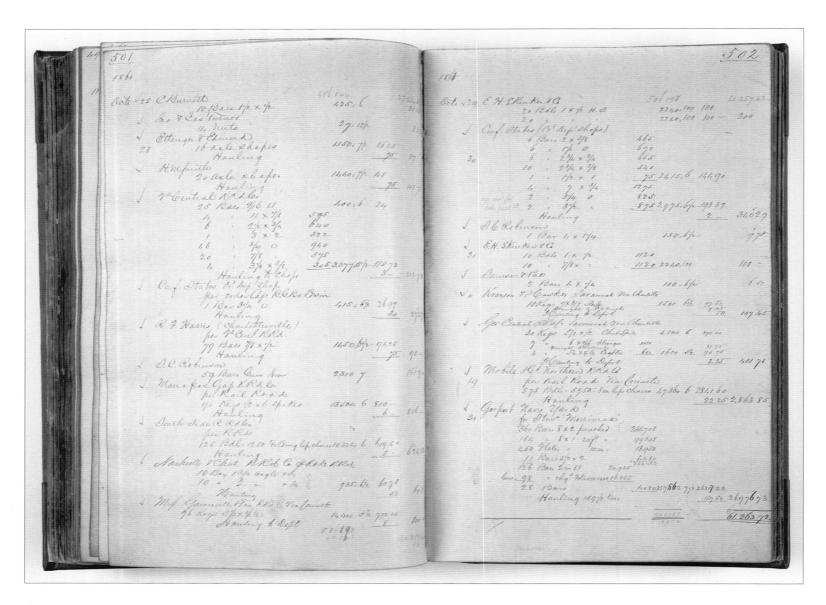

▲ Tredegar Iron Company, Richmond. Sales Book, February 1858–September 1865. Bound printed volume with manuscript notations. Acc. 23881e.

Famed as the "Ironmaker to the Confederacy" and essential to the expansion of southern railroads, the immense Tredegar Iron Works flourished for more than one hundred years on Richmond's riverfront. The ironwork's founders, Francis B. Deane Jr., an experienced Virginia blast-furnace operator, and a group of Richmond businessmen, honored the foundry's builder, Rhys Davies, by adopting the name of an ironworks in his native Wales. Created by an act of the General Assembly in 1837, the Tredegar Iron Company soon thereafter merged with the contiguous Virginia Foundry Company. Tredegar dominated the Confederate munitions industry during the Civil War and was virtually the sole source of heavy guns, projectiles, gun carriages, plates for ironclad vessels, wheels and axles for railroad rolling stock, and furnace machinery for the Confederate war effort. The company also

furnished a variety of products to other Confederate munitions factories and navy yards.

After the war, the company made a swift transition to peacetime production, manufacturing products for railroad and agricultural uses. The rise of the Tredegar Iron Works prior to the Civil War and its restoration afterward can be attributed largely to Joseph Reid Anderson (1813–1892), a United States Military Academy graduate from Fincastle, Virginia, who in 1841 assumed the management of the business. In 1848 he became owner of the plant, and the Anderson name remained virtually synonymous with Tredegar throughout its illustrious history.

Between 1952 and 1966, the Library of Virginia added substantially to its records relating to the operation of the Tredegar Iron Company, bringing the collection to more than one thousand volumes and a half million additional items. One such volume, a sales book, includes the entry for a shipment of iron "bars" and "plates" to "Gosport Navy Yard for Stmr. 'Merrimac'" to be used for refitting the vessel soon to become known as the famed CSS *Virginia*. GK

▶ Recent conservation efforts at the Library of Virginia have allowed the restoration of many items in various collections. Among them is the Tredegar Iron Company sales book dating from February 1858 to September 1865. The volume now has a new leather binding and spring-enforced spine, both of which had deteriorated over the past 130 years. The spring enables the ledger to open fully without stressing the spine so that the accountant could make notations right up to the inside edge of the paper.

and assistance, as circumstances may seem by them required, to any of our members, who may be brought into difficulty or suffering, for conscience sake, or any thing connected with Military Operations.

To wit

Benjamin Hallowell, Samuel Townsend,
Benjamin P. Moore Levi K Brown
Chalkley Gillingham Richard T Bentley &
Thomas Shepperd Gerard H Reese

The clerk was directed to send a copy of this Minute to each of our Monthly Meetings.
Extracted from the Minutes.

   Gerard H Reese: Clerk for the day.

    Then Concluded

At Fairfax Monthly Meeting of Women Friends held the 13th day of 4th Month 1864.

The Representatives are present.

Mary T. Bond (formerly Steer) having accomplished her marriage in violation of our discipline, has sent to this meeting a written acknowledgement and requests that she may retain her right of Membership —

The unhappy civil war that now afflicts our country and causes much difficulty in travelling or communicating with different Sections — being the cause of the transgression of Discipline; This meeting cordially accepts her acknowledgement — And Rebecca K Williams is requested to inform her that her request is granted & she is continued a member.

The time having expired for which the clerk and assistant were appointed (the clerk requests to be released. Rebecca K Williams. Elizabeth Scott Hannah Atkinson and Sarah G White are appointed to propose the names of persons to serve the ensuing year.

Eliza H Walker. Rachel Steer Mary R Walker, Mary E Williams. and Rachel N Williams are appointed to revise and record the minutes of this meeting.

    Then Concluded.

Recorded to this date
  4/13/64.

At Fairfax Monthly ...
the 13th day of 4th m...
The Representati...
Mary S. Bond (form...
her marriage in violatio...

CHURCH RECORDS

Religion played a central role in the life of Virginia from the colony's founding in 1607. Much of the history of the Old Dominion, therefore, can be found in the minute books, registers, and other records of its many congregations. The Library of Virginia's Church Records Collection includes originals, microfilm, or photocopies of the official records of more than three hundred Virginia churches, ranging in date from the early seventeenth to the twentieth century. The records include documents from all the major Protestant denominations as well as materials from Catholic and Jewish religious bodies and Quaker congregations in Virginia.

Following the English pattern, early settlers established Anglican (Church of England) parishes that functioned as both ecclesiastical and community organizations. But while parish lines in England had been established primarily by custom rather than by acts of Parliament, it was the General Assembly that fixed parish lines in colonial Virginia, often at the same time that it created or altered county boundaries. The Anglican Church in the colonial era assumed a wide influence in both religious and civil affairs. So important was the church as an adjunct of government that each parish was required to keep a register, or record of vital statistics; indeed, it would be two and a half centuries after the landing at Jamestown before civil authorities began systematically keeping such records.

◀ Fairfax Monthly Meeting of Women Friends, Record Book, Loudoun County, 1857–1871. Bound manuscript volume. Acc. 24309a.

On 13 April 1864, the Quaker women of Loudoun County met to discuss the case of Mary S. Bond. Although the exact nature of her offense is unknown, Bond had been found to be in "violation of our discipline." It is probable, though, that she had failed to attend worship services often enough. Married, she had evidently moved some distance away from the Quaker meetinghouse and had found it increasingly difficult, and dangerous, to travel to meetings while "the unhappy civil war that now afflicts our country" still raged. After considering her explanation and the circumstances, the meeting allowed Bond to remain a member of the congregation.

It was not unusual that Bond was judged by the women of the meeting. Each Quaker congregation sent representatives from a particular geographic area to a larger monthly meeting where members decided matters concerning the various churches and addressed complaints or concerns about particular worshipers. Only men attended the first monthly "meetings for business."As early as 1656, however, women had begun convening their own meetings in which they were equally responsible for the spiritual and moral life of their fellow female members.

The Fairfax Monthly Meeting to which Bond belonged had been established in 1744 from a far-larger congregation dating back to 1730. When Loudoun County was formed from a portion of Fairfax in 1757, the meeting found itself within the new county but retained its traditional name. Eventually the Fairfax Monthly Meeting became known as the Waterford meeting, named for the meetinghouse in which its members had worshiped for many years. In time, rapid growth led to yet another separation, with the formation of the Goose Creek Monthly Meeting in 1785. By the late nineteenth century, however, the migration of so many of the Fairfax meeting's members had reversed its fortunes. After many years of struggle, the meeting was discontinued in 1929. KH

Local churches of other denominations often recorded similar information, carefully documenting the passage of time within their tightly knit congregational communities. Many of those churches' records contain detailed listings of births, baptisms, marriages, deaths, and burials that were never recorded in any other source.

In addition, the records of Virginia's churches preserve valuable information about the daily lives of their members. For example, the records of Richmond's First African Baptist Church comprise one of the most valuable sources in existence for studying the interactions and concerns of the slave and free members of the largest black congregation in antebellum Virginia, numbering almost three thousand congregants by 1860. The members of that church, as well as those of many other churches, ministered to the spiritual and also the temporal needs of their fellow worshipers. This church's records—like many others in the Library's collection—contain information about economic hardship and self-help, about the resolution of family problems and business disputes, about the chastisement of members whose conduct fell far short of the congregation's ideals, and also about the spiritual growth and institutional health of the church itself.

Along with church records, the Library of Virginia also has a collection of more than four thousand family Bible records, primarily photocopies, that contain unique records of births, marriages, and deaths. Moreover, the Bibles often include a wealth of information not only on the immediate family circle of relatives, but also on the larger community. Some, for example, mention events in the lives of neighbors; others include details and vital records of the lives of slaves. By custom, each family's notations were usually made on blank pages in the front or back of a Bible, or on blank pages between the Old and New Testaments, continuing as the book passed from generation to generation. By the mid-nineteenth century it was not unusual for some printers to include specific pages designed for better organization of inscriptions of important dates and events. In many instances, a family's records were carefully maintained over multiple generations, and the variations in handwriting speak to the long passage of time and the individual family's commitment to remembering its past.

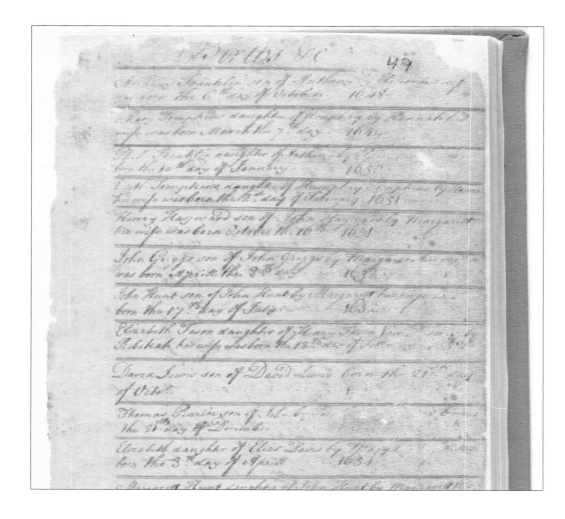

◀ Charles Parish, Register, York County, 1648–1800. Bound manuscript volume. Acc. 30089.

Of the many Church of England parishes established in Virginia between 1607 and 1785, Charles Parish was among the very oldest. The exact date of its creation is unknown, but the first recorded mention of the New Poquoson Parish, as it was originally called, occurred in February 1635. The parish was located in what was then Charles River County, which was named for Charles I, who lost the English Civil War in 1645 and was beheaded in 1649. Charles River was one of the colony's original eight shires, which had been established by the General Assembly sometime after the beginning of the first Anglo-Powhatan War in 1622. Twenty-one years later the assembly renamed the county York—in honor of James, duke of York, the second son of Charles I. In 1692, at the request of New Poquoson's parishioners, the assembly gave the parish itself the new designation Charles Parish.

Charles Parish's 128-page register of births and deaths is the earliest-known surviving church–record book in Virginia. It consists, in part, of entries copied from an even earlier compilation and is organized as two registers: birth records begin in 1648, and deaths in 1665; no marriage records were included. EC

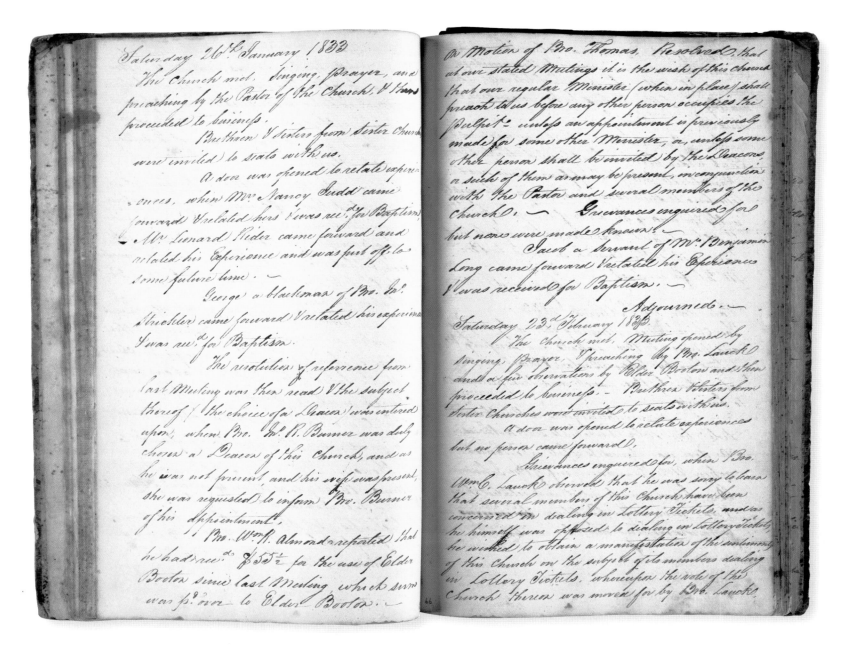

▲ Mount Carmel Baptist Church, Minute Book, Page County, 1828–1846. Bound manuscript volume. Acc. 28089a.

The Mount Carmel Baptist Church minute book offers insights into the everyday life of both whites and blacks within its members' Page County community. Its straightforward, business-like record includes the names of those present at church conferences, specific grievances, as well as deaths and baptisms. Among the latter are occasional mentions of slave baptisms. On 26 January 1833, for instance, "George a blackman of Bro. Jno. Strickler came forward & related his experience & was recd. for Baptism."

The practice of baptizing slaves was not uncommon in Virginia, and, in fact, was often encouraged. Many white southerners believed that, by adopting the Christian faith, slaves would be more resigned to their situation, which many slaveholders and others perceived as

ordained by God. Moreover, these same observers were secure in the belief that any single African American's conversion to Christianity would in no way alter the status of the individual slave from an article of property to an independent-thinking, rational human being. The Virginia General Assembly had addressed the issue as early as 1667 by declaring that a baptized slave remained a slave.

African Americans began joining Baptist congregations as the sect spread across the South in the middle of the eighteenth century. Sometimes, with the permission or the forbearance of the local white community, they were able to form their own black Baptist churches. In Virginia, Baptists generally maintained black churches as adjunct congregations, separate from white churches. In other instances, African Americans worshiped within white churches but in seating areas specifically assigned to them. After the Nat Turner slave rebellion in 1831,

Virginia law required that white churches provide official white pastors for any separate black congregations. Not until ten years later were any new black churches formally established in the state. After 1841, however, African American Baptist churches again began to grow in number, so that by the eve of the Civil War they were the largest black denomination in Virginia. SM

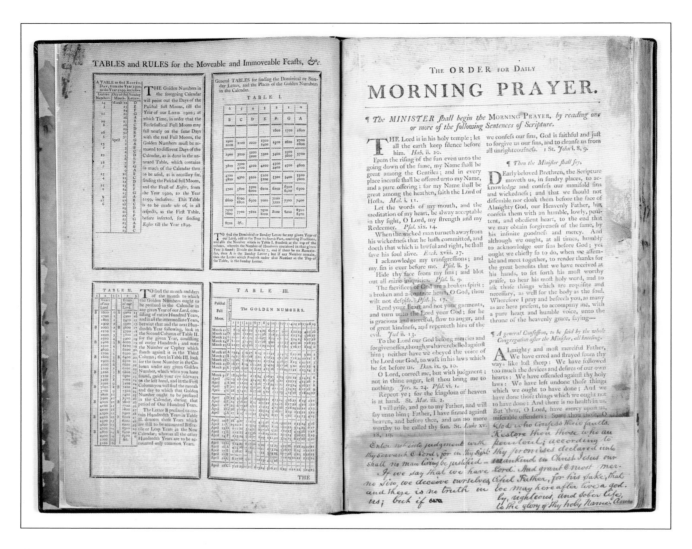

▲ *The Book of Common Prayer and Administration of the Sacraments and Other Rites and Ceremonies of the Church According to the Use of the Protestant Episcopal Church in the United States of America.* New York: Hugh Gaine at the Bible, Hanover Square, 1795.

The Library of Virginia's 1795 copy of *The Book of Common Prayer*, the official liturgical text of the Episcopal Church, carries with it an intriguing provenance. According to the inscription on the lining paper, it was "in use in St. Johns Church, Richmond, until the year of Our Lord 1850, when the church, then much dilapidated and ready to fall down, was repaired, and the desk resupplied with books." The wood-frame

Saint John's Church, the oldest place of worship in the city, was erected in 1741, and it was there on 23 March 1775 that Patrick Henry made his celebrated "liberty or death" speech. Henry's words were like fire: Edward Carrington, who had listened outside a window, left instructions that he be buried on the spot where he had stood that day.

The Reverend Henry S. Kepler, who served the church from 1848 to 1859, is said to have preserved the prayer book and presented it to his friend, Thomas Hicks Wynne, of Richmond. Sometime after Wynne took possession of the volume, it became part of the Library's collections. A number of damaged pages have mended margins, with the missing text supplied in manuscript—probably by the Reverend Kepler. SM

▶ Bailey Family Bible, 1820–1941. Bound, printed volume with manuscript notations. Acc. 22249.

Traditionally, families have recorded vital statistics—births, deaths, and marriages—in their Bibles. The Bailey family, of Virginia, recorded such significant events for more than one hundred years, from 1820 to 1941, on the pages between the Old and New Testaments. Historically, Bible records such as this have proved to be an invaluable resource for genealogical researchers and historians tracing family origins, constructing family trees, or gathering general biographical information. Currently, the Library's collection of Bible records represents more than four thousand different families. The records consist of a small number of original volumes, such as the Bailey family's Bible; the remainder are photocopies of pages from Bibles belonging to individuals who have generously shared their family records with the commonwealth of Virginia. SM

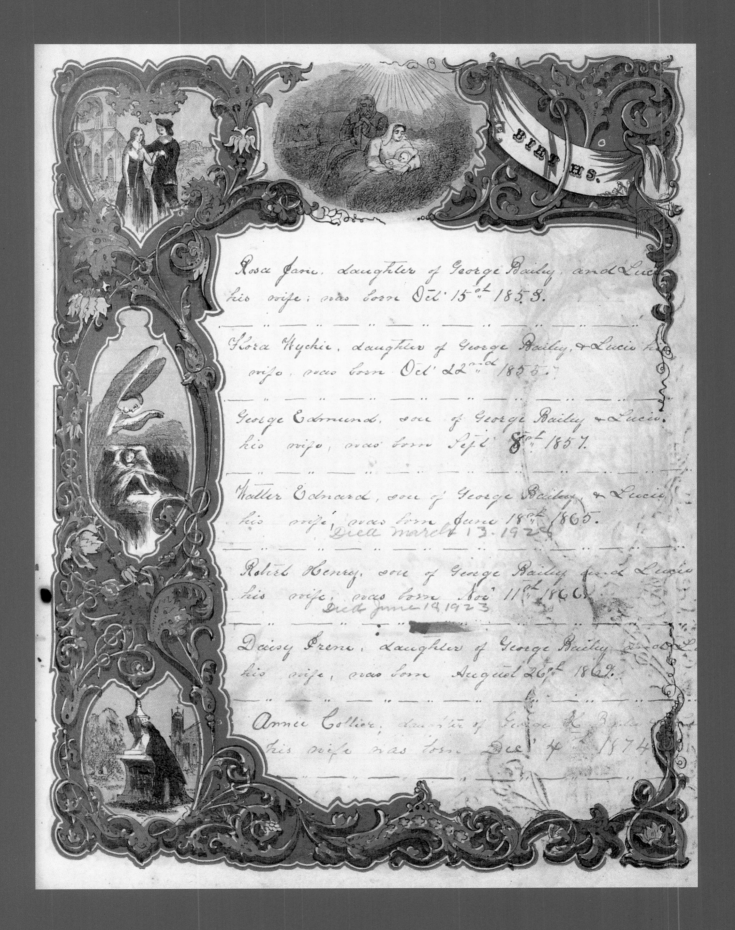

Rosa Jane, daughter of George Baily, and Lucie
his wife, was born Oct 15th 1853.

Kora Wyckie, daughter of George Baily, & Lucie his
wife, was born Oct 22nd 1855.

George Edmund, son of George Baily & Lucie
his wife, was born Sept 8th 1857.

Walter Edward, son of George Baily & Lucie
his wife, was born June 18th 1865.
Died march 13-192_

Robert Henry, son of George Baily and Lucie
his wife, was born Nov 11th 1866.
Died June 19, 1923

Daisy Irene, Daughter of George Baily and
his wife, was born August 26th 1869.

Annie Collier, daughter of George H. Baily
his wife was born Dec 4th 1874

CONFEDERATE IMPRINTS

From the earliest days of the Civil War, the art and business of printing were inexorably linked to the Confederate war effort. The new nation needed broadsides—"Men of Virginia, to the rescue!"—to fuel its patriotic fervor; it needed literary and practical periodicals to remind its citizens that, as Richmond's *Southern Literary Messenger* remarked, "a nation cannot live by bread alone." And it needed thousands of newspapers as well as official reports, texts, and announcements to ensure its populace remained informed, even when the news was unrelentingly grim. In 1864, for example, Virginians were reminded that they could indeed expect to make even "further extraordinary exertions and sacrifices." The short-lived Southern nation, moreover, perhaps needed most to be able to purchase, and find solace in, literature, children's stories, biographies, religious tracts, history, schoolbooks, playbills, humor, poetry, drama, music, and art—to find fact and fiction that confirmed the "flight of the genius of liberty from the Potomac, southward." And, finally, the Confederacy needed its own military manuals and guides, texts "put in harmony with the knowledge and organization of the present day."

The Library of Virginia's extensive collection of Confederate imprints—those items published within the Confederate States from secession until Federal occupation—encompasses every facet of the conflict from the war-torn South's perspective. The collection in a unique way also documents the development, decline, and death of the Confederacy. When the conflict began, Southerners could point to only a few major regional publishers, such as the well-known printing firms of J. W. Randolph and West and Johnston, both of Richmond. It was not long, though, before hundreds of smaller companies grew to meet the demand and the extraordinary enthusiasm for a distinctly regional source of information and education. The cause of publishing was no doubt boosted, too, when the Confederate government eventually exempted printers from military service.

◄ *Magnolia Weekly: A Home Journal of Literature and General News.* Richmond: 4? October 1862–11? March 1865.

From the first days of the war, Richmond served as a center of publishing activity. Of particular interest to many readers were the numerous periodicals, including, for example, the *Age: A Southern Monthly Eclectic Magazine, Smith and Barrow's Monthly*, and the *Sentinel*. Also printed in Richmond were the *Bohemian*, which quickly disappeared; the *Confederate States Medical and Surgical Journal*, not inaugurated until early in 1864; and *Southern Punch*, a magazine of humor first issued in 1863 and closely modeled after the famed and long-standing English publication known simply as *Punch*. Easily the best known, however, were the *Southern Illustrated News* and the *Magnolia Weekly*, the latter variously subtitled as *A Home Journal of Literature and General News* and as *A Southern Home Journal*. There were other changes, too: the issues for 25 October 1862 and 12 March 1864, for example, depict two variations in the magazine's design. The *Magnolia Weekly* attracted numerous subscribers from across the Confederacy, particularly, as in the words of one Richmonder, because the South's readers should "no longer be compelled to read the trashy publications of itinerant Yankees."

No matter how difficult it became to amass the necessary paper and ink to print thousands of issues each week, or to arrange for deliveries by the always-harried and overextended Confederate postal system, the *Magnolia Weekly* was somehow among the very few Southern periodicals to survive until nearly the end of the war, issuing copies as late as March 1865, barely a month before the surrender at Appomattox. Even as the quality of the magazine's appearance and content gradually declined, prospective subscribers were so numerous that the publisher repeatedly had to turn them away. EC

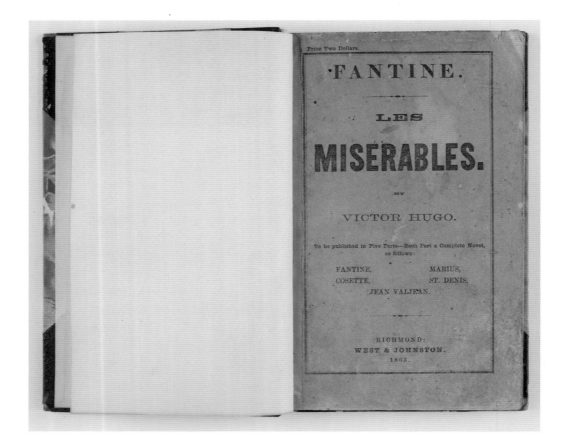

◀ Victor Hugo (1802–1885). *Les Miserables.*
(The Wretched.) A Novel. Richmond: West and
Johnston, 1863–1864.

First published in France in 1862, Victor
Hugo's famed novel, *Les Miserables*, attracted considerable attention throughout the Confederacy
and eventually proved to be the most famous foreign title published during the war. The prolific
Richmond firm of West and Johnston published
an English translation in five parts over a two-
year period. The book's publication in so many
distinct parts met several needs: besides conform-
ing to the work's logical divisions and also practically guaranteeing continuing and multiple sales,
the phased schedule reduced the amount of
paper, ink, and binding materials required at any
one time—although the publisher remained
exposed to the very real risk that supplies might
become unavailable at any moment, leaving the
profitable project incomplete.

The "new translation, revised," quickly proved
to be widely popular and also gave rise to a mar-
velous bit of dark humor applicable to the times
and the particular spirit of the title. Supposedly,
so the widespread story went, a woman in the
early summer of 1863 entered the Richmond
bookshop of West and Johnston in search of "a
copy of that book about Gen. Lee's poor miserable soldiers faintin'." The befuddled clerk, after
struggling a bit to discern what she might mean,
cautiously asked if she was, in fact, looking for a
copy of *Les Miserable: Fantine*, the title of the
novel's first part. No doubt flustered, she insisted
that something so odd could not possibly be the
book in question, refused to buy it, and left the
shop. EC

At first, Southern publishers and printers had little problem, as they quickly and efficiently
filled orders "for plain, fancy, and ornamental printing." Even as late as 1863, the Confederacy
was producing carefully crafted examples of the printer's art. The Library of Virginia's collection, for instance, includes a finely detailed "Catalogue of Sheet Music" issued in 1863 by a
company with stores in both Macon and Savannah, Georgia; that the business could in the
third year of the war still offer such an extensive selection of printed materials says much about
the health and adaptability of the Southern publishing industry.

As early as 1862, however, printers had begun to confront immense difficulties, and by late
1863 printing supplies were often nonexistent in many parts of the South. Everywhere else,
they were little better than always scarce. Typesetters, for example, were soon compelled to
invert the less-used letter *q* to serve as a makeshift *b* or to substitute all manner of odd liquids—
fig or pomegranate juice, to name but two—for hopelessly inadequate stores of ink. At the end
of 1863, printing equipment was almost impossible to find, much less repair. As for paper, by
1864 it was in such short supply that printers begged for "rags—rags of cotton, linen, flax, old
rope, etc.," anything that might serve better than odd-sized and secondhand scrap paper, or
ruled notebooks unbound and put to a second use, or, worse, even the back of wallpaper.

The noted historian Francis Parkman is often credited with making the first serious
attempt to collect and assess these remarkably hardy, even stubborn, publications of the
Confederate States of America. A member of the library committee of the famed Boston
Athenaeum, Parkman arrived in Richmond in June 1865 and gathered up as much as he could
of "these fugitive publications," printed materials he knew "had a peculiar historical interest"
and that, "unless secured promptly, before they were destroyed" or had "fallen into the hands
of collectors," would undoubtedly "be forever beyond our reach." As an agency of the commonwealth, the State Library had already undertaken the same task. Beginning in 1861, and
continuing throughout the war, the Library had collected those documents issued by the state
government as well as many unofficial materials both significant and ephemeral. Since then,
the Library of Virginia has continued to collect and preserve the rare and revealing printed vestiges of the Confederacy's literary and political self.

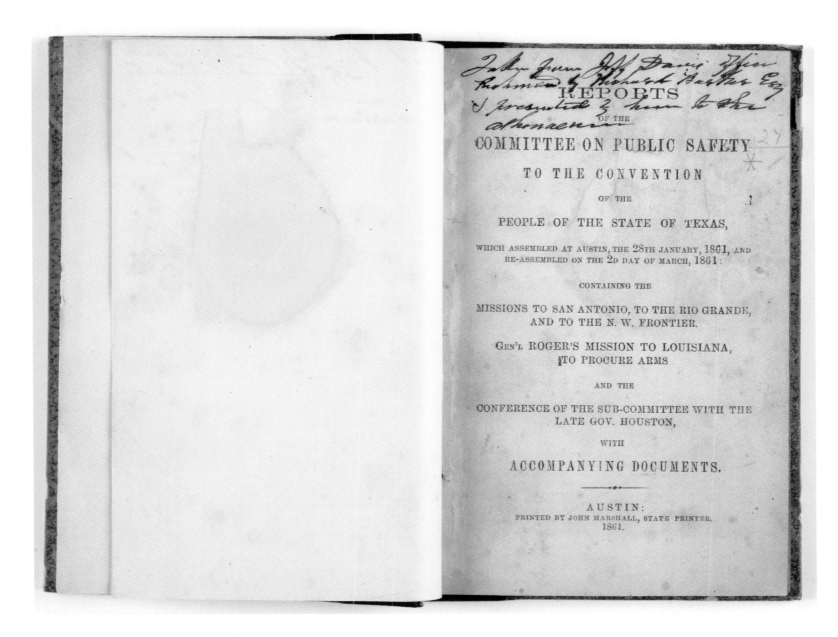

REPORTS

OF THE

COMMITTEE ON PUBLIC SAFETY

TO THE CONVENTION

OF THE

PEOPLE OF THE STATE OF TEXAS,

WHICH ASSEMBLED AT AUSTIN, THE 28TH JANUARY, 1861, AND
RE-ASSEMBLED ON THE 2D DAY OF MARCH, 1861:

CONTAINING THE

MISSIONS TO SAN ANTONIO, TO THE RIO GRANDE,
AND TO THE N. W. FRONTIER.

GEN'L ROGER'S MISSION TO LOUISIANA,
TO PROCURE ARMS

AND THE

CONFERENCE OF THE SUB-COMMITTEE WITH THE
LATE GOV. HOUSTON,

WITH

ACCOMPANYING DOCUMENTS.

AUSTIN:
PRINTED BY JOHN MARSHALL, STATE PRINTER.
1861.

▲ *Reports of the Committee on Public Safety to the Convention of the People of the State of Texas.* Austin: Printed by John Marshall, State Printer, 1861.

As important as a particular imprint might be in its own right, its more day-to-day history is often as intriguing. Who first owned it? How did it reach its present state? And who else might have turned its pages, and to what purpose? One such Confederate imprint, *Reports of the Committee on Public Safety,* issued by the state of Texas in 1861, bears two inscriptions that reveal much of one title's unusual story.

The Confederate government had already evacuated Richmond as the Union army began its final assault on the city on 3–4 April 1865. Regiments raced one another to see which one could arrive first. A Union officer wrote that when his men reached the abandoned defense works, they leaped over and "rushed wildly in

every direction." Some units then broke into a headlong run toward the burning streets around Capitol Square. Just south of the Capitol, one particular building, the former United States Custom House, attracted the attention of several Federal units. First, the building was supposedly of fireproof construction; from there the Union soldiers could blow up or torch other buildings around it and create a firebreak. And it was there on Main Street, too, that Jefferson Davis and the Confederate Treasury and State Departments had maintained offices—offices filled with everyday reference materials and reports.

The building was soon crowded with a melee of soldiers, some hard at work and some eagerly ransacking offices looking for souvenirs. One of them, Richard Barker, grabbed a copy of the Texas report, later inscribing it: "Taken from Jeff Davis' office, Richmond . . . & presented by him to the Athenaeum." The second inscription

pointedly described the donated book as one taken from Davis's office within "the executive dept of the so-called Confederate States govt." The report eventually made its way to the Reynolds Library in Rochester, New York. In 1940, the director of the Rochester Public Library returned the volume to the Library of Virginia. The Texas report is among a number of Library of Virginia titles with a similar Civil War provenance: capture, donation to an institution near the soldier's home, and eventual sale or transfer to the Library. EC

◀ A. W. Kercheval and A. J. Turner. *Pray, Maiden, Pray! A Ballad for the Times, Respectfully Dedicated to the Patriotic Women of the South.* Richmond: George Dunn and Company, 1864.

▶ Charles Chaky de Nordendorf. *Old Dominion March; Dedicated to General William Smith, Governor of Virginia.* Richmond: George Dunn and Company, 1863.

▶ Henry Clay Work. *Just Before the Battle Mother; A Ballad for the Piano Forte.* Richmond: J. W. Davies and Sons, 1863.

"If all the music manufactured in the South found a market," remarked a Richmond editor, "we should certainly be a very musical people." It was not for want of trying. Almost immediately after the outbreak of war, Confederate publishers rushed to meet, or create, a demand for music. Among the first publications were songsters, collections not of single tunes, but of several and sometimes many songs. The Library of Virginia's collection includes several, such as the eighteen-page *Hopkins' New-Orleans 5 Cent Song-Book*, issued in 1861, and *War Songs of the South*, published the next year and edited by William G. Shepperson, a correspondent for the *Richmond Dispatch*. The latter offered more than two hundred pages of music. As late as 1865, the Richmond firm of West and Johnston was somehow able to print and market a remarkable "Eleventh edition! Enlarged" of *The Stonewall Song Book, Being a Collection of Patriotic, Sentimental and Comic Songs.*

Besides the larger songbooks, there were hundreds of sheet-music titles, many of them now part of the Library's imprint collection. Some—such as *Who Will Care for Mother Now?*—spoke of home and family; others—such as *Her Bright Smile Haunts Me Still*, published in Macon, New Orleans, Savannah, and Richmond—captured another side of the soldier's life left behind. And still others—such as *The Vacant Chair; or, We Shall Meet, But We Shall Miss Him*—were grim admissions of the reality that many faced. While most sheet music failed to capture a wide audience, some fared well, aided in large part by effective designs and skillful printing. Henry Work's *Just Before the Battle Mother*, Charles Nordendorf's *Old Dominion March*, and *Pray, Maiden, Pray!*, with lyrics by A. W. Kercheval and music by A. J. Turner, are all examples of the engraver's and printer's craft. Two of them were printed by George Dunn and Company, of Richmond, well-known for music publishing.

Nordendorf, compiler of *The Old Dominion March*, especially epitomized the freewheeling nature of Southern music-publishing. In copies of another tune, *Oh! Bring My Brother Back to Me!*, he included an invitation to the public to "send original poems in, to be set to music." Those he found particularly suitable and potentially profitable would "be copyrighted by the composer." Then, after investing in the publication of the new song and pocketing any profits, he promised to present "25 copies to the author of the verses" as compensation. Any "rejected poems," he added, "will not be returned." Perhaps no matter. As one historian of the Confederate home front has remarked, "there was hardly anyone who was so inhibited as not to feel that he could write a song, either the words or music, and frequently both." EC

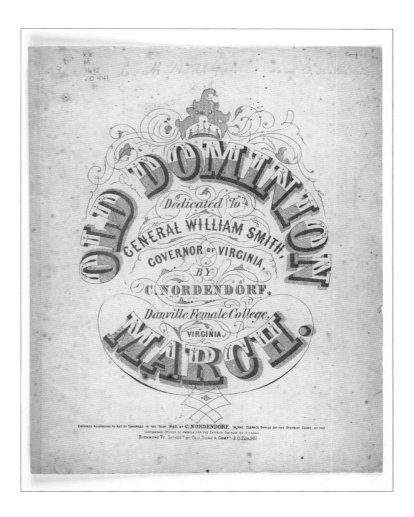

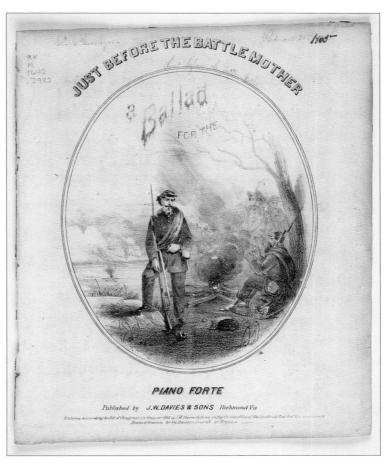

Accordinge to my former letter I haue sent home to the handes of my lo: of Dorchester, the answere to his Ma:tie letter concerninge William Capps, made by the Gouernor and Counsell then resident to their lo:ps But Docter John Pott whome I found Gouernor, had conuerted the fines laid vpon Capps his freindes to his owne priuate vse: the w:ch I will cause to be repaid them out of the said Doctors estate, I haue allso receaued diuers foule complaints, against the said Docter for manie disorders in the tyme of his gouernment by him done, as the pardoninge a wilfull murtherer, after he was legallie condempned, then inrestinge him into his former estate vpon composition, and afterward giuinge him his pass for England, a copie of w:ch inuestment I haue sent to S:r John Brooke. At the Assemblie It was generallie concluded to build a forte at Poynte Comforte, capeable of 16 peece of Ordnance, most of w:ch I hope will be mounted before Christmas next. By w:ch yo:u may perceaue, that the people are nowe more cheerefull disposed to make this, their Countrey, beinge at their owne charges, they haue vndertaken soe great a worke as is this fortification. Some potashes I haue sent home for a triall, and that is 100 pounds out of wood ashes, the other of tobacco stalkes consigned to S:r John Wolstonholme for approbation, for the rest of the affaires I commend me to my former letter, and to my brother Jennens relation, whom I haue sent home to attend the lo:ps of the Counsell, and he shall allso waite vpon yo:u to entreate yo:r best assistance on my behalfe, and acquainte yo:u w:ch the particulers therof. Soe wishinge yo:u all happines I rest

VIRGINIA'S OFFICIAL RECORDS

The official records of the colony and, later, the commonwealth of Virginia together form the Library of Virginia's single largest collection. As the designated repository of the Old Dominion's archival records, the Library contains more than eighty-three million unique and irreplaceable original documents, an incomparable public record of the history and development of Virginia.

The earliest archival materials include, for example, the surviving records of the secretary of the colony, dating from 1623 to 1776, as well as the correspondence, journal, and letter book of the short-lived and little-known Board of War, formed in 1779 and abolished a year later. Far more recent records include those of the Office of Civilian Defense during World War II and the Division of Motion Picture Censorship, active between 1927 and 1966. Besides including these and other records of most of the executive, legislative, and regulatory agencies of state government, the Library of Virginia's archival collection also includes many of the state's nineteenth-century judicial records, the surviving journals and papers of the Virginia constitutional conventions, and the papers of the secession convention of 1861. The Department of Education's voluminous files contain documentation about the founding and growth of Virginia's public school system, while the records of the adjutant general include numerous military-related manuscripts, including some muster rolls for the period 1795–1809. The enormous files of the nineteenth-century Board of Public Works contain extensive reports concerning the many canal, railroad, and turnpike companies, corporations, and partnerships that constructed and operated Virginia's first bridge, ferry, and other transportation services.

Most of the archival records in the Library of Virginia are one-of-a-kind, original documents. Other records, such as the collection of microfilmed county records or the abstracts of seventeenth- and eighteenth-century documents amassed by the Library's Virginia Colonial Records Project, are copies prepared for the express purpose of making available additional texts of valuable historical records. During the twentieth century, the Library has also become the official repository of the archival records of many of Virginia's counties and cities, providing essential documentation for the study of genealogy, local history, and the development of Virginia's institutional, legal, and political character.

In addition to its numerous manuscript collections, the Library of Virginia also offers researchers the largest extant collection of printed government documents relating to the commonwealth, ranging from the annual journals of the two houses of the General Assembly to the reports and other publications of the state's various agencies. The Library's collection includes copies of the first compilation of Virginia laws ever printed in the Old Dominion as well as several copies of a rare, and unofficial, assemblage of Virginia statutes published by John Purvis in London in 1684. And as the public institution charged with administering an extensive government documents program, the Library of Virginia maintains a broad and significant collection of contemporary state-sponsored publications.

◀ Sir John Harvey (died ca. 1646), Jamestown, Virginia, to Sir Robert Heath, London, England, 31 May 1630. Manuscript. Colonial Papers Collection, Folder 1, no. 1A, Record Group 1.

Governor John Harvey's one-page letter to Sir Robert Heath, His Majesty's attorney general in England, is the oldest official government document in the collections of the Library of Virginia. Written soon after Harvey's arrival in the colony in April 1630, the letter includes critical comments on the behavior of Harvey's predecessor, Dr. John Pott, and the controversy surrounding the king's agent in the colony, William Capps. Harvey also commented on two types of potash he had sent to England for further study.

More significant, Harvey wrote of preparations being undertaken for the defense of the colony, in particular the construction of a major fortification at Point Comfort. To Harvey, the project signaled the colonists' growing acceptance of Virginia as their adopted homeland rather than as a temporary settlement. Harvey wrote that "the people are nowe more than ever resolved to make this, theire Countrey, seinge at their owne Charges, they have undertaken soe greate a work as is this fortification." DSG

▲ Charles I (1600–1645). Commission to Sir
Francis Wyatt, Governor of the Royal Colony of
Virginia, 11 January 1639. Manuscript on vellum.
Acc. 24702.

With this 1639 commission, a parchment
bearing the king's royal seal and signature, or
sign manual, Charles I appointed Sir Francis
Wyatt to the position of governor of the royal
colony of Virginia to replace the unpopular Sir
John Harvey. Royal commissions were among
the most important documents under which the
colony functioned. The colonial charter, also
issued by the king, created the government of
the colony, while the royal commission formally
placed the responsibility for its administration in
the hands of a governor, who served as a vice-
regent, or personal deputy, of the king. From
time to time the king's ministers sent instructions
to the governors. Together, the charter, commission, and ministerial instructions formed the
constitution of government for the colony. Each
document derived its power and authority
directly from the Crown, not from the people of
Virginia, nor from Parliament. The Library of
Virginia purchased the faded but magnificent
parchment commission from the estate of
Somerton Erleigh, of Somerset, England, in 1957.

Wyatt, a native of Boxley in the county of
Kent, England, twice served as governor of
Virginia. In February 1621 the council of the
Virginia Company awarded him his first appointment. Wyatt arrived in Virginia in October 1621
and succeeded Sir George Yeardley on 18
November that same year. After the dissolution
of the Virginia Company in May 1624, Virginia
became a royal colony, and both King James I
and his son and successor, Charles I, retained
Wyatt in office. In September 1625 Wyatt
requested to be retired as governor. His father
died that same month and Wyatt returned to
England by May 1626. Reappointed in 1639,
Wyatt served for only a brief period in Virginia
during his second administration, which ended
in February 1642. He died in England late in the
summer of 1644. DSG

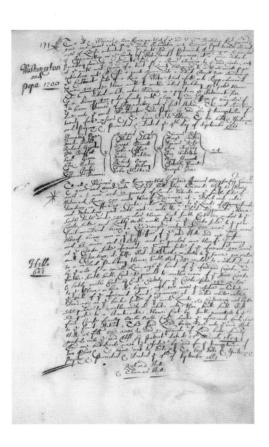

◀ Land Patents with List of Headrights, 1661 and 1666. Bound manuscript. Land Office Records, Patent Book 5, p. 171, Record Group 4.

On 4 September 1661, Governor Sir William Berkeley signed a patent for Major John Washington and Thomas Pope for twelve hundred acres on the south side of the Potomac River in Westmoreland County. John Washington, who with his brother Lawrence arrived in Virginia about 1655, was the great-grandfather of George Washington. Thomas Pope was the brother of John Washington's wife, Ann. The document lists the names of twenty-four persons, or headrights. A second patent, dated 4 September 1666 and entered on the same page, was issued to Richard Hill under the signature of Lieutenant Governor Francis Moryson.

The headright system, used as early as 1618 and reconfirmed by the Privy Council in July 1634, governed how most virgin land was obtained during the seventeenth and early eighteenth centuries in Virginia. As an inducement to immigration, each person who arrived in Virginia was due fifty acres of unclaimed land; in practice, however, the person who paid the immigrant's passage usually received the land.

After obtaining a certificate from a county clerk stating that the bearer was due land on the basis of having paid the passage of specific persons, the investor commissioned a survey of the land he wanted. With the headright certificate and the survey in hand, he then went to the office of the secretary of the colony from which the patent was issued over the governor's signature. Headright certificates could be accumulated and saved over time allowing the holder to receive a large parcel of land at once, as did Washington and Pope. Those headright certificates collected in the secretary's office were destroyed on an annual basis.

In 1924, the General Assembly transferred the duties of the register of the Land Office to the secretary of the commonwealth and by similar action in 1952 to the state librarian. Received by the Library of Virginia in 1948, the Land Office records total more than three hundred linear feet and include more than five hundred volumes. DSG

▶ Nathaniel Bacon (1647–1676). Promissory note to Thomas Ballard, 27 October 1674. Manuscript. Colonial Papers Collection, Folder 2, no. 11, Record Group 1.

In 1674 twenty-seven-year-old Nathaniel Bacon signed a promissory note to purchase Curle's Neck Plantation from its owner, Thomas Ballard. Bacon, recently arrived in Virginia from his family's seat in Suffolk County, England, promised to pay Ballard £200 sterling in "good bills of Exchange" as soon as the deed was executed, with another £100 due in 1675 and the remaining £200 in 1676. The promissory note, which has been in the collections of the Library of Virginia since the late nineteenth century, includes the earliest-known autograph signature of Nathaniel Bacon the Rebel, as he is usually known in Virginia history.

Bacon also acquired a large Henrico County property, soon thereafter known as Bacon's Quarter. As the owner of two such large estates and as a well-connected young colonist, Bacon won an appointment to the governor's prestigious executive Council at Jamestown. In 1676, in part in response to perceived threats against their frontier lands, Nathaniel Bacon and many of his neighbors joined in what became known as Bacon's Rebellion, the most serious challenge to Virginia's government during the entire colonial period. By September 1676, Bacon's rebels had driven the governor, Sir William Berkeley, and his followers across the Chesapeake to the Eastern Shore and had burned the capital town

of Jamestown. But when Bacon died of a fever in October, the rebellion collapsed. In spite of the central role that Nathaniel Bacon played in several of the most dramatic incidents in seventeenth-century Virginia, very few records survive to document the important parts of his life. BT

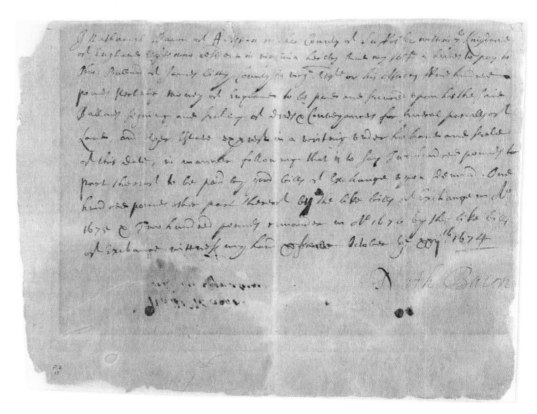

▶ Francis Nicholson (1655–1728).
Proclamation, 4 September 1700. Manuscript.
Essex County Circuit Court Papers.

By proclamation, Governor Francis Nicholson
in 1700 informed the population of Virginia that
while he was absent from the colony on official
business in New York his executive duties would
be exercised by William Byrd (1652–1704), president of the Council, the governor's executive
advisory body.

Nicholson had no way of communicating the
news directly to all of the people at one time: there
was no newspaper, not even a printing press for
producing a large number of copies for mass distribution. So Nicholson issued an official announcement in the form of a handwritten proclamation,
read before the public at the Capitol. To reach
the vast majority of the population, several
scribes duplicated the text. The secretary of the
colony authenticated the individual copies, then
sent one to each of the county courts. There, the
local justices had the proclamation read aloud to
the assembled freeholders. By these several public
steps, the official acts of the government at
Jamestown, and later at Williamsburg, were eventually communicated to the people throughout
Virginia's various jurisdictions.

The official copy, bearing Nicholson's autograph signature and the seal of the colony, also
includes the signature of Edmund Jenings, the
deputy secretary of the colony, attesting to the
document's authenticity, as well as the signature
of Francis Meriwether, the clerk of Essex County,
verifying that the proclamation had been publicly
read in that county. It is one of many thousands
of documents originally preserved in the Essex
County courthouse and later transferred to the
Library of Virginia where, under the provisions of
an act of the General Assembly creating the
Circuit Court Records Preservation Program, the
documents have been filed and described in
accordance with modern archival practices. BT

▲ Phillip Cowen (fl. 1675). Petition to
Governor Sir William Berkeley, 16 June 1675.
Manuscript. Colonial Papers Collection, Folder
19, no. 2, Record Group 1.

In 1675, Phillip Cowen, an African American
indentured servant, petitioned the governor of
Virginia. In outlining his master's abuses regarding the terms of his service, Cowen provided one
of the earliest-known surviving documents
regarding the slowly evolving nature of African
American servitude in the colony. The petition
was almost certainly prepared by an attorney acting on behalf of the petitioner. In spite of pecu-
liarities of spelling common to the time, the

document follows the traditional forms of petitions with which most people, especially servants, would probably not have been familiar.
The petition states that Phillip Cowen's master
had attempted by fraud and threats to lengthen
the term of Cowen's service by twenty additional
years, in effect, given the life expectancies of the
time, to convert an indenture for a limited time
of service into an early approximation of lifetime
slavery.

Because so few records of the early colonial
government exist, the response of the governor
and his Council is unfortunately unknown. It is
clear from the text of the petition, however, that
at least some African Americans during the late

1600s were indeed regarded as similar in status to
Virginia's white indentured servants. But it is
also clear, by the very fact that the petition had
to be prepared and submitted to the governor
and Council, that indentured servitude presented
a unique and especially precarious situation for
Virginia's African Americans. BT

By his Excellency

A Proclamation

Whereas his most Sacred Majesty by his Royall Letters Patents bearing date at Westminster the [ ] day of July in the tenth year of his Reigne, was graciously pleased to constitute & appoint Francis Nicholson Esqr to be his Majties Leivt & Governor Genll of his & her Majties Colony & Dominion of Virginia And whereas his Majesty by his aforesaid Royall Commission to me given was pleased to declare his Royall Will & pleasure That in Case of my death or absence from his Colony and Dominion aforesd And that there be noe other person upon the place Comissionated by his Majesty to be his Majties Leivetenant Governor or Comander in Cheif That then the present Councill of Virginia do take upon them the Administration of the Government and Execute the aforesd Commission and the severall powers and authorities therein contained And that the first of the Councill shall Preside with such power and preeminence as any former President heretofore used & Enjoyed And whereas his Majties Royall Comands hath been Signified to me by the Rt Honble the Lords Comissioners of Trade & Plantations by their Letter dated 12th Aprill 1700 to goe to New York I have therefore thought fit to publish and declare and by this Proclamation in his Majties name do publish & declare That the Administration of ye Government and the Execution of the aforesd Commission and the severall powers & authorities therein contained is dureing such my absence in his Majties President and Councill of his his & her Majties Colony and Dominion of Virginia And that William Byrd Esqr is at this present the first in the Commission of his Majties said Councill, and so by reason thereof President I do therefore hereby in his Majties name hereby strictly Charge require & Comand all his Majties Loveing Subjects of what station or Qualification soever within his Colony & Dominion aforesd to Yeild all due honor and obedience to his Majties aforesd President and Councill pursuant to his aforesd Royall Commission in the Administration of the Government untill my Arrivall here, as they will answer the Contrary at their utmost peril Given under my hand & the Seale of the Colony this 4 day of September 1700 in the twelfth year of his Majties Reign

ffr: Nicholson

A Proclamation declareing Wm
Byrd Esqr President [ ]

Published in this County Court ye 10th day of [ ] 1700
Truly Recorded [ ]

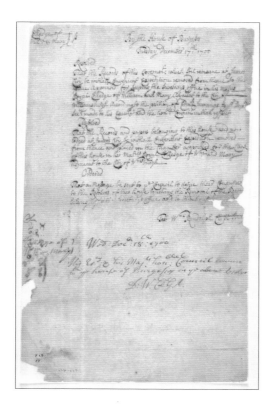

▲ Virginia House of Burgesses. Resolution, 18 December 1700. Manuscript. Colonial Papers Collection, Folder 13, no. 17, Record Group 1.

When the Capitol building, or State House as it was then known, burned in Jamestown on 20 October 1698, the records and papers of the House of Burgesses, the governor's Council, and the secretary of the colony, as well as other government documents and books of the Council's library, were thrown out of the windows of the blazing building and saved from the flames. Two former clerks of the General Court and the secretary's office, Peter Beverley and his brother Robert Beverley (later known as Robert Beverley the historian), spent long hours laboriously arranging and filing the papers while the government decided whether to rebuild the State House in Jamestown or move the capital to a healthier site at Middle Plantation, adjacent to the new College of William and Mary.

When the General Assembly convened in December 1700, it met in rooms at the College. There the House of Burgesses adopted the resolution ordering that all government records be transferred to the new seat of government. The upper house of the assembly, the governor's Council, concurred on the next day. By the authority of the resolution, the colony's public records were moved by wagon from Jamestown to Williamsburg late in 1700. BT

▼ Petition of the Queen and the great men of Pamunkey town, ca. 1705–1706. Manuscript. Colonial Papers Collection, Folder 17, no. 27, Record Group 1.

In the early 1700s, the Pamunkey Indians became increasingly concerned with the encroachment of English settlers on their Virginia lands. By the terms of a peace treaty signed 29 May 1677, the Pamunkey tribe had been assured that no English colonists would settle or plant within three miles of any Indian town. In an attempt to obtain a clear title to their lands on the Pamunkey Neck in King William County, the tribe addressed a petition to Governor Edward Nott. The document bears the marks of Ann, queen of the Pamunkey, and six of the "great men," or tribal leaders, of Pamunkey Town. The rare official document not only records the ultimately doomed struggle faced by Native Americans to retain their lands, but also the powerful position of women within Indian society and culture.

This was not the first attempt by the Pamunkey to protect their landholdings. Mrs. Betty, then queen of the Pamunkey, and four tribal leaders had previously petitioned Governor

Francis Nicholson in 1701, asking that he confirm their title to the Pamunkey lands by issuing a patent. The House of Burgesses passed and the Council approved a bill in September 1701 for "quieting possession of several persons seated within bounds of land laid out for Pamunkey Indians," but Nicholson refused to give his approval. On 22 October 1701, the General Court finally agreed to respond to the 1701 petition and ordered that the several parcels leased by the Indians to British subjects be certified by patent and that another patent be issued to the tribe for the remainder of their lands. The order resulted in seventeen individual patents. However, no patent was issued expressly confirming title to the Pamunkey tribe, although a survey of the Indian lands is mentioned in extant records. The 1706 petition was yet another attempt to gain some assurance that the Pamunkey lands might somehow remain secure. There is no record that either the House of Burgesses or the Council ever considered the petition to Governor Nott. DSG

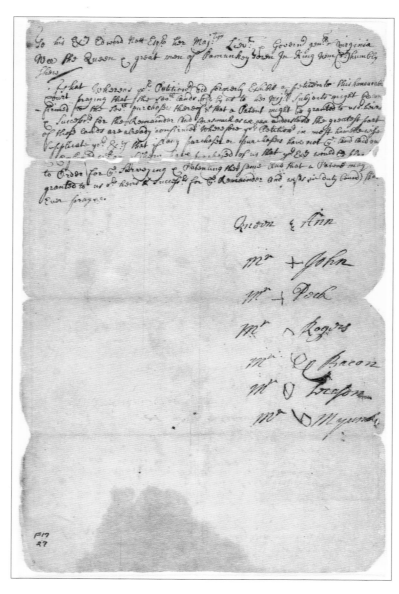

▶ Elizabeth Burwell Harrison (fl. 1710). Petition to the Virginia House of Burgesses, ca. 1710. Manuscript. Colonial Papers Collection, Folder 22, no. 8, Record Group 1.

Women in colonial Virginia could neither buy nor sell property with the same freedom as men, and it was frequently necessary to petition the General Assembly for a special dispensation enabling them to administer property bequeathed to them. Elizabeth Harrison faced just this situation after her husband's death in April 1710. Benjamin Harrison, called by Governor Francis Nicholson one of the two ablest lawyers in the colony, served at various times as clerk of the Council, member of the House of Burgesses for James City and Charles City Counties, Speaker of the House of Burgesses, acting attorney general, and treasurer. Harrison owned more than twenty thousand acres of land in four counties as well as numerous slaves. If he wrote a will, it has not survived. Harrison had, however, confided to his wife how he wanted certain of his properties to be divided, including three plantations and twenty slaves in Surry County. He was considerably in debt at his death.

Despite her husband's expressed wishes, Elizabeth Harrison—as a woman—was powerless to dispose of his various holdings without the approval of the General Assembly, to which she petitioned for permission to sell specified properties. Although the document itself is undated, the journals of the House of Burgesses state that the petition was brought before the legislative body on 16 November 1710. The resulting act granting her sufficient authority to conduct necessary business was passed by the burgesses and approved by the governor on 9 December 1710. DSG

▶ *A Collection of All the Acts of Assembly, Now in Force, In the Colony of Virginia.* Williamsburg: Printed by William Parks, 1733.

William Parks (ca. 1698–1750) printed the first collected edition of the laws of colonial Virginia to be published in the colony. Parks had established the first newspaper in the southern colonies and the first successful printing business in Annapolis, Maryland, before opening a printing office in Williamsburg in 1730. Under an agreement formalized by an act of the General Assembly, Parks in 1733 published the official edition of the Virginia statutes then in force. Between 1732 and his death in 1750, Parks at the conclusion of each legislative session regularly published the official journals of the House of Burgesses and the laws enacted by the General Assembly.

In order to supply his busy printing shop, Parks established the first paper mill in Virginia. Further, he founded the colony's first newspaper, the *Virginia Gazette*, in 1736. In addition to issuing the first almanac in the South, he also published the first book in the English colonies about printing, John Markland's *Typographia. An Ode, on Printing* (1730); the earliest books published in America on the subjects of sports, Edward Blackwell's *A Compleat System of Fencing; or, the Art of Defence* (1734), the law of Virginia, George Webb's *The Office and Authority of a Justice of Peace* (1736), and cookery, *The Compleat Housewife; or, Accomplish'd Gentlewoman's Companion* (1742). In 1747 Parks published William Stith's lengthy *History of the First Discovery and Settlement of Virginia*, the first full-length book of history to be printed in the Old Dominion. The Library of Virginia's collections include more than twenty imprints from the pioneer Williamsburg printing press of William Parks. BT

A

COLLECTION

OF ALL THE

ACTS of ASSEMBLY,

Now in Force, in the Colony of

VIRGINIA.

WITH THE

TITLES of Such as are Expir'd, or Repeal'd. And NOTES in the Margin, ſhewing how, and at what Time, they were Repeal'd.

Examin'd with the Records,

By a COMMITTEE appointed for that Purpoſe.

Who have added

Many uſeful *Marginal Notes*, and *References:* And an exact TABLE.

Publiſh'd, purſuant to an Order of the GENERAL ASSEMBLY, *held at* WILLIAMSBURG, *in the Year* M, DCC, XXVII.

WILLIAMSBURG:

Printed by WILLIAM PARKS. M, DCC, XXXIII.

▶ The Surrender of Fort Necessity, 3 July 1754. Manuscript translation from the French document. Colonial Papers Collection, Folder 44, no. 14, Record Group 1.

The initial battle for control of the Ohio Valley during the French and Indian War, known in Europe as the Seven Years' War, took place at Fort Necessity, near the Great Meadows in southwestern Pennsylvania. The aptly named but small and hastily constructed fortification was under the command of an ambitious and promising officer of the Virginia militia, Colonel George Washington. Leading the nine-hundred-member French force, reinforced by more than thirteen hundred Indians, was Louis Coulon de Villiers. The French commander was especially intent on revenging the death of his brother, Joseph Coulon de Villiers, sieur de Jumonville, killed five weeks earlier, on 28 May, in a sharp but brief clash with a small force of Virginians—led by the same Colonel Washington.

The battle at Fort Necessity began on the morning of 3 July 1754 and continued throughout a day of rain until about eight o'clock that night. After requesting a meeting with Washington, de Villiers presented a list of seven articles of capitulation. Washington—his men greatly outnumbered, without adequate supplies for his troops, and with no hope of rescue—had little choice. His French foe had at least presented him with a proposal that allowed him to withdraw with his honor intact. Washington, after some little negotiation, accepted the terms of the capitulation just before midnight. The next morning, Washington and his remaining soldiers—with all their supplies and most of their equipment—left the fort, which was then razed by the French. By the terms of the surrender, Washington left his artillery behind, as well as several French officers captured on 28 May.

The English-language translation of the surrender document was made shortly after the completion of the original instrument of capitulation just before midnight on 3 July. The Library of Virginia's copy, signed by the French commander, was exhibited at the Virginia booth at the 1907 Jamestown Ter-Centennial Exposition. The original French-language document, with all signatures, is included in the collections of the Centre d'Archives de Montréal, Montreal, Canada. DSG

▶ Virginia House of Burgesses. Resolution, 30
May 1774. Manuscript. Colonial Papers
Collection, Folder 50, no. 17, Record Group 1.

Early in May 1774, shocking news reached
Williamsburg. Parliament, Virginians learned,
had voted to close the port of Boston in retaliation for the December 1773 Boston Tea Party
and was, moreover, preparing to pass additional
coercive acts to put a stop to colonial protests
against British policies. With the news, Thomas
Jefferson, Patrick Henry, Richard Henry Lee,
Francis Lightfoot Lee, and several other members of the House of Burgesses met privately in
the library of the royal governor's advisory
Council to prepare a response to the British
actions. The resulting resolutions so offended the
governor, John Murray, earl of Dunmore, that he
put an end to the current session of the General
Assembly and sent the burgesses home.

At the end of the month, on 29 May 1774,
an express rider arrived in Williamsburg bringing
a report and resolutions from Samuel Adams's
Committee of Correspondence in Boston. Paul
Revere had relayed the messages from Boston to
Philadelphia, and a succession of other riders
had carried the Bostonians' request for assistance
to Virginia and the other colonies. Peyton
Randolph, as Speaker of the House of Burgesses,
hastily rounded up those legislators who were
still in Williamsburg. With Randolph as modera-
tor, twenty-five men met on 30 May 1774 and
signed this resolution.

The document inspired the organization of
the first of five revolutionary conventions that
met in Virginia between August 1774 and July
1776. The first convention issued the official call
for the initial meeting of the First Continental
Congress, of which Peyton Randolph would be
president. Among the signers of the 1774 resolution were Edmund Pendleton and George
Washington, who also attended the Congress in
Philadelphia; Thomas Jefferson, Francis Lightfoot
Lee, and Thomas Nelson Jr., who were members
of the Second Continental Congress and signers
of the Declaration of Independence; Robert
Carter Nicholas, the treasurer of Virginia; and
James Wood, who like Jefferson and Nelson later
served as governor of the commonwealth of
Virginia. BT

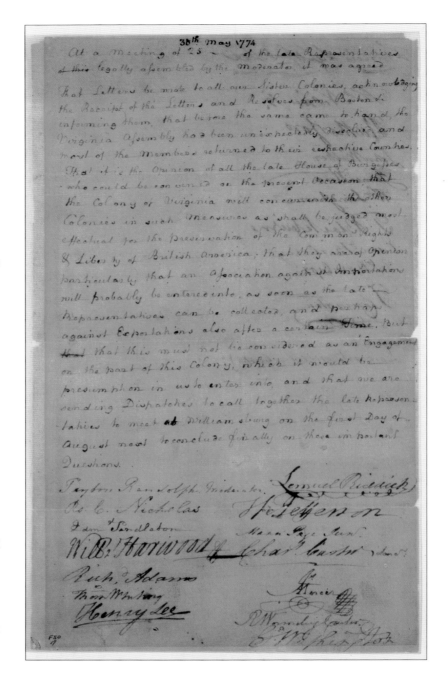

▶ Virginia House of Burgesses. Journal, 6 May
1776. Bound manuscript. Colonial Government,
House of Burgesses, Record Group 1.

On 6 May 1776, during the sixteenth year of
the reign of King George III, assistant clerk
Jacob Bruce made the last entry ever recorded in
the official journals of the Virginia House of
Burgesses. The clerk, George Wythe, was absent
in Philadelphia representing Virginia in the
Continental Congress. With the stark prospect
of revolution looming over the colonies, Bruce
wrote that "Several Members" of the House of
Burgesses met in the Capitol in Williamsburg in
response to the order of adjournment adopted on
7 March 1776. Symbolically caught between an
age then passing and another not yet begun, the
legislators seemed somewhat at a loss: they "did
neither proceed to Business" nor formally
adjourn as a House of Burgesses. One of their fellow members, Edmund Pendleton, of Caroline

County, explained that the members of the colonial legislature, by not setting a date for another
meeting, intentionally "let that body die." The
long-standing legislature as a part of the colonial
empire in North America was, as Bruce expressed
it in his brief account of the day's deliberations,
simply "finis."

In 1905 the first state librarian, John Pendleton
Kennedy, began the publication of the *Journals
of the House of Burgesses*. The ten-year, thirteen-
volume project marked the beginning of the
Library's modern program of publishing Virginia's
historic records. Inaugurated at the same time
that the Library of Congress began its distinguished publications program with the first volumes of the *Journals of the Continental Congress*,
the books issued by Kennedy and his successor,
Henry Read McIlwaine, placed the Library in the
forefront of a new national movement to preserve
and publish the most important records of the
nation's past. BT

Whereas several Companies of the Militia of this Colony have been drawn out into actual Service, by command of his Excellency the Governor, for the defence and protection of the Frontier against the Incursions and depredations of the Indians, and there are now, owing several large sums of Money, as well for the pay of such Militia, as for Provisions, Arms, and other necessaries furnished them; and it will be a great saving to this Colony, as well as ease to the Claimants, to have such Accounts adjusted by Commissioners in the Country.

Resolved, therefore, that Archibald Cary, William Cabell, William Fleming, John Ireson, and John Mitchell, Gentlemen, or any three or more of them, be, and they are hereby appointed, Commissioners for the Counties of Fincastle, Botetourt, Culpeper, Pittsylvania, Halifax, and Bedford, and for that part of the County of Augusta which lies of the Eastward of the Allegany Mountains; and that Richard Lee, Francis Peyton, Josias Clapham, Henry Lee, and Thomas Blackburn, Gentlemen, or any three or more of them be, and they are hereby appointed, Commissioners for the other Counties, and for that part of the County of Augusta which lies to the Westward of the Allegany Mountains, and for the Provinces of Maryland and Pennsylvania, to examine, state, and settle the Accounts of the pay of the Militia, and of all Provisions, Arms, Ammunition, and other necessaries furnished the said Militia of the Counties, for which they are appointed Commissioners, and report the same to the General Assembly.

And then the House adjourned until Thursday, the twelfth day of October next, at ten of the Clock, in the Morning.

Thursday

Thursday the 12th of October 15 Geo. III. 1775.

The House met according to their Adjournment: but no more than thirty seven Members appearing, which was not a sufficient number to proceed to Business.

The House adjourned til the first Monday in March next.

Thursday the 7th of March 16 Geo. III. 1776.

The House met according to their Adjournment: but no more than thirty two Members appearing, which was not a sufficient number to proceed to Business.

The House adjourned til the first Monday in May next.

Monday, the 6th of May, 16 Geo. III. 1776.

Several Members met, but did neither proceed to Business, nor adjourn, as a House of Burgesses.

FINIS.

▲ Proceedings of the Convention of Delegates, 29 June 1776. Manuscript. Revolutionary Government, Revolutionary Conventions, Record Group 2.

The official journal of the fifth and last of the Virginia revolutionary conventions, which met in the Capitol in Williamsburg from 6 May through 5 July 1776, records some of the most momentous decisions made in Virginia's and the nation's history. The manuscript journal penned by assistant clerk Jacob Bruce contains the earliest-known full text of the Virginia resolutions of 15 May instructing Virginia's representatives to the Continental Congress to introduce a declaration of independence. Bruce also recorded the earliest-known full text of George Mason's Virginia Declaration of Rights, unanimously adopted on 12 June, and later a model for the United States Bill of Rights and the French Declaration of the Rights of Man and of the Citizen adopted in 1789. On 29 June, the convention delegates unanimously ratified Virginia's first constitution and elected Patrick Henry governor of the newly independent commonwealth of Virginia.

In April 1865, shortly after the end of the Civil War, a Union soldier removed the journal from the state archives in the Capitol in Richmond and took it home with him. His descendants sold the manuscript journal in 1942 to a Philadelphia dealer in rare books and manuscripts. When the dealer, in turn, attempted to sell the volume to the Colonial Williamsburg Foundation, the state librarian and the attorney general of Virginia intervened to ensure the document's safe return to the archives, by then part of the Virginia State Library. Virginia reimbursed the dealer in the amount of his original purchase price. The transaction was one of several during the same period that established the precedents by which the commonwealth of Virginia has been able to recover a large number of lost public documents. BT

▼ Charles Cornwallis, earl Cornwallis (1738–1805). Acknowledgment of His Status as a Prisoner of War, 28 October 1781. Manuscript. Special Collections.

Lord Cornwallis, the British commander at the Battle of Yorktown, signed this document more than a week after he had surrendered his army. Under the terms of the surrender agreement, Cornwallis and his army became prisoners of war. As such, the general formally acknowledged his status so that he could be paroled and return to England, first pledging his "Faith & Word of Honor" not to take any action injurious to the United States until properly exchanged under an agreement to be formulated at the end of the war. Cornwallis's surrender on 19 October 1781 effectively ended the military phase of the American Revolution, although the peace treaty was not concluded and the last British army units withdrawn until 1783.

The copy of the Cornwallis parole was one of the many historic documents and books that the Virginia State Library displayed at the 1907 Jamestown Ter-Centennial Exposition in celebration of the three-hundredth anniversary of the first settlement of Virginia. BT

▶ Virginia General Assembly. The Deed of Cession of the Northwest Territory, 1 March 1784. Records of the General Assembly, Executive Communications Collection, 3 May 1784, Record Group 78.

Virginia's deed of cession of the Northwest Territory stands as a monument to the strength of national fervor in the post-Revolutionary period. Under the terms of its early charter, Virginia since 1609 had claimed title to the vast and valuable lands northwest of the Ohio River. In 1784, however, there was a larger purpose to consider. For the betterment of the United States and in recognition of its place within the greater whole, the Old Dominion freely relinquished its claim to the immense territory stretching beyond its farthest settlements. Virginia thereby established the precedent of national domain.

Thomas Jefferson had transmitted Virginia's first act of cession to the Continental Congress on 2 January 1781. That first proposal, however, stipulating several conditions for granting lands within the territory, attracted considerable opposition from influential land companies eager to control access to the new frontier. The issue was further complicated by the land bounties the commonwealth had offered Virginia officers and troops of the Continental and State Lines during the Revolution. After three years of intense political struggle, the various issues were at last reconciled and the delegates of the Confederation Congress enthusiastically accepted Virginia's offer on 1 March 1784.

Virginia's copy of the deed of cession, with its wax seal impressed on paper and with ribbon attached, and authenticated by Thomas Jefferson, was enclosed in a letter from Virginia's five delegates to Congress to Governor Benjamin Harrison on 22 March 1784. Harrison forwarded both the letter and the document to the Speaker of the House of Delegates on 3 May 1784. The other copy, intended for the national record, is among the collections of the Library of Congress. DSG

To all to whom these presents shall come

Know Ye, that among the Archives of the United States in Congress Assembled is lodged a Deed or Instrument in the words following

"To all who shall see these Presents,

We Thomas Jefferson, Samuel Hardy, Arthur Lee and James Monroe the underwritten, Delegates for the Commonwealth of Virginia in the Congress of the United States of America send Greeting

Whereas the General Assembly of the Commonwealth of Virginia at their sessions begun on the twentieth day of October one thousand seven hundred and Eighty three passed an Act entitled "An Act to authorize the Delegates of this State in Congress to convey to the United States in Congress Assembled all the Right of this Commonwealth to the Territory north-Westward of the River Ohio" in these words following to wit—

"Whereas the Congress of the United States did by their Act of the sixth day of September in the year one thousand seven hundred and Eighty recommend to the several States in the Union having Claims to waste and unappropriated Lands in the Western Country a liberal Cession to the United States of a portion of their respective Claims for the common Benefit of the Union; And Whereas this Common-

-wealth/

▲ Thomas Jefferson (1743–1826). "An Act for Establishing Religious Freedom," 16 January 1786. Manuscript. Records of the General Assembly, Enrolled Bills, Record Group 78.

The Virginia General Assembly during its session of 17 October 1785 to 21 January 1786 passed "An Act for Establishing Religious Freedom." The formal, enrolled bill of the Virginia Statute for Religious Freedom includes the signatures of Archibald Cary, Speaker of the Senate of Virginia, and Benjamin Harrison, Speaker of the House of Delegates. The act, abrogating all connection between church and state, assured citizens the freedom to follow their own religious beliefs and opinions unencumbered by any compulsion. The statute's author, Thomas Jefferson, ranked it in importance with the Declaration of Independence and, indeed, considered it a necessary companion to the earlier document. When writing his own epitaph, Jefferson listed his authorship of the 1786 statute as one of the three achievements for which he wished to be remembered.

Jefferson drafted his bill for establishing religious freedom in 1777 but did not introduce it in the General Assembly until 12 June 1779. The

House of Delegates, though, postponed consideration of the measure, effectively blocking its passage. The document was then printed as a broadside in an effort to gain popular support, but the attempt to have it considered in the October 1779 session also met with no success. James Madison reintroduced the bill on 31 October 1785, which the General Assembly passed on 16 January 1786. Without Madison's leadership and support, the measure might not have succeeded.

No manuscript copy of the draft bill has been found. As for the final version, the text appeared in the General Assembly session laws of October 1785 and in volume twelve of William Waller Hening's *Statutes at Large*. Both texts are identical to the Library of Virginia's parchment copy of the completed, enrolled bill—the earliest-known text of the statute as adopted. DSG

▶ Bill of Rights to the United States Constitution, 1789. Manuscript. Records of the General Assembly, Executive Communications, Record Group 78.

In 1789, Congress asked that the states consider several changes to the United States Constitution and in September sent a copy of twelve proposed amendments to the Virginia General Assembly. Early in December 1791 the House of Delegates voted approval of all twelve. The Senate of Virginia, however, on 15 December approved only ten, rejecting the first and second proposals. The remaining ten amendments—known from their inception as the Bill of Rights—thereupon became part of the federal Constitution.

Virginia's 1789 copy of the proposed Bill of Rights, with its original twelve amendments, bears the authenticating signatures of the Speaker of the House of Representatives, Frederick Augustus Conrad Muhlenberg; the vice president of the United States and president of the Senate, John Adams; the clerk of the House of Representatives, John James Beckley; and the secretary of the Senate, Samuel Allyne Otis. The document is one of only twelve surviving original signed copies of the Bill of Rights.

The first of the twelve amendments, restricting the size of the House of Representatives, never received the approval of enough state legislatures to become a part of the Constitution. The second was meant to prevent members of Congress from receiving an increase in pay until after a congressional election, so that voters had a chance to reconsider the merits of candidates who might have agreed to raise their own salaries. It, too, failed to win approval. In recent years, however, a renewed interest in congressional pay and benefits led to a revival of interest in the amendment, and on 7 May 1992 Michigan became the thirty-eighth state to approve the article. On that date it became the Twenty-Seventh Amendment to the Constitution. BT

Congress of the United States.

begun and held at the City of New York, on
Wednesday the fourth of March one thousand seven hundred and eighty nine.

THE Conventions of a number of the States, having at the time of their adopting the Constitution, expressed a desire, in order to prevent misconstruction or abuse of its powers, that further declaratory and restrictive clauses should be added: And as extending the ground of public confidence in the Government, will best ensure the beneficent ends of its Institution.

RESOLVED, by the Senate and House of Representatives of the United States of America, in Congress assembled, two thirds of both Houses concurring, That the following Articles be proposed to the Legislatures of the several States, as amendments to the Constitution of the United States, all or any of which Articles, when ratified by three fourths of the said Legislatures, to be valid to all intents and purposes, as part of the said Constitution; viz.

ARTICLES in addition to, and amendment of the Constitution of the United States of America, proposed by Congress, and ratified by the Legislatures of the several States, pursuant to the fifth Article of the original Constitution.

Article the first. After the first enumeration required by the first Article of the Constitution, there shall be one Representative for every thirty thousand, until the number shall amount to one hundred, after which the proportion shall be so regulated by Congress, that there shall be not less than one hundred Representatives, nor less than one Representative for every forty thousand persons, until the number of Representatives shall amount to two hundred; after which the proportion shall be so regulated by Congress, that there shall not be less than two hundred Representatives, nor more than one Representative for every fifty thousand persons.

Article the second. No law varying the compensation for the services of the Senators and Representatives, shall take effect, until an election of Representatives shall have intervened.

Article the third. Congress shall make no law respecting an establishment of religion, or prohibiting the free exercise thereof; or abridging the freedom of speech, or of the press; or the right of the people peaceably to assemble, and to petition the Government for a redress of grievances.

Article the fourth. A well regulated Militia, being necessary to the security of a free State, the right of the people to keep and bear arms, shall not be infringed.

Article the fifth. No Soldier shall in time of peace be quartered in any house, without the consent of the owner, nor in time of war, but in a manner to be prescribed by law.

Article the sixth. The right of the people to be secure in their persons, houses, papers, and effects, against unreasonable searches and seizures, shall not be violated, and no warrants shall issue, but upon probable cause, supported by oath or affirmation, and particularly describing the place to be searched, and the persons or things to be seized.

Article the seventh. No person shall be held to answer for a capital, or otherwise infamous crime, unless on a presentment or indictment of a Grand Jury, except in cases arising in the land or naval forces, or in the Militia, when in actual service in time of war or public danger; nor shall any person be subject for the same offence to be twice put in jeopardy of life or limb; nor shall be compelled in any criminal case to be a witness against himself, nor be deprived of life, liberty, or property, without due process of law; nor shall private property be taken for public use, without just compensation.

Article the eighth. In all criminal prosecutions, the accused shall enjoy the right to a speedy and public trial, by an impartial jury of the State and district wherein the crime shall have been committed, which district shall have been previously ascertained by law, and to be informed of the nature and cause of the accusation; to be confronted with the witnesses against him; to have compulsory process for obtaining witnesses in his favor, and to have the assistance of counsel for his defence.

Article the ninth. In suits at common law, where the value in controversy shall exceed twenty dollars, the right of trial by jury shall be preserved, and no fact tried by a jury, shall be otherwise re-examined in any Court of the United States, than according to the rules of the common law.

Article the tenth. Excessive bail shall not be required, nor excessive fines imposed, nor cruel and unusual punishments inflicted.

Article the eleventh. The enumeration in the Constitution, of certain rights, shall not be construed to deny or disparage others retained by the people.

Article the twelfth. The powers not delegated to the United States by the Constitution, nor prohibited by it to the States, are reserved to the States respectively, or to the people.

ATTEST,

Frederick Augustus Muhlenberg, Speaker of the House of Representatives.

John Adams, Vice President of the United States, and President of the Senate.

John Beckley, Clerk of the House of Representatives.

Sam. A. Otis Secretary of the Senate.

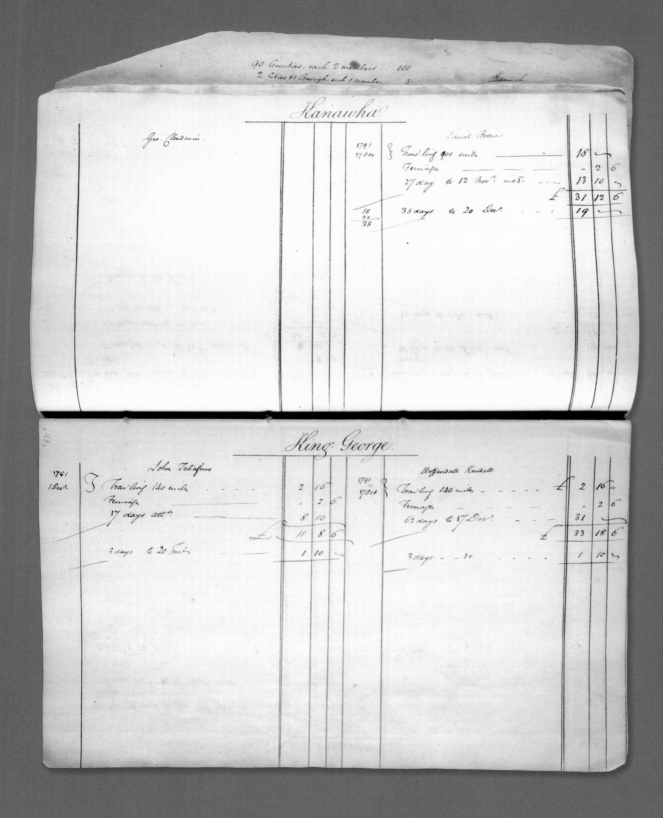

Kanawha

Geo. Clendenin

Samuel Boone

1791 17 Octr	Trav'ling 900 miles		18	
	Ferriages		~ 2 6
	27 days to 12 Novr. met.		13 10 ~
		£	31 12 6
18 20 / 38	38 days to 20 Decr.		19 ~

King George

1791 18 Octr John Taliaferro

	Trav'ling 140 miles	2 16 ~
	Ferriage	~ 2 6
	17 days attd.	8 10
	£	11 8 6
	3 days to 20 ditto	1 10 ~

1791 17 Octr Wiffendale Kendall

	Trav'ling 140 miles	£ 2 16 ~
	Ferriage	~ 2 6
	62 days to 17 Decr.	31 ~
	£	33 18 6
	3 days ~ ditto	1 10 ~

◄ Daniel Boone (1734–1820). Expenditure Account, October 1791. Bound manuscript. Records of the General Assembly, House of Delegates Attendance Books, 1776–1884, Record Group 79.

The legendary frontiersman Daniel Boone (1734–1820) on three occasions served in the Virginia General Assembly's House of Delegates, each time representing a different county. He first represented Fayette County, district of Kentucky, during the session of 7 May to 23 June 1781 and again from 1 October 1781 to 5 January 1782. The citizens of the newly created county of Bourbon, district of Kentucky, sent Boone to the session of 15 October 1787 to 8 January 1788. Finally, he was elected, along with George Clendinen, to represent another newly formed county, Kanawha (now in West Virginia), in the legislative session of 17 October to 20 December 1791. In 1792, both Fayette and Bourbon Counties became part of the new state of Kentucky.

The page from the 1791 session's attendance book shows that Boone was present throughout the sixty-five-day session. In contrast, George Clendinen was never present. In addition to a per diem allowance, Boone received a fee to cover the travel expenses incurred on his nine-hundred-mile journey to and from Richmond and an allowance for ferry fares. Attendance books for the years 1776–1884 account for 78 of the 348 volumes in the Library's records of the Virginia House of Delegates; there are, in addition, approximately six hundred linear feet of manuscript materials. DSG

▲ Judith Hope (fl. 1818). Petition to the Virginia House of Delegates, ca. 1819. Manuscript. Records of the General Assembly, Legislative Petitions, City of Richmond, Record Group 78.

Among the more than twenty-one thousand petitions presented to the Virginia General Assembly between 1776 and 1865 is an unsigned, undated plea presented to the House of Delegates in December 1819 on behalf of Judith Hope, "a woman of color." Although still a slave, Hope inquired whether she could receive an exemption from a law passed on 25 January 1806 requiring any slave freed after 1 May 1806 to leave the state within twelve months of being emancipated or face reenslavement. Judith Hope's mother had purchased her, and "was desirous to give her freedom if the permission of the Legislature can be obtained for her remaining in the land of her nativity." Judith Hope cited a subsequent law passed 24 January 1816 allowing any slave emancipated for "extraordinary merit" to remain in the state; she hoped that her well-known good character and deportment would suffice for "extraordinary merit."

The House of Delegates received the petition on 23 December 1819 and referred it to the Committee on Courts of Justice the next day. Notes on the petition itself indicate that the legislature rejected the request on 17 January, although no such entry appears in the journal of the House of Delegates.

There was, though, more to her story. In her petition, Judith Hope identified her late father as Caesar Hope, a former barber in Williamsburg and Richmond. The records of the city of Richmond in the Library of Virginia's collections include Caesar Hope's will, which instructed his executor, Edmund Randolph, to purchase and set free his two young children, Nelson and Judith. Caesar Hope's intentions were frustrated by the 1806 law, and Judith remained a slave. His will also made provision for Teenar, "the woman who lives with me as my wife." In turn, the later will of one Tenah Hope, dated 1828, "emancipates and sets free my daughter Judy who is also my slave." At last, more than twenty years after her father's will provided her with her first step toward emancipation, Judith Hope was free. DSG

▶ A List of Free Negroes and Mulattoes residing within the District of Richard Perkins Commissioner of the Revenue in the County of Campbell North District for the Year 1833. Manuscript. Auditor of Public Accounts, Entry 757, Reports of Free Negroes and Mulattoes, 1833–1836, Record Group 48.

In the aftermath of the Nat Turner insurrection in 1831, the General Assembly enacted several statutes with the intent to compel blacks to leave the commonwealth. One such law, passed 4 March 1833 "making appropriations for the removal of free persons of colour" to the western coast of Africa, established a board of commissioners charged with carrying out the provisions of the act. Lists, such as the one submitted by Richard Perkins in 1833, were meant to assist the commissioners in determining who might be encouraged to immigrate. Perkins's list includes the names of free African Americans within a specific section of Campbell County and identifies each individual by name, color, sex, age, and occupation.

Restrictive laws against Virginia's free blacks had been in force for more than a quarter century. On 25 January 1803, the General Assembly had passed a law "more effectually to restrain the practice of Negroes going at Large." The act required localities to register every free Negro or mulatto living within their jurisdiction. County court clerks kept books listing free blacks by name, age, color, and stature, and by distinguishing marks or scars on the face, head, or hands. Clerks also noted the court in which an individual had been emancipated, or whether the person had been born free. Unfortunately, few of these informative lists survive. Those that do contain some of the earliest-surviving registers of African American families in Virginia. DSG

A List of Free Negroes and Mulattoes residing within the District of Richard Perkins Commissioner of the Revenue in the County of Campbell North District for the Year 1833

Names of Negroes	Colour	Sex	Ages	Occupation
Ash Peter	Black	Male	30 years	Boatman
Ash James	do	do	33 "	ditto
Ash Chanty	do	Female	27 "	
Ash Mariah	do	do	31 "	
Adams Edward	do	Male	29 "	Cooper
Bobron Israel	do	do	48 "	Shoemaker
Bobron Hannah	do	Female	43 "	
Bobron Allen	do	Male	25 "	Boatman
Bobron Lyndsey	do	do	21 "	ditto
Bobron Mary	do	Female	18 "	
Bobron Lucinda	do	do	16 "	
Bobron Mariah	do	do	14 "	
Butler William	do	Male	30	Black Smith
Burns Pleasant	Mulatto	do	23	ditto
Battles James	do	do	36	Cooper
Cole Thomas	do	do	27	days labourer
Campbell Joseph	do	do	31	ditto
Christian Mourng	do	Female	60	
Christian Lucy	do	do	5	
Couison William	do	Male	30	Ditcher
Douglass Murray	do	do	40	Waggoner
Evans John	do	do	19	Cart driver
Evans Juda	do	Female	47	
Evans Albert	do	Male	16	
Evans Mary	do	Female	12	
Evans Martha	do	do	25	
Evans Lewis	do	Male	6	
Evans Littleberry	do	do	4	
Evans David	do	do	23	Painter
Frumam John	Black	Male	36	Blacksmith
No 30. Carried over				

► Virginia Ordinance of Secession, 17 April 1861. Printed form with manuscript. Convention of 1861, Record Group 93.

On 17 April 1861, and after considerable debate, a convention of Virginians meeting in Richmond voted eighty-eight to fifty-five to repeal the commonwealth's ratification of the Constitution of the United States and to secede from the Union. Only five days earlier, Confederate forces had opened fire on Fort Sumter in Charleston harbor; President Abraham Lincoln had already reacted by issuing a call for seventy-five thousand troops to suppress "combinations too powerful" to respond to ordinary measures. The final decision whether to secede, though, was not the convention's alone. In order to submit the question to a public referendum, the delegates formally adopted the ordinance as the official instrument to which Virginians could respond. On 23 May, the voters ratified the commonwealth's Ordinance of Secession.

On 14 June 1861, those members of the convention who favored secession, or who were at least willing to acquiesce in the final decision, signed the formal parchment text of the ordinance. Some members of the Virginia Convention who were not in Richmond in April 1861 later signed the Ordinance of Secession. One such man was James Vass Brooke (1824–1898), of Fauquier County, who was elected to the convention in June 1861 to fill a vacant seat. He signed the Ordinance of Secession on 26 June; his signature is near the bottom of the sixth column.

During the Civil War, a skillful lithographer produced an excellent print of the ordinance, and in 1869 and 1873 two other lithographers, working from the first print, produced yet more copies. From time to time after the 1860s, people excitedly announced that they had discovered Virginia's Ordinance of Secession. Each one was, in fact, one of the copies. The discoveries merited attention, however, because the original had long since disappeared from Virginia's archives.

In the days and weeks that followed the evacuation of Richmond on 2 April 1865, Union military and civil officials had freely roamed through the Capitol—and its state library. There, a Union soldier, Charles W. Bullis, removed the unique parchment and later carried it home. In 1887, his widow sold the Ordinance of Secession to a collector. Following the death of the collector and of his son, the collector's daughter-in-law sent the valuable document to Richmond, where it was authenticated and at last returned to the archives late in December 1929. BT

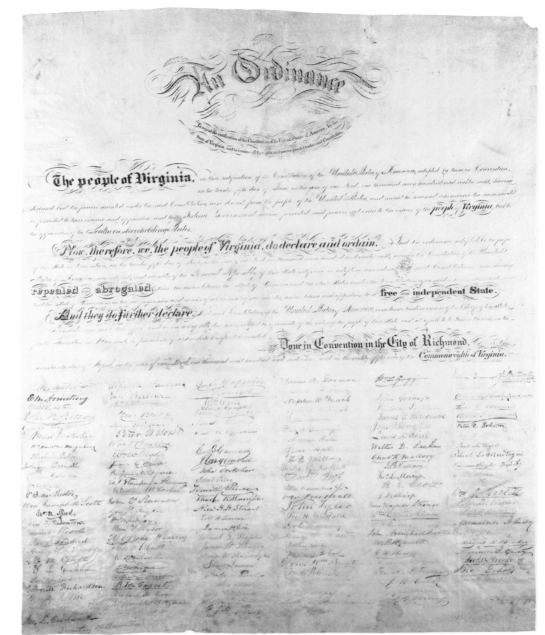

▲ Names of Electors who have cast their Ballots in 3rd. District County of Southampton State of Virginia at an election held Oct. 22nd. 1867 for and against a Convention and for a delegate to the same. Manuscript. Secretary of the Commonwealth, Election Records, 1776–1946, Record Group 13.

In a statewide election to be held on 22 October 1867 Virginia voters were to decide whether to hold a constitutional convention and, if so, who would represent them at the meeting. The United States Army, as part of its supervision of Virginia's civil government during Reconstruction, directed that the poll lists and voter returns be reported separately for black and white voters. Assembled only two and half years after the Civil War, the surviving pollbooks, ballots, and other records of the election thus document a profound redefinition of the Old Dominion's democratic process: the first mass political participation of African Americans in Virginia politics. The election documents are part of the Library of Virginia's extensive archival collection of original election records and returns from the eighteenth through the twentieth centuries.

Most of the African American voters—and many of the candidates—were former slaves and for them the election was especially significant. The divisive impact of the outcome of the war is particularly evident in the results of the elections in Southampton County. Almost 98 percent of the eligible African American men eagerly seized their first opportunity to vote. In contrast, because of widespread opposition among white citizens to the proposal to hold a convention and to the participation of blacks in the political process, only about 56 percent of the eligible white males voted. Southampton County's voters approved the referendum by a vote of 1,262 (with 1,242 black voters and 20 white voters) to 612 (all white).

John Brown, a former slave, was a candidate for convention delegate on "the regular Union Republican Ticket." Many of the ballots cast for him are filed with the pollbooks; they record his political identification and preserve the only evidence of his campaign slogan: "Thou shalt love thy neighbor as thyself." Brown received every black vote cast plus a vote from one white man. Two white candidates split the small number of remaining votes. John Brown represented Southampton County in the Virginia constitutional convention of 1867–1868. BT

▶ Robert E. Lee Camp Confederate Soldiers' Home (1884–1941), Richmond. Application for admission, 1915. Printed form with manuscript notations. Acc. 24736, Record Group 52.

N. Johnson Agnew, of Floyd County, submitted his application for admission to the Robert E. Lee Camp Confederate Soldiers' Home, in January 1915. The Richmond institution's records include thousands of such applications, a detailed source of information on the families, military service, physical description and health, even the financial status of numerous Confederate veterans in Virginia. The collection also includes registers of residents, applications for leaves of absence and discharges, and the minutes of the home's board of visitors. The materials, totaling more than twenty-two linear feet and nine volumes, were presented to the Library by the Virginia Division, United Daughters of the Confederacy, in March 1958.

Concerned with the plight of so many "invalid and infirm" former comrades, a group of Confederate veterans had met in Richmond on 18 April 1883 to form the Robert E. Lee Camp as a benevolent society "minister[ing] . . . to the wants" of disabled and indigent veterans who had fought with Virginia units during the Civil War. The organization was incorporated on 13 March 1884 and opened its soldiers' home on 1 January 1885 at a site in western Richmond. Despite significant donations, the veterans' residence was in financial distress from its formation. On 12 February 1886, the General Assembly passed an act authorizing a small annual appropriation and appointed several state officers as ex officio members of the institution's board of visitors. Even with a membership that by the 1890s included such prominent and well-to-do Richmonders as tobacconist Lewis Ginter and bank president James B. Pace, the Robert E. Lee Camp found that fund-raising for its principal program remained modest. It became increasingly difficult to maintain such a large number of sick, disabled, and elderly veterans in adequate fashion. A sympathetic legislature agreed to increase its annual appropriation substantially by an act passed on 3 March 1892. In return, the Robert E. Lee Camp deeded its property to the state. The home remained open until the last resident died in 1941. Now on the grounds of the Virginia Museum of Fine Arts, a wood-frame chapel and a mansard-roof building are all that remain of the once extensive complex of buildings. DSG

APPLICATION FOR ADMISSION
TO THE
Soldiers' Home of R. E. Lee Camp, No. 1
Confederate Veterans
AT
RICHMOND, VIRGINIA

BRANCH B. MORGAN, President

BOARD OF VISITORS
WM. F. RHEA, 1st Vice-President

G. K. ROPER,   JOHN LAMB,   JULIEN H. HILL, Secretary-Treas.

W. S. ARCHER,   P. J. WHITE,   JOHN W. GORE,   W. B. FREE...

---

rules and regulations made by the proper authorities of the Home for its government and that I will perform all duties required of me, and obey all lawful orders of the officers of the said Home; **and I sign this application with the full knowledge that any violation of the rules will subject me to punishment or dismissal, at the discretion of the Board of Visitors.**

assessed Value of my Property is $650

Witness the following signature this *19th* day of *January* A. D., 1915

(Applicant sign here) *N Johnson Agnew*

(Post-Office) *Floyd, Va*

STATE OF *Virginia*

County of *Floyd*

This day personally appeared before me, *J E Burwell*, a Notary Public in and for the County and State aforesaid, *N Johnson Agnew*, whose name is signed to the foregoing application, and made oath that the statements therein contained are true.

Given under my hand this *19th* day of *January* 1915

J E Burwell, N.P. ———— N. P.

CERTIFICATE OF WITNESSES

We, *B Bishop* and *G M Whitlow*, certify that we know the above applicant *N Johnson Agnew*; that he was during the war enlisted and served honorably in the same regiment with us—namely, in the *Company G 21st Va Cavalry*, and that we believe the statements contained in his above application to be true.

B Bishop
G M Whitlow

CERTIFICATE OF JUDGE

STATE OF *Virginia*

County of *Floyd*

This is to certify that I have examined into the statements contained in the foregoing application of *N Johnson Agnew*, and that I am satisfied from the evidence adduced before me that the said *N Johnson Agnew* served honorably during the late war in the Confederate army or navy; that he was loyal to the government of the Confederate States to the end of the war; that he has borne a good character ever since, and that his present condition is such as to render him unable to provide for himself unaided.

Given under my hand as Judge of *Circuit Court of Floyd County*

W W Moffett Judge.

I, *M. L. Dalton* certify that the applicant *N. J. Agnew* is of sound mind, and not an habitual drunkard, nor has he ever been an inmate of an insane asylum.

M. L. Dalton

Medical Doctor

No veteran will be admitted to the Home, who has Five Hundred Dollars or an estate of that amount.

INSANE PERSONS, HABITUAL DRUNKARDS, PERSONS SUFFERING WITH CANCEROUS AFFECTION OR CONTAGIOUS DISEASE WILL NOT BE ADMITTED UNDER ANY CIRCUMSTANCES.

ORDER OF ADMISSION

The above application having been approved by the Board of Visitors, the said applicant is admitted to the Soldiers' Home.

———————————————
President Board of Visitors of Home.

Have you drawn a Pension in the last twelve months? *yes*

At what time? *Sept 1st 1914*

Give amount *$28 80*

☞ Applicants will remain at their homes till notified that they will be admitted.

▶ Colgate Whitehead Darden Jr. (1897–1981). Virginia War History Commission, Military Service Record, 29 June 1921. Printed form with manuscript notations. Virginia War History Commission Collection, Record Group 66.

Like thousands of other Virginia veterans of the Great War, former second lieutenant Colgate Whitehead Darden Jr., United States Marine Corps Reserve Flying Corps, took time early in the summer of 1921 to complete a four-page questionnaire for the Virginia War History Commission. Darden, a native of Southampton County, submitted his report to be filed "as a permanent record in the State Library . . . of the deeds of Virginia soldiers and sailors in the service of federal, state, and allied governments during American participation in the World War." And, as requested, he also enclosed a photograph, taken in uniform on 4 July 1918.

Governor Westmoreland Davis had created the Virginia War History Commission on 7 January 1919, with the General Assembly appropriating funds for its work on 10 September. Veterans were asked to provide considerable pre-war biographical detail, even the college fraternity to which they belonged. Most of the more than four dozen questions, however, elicited details about each person's wartime experiences. On the final page, for example, six questions probed the veterans' emotional state as they emerged from the war's horrors.

Darden said little about that. He did, though, outline his considerable service. He began the war as a member of the American Volunteer Motor Ambulance Corps, serving with the French at Verdun in 1916, for which he received the Croix de Guerre for his actions under fire. By the autumn of 1917 he was in the U.S. Navy, first in Boston, then as an aviation cadet in Miami and Pensacola, Florida. Transferred to the Marine Corps, Darden arrived in France in August 1918. That October he was severely injured in an "aeroplane accident." After eight months in military hospitals, Darden received his discharge in Washington, D.C., on 6 August 1919.

The War History Commission ceased operations on 1 July 1928, after which the State Library received its voluminous records. The commission's papers include records of most Virginians who served in the war as well as detailed reports on community efforts on behalf of the Red Cross and other volunteer agencies, fund-raising drives, and other local war-related work.

As for Colgate Whitehead Darden, he returned to the University of Virginia and then earned master's and law degrees from Columbia University. In addition, he studied international law at Oxford University in 1923 and 1924. Darden was a member of the Virginia House of Delegates from 1930 to 1933. Thereafter, he served three terms in the U.S. House of Representatives between 1933 and 1941, one term as governor of Virginia from 1942 to 1946, and twelve years as president of the University of Virginia from 1947 to 1959.

While Darden was governor, the General Assembly created the Virginia World War II History Commission to preserve the records and commemorate the participation of Virginians in the Second World War. Its records, too, are part of the Library of Virginia's archival collections. The staff of the World War II History Commission joined the Virginia State Library in 1948, forming the nucleus of a new History Division. BT

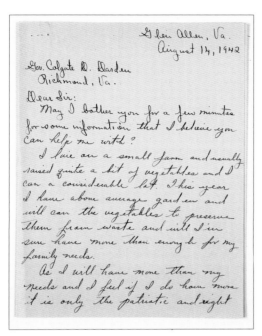

▲ Mrs. M. A. Thomas, Glen Allen, Virginia, to Governor Colgate Darden, Richmond, Virginia, 14 August 1942. Executive Papers of Colgate Whitehead Darden Jr., Box 59, Folder: State and Regional Defense, Office of Civilian Defense Suggestions, Record Group 3.

In the summer of 1942, in only the ninth month of U.S. participation in World War II, Naomi Lovelace Thomas from her Glen Allen home several miles north of Richmond sent a brief letter to Virginia governor Colgate Darden. With two sons already in the army, she was particularly eager to help in whatever way she could. Thus, with an "above average" vegetable crop, she graciously offered to continue "canning as much as possible" for the war effort—that is, if "the Army will accept" her donations of canned goods. Filed with Mrs. Thomas's letter is a carbon copy of Governor Darden's reply, informing her that he would inquire whether the armed services would indeed accept privately canned foods. Spurred on by their wartime patriotism, Virginians such as Mrs. Thomas while unable to supply the armed services directly with food did manage to do so indirectly. The state's various rationing boards and other agencies increasingly encouraged citizens to plant "victory gardens"— what each family grew for itself left more commercial crops for use by the military. In central Virginia, for example, the Victory Crop Corps proved particularly popular, especially after canned goods were added to the list of rationed foodstuffs only several months after Mrs. Thomas's letter. BT

▼ Charles H. Nichols Jr., Hampton, Virginia, 28 January 1959; Catherine M. Briggs, Vienna, Virginia, 29 January 1959; Mrs. James Edwin Bear, Richmond, Virginia, 12 February 1959; to Governor J. Lindsay Almond Jr. Executive Papers of Governor James Lindsay Almond Jr., Box 136, Acc. 26230, Record Group 3.

Few issues in modern Virginia history aroused such intense emotions as did the Civil Rights movement. Particularly dramatic was the question of court-ordered school desegregation during the 1950s, to which many of the state's political leaders responded by adopting a policy of Massive Resistance. As the state's attorney general, for example, J. Lindsay Almond Jr. in 1952 had in open court declared segregation to be "morally and legally defensible." And as governor, Almond in September 1958 closed nine public schools rather than comply with federal orders. But in a January 1959 special session of the General Assembly he signaled a significant change of heart. "The time has arrived," he admitted, "to take a new, thorough, and long look at the situation which confronts us." To many observers, it represented a sudden and dramatic break with his old friends and political allies: keeping the public school system open and functioning was more important than attempting to block desegregation. Among the many letters of support that Almond received were those from Charles H. Nichols Jr., professor of English at Hampton Institute; Catherine M. Briggs, the "Mother of five young Virginians," of Vienna, Virginia; and Margaret W. Bear, wife of a professor at Union Theological Seminary in Richmond.

These and many hundreds of other letters expressing differing views on school desegregation and the Civil Rights movement are part of the executive papers of Governor Almond. The Library of Virginia's archival collections contain official papers of all of Virginia's governors since Patrick Henry, from 1776 to the present. In addition, the Library's collections include other materials relating to the Massive Resistance period, such as the records of the Pupil Placement Board, the Commission on Constitutional Government, and the Department of Education. BT

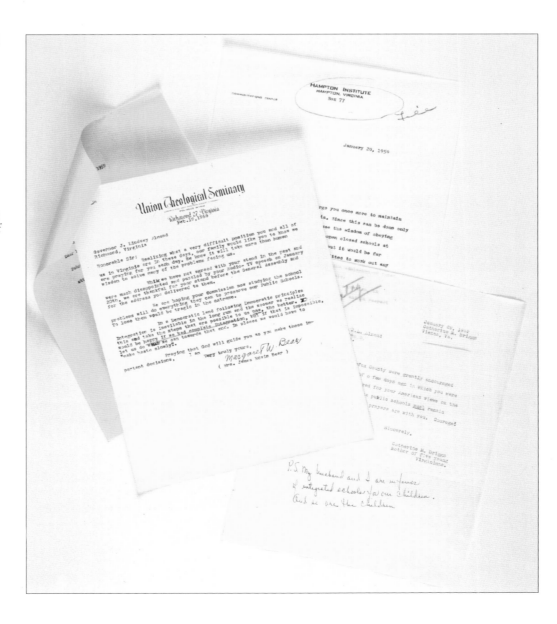

greſs, together with the Preſident, ſhould, without delay, proceed to execute this Conſtitution.

By the unanimous Order of the Convention,

GEORGE WASHINGTON, Preſident.

William Jackſon, Secretary.

In Convention, September 17, 1787.

SIR,

WE have now the honor to ſubmit to the conſideration of the United States in Congreſs aſſembled, that conſtitution which has appeared to us the moſt adviſeable.

The friends of our country have long ſeen and deſired, that the power of making war, peace and treaties, that of levying money and regulating commerce, and the correſpondent executive and judicial authorities ſhould be fully and effectually veſted in the general government of the union: but the impropriety of delegating ſuch extenſive truſt to one body of men is evident—Hence reſults the neceſſity of a different organization.

It is obviouſly impracticable in the fœderal government of the ſtates, to ſecure all rights of independent ſovereignty to each, and yet provide for the intereſt and ſafety of all—Individuals entering into ſociety, muſt give up a ſhare of liberty to preſerve the reſt. The magnitude of the ſacrifice muſt depend as well on ſituation and circumſtance, as on the object to be obtained. It is at all times difficult to draw with preciſion the line between thoſe rights which muſt be ſurrendered, and thoſe which may be reſerved; and on the preſent occaſion this difficulty was encreaſed by a difference among the ſeveral ſtates as to their ſituation, extent, habits, and particular intereſt.

In all our deliberations on this ſubject we kept ſteadily in our view, that which appears to us the greateſt intereſt of every true American, the conſolidation of our union, in which is involved our proſperity, felicity, ſafety, perhaps our national exiſtence. This important conſideration, ſeriouſly and *deeply*

deeply impreſſed on our minds, led each ſtate in the convention to be leſs rigid on points of inferior magnitude, than might have been otherwiſe expected; and thus the conſtitution, which we now preſent, is the reſult of a ſpirit of amity, and of that mutual deference and conceſſion which the peculiarity of our political ſituation rendered indiſpenſible.

That it will meet the full and entire approbation of every ſtate is not perhaps to be expected; but each will doubtleſs conſider, that had her intereſts been alone conſulted, the conſequences might have been particularly diſagreeable or injurious to others; that it is liable to as few exceptions as could reaſonbly have been expected, we hope and believe; that it may promote the laſting welfare of that country ſo dear to us all, and ſecure her freedom and happineſs, is our moſt ardent wiſh.

With great reſpect,

We have the honor to be, SIR,

Your EXCELLENCY's moſt

Obedient and humble Servants,

George Waſhington, Preſident.

By unanimous Order of the CONVENTION.

HIS EXCELLENCY

The Preſident of Congreſs.

RICHMOND: Printed by AUGUSTINE DAVIS.

In Convention, Sept

S I R,

WE have now the honor to submi
States in Congrefs affembled, to
to us the moft advifeable.

THE PUBLICATIONS OF THE UNITED STATES GOVERNMENT

The Library of Virginia has been an officially designated recipient of United States government publications since the establishment of the federal depository-library program in the late nineteenth century. Between the 1890s and 1950 the State Library received at least one copy of every publication issued by the national government. Since then, the Library of Virginia has received nearly 50 percent of the many thousands of federal titles issued each year—from the proceedings of Congress to the reports of the Department of Agriculture, from the records of the Weather Bureau to copies of treaties and patent office reports, and from the debates of post–World War I disarmament conferences to U.S. Navy medical bulletins.

Virginia's first efforts, however, to collect and preserve an official printed record of the nation—its legislative deliberations, scientific expeditions, diplomatic and military endeavors, economic and social programs, and even its aesthetic and intellectual yearnings—began far earlier than the 1890s. Almost as soon as a central government under the newly ratified U.S. Constitution began to function in the spring of 1789, agents of the commonwealth of Virginia set about collecting official—and, when necessary, even unofficial, privately printed—copies of U.S. government documents. Soon thereafter, too, the General Assembly and the office of the governor instituted an exchange program by which the Old Dominion offered copies of Virginia's legislative journals, acts of assembly, and published court reports in return for similar materials from the federal government as well as from various other states. The exchange program enabled the government of Virginia to acquire an extraordinarily large number of invaluable published materials, often without having to appropriate any funds to do so.

The extensive range of government publications in the collections of the Library of Virginia provides significant evidence of the expanding role the federal government played in American life throughout the nineteenth and twentieth centuries. There are, for example, detailed surveys of the Mississippi River rapids completed by a young lieutenant of engineers, R. E. Lee, in 1838 as well as War Department seniority lists for the 1850s, proceedings for the Pan-American Scientific Conference in 1915–1916, and annual reports of the Smithsonian Institution beginning in the 1840s. The variety of titles also demonstrates that from the very earliest days Virginia participated in a nationwide program to disseminate and preserve useful publications of official documents.

◄ *The Federal Constitution for the United States of America. &c.* Richmond: Printed by Augustine Davis, 1787.

Before the establishment of the Government Printing Office in 1860, the federal government often relied on the public spirit, and entrepreneurial drive, of individual local printers to disseminate significant documents. On Wednesday, 26 September 1787, for example, Richmond postmaster and printer Augustine Davis (ca. 1755–1825) hurriedly inserted a small but momentous item in his newspaper, the *Virginia Independent Chronicle*, informing his readers that he had learned "from good Authority, that the FEDERAL CONSTITUTION was unanimously passed on the 17th Instant, when the Hon. Convention of the United States closed their deliberations." In fact, the passage was not unanimous. Two Virginians, George Mason and Governor Edmund Randolph, were among the several delegates who had refused to sign the document. The document, though, had been approved by an overwhelming majority of the delegates and was to be presented to the states for ratification.

Seeing an opportunity, Davis informed his readers that because the text of the Constitution "was received too late to be published in this day's Chronicle, it will be printed in a pamphlet, and handed to them on Thursday." Rather than include the document in the next week's issue of his paper, Davis announced on 3 October that he had indeed, as promised, "Just Published" the text of the Constitution in a small, eleven-page pamphlet, which was for sale at his post office for one shilling per copy. The pamphlet also included the text of a resolution of the convention suggesting procedures for how the Constitution should be put into operation and the text of the formal letter by which George Washington, president of the convention, forwarded the document to the United States Congress. The Library of Virginia owns the only known copy of Augustine Davis's pamphlet edition of the new Constitution. BT

▼ *Journal of the House of Representatives of the United States: Anno M,DCC,LXXXIX, and of the Independence of the United States the Thirteenth.* New-York: Printed by Francis Childs and John Swaine, 1789.

The Library of Virginia's copy of the earliest printed edition of the *Journal of the House of Representatives of the United States* documents the inaugural meeting of the First Congress under the authority of the Constitution of the United States. The 164-page volume includes the autograph signature of Charles Hay (1764–1795), of Richmond, who was elected clerk of the Virginia House of Delegates in 1789. Beginning sometime in the 1790s, Congress and the states initiated a program of providing one another printed copies of the journals and laws from their respective legislative sessions. Hay may well have received Virginia's copy of the *Journal of the House of Representatives* under the exchange program.

Virginians played prominent roles in the First Congress, which opened in New York in March 1789. James Madison, of Orange County, was widely regarded as the most influential member of the House of Representatives. Another Virginian, John James Beckley, a former mayor of Richmond and Hay's predecessor as clerk of the House of Delegates, won election as clerk of the House. In the Senate were William Grayson, of Prince William County, and Richard Henry Lee, of Westmoreland County; Lee had been a signer of the Declaration of Independence in 1776 and served as president of the Congress in 1784 under the Articles of Confederation. Foremost among the Virginians, however, was George Washington, of Fairfax County, sworn in as the first president of the United States several weeks after the opening session of the First Congress. BT

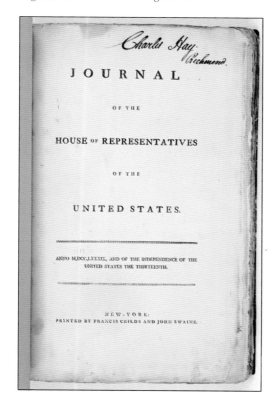

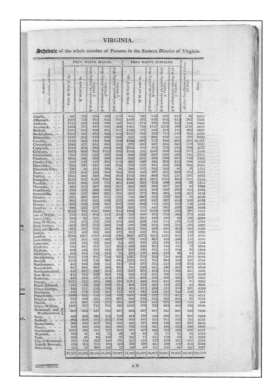

▲ *Return of the Whole Number of Persons Within the Several Districts of the United States, According to "An Act Providing for the Second Census of Enumeration of the Inhabitants of the United States."* Washington, D.C., 1801.

In accordance with a provision of the newly ratified Constitution, the First Congress passed a census act that was signed by President George Washington on 1 March 1790. Printed eleven years later by order of the House of Representatives, the first *Return of the Whole Number of Persons*, enumerating the young nation's population, was sent to each state, probably to the attention of the governor.

The 1790 census was much less detailed than later ones. It listed the names of heads of households, and within the household the number of free white males in categories for those both above and below sixteen years of age, an aggregate count of free white females (without specify-

ing their ages), and the number of all other free persons (such as free African Americans) and slaves. To many observers, the detail provided a useful gauge of the country's military and industrial capacity. Others were not so sure. In a mid-February 1790 letter to Thomas Jefferson, James Madison wrote that a bill to take a census—containing "a schedule for ascertaining the component classes of the Society, a kind of information extremely requisite to the Legislator, and much wanted for the science of Political Economy"—had passed the House of Representatives. Madison had to report, however, that the bill "was thrown out by the Senate as" simply "a waste of trouble"—merely a collection of "materials for idle people to make a book." The bill finally passed at the end of the month.

In order to compile the statistics, marshals from each judicial district appointed assistants. As they progressed through various communities, the assistants made two copies of their work, one posted in the immediate neighborhood, and the other sent to the federal government. The local assistants recorded the returns on all manner of paper, from sheets only three inches wide to some three feet long, and with odd covers, including wallpaper. Listing 3,929,214 people, with Virginia by far the most populous state, the first census cost $44,377 to complete. Although the census of 1800 was more detailed, it was not until the seventh census in 1850 that the report gave the name of every person in each household.

During the War of 1812 the federal government's copies of Virginia's manuscript census returns for 1790 and 1800 were destroyed when the British attacked Washington, D.C. While Virginia's copies likewise do not survive—except the 1800 returns for Accomack County—fortunately the commonwealth had conducted its own enumerations in 1782, 1783, 1784, and 1785. In the early 1900s, Virginia's Library Board obtained permission from the General Assembly to lend the Bureau of the Census the four eighteenth-century "lists for the purpose of making copies and publishing the names" as a substitute for the long-lost census records. The result, duly printed in 1908, remains a valuable research resource. DSG

◄ *United States Exploring Expedition. During the Year 1838, 1839, 1840, 1841, 1842. Under the Command of Charles Wilkes, U.S.N. . . .* Atlas to Volume 7. Philadelphia: Printed by C. Sherman, 1849.

The United States Exploring Expedition of 1838–1842 was the largest—and most successful—scientific enterprise undertaken by the federal government to that time. Under the command of Lieutenant Charles Wilkes, of the United States Navy, the explorers mapped portions of the South Atlantic Ocean, the Pacific Northwest, and Polynesia, even the Antarctic Ocean, becoming the first Americans to venture into the polar region. The expedition's members collected thousands of geological, botanical, and zoological specimens and made the largest contribution to scientific knowledge of any American enterprise to that date. Moreover, the specimens that the explorers brought back to the United States became the nucleus of the collections of the then-new Smithsonian Institution.

Congress ordered that the explorers and a team of scientists publish the findings in a limited edition of one hundred copies. Originally planned as a twenty-four-volume work, four of the volumes were never printed and a fifth never officially distributed; a fire at the printing house destroyed a portion of the press run of several of the other volumes. Per the instructions of Congress, Virginia received a nineteen-volume-set of the extremely rare, and magnificent, compilation, now part of the Library of Virginia's collections.

Volume seven of the set, James D. Dana's 1846 work on zoophytes, was one of the first books of the edition to be printed. The engraving of sea anemones is from the atlas issued in 1849 to accompany Dana's volume. Dana's work completely revolutionized scientific understanding of zoophytes—invertebrate animals such as sea anemones, coral, and sponges. Later one of the greatest of all nineteenth-century American scientists, Dana also prepared the volume on geology and the two volumes on crustacea. Of the 680 species of crustacea that the expedition collected, fully 500 were of species previously unknown to science. BT

▶ John Charles Frémont (1813–1890). *Report of
the Exploring Expedition to the Rocky Mountains in
the Year 1842, and to Oregon and North California
in the Years 1843–'44.* Published as Senate
Executive Document No. 174, Twenty-Eighth
Congress, Second Session. Washington, D.C.:
Gales and Seaton, 1845.

In 1842–1844, a twenty-nine-year-old topographical engineer, John C. Frémont, led a trail-
blazing expedition from the Missouri River to
the Rocky Mountains and beyond. Nicknamed
"the pathfinder," Captain Frémont became a
national hero for his exploration of the Oregon
Trail and the Pacific Northwest, meticulously
recounted in his official *Report of the Exploring
Expedition.* Included in his description of the
expedition along the Snake River at the end of
September 1843 is an illustration of Shoshone
Falls in what is now Twin Falls County, Idaho.
One of many works on the westward movement
acquired by the State Library during the nineteenth century, Frémont's *Report* bears an inscription on the original wrapper reading "For Mr
Lyons from Danl Webster," which was pasted into
the volume. The book's recipient was probably
Richmond lawyer James Lyons, a Whig Party veteran of the Senate and House of Delegates who
entertained Massachusetts's Senator Daniel
Webster on his visit to Richmond in 1847.

A confident and ambitious army officer of
considerable charm, Frémont found his military
career no doubt further enhanced by his marriage
to Jessie Benton, the daughter of U.S. Senator
Thomas Hart Benton, of Missouri. Frémont's
father-in-law helped him to obtain choice
appointments on several missions to explore the
West, while Frémont's brilliant wife much
improved the literary style of his published journals. Frémont's exploits in California later in
the decade paved the way for a wave of new
immigrants after the discovery of gold there in
1848. In 1856 Frémont was the first presidential
nominee of the new Republican Party; five years
later, President Abraham Lincoln—at the insis-
tence of the officer's many friends—appointed
Frémont to the rank of major general. Frémont
had reached too far. The appointment was a disaster. After his defeat by Thomas J. Jackson in
the famous Valley Campaign of 1862, Frémont
asked to be relieved of duty. In 1864, he led a
half-hearted attempt to form a third political
party and during 1878–1883 recouped his reputation somewhat by serving as territorial governor
of Arizona. Although Frémont continued to
write about his exploits as an explorer, in his last
years it was his wife's income as a writer that sustained the family. BT

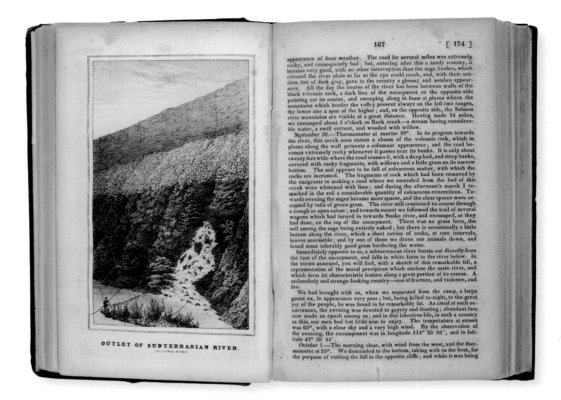

OUTLET OF SUBTERRANIAN RIVER.

▶ Matthew Fontaine Maury (1806–1873).
*Explanations and Sailing Directions to Accompany
the Wind and Current Charts. . . .* Washington,
D.C.: William A. Harris, Printer, 1858.

The vibrant color plate of four crustaceans is
from the eighth, and final, edition of Matthew
Fontaine Maury's *Explanations and Sailing Directions
to Accompany the Wind and Current Charts.* First
published in 1851, the updated two-volume edition of 1858 provided a greatly enlarged text.
Maury's widow, Ann Hull Herndon Maury, presented the volumes to the Virginia exhibit at the
World's Columbian Exposition in Chicago on 20
May 1892. The set is inscribed by the donor,
"Mrs. Comr M. F. Maury." The Library of Virginia's
collections also include a copy of the fourth edition, published in 1852.

Born near Fredericksburg, Virginia, and reared
and educated near Franklin, Tennessee, Maury
joined the United States Navy in 1825 as a mid-
shipman. For nine years he served on three
extended cruises, including one around the world,
and in 1842 was appointed superintendent of the
navy's Depot of Charts and Instruments, a post
that included the superintendency of the new
Naval Observatory. Maury, though, was far more
interested in the hydrographic and meteorological
aspects of his duties and soon embarked on extensive research on winds and currents. He predicted

that, using his own carefully devised charts and
sailing directions, it would be possible for mariners
to save between ten and fifteen days in the passage between New York and Rio de Janeiro.
After his predictions proved accurate, ships' captains began assisting his work by reporting the
wind and current patterns they encountered on
their voyages.

The cooperative oceanographic observations
proved invaluable, so much so that an international congress held in Brussels in 1853 adopted
Maury's uniform system whereby the world's naval
and merchant-marine vessels would record
oceanographic data. The resulting information
enabled Maury to revise his charts of winds and
currents for both the Atlantic and Pacific Oceans.
The revisions significantly shortened the duration
of voyages and, in turn, the amount of money
required to fund each one. In 1855, Maury also
published a textbook of modern oceanography—
establishing the study of the sea as a distinct
branch of science.

After service in the Confederate navy, Matthew
Fontaine Maury in 1868 accepted the professor-
ship of meteorology at the Virginia Military
Institute in Lexington. There he undertook a survey of the state in which he stressed the importance of establishing a system of meteorological
observations, transmitted by telegraph, as a means
of aiding farmers across the Old Dominion. DSG

Plate XXII

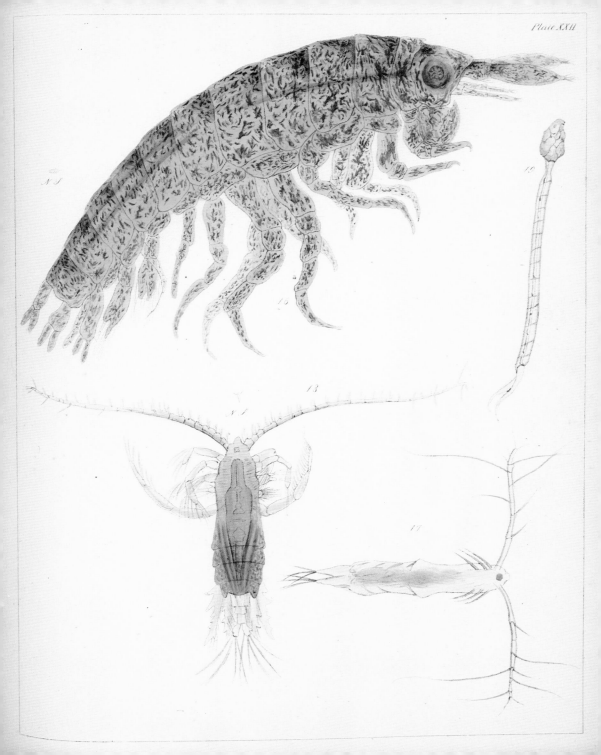

John Chartier Jerson one of the most eminent
theologians of his time was born in 1363
at Jerson a village in Champagne near
Retel. He was educated at the College
Navarre in Paris & afterwards was
Chancellor & Canon of the Church of Paris.
He died in 1429.
He wrote a great many works, which
have been justly valued & frequently
printed. The best edition of them was
printed at Antwerp in 1706 in 5 folio
vols —

Incipit Tractatus venerabilis doctoris magistri
Johannis Jarson Cancellarii parisiensis De o-
ratione et suo valore, continuatione et
intensione sub pluribus considerationibus.
Incipit prima pars et manuductio in ipsas
considerationes, ostendens que pertinere
ad monachi vocationem et professionem
ordinum insistere, in qua qualis esse debe-
at ipsum construit.

Oportet semper orare, et non
deficere. Scripsit tullius ac-
curatissime commentarium
fratri suo de petitione consulatus, suadens ut in om-
ni loco sedens et ambulans recogitet
secum assidue quis es tu qui petis, et a
quibus petis. Subiit animo tibi scribere
germane carissime de petitione non for-
ensis consulatus, sed celestis incolatus.
Ad hoc enim professionem tuam vocationem
tuam sacerdotium tuum dedicata esse memi-
neris, apponas igitur in omni meditatione tua
in omni operatione tua, loco et tempore, quis et
qualis es qui oras. quem vel quas oras.
quid vel per quos oras. Certum quodlibet hor-

BOOK ARTS

Among the approximately eight hundred thousand volumes in the collections of the Library of Virginia are many extraordinarily fine examples of the printer's and engraver's arts. The Library is particularly fortunate, for example, to have four *incunabula*—books printed before 1501 when the art of printing was still in its infancy. Among the oldest of these is the first Italian-language publication of Pliny the Elder's *Historia Naturale*, printed in Venice in 1476. The Library's collection also includes a mammoth first edition of Hartmann Schedel's *Liber Chronicarum*, published in Nuremberg in 1493 and popularly known as the *Nuremberg Chronicle*, the first printed history of the world. Within only days of its publication, the volume was quickly outdated by the arrival of startling news—Christopher Columbus had returned from a successful voyage of discovery to a new world.

Among the Library's most unusual volumes are several books embellished with elaborate fore-edge paintings, such as a 1796 edition of the *Book of Common Prayer* and an 1857 copy of the *Annotated Paragraph Bible*. On the edges of each volume's pages, artists painted small, yet detailed illustrations viewed best when the books are partly opened and the pages slightly fanned. The Library also has an excellent collection of miniature books, some relating to Virginia subjects, such as a number of diminutively sized, yet remarkably complete biographies of Civil War generals. The rare book collection, in addition, includes especially fine examples of the bookbinder's art, as well as numerous volumes enhanced with early woodcuts, engravings, and lithographs. Together, the thousands of rare and unusual volumes reflect the range of literary, historical, philosophical, and aesthetic subjects long pursued by Virginia collectors, writers, printers, and educators.

◀ Jean Gerson (1363–1429). *De Oratione et Valore Eius: De Arte Audiendi Confessiones; De Remediis Contra Recidivium Peccandi*. England, fifteenth century. Manuscript, in Gothic script, on vellum.

For centuries before the invention of printing, books were the work of individual copiers, or scribes, who produced or duplicated texts in meticulous manuscript. Usually members of religious orders, they were especially intent on ensuring that important ecclesiastical and other works reflective of their particular faith or perspective survived for the ages.

De Oratione et Valore Eius, for example, provided an explication for the hearing of confessions and the remission of recurring sins, complete with marginal notations. The red-colored initials and headings characteristic of such volumes are known as "rubrication" and were much favored as a stylistic device of the time. The volume's parchment pages are made of vellum, or animal skin that was soaked in lime and dried under tension, as is the book's later nineteenth-century binding. Although a handwritten note in the book states that the "Ms. was wrote about A.D. 1360," the declaration is undoubtedly a misreading of an earlier owner's shelf-location mark on the volume's spine: "No. 1360." HG

▶ Saint Bonaventura (1221–1274). *Opuscula*.
Cologne: Printed by Bartholomaeus de Unkel, 28
June 1484.

Johannes Nider (ca. 1380–1438). *Formicarius*.
Probably Cologne, ca. 1470.

Bound together as a single volume, the two
texts are examples of *incunabula*, books produced
in the earliest decades after the invention of the
printing press in 1447. Several traditions long
associated with manuscript volumes nevertheless
survived: both texts, for example, are highlighted
by the red lettering, known as rubrication, of initial letters and headings. Thus each decorated
page, after printing, was embellished by hand,
either with a brush or pen.

The first of the two volumes is a collection of
the *opuscula*, or minor works, of Saint Bonaventura.
A Franciscan and one of the greatest intellects of
the medieval church, Bonaventura studied in
Paris and authored numerous theological texts,
biblical commentaries, a life of Saint Francis of
Assisi, and nearly five hundred sermons. The
second volume, a book of instruction, is by
Johannes Nider. Born in Swabia, Nider was a
member of the Dominican Order, studied in
Vienna and Cologne, and was, like Bonaventura,
a noted theologian as well as a teacher.

Much of the dual volume's original binding
remains intact. The covers are fashioned of oak
or beech boards, with the book block sewn onto
leather bands, then covered with stamp-decorated
leather. Protruding metal "bosses" allow a reader
to slide the book easily on wooden bookshelves
and tables without marring the leather cover.
The remnants of metal clasps, used to hold the
book closed when not in use, are still present.
So, too, are the remains of a chain attachment:
because of their scarcity and value, books of this
period were often securely affixed to a library
bookcase or table. On one cover is a metal-framed
label, under a window made of cow horn shaved
thinly enough to be transparent.

Two notations inside the volume—"15 March
1877" and "Source unknown"—provide little
information as to how the Library of Virginia
received the joined texts. There are only ten
other copies of *Opuscula*, and no other copies of
this edition of *Formicarius*, known to exist in the
United States. HG

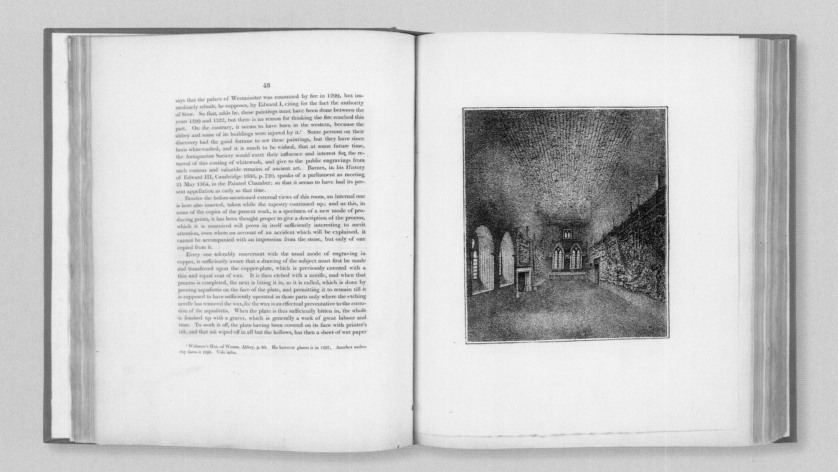

▲ John Thomas Smith (1766–1833). *Antiquities of Westminster; The Old Palace; St. Stephen's Chapel (Now the House of Commons)*. London: Printed by T. Bensley for J. T. Smith, 1807.

The celebrated early-nineteenth-century volume is unique in the history of printing: it is the first book to be illustrated with a lithograph. Employing a method perfected in Germany by Aloys Senefelder in the late 1790s, the earliest lithographers drew pictures on the polished surface of extremely fine-grained Bavarian limestone with a grease crayon. They then employed an alternating process of oil-based ink and water—relying on the principle that oil (or grease) and water do not mix—to confine the details of the image. The lithographer was then able to print the image on paper, one copy at a time. It is difficult to overstate lithography's importance

as an illustration process: besides being a still-significant artistic medium, it was the precursor of many modern printing methods.

In 1807, however, the process of lithography remained a difficult one. John Thomas Smith explained in a note to his study of Westminster that he had intended to include a particular view of the celebrated Painted Chamber. The printer's workmen, however, were unfortunately careless and after one day's labor had neglected to clean the lithograph print-stone; the ink dried and crusted and the stone broke when handled the next day. With only some three hundred of the lithographs completed, the printer had little choice except to bind most of the volumes without the interior view Smith had intended. The Library's copy of *Antiquities of Westminster* includes the rare image. HG

𝕬 𝕭 𝕮 𝕯 𝕰 𝕱 𝕲 𝕳

A B C D E F G H

𝕵 𝕶 𝕷 𝕸 𝕹 𝕺 𝕻 𝕼

I K L M N O P Q

𝕽 𝕾 𝕿 𝖀 𝖁 𝖂 𝖃 𝖄 𝖅.

R S T U V W X Y Z.

———

Lern' den Buchstab' erst recht kennen,
Daß du kannst ein'n jeden nennen;
Alsdann fleißig buchstabier,
So fällt's Lesen dir nicht schwer.

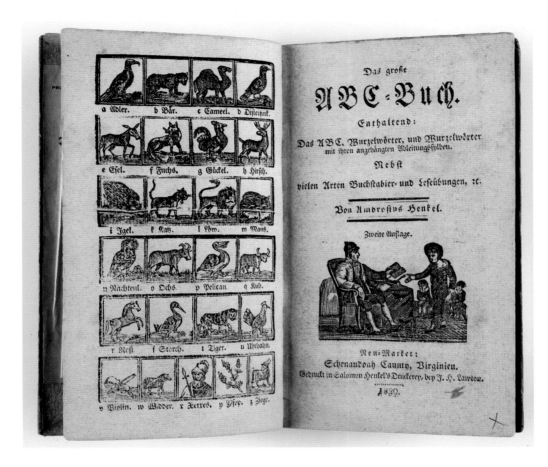

◀ Ambrose Henkel (1786–1870). *Das grosse A B C-Buch.* New Market, Va.: Henkel Press, 1820.

▼ Ambrose Henkel (1786–1870). *A B C-und Bilder-Buch.* New Market, Va.: Henkel Press, 1817.

During the eighteenth century, German settlers followed the primitive roads from Pennsylvania and western Maryland into the Valley of Virginia, founding and populating a thriving German-American community of farms and villages that eventually stretched through the rich Virginia farmland into western North Carolina and eastern Tennessee. Among the earliest German-language printers to serve the many scattered settlements was Matthias Bartgis (1759–1825), who worked in Lancaster, Pennsylvania, and Hagerstown, Maryland, and, by 1787, in Winchester, Virginia, as well. It was the Henkel family, however, that in the early 1800s began what became the largest and most-enduring of the German printing establishments. The Henkel Press remained in business until the 1930s.

Born in 1754, the Reverend Paul Henkel served as a circuit preacher and Lutheran missionary throughout Virginia and North Carolina, always adhering to the traditions of German culture as he made his way along the frontier. It was in large part to carry on the family's and their forebears' heritage that two of the Reverend Henkel's six sons, Ambrose and Solomon, established a German-language press in the Shenandoah County town of New Market. The press issued its first title, a broadside of religious hymns and prayers, on the occasion of the dedication of Rader's Lutheran Church in nearby Rockingham County on 6 October 1806.

In addition to broadsides, the Henkel brothers between 1806 and 1820 published a variety of religious tracts, conference minutes of the Lutheran Church, and other denominational titles—and a children's book, *Die fromme Zwillinge.* Subtitled *Das erste deutsche Virginische Kinderbuch,* it was the first German-language children's book printed in the Old Dominion, and was probably the first juvenile work in any language issued by a Virginia press. The Henkels continued to publish materials for children, including a series of spellers. The *A B C-und Bilder-Buch* (or alphabet and picture book), for example, combined illustrations of everyday objects, farm animals, and plants with German- and English-language descriptions, reflecting the bilingual nature of Valley society in the early 1800s as well as the agricultural and craft-based culture of the German community. The Henkel brothers also issued multiple editions of their popular *Das kleine A B C-Buch,* or small spelling book, and *Das grosse A B C-Buch.* Many of the little books remained securely stored away in the Henkel family's possession until the 1960s. The Library purchased several of the pristine, brightly bound spellers in the early 1970s. GK

▼ Virginia Institution for the Education of the Deaf and Dumb and of the Blind. *The Little Story Book. Compiled for the Use of the Pupils of the Blind Department of the Virginia Institution. . . .* Staunton: Virginia Institution for the Education of the Deaf and Dumb and of the Blind, 1851.

When founded in Staunton in 1839, the Virginia Institution was one of only five schools for the deaf and four for the blind in the United States. The school owned a printing press, which, besides offering vocational training opportunities, provided a needed source of income and a means by which the institute could produce its own specialized textbooks for its sight-impaired students. A report of the board of visitors in the early 1850s charted some of the shop's activities: in 1851, for example, the Virginia Institution published two schoolbooks with raised print, one of which was *The Little Story Book*.

The method of stamping standard alphabetic characters on paper in pronounced relief, such as in *The Little Story Book*, was introduced in Paris

in 1784 by Valentin Haüy (1745–1822). His simple, yet innovative technique was the most widely used system for creating books for the blind until the early 1900s. Although Louis Braille (1809–1852) had by 1829 perfected the system of raised dots that bears his name, a universal Braille code for the English-speaking world was not adopted until the twentieth century. Despite its longer-standing popularity, examples of the earlier, raised-lettered text are nevertheless now rare.

The Library of Virginia for many years maintained a collection of books for the blind, even listing its titles in the State Library's annual *Bulletin* for 1912 and 1920. In 1942, the Library transferred all but a few of the titles to the Virginia Commission for the Blind. NB

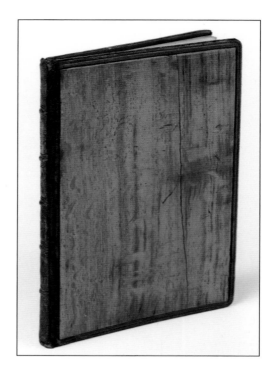

▲ William Perry (fl. 1860s). *A Treatise on the Identity of Herne's Oak, Shewing the Maiden Tree to Have Been the Real One.* London: Printed by L. Booth, 1867.

In his comic play *The Merry Wives of Windsor*, William Shakespeare wrote of a tree near Windsor Castle known as Herne's Oak. There, two of his characters, Mistresses Page and Ford, plotted to deceive "fat Falstaff" and "mock him home to Windsor." In act four, scene four, the playwright also recounted how "Herne the hunter, sometime a keeper here in Windsor forest," haunted the spot, walking "round about an oak, with great ragg'd horns" and shaking "a chain in a most hideous and dreadful manner." Shakespeare evidently embellished a popular local story about a gamekeeper who had hanged himself from an oak, perhaps in remorse over his conviction for poaching, and thereafter was believed to haunt the spot.

Perry's 1867 *Treatise on the Identity of Herne's Oak* was an attempt to identify the specific tree. Confident he had found it, the author also hoped to preserve a bit of it for posterity. Thus, according to a signed certificate included with the volume, the book is bound in boards from the actual great oak after it was felled in the Royal Gardens at Windsor. HG

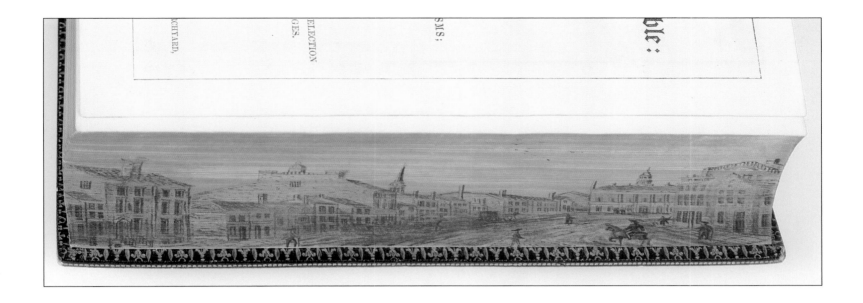

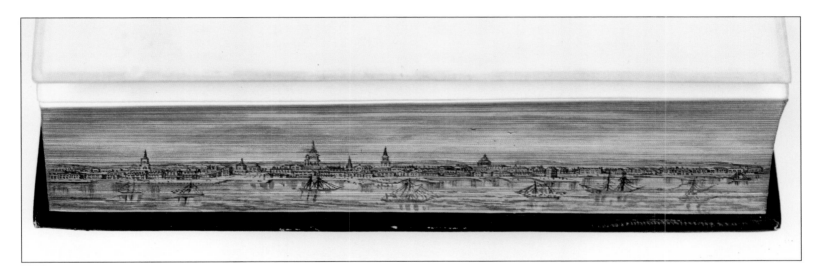

▲ *The Annotated Paragraph Bible, Containing the Old and New Testaments According to the Authorized Version, Arranged in Paragraphs and Parallelisms.* London: Religious Tract Society, 1857.

The Book of Common Prayer and Administration of the Sacraments, and Other Rites and Ceremonies of the Church, According to the Use of the Church of England. Cambridge: Printed by J. Burges, printer to Cambridge University and sold by C. Dilly et al.; London: 1796.

Both religious volumes have been embellished with a fore-edge painting, a form of decoration perfected by a British bookbinder around 1750. By slightly fanning out the pages of a volume and painting the extended surfaces in watercolor, a careful artist was able to depict detailed landscapes, street scenes, nautical motifs, or historical events, whatever might best embellish and personalize a particular volume. The small and elongated paintings were often purposely obscured by gilding or marbling the outermost edges of the closed pages, with the delicately rendered views visible as a delightful surprise only when the book's pages were fanned. Fore-edge painting was an almost exclusively British fancy and remained most popular from 1785 to 1835.

The scene on *The Book of Common Prayer* is of London, depicting Saint Paul's Cathedral and the Tower as well as the River Thames dotted with sailing ships. The view on *The Annotated Paragraph Bible* is probably a New York street scene, complete with tiny pedestrians and travelers on horseback and showing Wall Street, Broad Street, and City Hall. The unusual fore-edge scene might have been rendered in the United States, or was perhaps executed in England for an American client. HG

▲ ▶ Andrew White Tuer (1838–1900). *History of the Horn-Book.* London: Leadenhall Press; New York: Scribner, 1897.

Andrew White Tuer began his publishing career as a partner in a London stationery store, established about 1862. By 1872 he was editing a journal devoted to the paper-and-printing trade and in 1879 published his first book, *Luxurious Bathing.* While his Leadenhall Press published many plainly bound volumes printed in the customary black ink on white or ecru-colored paper, Tuer is far better known for his striking and imaginatively designed works that deviated from the ordinary. He used dark blue ink on light blue paper, multicolored pages, and even printed an advertisement on Japanese handkerchiefs. He even bound several of his books, such as *Our Grandmothers' Gowns* (ca. 1885), in patterned cloth.

Two of the titles for which he is perhaps best remembered featured pockets filled with miniature hornbooks. Originally devised as a small handheld, paddle-shaped primer for children, hornbooks were traditionally inscribed with the alphabet, numerals, the Lord's Prayer, or other rudimentary lessons. When covered with a thin coating of translucent animal horn, the "books" were thus able to withstand "the innocent mischief resulting from damp and grubby paws." The first of the two titles, *History of the Horn-Book* (issued in 1896 in two volumes), contained seven diminutive hornbooks. A year later, Tuer published a one-volume abridgment, with a pocket in the back containing "three horn-books, one of oak, one of card and one of ivory." ES

Miss Campion.

HISTORY

OF

THE HORN-BOOK

BY

ANDREW W. TUER, F.S.A.

AUTHOR OF 'BARTOLOZZI AND HIS WORKS,' ETC.

WITH THREE HUNDRED ILLUSTRATIONS

1897

LONDON : PUBLISHED BY

THE LEADENHALL PRESS, LTD., 50 LEADENHALL STREET, E.C.

SIMPKIN, MARSHALL, HAMILTON, KENT & CO., LTD.

NEW YORK : CHARLES SCRIBNER'S SONS, 153-157 FIFTH AVENUE

Painted by J. Shaw.   Engraved by J. Hill.

NORFOLK; FROM GOSPORT, VIRGINIA.

PRINTS, PHOTOGRAPHS, AND POSTCARDS

Among the most valuable and frequently used resources in the Library of Virginia are its files of several hundred thousand prints, photographs, and postcards. From early engravings and lithographs to late-twentieth-century photographs and postcards, the collection traces the development of American image-making both as art and as popular culture.

During the nineteenth century, engravings of the work of prominent artists graced both books and parlor walls. Examples of prints in books are illustrated throughout this volume; presented here are works produced for display as art in portfolios or in the home. Engravers, such as John Hill, and lithographers, such as Edward Beyer and Louis Prang, based their work on their own drawings or paintings or on those by other artists. The Library's collection of Virginia scenes produced by Hill, Beyer, and Prang, as well as many others, includes a wide range of popular tastes, from landscapes and familiar landmarks to Civil War battles.

With the advent of photography in 1839, printmakers had another source for their work and the public another popular graphic medium for preserving remarkably detailed vestiges of a culture and its history. Among the Library of Virginia's most notable photographic collections is the extensive series of images made by the United States Army Signal Corps of the Hampton Roads Port of Embarkation during World War II. The Library's pictorial collections also include photographs taken in Virginia by the federal government's New Deal programs—the Farm Security and Work Projects Administrations—during the 1930s. Among other photographic collections are the extensive pictorial archives of the Virginia State Chamber of Commerce, images of Virginia displayed by the commonwealth at the World's Fair in New York in 1939, as well as the original negatives of several of the Old Dominion's most-distinguished photographic artists, most notable among them the large collection of early-twentieth-century glass-plate negatives of Norfolk photographer Harry C. Mann.

Picture postcards employed photography in a novel way and reached their greatest popularity in the United States between 1901 and 1915. The majority of the Library of Virginia's collection of more than five thousand cards documents those early years, but there are also numerous examples of the popular art form from the 1920s, the Great Depression, and thereafter. The images of Virginia cities, landscapes, and natural and historical attractions first published as penny postcards and later as more expensive and elaborate souvenirs provide a visual record of the changing face of the commonwealth throughout the twentieth century.

◀ Joshua Shaw (1776–1860). *Norfolk; from Gosport, Virginia.* Philadelphia: Engraved by John Hill, ca. 1820. 13 ⅝ x 17 ⅛ inches.

Joshua Shaw began his artistic career as a sign-painter's apprentice in Manchester, England. While completing his apprenticeship, he continued his art studies, and it was not long before he was exhibiting his work at the Royal Academy of Arts. In 1817, at about the age of forty, Shaw came to the United States and settled in Philadelphia. Two years later, he traveled throughout the South taking subscriptions for his *Picturesque Views of American Scenery* (1820). Shaw admired the unspoiled American landscape, writing that "in no quarter of the globe are the majesty and loveliness of nature more strikingly conspicuous than in America."

Shaw was fortunate to collaborate with John Hill (1770–1850), a fellow Philadelphian and a master engraver, to reproduce his portfolio. Shaw and Hill intended to issue six different collections, each containing a half-dozen views, but only three of the planned collections actually appeared. Included among the Virginia views were scenes of Norfolk from Gosport (Portsmouth), Lynnhaven Bay, and Bolling's Dam, Petersburg. The beauty and popularity of Joshua Shaw's landscapes, enhanced by John Hill's craftsmanship, helped to lay the foundation for a landscape tradition in America. Their collection, moreover, formed one of the first portfolios of American views not produced in Europe. JK

▲ Edward Beyer (1820–1865). *Natural Bridge*.
Tinted lithograph with additional hand-coloring.
Plate 1 from *Album of Virginia; or, Illustration of
the Old Dominion*. Richmond, 1858.

Born in Germany in 1820, Edward Beyer
studied art in Düsseldorf and worked in Dresden
during the 1840s before journeying to America
about 1848. In 1856, after spending two years
traveling, sketching, and painting throughout
the commonwealth, Beyer announced his plans
to issue his Virginia works in an album of lithographs. By 1857, the artist had returned to
Germany to oversee the printing of his album at
Berlin and Dresden. Copies of the forty color-
plates and an illustrated title page were shipped
to Richmond, where the *Album of Virginia* was
entered for copyright in 1858.

Befitting its status as Virginia's best-known
natural landmark, Beyer included three different
views of Rockbridge County's Natural Bridge in
his published collection. Although the album
contained no written descriptions except for the
titles on the plates, a separate *Description of the
Album of Virginia; or, The Old Dominion, Illustrated*
was issued in two pamphlets in 1857 and 1858.
The text described Natural Bridge as a towering
wonder "so simple, yet so grand as to assure you
that it is the work of God *alone*." JK

◄ William Goodacre (fl. 1829–1835). *University of Virginia, Charlottesville*. New York: Engraved and printed by Fenner Sears and Company; London: Published by I. T. Hinton and Simkin and Marshall, 1 Dec. 1831. 7 x 10 ½ inches.

The artist William Goodacre, a landscape and still-life painter, worked primarily in New York City. He did, though, complete a number of Virginia scenes, including one of the State Capitol, for John Howard Hinton's *History and Topography of the United States*, published in both Philadelphia and London and first issued in installments between 1830 and 1832. Prepared in New York and published in London on 1 December 1831, Goodacre's finely detailed view of the *University of Virginia, Charlottesville* appeared as a single work for sale during the same period. The artist later completed views of Natural Bridge, Harper's Ferry, and Richmond's Monumental Church, all of which were published as engravings by Samuel Walker, of Boston. EC

► Edward Beyer (1820–1865). *Old Point Comfort. Hygeia Hotel.* Tinted lithograph with additional hand-coloring. Plate 32 from *Album of Virginia; or, Illustration of the Old Dominion.* Richmond, 1858.

Virginia's early settlers named Point Comfort (now Old Point Comfort), situated at the mouth of the James River, for its deep channel and safe anchorage. The colonists also established a fort there as early as 1609 to defend the Virginia settlement against Spanish attack. It was there, too, that the U.S. Army between 1819 and 1834 constructed Fort Monroe to protect the thriving Hampton Roads area. In 1833 the federal government imprisoned the Indian chief Black Hawk at the new fort. So many curiosity seekers came to see the famous prisoner, the leader of an uprising of Sauk, Winnebago, and Fox Indians in the upper Mississippi Valley the year before, that they overflowed the small, nearby Hygeia Hotel. The proprietor, Harrison Phoebus, eventually developed the Hygeia into one of the antebellum South's most fashionable resorts.

Of the forty plates included in Edward Beyer's *Album of Virginia*, the lithograph of Old Point Comfort, with its view of Fort Monroe, and the Hygeia Hotel is the only one to depict a Virginia scene east of Richmond. Beyer entered Virginia from the west by way of the Ohio River and leisurely made his way to and from a number of the popular resort hotels that featured the Old Dominion's famous medicinal springs. He often painted pictures of the resorts in return for accommodations, and may have done the same at the Hygeia Hotel. Although many of the paintings Beyer made of his travels have survived, none of the originals on which he based his series of forty lithographs is known to exist. JK

ALBUM OF VIRGINIA.

OLD POINT COMFORT.

HYGEIA HOTEL.

THE FALL OF RICHMOND, VA. ON THE NIGHT OF APRIL 2d 1865.

This strong hold the Capital City of the Confederacy, was evacuated by the Rebels in consequence of the defeat at "Five Forks" of the Army of Northern Virginia under Lee, and capture of the South side Rail-Road by Genl Grant... Before abandoning the City, the Rebels set fire to it, destroying a vast amount of property, and the conflagration continued until it was subdued by the Union troops on the following morning.

▲ Nathaniel Currier (1813–1888), and James Merritt Ives (1824–1895). *The Fall of Richmond, Va. On the Night of April 2d, 1865.* New York: Currier and Ives, 1865. 23 ¼ x 28 ½ inches.

On 2 April 1865, a military courier entered Richmond's Saint Paul's Episcopal Church, across from the entrance to Capitol Square. The messenger informed Confederate president Jefferson Davis that Petersburg could no longer be defended and that R. E. Lee recommended that the government abandon Richmond. Throughout that day and into the next, officials, local defense troops, and numerous civilians evacuated the city—hampered by a huge fire, buffeted by high winds, set by the retreating Confederate troops. It was just the sort of dramatic scene to attract the attention of the New York firm of Currier and Ives.

Often regarded principally as a purveyor of popular art for the masses, Currier and Ives served as a crucial factor in the evolution of the American news media. In 1840, Nathaniel Currier was commissioned by a New York newspaper to produce a print of a Long Island steam-

boat disaster. Currier, in business since 1835, had the scene ready within a week of the incident; it was for its day a remarkably current illustrated news-feature.

Currier quickly realized the economic potential of such scenes and over the next several years established a nationwide business in the print trade. The company often published series, so as to generate additional sales, and frequently adopted emotion-charged titles in order to attract further interest in particular scenes. The prints, available at the company's New York store or by mail order, sold for twenty cents each or six for a dollar; larger scenes cost as much as one to four dollars. It was not until 1852 that Currier hired the multitalented James Merritt Ives, a relative, as a clerk, bookkeeper, artist, and lithographer. Ives became a partner in 1857. The firm remained active until 1907.

Currier and Ives issued two editions of the Richmond view, both published in 1865. In the second, the company made several changes in the composition of the carriages, wagons, and pedestrians depicted crossing the James River bridge. Both prints have long been rare. EC

▶ Louis Prang (1824–1909). *Laying the Pontons at Fredericksburg.* Boston: L. Prang and Company, 1887. 17 x 23 ½ inches.

Louis Prang pioneered the development of chromolithography in America. Well-known for his elaborate greeting cards, Prang believed a demand existed for high-quality color reproductions of paintings and for many years worked to supplant the popularity of the simpler, and less expensive, illustrations offered by the New York firm of Currier and Ives.

A native of Breslau, Silesia, Prang served as an apprentice engraver for his father and later traveled throughout Europe working as a printer and dyer of color textiles, excellent training for his later work in lithography. Prang, however, was forced to flee Europe after the 1848 revolutions against the German monarchies failed, settling in Boston in 1850. After four years as a partner in the firm of Prang and Mayer, he established L. Prang and Company in 1860. The Civil War played an especially important role in the early history of the firm, and Prang's scenes of battles, camp life, and maps of engagements proved to be consistently popular. In a shrewd bit of marketing, Prang also sometimes printed battle plans and maps for mass distribution with the wartime newspapers, helping to sustain a demand for the new company's Civil War themes.

After 1865, Prang became famous for his chromolithographs. While standard lithographs were printed from a single stone, a Prang chromolithograph might require as many as twenty printing stones to create the exact shading and color of an original painting. Prang intended his postwar series of Civil War images, such as *Laying the Pontons at Fredericksburg*, to be particularly suitable for display in the home, providing high-quality art for the growing American middle class.

The Prang view of Fredericksburg depicts an early moment of the Federal attack on the town. On 11 December 1862, the Union army deployed several pontoon bridges across the Rappahannock River; soldiers then crossed the stream to drive Confederate sharpshooters from their hiding places and establish a bridgehead on the south bank. Although the Federal army was initially able to occupy the town itself, it lost nearly eleven thousand men in repeated frontal assaults against the Army of Northern Virginia, well entrenched along Marye's Heights behind the town. GK, DWG

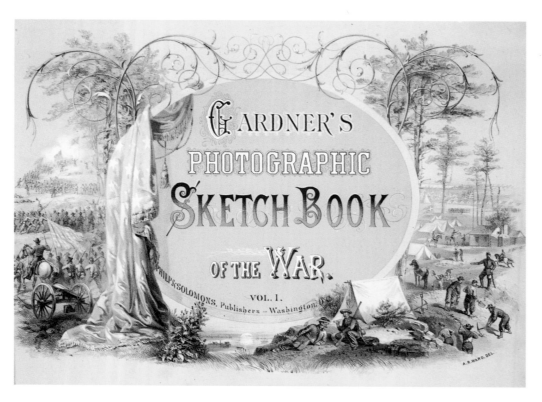

Alexander Gardner (1821–1882). *Gardner's Photographic Sketch Book of the War.* 2 vols. Washington, D.C.: Philp and Solomons, 1865–1866.

Gardner's Photographic Sketch Book of the War was a remarkable achievement in photojournalism. The two-volume work included a hundred mounted photographs selected from the approximately three thousand glass-plate negatives taken by Alexander Gardner and his colleagues. The published collection included battlefield views, camp scenes, and famous personalities and generals. The images of the dead at Gettysburg form the climax of the work, which is essentially a narrative of the war following the Army of the Potomac from First Manassas to Appomattox. Gardner intentionally designed the volume as a photo-essay—a revolutionary concept—writing a narrative to accompany the photographs. The stark image of members of the U.S. Military Telegraph Construction Corps is by Timothy O'Sullivan (1840–1882), one of Gardner's most-prolific and -talented colleagues.

Gardner, a pioneer of American photography, was born in 1821 just north of Glasgow, Scotland. Apprenticed as a jeweler, he followed a number of pursuits in his early years and opened his first photographic studio in Dumbarton, Scotland, in 1856. Soon thereafter, he immigrated to America and began work in

New York at the studio of Mathew Brady. It was with Brady that Gardner began to document the American Civil War. In 1862, however, Gardner and several other photographers left Brady's employ in a dispute over the attribution of their work. Despite Brady's considerable postwar reputation, the majority of the wartime images so familiar today were the work not of Brady, but of Gardner and his colleagues. Gardner initially spent his time photographing campsites, significant locales, and battlefields—most memorably Gettysburg—but after 1863 worked principally at his Washington, D.C., studio, collaborating with photographers in the field. Gardner made more images of Abraham Lincoln than any other photographer. He also documented the war's aftermath, capturing the ruins of Richmond and serving as the photographer of record for the execution of the Lincoln assassins and of Captain Henry Wirz, the commander of Andersonville Prison. GK

Negative by T. H. O'SULLIVAN.   Entered according to act of Congress, in the year 1866, by A. Gardner, in the Clerk's Office of the District Court of the District of Columbia.   Positive by A. GARDNER, 511 7th St., Washington.

U. S. MILITARY TELEGRAPH CONSTRUCTION CORPS.

No. 62.   April, 1864.

◄ Harry C. Mann (1866–1926). "Jimmie at the Table," James Mann Jr., ca. 1912. Harry C. Mann Photograph and Glass-Plate Negative Collection.

The Library of Virginia's picture collections include more than twenty-four hundred commercial as well as personal and family photographs by Harry C. Mann. The photographer's brother, Colonel James Mann, presented the negatives and prints to the Virginia Chamber of Commerce in 1939, which in turn transferred the superb collection to the Library in 1940. Colonel Mann's son, James Mann Jr. (1911–1977), was photographed by his uncle about 1912. An excellent documentary record of life and landscapes throughout tidewater Virginia, the Mann collection also stands out as a significant artistic achievement.

Harry C. Mann, born in Petersburg in 1866, began taking pictures in the 1890s while employed as a government clerk, but few examples of his early work survive. Mann launched his short, but highly successful professional career behind the camera as an official photographer for the Jamestown Ter-Centennial Exposition of 1907 and in 1910 opened a studio in Norfolk. Mann's work included family portraits, community groups, businesses, churches, schools, and historic buildings. While his subjects were the typical fare for a commercial photographer, Mann's eye for aesthetically pleasing composition set him far apart from many of his contemporaries. In September 1915, for example, the *National Geographic Magazine* published twenty-two of Mann's views of the Virginia coast. Mann also exhibited his work in competitions in Paris, London, and New York, winning awards for his artistry. Tragically, by 1924 Mann's health had become so precarious that he was forced to retire to the Virginia mountains. He died in 1926 in a hospital in Lynchburg, Virginia. SM, EC

◄ Harry C. Mann (1866–1926). "Baptist Church Watermelon Picnic at Ocean View, Norfolk." Harry C. Mann Photograph and Glass-Plate Negative Collection.

During the early 1900s many churches, clubs, and other social and religious organizations sponsored family outings and train excursions to the Virginia seaside. Cheap transportation and increased leisure time fueled the growth of beach resorts and entertainment in places like Virginia Beach. Mann often worked at the beaches in the tidewater area, recording social events as well as the rugged beauty of the Virginia shore and the Atlantic Ocean. His work drew considerable attention and in August 1922, for example, the magazine *Country Life* published a photo essay devoted to his seascapes. GK

◄ Harry C. Mann (1866–1926). "Sansone Fruit Company, 410 East Main Street, Norfolk." Harry C. Mann Photograph and Glass-Plate Negative Collection.

Harry Mann's photograph of Antonio and Augustus E. Sansone and Thomas L. Amato posed in front of their unimposing, but vibrant downtown store captured a typical small business in early-twentieth-century Norfolk. Like most photographers, Mann relied on commercial work for much of his income, but he probably enjoyed taking the photograph of the proud owners of the Sansone Fruit Company. The image also documents the ethnic diversity of the Virginia port city. While Richmond and most other Virginia cities saw small increases in their immigrant populations after the 1870s, Norfolk's growth as a major eastern port attracted far greater numbers of newcomers from eastern and southern Europe. GK

United States Army Signal Corps, Hampton Roads, Virginia. United States Army Signal Corps Photograph Collection, Hampton Roads Embarkation Series, 1942–1946.

The winter and spring of 1942 found the United States Army rushing to prepare for what promised to be a protracted war in Europe. Establishing immense staging areas and port facilities from which to ship troops and supplies overseas was a particularly urgent need. Just as it had been in the First World War, Virginia's vast Hampton Roads became a crucial base in the war against Germany. On 15 June 1942, the army officially activated the Hampton Roads Port of Embarkation, under the command of the army's Transportation Corps, with its headquarters in Newport News. Newport News provided several advantages over other tidewater cities: as the eastern terminus of the Chesapeake and Ohio Railroad, the city had six large railroad piers, some already equipped with thirty-ton cranes, and more than a hundred warehouses with approximately two million square feet of sheltered storage space. It also had maritime repair facilities, including the Warwick Machine Company and the Newport News Shipbuilding and Dry Dock Company.

By war's end, more than 772,000 men and women had gone to war through the port's various facilities. Besides embarkation, Hampton Roads saw even more arrivals—915,116, including the wounded and even prisoners of war. To document all this, the Transportation Corps maintained a port historian's office and regularly assigned Signal Corps photographers, regardless of time or weather, to document as much activity and as many representative sailings and debarkations as possible. More than thirty-five hundred of the black-and-white images, complete with the photographers' interview notes, are included in the Library of Virginia's picture collections.

Many of the images are of soldiers, airmen, Medical Corps personnel, USO and Red Cross workers, and even French colonial troops waiting nervously to board ships for overseas duty. To help ease the tension, an army band was usually there, too, playing a variety of rousing military marches and lively swing tunes. On 4 September 1943, a Signal Corps photographer recorded Private R. A. Smith, of New York City, and Private M. Prudent, from New Jersey, jitterbugging on Pier 6.

Many of the Hampton Roads photographers—as well as mechanics, clerks, medical personnel, and administrators—were women. One of them, Private First Class Dorothy Baker, of Philadelphia, camera at the ready, was pictured in the pier area by a fellow photographer on 11 May 1945, three days after Germany surrendered.

Four months later, on 8 September, another Signal Corps photographer captured the arrival of First Lieutenant James D. Clark, of Richmond, Virginia. A communications officer with the 508th Fighter Squadron, 404th Fighter Group, Clark had sailed overseas on 23 March 1944 and returned home aboard the SS *Montclair Victory*, which departed Antwerp, Belgium, on 30 August 1945 with more than nineteen hundred passengers aboard. First bound for Boston, the ship while at sea had been ordered to Newport News instead. There Clark was surprised by his family, including his young daughter, Sharon; he had last seen her when she was seven days old. JK, EC

T. Beverly Campbell (1892–1964), compiler. Virginia State Chamber of Commerce, New York World's Fair Photograph Collection.

Virginia was one of twenty-two states represented in the Court of States at the New York World's Fair in 1939. The commonwealth's presentation was, however, unlike any other there. Located close to the main entrance, the Virginia Room was to be a place where footsore visitors could recuperate, enjoy a complimentary glass of ice water served by white-jacketed waiters, and peruse an array of 227 photograph albums prepared by the Virginia State Chamber of Commerce.

Beverly Campbell, an editor and playwright from Richmond who managed the Virginia Room during the fair's run, selected more than fifty-six hundred images submitted by corporations, government agencies, and individual photographers. Campbell then organized the images within subject groups and added brief descriptive captions. As a collection, the optimistic, flattering pictures of the Old Dominion form an interesting and pronounced contrast to the many depression-era documentary photographs of Virginia produced by such federal agencies as the Farm Security Administration. Views of an angler wading a mountain stream, a group of dancers, or an oysterman, for example, served as a public relations boost to Virginia's ailing economy and image. At the conclusion of the World's Fair, the Virginia State Chamber of Commerce donated the albums to the Library of Virginia. JK

◄ ▼ W. Lincoln Highton (1906–). "Daffodils for the Market, Gloucester County" and "Farmer along Route 52, south of Hillsville, Carroll County." Work Projects Administration, Virginia Federal Writers' Project, American Guide Series.

As part of the depression era's broad Work Projects Administration, the Federal Writers' Project provided jobs to writers, teachers, editors, and other unemployed white-collar workers. Besides compiling numerous local inventories of historic sites, documenting the life experiences of a wide range of people, and writing local histories, the Federal Writers' Project employees also embarked on an American Guide Series, with book-length guides to major cities, selected regions, and particularly individual states. Under the supervision of Eudora Ramsay Richardson, the Virginia Writers' Project in May 1940 published *Virginia: A Guide to the Old Dominion*. So popular did the book become that it was reprinted in 1941, 1946, and yet again in 1947; the Library of Virginia reissued the volume in 1992.

The principal photographer for the Virginia guide was W. Lincoln Highton. During the late 1930s, as the chief still photographer for the U.S. Information Service, Highton was assigned to contribute pictures to several Federal Writers' Project titles. At least thirty-five of the one hundred photographs in the Virginia guide are by Highton, including his striking photograph of a Gloucester County laborer carrying a basket of harvested daffodils. Highton usually took variant views of his subjects. He photographed a Carroll County farmer, for example, within a stark and tightly framed perspective as well as within a wider composition that included the farmer's team of oxen; only the latter was included in the guide. Among the Library's other Highton photographs are several views of Virginia watermen and storekeepers, rural villages and pastimes, historic sites, and Shenandoah Valley farms. JK

◄ Arthur Rothstein (1915–1985). "Mrs. Dodson and one of her nine children, Shenandoah National Park, Va." Historical Section, Farm Security Administration Photograph.

For eight years between 1935 and 1943, the Historical Section of the federal government's Farm Security Administration, under the direction of Roy Emerson Stryker, documented the social need behind the FSA's numerous programs to assist poor, unemployed, or migrant farmers. An economist, Stryker concluded that photography was the best way to complete the task. The results were overwhelming: some 270,000 pictures over eight years produced by a superb staff that included Walker Evans, Ben Shahn, Dorothea Lange, Marion Post Wolcott, and Arthur Rothstein.

Rothstein, a former student of Stryker at Columbia University, was the first photographer hired by the FSA. His genius in the mechanics of camera work and his efforts to organize the Historical Section's photography laboratory in Washington, D.C., won him a chance at fieldwork. His photograph of a mountain woman and her toddler is from one of his first assignments: to record a rapidly disappearing way of life as the federal government removed Virginia families from their land to establish Shenandoah National Park. With its simple artistry and unblinking depiction of rural hardship and poverty, the photograph of the barefoot mother and child is typical of the FSA's remarkable pictorial work. JK

HUMAN CONFEDERATE FLAG   "And 'Twill Live In Song and Story Though Its Folds Are In the Dust"

◀ "The James River, Lynchburg, Va."
Postcard Collection. New York: Rotograph
Company, 1906.

▼ "Natural Tunnel, Bristol, Va. Tenn." Postcard
Collection. New York: Souvenir Post Card
Company, postmarked 1908.

The first commercially produced "picture
postcards" were printed in the United States in
1893. Until World War I, however, it was
Germany, with its superior printing industry and
lower labor costs, that supplied the United States
with most of its postcards. The early-twentieth-
century views of the James River at Lynchburg
and the Natural Tunnel, for example, were published in New York but printed in Germany.
Since postal regulations required that one side of
the postcard include only the recipient's name
and address, printers provided a small space along-
side the picture for brief messages. Not until
1907 could manufacturers include space for the
address and message on a single side and thus
devote the entire front to the picture. KH

◀ "Human Confederate Flag.", ca. 1907.
Richmond: Southern Bargain House, [1907].
Postcard in *Have a Look at Our City* scrapbook,
ca. 1920.

The equestrian statue of R. E. Lee on
Monument Avenue in Richmond served as the
backdrop for the "Human Confederate Flag."
Composed of boys dressed in white and girls in
red and blue, the flag was part of a massive five-
day celebration in 1907, beginning with the
unveiling of the J. E. B. Stuart monument on
30 May and ending with the unveiling of the
Jefferson Davis monument on 3 June. The festivities also coincided with the seventeenth annual
reunion of the United Confederate Veterans in
Richmond. This postcard is based on a photograph by Huestis Pratt Cook (1868–1951), of
Richmond. Cook had continued the business
begun by his father, George Smith Cook (1819–
1902). Their work became the basis for numerous
postcards, many of which were made, like those
of other photographers of the period, without
their consent. The lack of copyright restrictions
only encouraged postcard companies to print
thousands of popular images without any attribution to the original photographer. KH

▲ "Feeding Sea-lions at City Park, Norfolk, Va." Postcard Collection. N.p., n.d.

▼ "Fortress Monroe and Entrance to Hampton Roads from Hotel Chamberlin, Old Point Comfort, Va." Postcard Collection. Detroit Publishing Company, ca. 1913.

The popularity of postcards exploded with the rapid development of inexpensive amusements and the accompanying growth of tourism after 1900. Visitors to Norfolk, for example, could purchase views of favorite attractions, such as the sea lions at the city park. So popular did the small

souvenirs become that the U.S. Post Office in 1908 processed more than 667 million postcards.

In addition to the basic postcard, tourists could also buy foldout versions with panoramic views of cities and landscapes. With one such card, the recipient seemingly peered out a window of the elegant Hotel Chamberlin, looking out over Fort Monroe and the entrance to Hampton Roads at Old Point Comfort. Resorts, hotels, railroads, and steamship companies often provided cards as a courtesy to guests, which, when mailed, became an effective and inexpensive means of advertising. The Hotel Chamberlin also published a card featuring its noonday menu, complete with a color view of the resort. KH

▶ "United States Government Pier, Jamestown Exposition, 1907." Postcard Collection. New York: American Colortype Company, 1907

In 1907 Virginians celebrated the 300th anniversary of the first permanent English settlement in North America with the grand Jamestown Ter-Centennial Exposition. Located on a point of land near Willoughby Spit on the Hampton Roads, the exposition opened on 26 April 1907 and closed in November. Attractions ranged from the largest gathering of naval warships in history to a re-created Eskimo village sweltering through the tidewater Virginia summer.

At a time when the popularity of the postcard had skyrocketed, the purchase of one or two of these souvenirs was no doubt an essential exposition transaction. Pictured on this postcard is a somewhat fanciful view of the Government Pier, "the great architectural and engineering triumph of the Exposition." The structure was dedicated on the evening of Saturday, 14 September, and festivities included a concert by the national band of Mexico stationed on top of the pier, a speech by exposition president, Harry St. George Tucker, and an elaborate fireworks display. The latter entertained visitors with such spectacles as the "National Bombs, opening Red, changing to White, finishing Blue," a "fire portrait of John Smith correctly reproduced in lines of fire," and the "Jamestown Bouquet, produced by the simultaneous flight of 200 large rockets." The Government Pier was actually three structures: the twin piers Godspeed and Susan Constant linked by what was "the largest concrete arch ever built." JK, SM

HOTEL CHAMBERLIN   703II FORTRESS MONROE AND ENTRANCE TO HAM

To decline — Love to all, Mary. and can find —

UNITED STATES GOVERNMENT PIER, JAMESTOWN EXPOSITION, 1907.

ROADS FROM HOTEL CHAMBERLIN, OLD POINT COMFORT, VA

17 9.

1. Avicula. 2. Meleagrina. 3. Pedum. 4. Lima. 5. Pecten
6. Plagiostoma. 7. Plicatula. 8. Spondylus. 9. Gryphea.
10. Ostrea. 11. Pedicella. 12. Placuna. 13. Anomia. 14. Crania.
15. Orbicula. 16. Terebratula. 17. Lingula. 18. Hyalea.
19. Cleodora. 20. Limacina. 21. Cymbulia. 22. Chitonellus.
23. Chiton. 24. Patella. 25. Pleurobranchus. 26. Umbrella.
27. Parmophorus. 28. Emarginula. 29. Fissurella.

P. S. Duval, Lith. Phil.ª

PRACTICAL GUIDES AND REFERENCE WORKS

From the early days of the Virginia colony, printed guides and other reference resources contributed much to the effective governance and well-being of the Old Dominion. The royal governor's Council, for example, maintained a carefully selected library of lawbooks, public records of all kinds, atlases, practical compendiums, and even titles to guide the colony's religious faith. There were also studies devoted to the natural sciences, especially volumes describing the plants, animals, and marine life found in such remarkable profusion within England's Atlantic and West Indian colonies. The governor and Council's increasing reliance on dependable and current information thus gave impetus to the formation of the first reference library in Virginia—the precursor to the Library of Virginia.

During the early nineteenth century, the General Assembly continued the practice begun by the colonial Council and funded the purchase of reference works of all kinds. It was, though, with the formal establishment of the State Library in 1823 that the legislature signaled Virginia's permanent commitment to the acquisition and accessibility of printed guides and reference resources. The publication of the Library's first printed catalog five years later, in 1828, presented further evidence of the commonwealth's sustained search for new and innovative titles essential to efficient government and the stewardship of the state's resources. The catalog, for example, confirmed the purchase of Alexander Wilson's nine-volume study, *American Ornithology; or, The Natural History of the Birds of the United States*, published in Philadelphia between 1808 and 1825 and at the time regarded as the first great book of American science.

The Library's extensive collections of eighteenth- and nineteenth-century guides and reference works include encyclopedias in several languages, volumes of collected British and American state papers and documentary histories, almanacs (including several rare examples compiled and printed in colonial Virginia), household and gardening guides, treatises on the cultivation of crops and animal husbandry, expositions on the sciences and engineering, and illustrated compilations of architectural styles. Among the thousands of titles is an almost-complete set of the English-language edition of Pierre Bayle's celebrated *General Dictionary, Historical and Critical*, published in London between 1734 and 1741 and acquired by the governor's Council before the mid-1770s. One of the most beautiful reference works is a three-volume edition of the earl of Clarendon's famous *History of the Rebellion and Civil Wars in England Begun in the Year 1641*. Together, the guides and reference resources reflect what Virginians since the early 1700s perceived as the most practical, necessary, and effective printed resources to aid them in the exploration and development of the commonwealth.

◄ Edgar Allan Poe (1809–1849). *The Conchologist's First Book: or, A System of Testaceous Malacology, Arranged Expressly for the Use of Schools.* Philadelphia: Published for the author, by Haswell, Barrington, and Haswell, 1839.

Struggling to earn a living as a writer and as editor of the Richmond-based *Southern Literary Messenger*, Edgar Allan Poe in 1839 eagerly accepted a fifty-dollar commission to compile a small schoolbook on sea mollusks. The year before, Thomas Wyatt had published a lengthy and highly regarded treatise on the same subject, *Manual of Conchology*. The volume was, however, expensive, and despite Wyatt's pleas the publisher refused to issue a less costly abridgment while sales remained steady. Eager to capture the wider student market, an enterprising Philadelphia company decided to issue a similar, but shorter text compiled from research already collected. To take on the task and to fend off any potential trouble, the printer determined to select a writer of relatively little stature—someone "whom it would be idle to sue for damages."

Poe wrote a brief preface and introduction, translated a treatise by Georges Cuvier on the small sea animals, and then filled the remainder of the text with the paraphrased work of several other writers. Poe openly acknowledged his debt to Wyatt, Cuvier, and others, and never implied his work was original, but he was nevertheless vigorously condemned in the press and literary circles for plagiarism. The book itself proved to be a great success as a basic textbook, sold out within two months, and was reprinted in 1840 and again in 1845. Poe, however, received no royalties. *The Conchologist's First Book* was Poe's only work to be issued in a second edition in his lifetime. EC

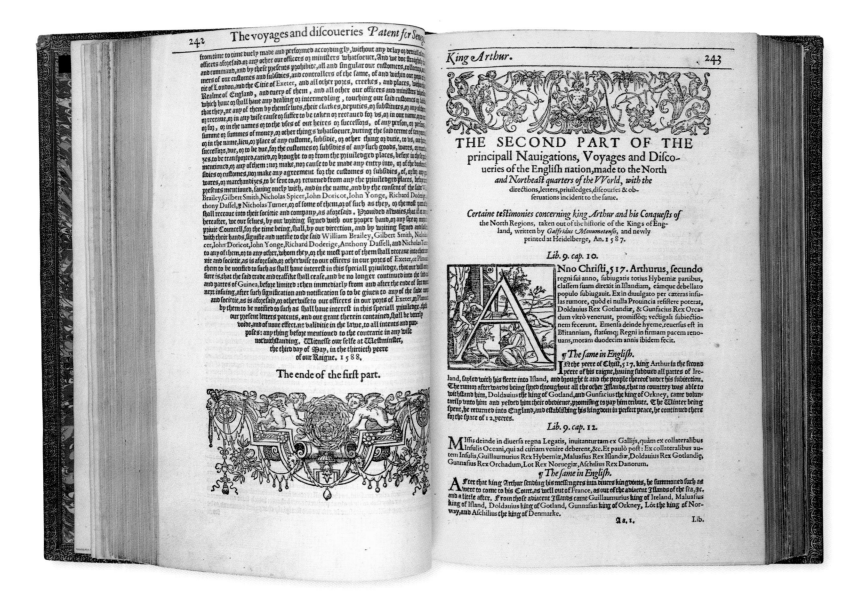

▲ Richard Hakluyt (1552?–1616). *The Principall Navigations, Voiages and Discoveries of the English Nation.* London: Imprinted by George Bishop and Ralph Newberie, deputies to Christopher Barker, printer to the Queenes most excellent Maiestie, 1589.

Recalling his earliest school days, Richard Hakluyt remarked that a lesson in geography had inspired in him a sense of "rare delight" and an ambition "to prosecute that knowledge and kind of literature." Pursuing that youthful interest, Hakluyt in 1570 entered Christ Church, Oxford University, where he studied accounts of the earliest voyages of discovery. After earning his master of arts degree in 1577, he taught geography at Christ Church and in 1582 published *Divers Voyages Touching the Discoverie of America.* The book won him the notice of Francis Howard, baron Howard of Effingham, and an appointment the next year as chaplain to the lord admiral's son-in-law, Sir Edward Stafford, the ambassador to France.

During Hakluyt's first year in Paris he read French, Italian, and Spanish accounts of the New World, consulted mapmakers, and questioned merchants and shipmasters about their overseas experiences. Drawing on this knowledge, he composed *A Discourse on Western Planting,* an argument for English participation in the exploitation of the trans-Atlantic world. In 1584, Hakluyt presented the document to Queen Elizabeth in support of Walter Ralegh's quest to establish a colony in Virginia.

A skilled editor who prized the literary qualities of the personal narrative, Hakluyt continued to collect numerous firsthand accounts from the seamen and gentlemen adventurers who traveled to the distant and remote quarters of the earth. He compiled these narratives into his great history of discovery and exploration, *The Principall Navigations, Voiages and Discoveries of the English Nation,* published in 1589 as a single volume and in an expanded, three-volume edition ten years later, *The Principall Navigations: Voyages, Traffiques and Discoveries of the English Nation.* DWG

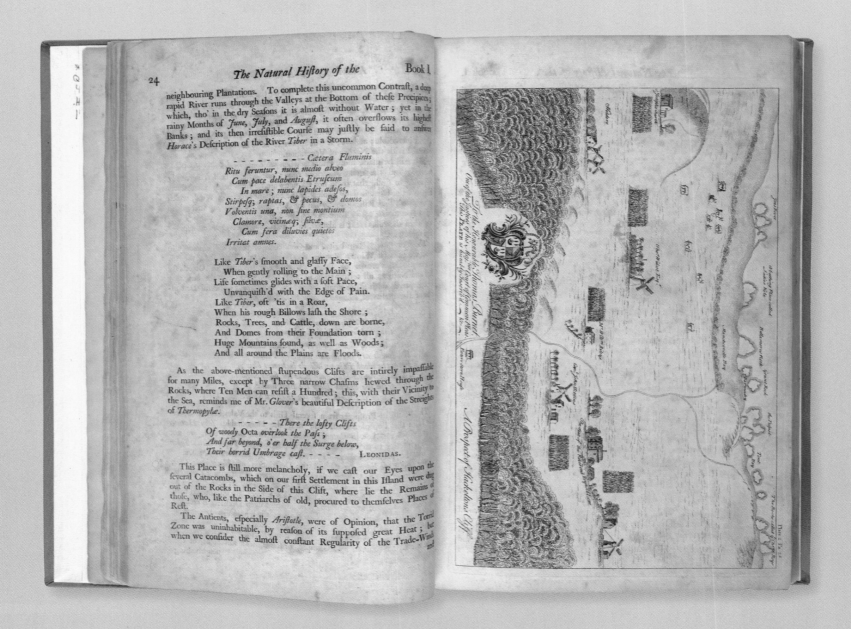

▲ Griffith Hughes (fl. 1750). *The Natural History of the Island of Barbadoes. In Ten Books.* N.p., ca. 1750.

The Natural History of the Island of Barbadoes is the earliest-recorded private donation to the State Library. An inscription in the volume reads, "Presented the Library of Virginia by Addison Hansford Esq., 1833." A resident of King George County, Hansford (1800–1850) succeeded his father as clerk of the Senate of Virginia and served from 1824 until 1849. Although there is no record indicating why Hansford donated the volume, it is possible that he wished to recognize the benefits of the state's ten-year-old reference library. He had probably made frequent use of its growing collection, housed in a room only a few steps away from the Senate chamber, as a part of his daily routine in the Capitol building.

The volume is by Griffith Hughes, probably the son of Edward Hughes, of Towyn, Merionethshire. That Griffith was born circa 1707 and entered Saint John's College, Oxford University, in 1729, where he received the bachelor's and master of arts degrees in 1748 In 1750 Griffith Hughes was a fellow of the Royal Society of London and rector of Saint Lucy's Barbados; his *Natural History of the Island of Barbadoes* was published about the same time. Among the volume's twenty-nine plates is the detailed depiction of "Hackelton's Cliff." BT

PLATE VII.

Drawn from Nature by J.J. Audubon, F.R.S. F.L.S.

Lith. Printed & Col.ᵈ by J.T. Bowen, Phila. 1843.

SCIURUS CAROLINENSIS. GMELIN.

CAROLINA GREY SQUIRREL.

Natural Size.

MALE AND FEMALE.

John James Audubon (1785–1851) and John
Bachman (1790–1874). *The Viviparous
Quadrupeds of North America.* 3 vols. New York:
J. J. Audubon, 1845–1851.

Best known for his massive series of watercolors of the birds of North America, John James Audubon collaborated with John Bachman in the preparation of another major scientific and artistic work—a superb three-volume study of the four-footed animals of North America. Bachman compiled the major portion of the text and Audubon executed the watercolors from which the book's engravings were made.

Audubon traveled widely throughout the eastern United States, completing a series of field sketches for many of the illustrations. He would certainly have seen the "Carolina Grey Squirrel" in its natural habitat many times. The "Polar Hare," however, is found only in the far north, and the "Collared Peccary" only in the desert Southwest; it is probable that he prepared the illustrations of those mammals from specimens he received from his many scientific-minded friends. The identifications on the book's individual color plates provides the common name of each animal as well as its binomial scientific name, as assigned by Georges Cuvier, William Elford Leach, and other leading taxonomists. Rare and valuable as works of art, Audubon's watercolors are among the most important artistic productions of any American naturalist during the first half of the nineteenth century and are equally valuable examples of the lithographer's art. BT

▲ Thomas Nuttall (1786–1859). *The North
American Sylva; or, A Description of the Forest
Trees of the United States, Canada and Nova
Scotia, Not Described in the Work of F. Andrew
Michaux.* 3 vols. Philadelphia: J. Dobson,
1842–1849.

The plate of the *Ficus aurea*, or "Strangler Fig,"
is one of more than a hundred illustrating
Thomas Nuttall's *North American Sylva*. As one
of the most influential scientists in the United
States during the first half of the nineteenth century, Nuttall published original studies in
ornithology, geology, mineralogy, and botany.
His three-volume "description of the forest trees,"
as a continuation of the pioneering work of the
European botanist François André Michaux,
completed the first systematic study of the trees
of eastern North America.

From the earliest years of the seventeenth
century, Virginians had contributed significantly
to the accumulation and classification of botanical information about North America, and the
libraries of colonial Virginians as well as that of
the governor's Council contained important
works on botany. Trees were crucial to the colonial economy. The British navy needed tall,
straight pines for ship's masts, strong oak and
other woods for hulls and decks, and pitch pines
for waterproofing tars. Other woods served as raw
material for the casks and barrels used to store
and ship tobacco, grain, and other commodities,
and many Virginians harvested chestnuts, acorns,
walnuts, and other forest products for nutritional
as well as medicinal uses. During the nineteenth
century, forest products became vital to Virginia's
lumber and papermaking industries. BT

▼ Alexander Wilson (1766–1813). *American
Ornithology; or, The Natural History of the Birds of
the United States.* 9 vols. Philadelphia: Bradford
and Inskeep, 1808–1825.

The detailed illustration of two of the most
colorful of Virginia's birds—the "Cardinal
Grosbeak" and the "Red Tanager"—is from volume two of the first edition of *American
Ornithology,* compiled by Alexander Wilson. The
Library of Virginia acquired the nine-volume set
soon after its publication and listed the title in its
first printed catalog, published in 1828, simply as
"Wilson's American Ornithology."

Wilson's monumental work predates that of
John James Audubon and includes far more birds,
and far more descriptive text, than did Audubon
in his later single-volume work. Moreover,
Wilson's compilation was the first multivolume
scientific publication of its kind in the United
States. During his research, Wilson traveled to
Virginia to collect specimens and to interview
persons who had made special studies of some of
the birds of eastern North America. Following
directions and suggestions that he obtained from
President Thomas Jefferson, Wilson acquired an
example of the ruby-throated hummingbird.

Wilson illustrated the northern cardinal and
scarlet tanager in a single plate. The tanager
arrives in Virginia from the tropics in the late
spring, nesting and raising its young in the tree-
tops of the Old Dominion's forests before depart-
ing for its winter home in the early autumn. The
cardinal is a year-round resident and has been
known by a variety of names, including "Virginia
Nightingale," "Virginia Redbird," "Virginia
Grosbeak," and "Cardinal Grosbeak." Now
known as the "Northern Cardinal," to distinguish
it from several Central and South American
cardinal species, it is the official state bird of
Virginia. BT

p. 15

SUILLUS.

The great Hog-Fish.   Le grand Pourceau.

THESE Fish are taken of several sizes ; but the largest that I have seen was between three and four feet, as this was : the iris of the eye red, the upper mandible of a fleshy callous substance and of a reddish purple colour ; which was guarded by a bony substance as by a shield ; the upper part of which to the eye was black, from under the eye to the angle of the mouth it was purple, sprinkled thick over with crooked blue lines in form of worms ; the end of the upper mandible was armed with four large teeth, at the end of the under mandible were also two of the like size ; the rest of the teeth were small, and in single rows : the inside of the mouth was of a blood-red colour, the under jaw yellow. From the eyes to the tail, the back was covered with large purple scales, those on the belly lighter with stains of yellow : on the back was a remarkable black fin dividing at the basis, and branching into four long pliant flagelli, large at the basis, and gradually decreasing to their points, and bending backwards. Behind the gills were two yellow fins, and another imperfect one, or rather beard, under the throat. The tail of this Fish being cut off before I had it, I cannot say of what form it was.

CES Poissons sont de grandeurs différentes ; mais les plus grands que j'aye vûs étoient entre trois & quatre piés, tel qu'étoit celui-ci. Il avoit l'iris des yeux rouge, la machoire supérieure d'une substance charnue & calleuse, & d'une couleur violette tirant sur le rouge : elle étoit défendue & couverte d'une substance offense, qui lui servoit comme de bouclier, dont le dessus jusqu'à l'oeil étoit noir, & depuis le dessous de l'oeuil jusqu'au coin de la gueule étoit violet, & tout parsemé de petites lignes bleues, ondées en forme de petits vers. Le bout de la machoire supérieure étoit armé de quatre dents fort grandes : il y en avoit aussi deux semblables au bout de la machoire inférieure : les autres dents étoient petites ; & il n'y en avoit qu'une rangée, tant en haut qu'en bas : le dedans de la gueule étoit d'un rouge de sang : la machoire inférieure étoit jaune. Depuis les yeux jusqu'à la queüe, le dos étoit couvert de grandes écailles violettes : celles du ventre étoient semblables, mais plus claires, & avoient quelques tâches jaunes : sur le dos il y avoit une nageoire noire, fort remarquable, qui se divisoit à sa base en quatre longues branches souples, qui s'étrécissoient toujours jusqu'à leurs extrémités qui se terminoient en pointes, & se recourboient vers la queüe : derriere des ouyes il y avoit deux nageoires jaunes, & une autre imparfaite, ou plûtôt une espece de barbe, sous la gorge. Comme on avoit coupé la queüe de ce Poisson, avant que je l'eusse vûe, je ne saurois dire quelle en étoit la forme.

▲ Mark Catesby (1683–1749). *The Natural History of Carolina, Florida, and the Bahama Islands.* London: Printed for C. Marsh et al., 1754.

Mark Catesby is regarded as the most important artist-naturalist of the American colonial era. Born and educated in England and a member of a prominent English family of historians and amateur botanists, Catesby was the first naturalist to illustrate an extensive array of American flora and fauna in which animals were combined with plants in a true-to-life relationship.

Catesby came to Virginia in 1712 because, he wrote, "my curiosity was such that I soon imbibed a passionate desire of viewing the animal and vegetable productions in their native countries. . . . Virginia was the place (as I had relations there), which suited most with my convenience to go." From Virginia he traveled southward, spending seven years compiling notes and drawings for his *Natural History of Carolina, Florida, and the Bahama Islands,* which contains numerous species indigenous to Virginia. His second trip to the colonies was sponsored by Virginia governor Francis Nicholson, who gave him an annual pension so that he might "observe the rarities of that country." While in Virginia he assembled an enormous collection of flora and fauna for his English patrons.

Catesby considered drawing and even printmaking part of the necessary skills of a naturalist and learned the art of etching for his *Natural History.* Of the book's lavishly colored 220 plates, he etched all but 2 and either hand-colored or supervised the coloring of the first set of prints; producing the first volume took twenty years. Based on his fieldwork, Catesby combined engravings with analytical and descriptive text in both English and French, a practice that later artist-naturalists would follow. Catesby wrote a detailed physical description of the "Hog-Fish," a species found in the waters around Florida and the Bahamas, but then noted: "The tail of this Fish being cut off before I had it, I cannot say of what form it was." SM, BB

Mary H. Willie's Milley born
_____ Laurne died
_____ Weather taken up

May 22. 18. 30 g. Wm Williams
Loaffed for Irregular marriages
also Connachan & Grierson
_____ of Parishes & Mint in Virginia
Receipt _____ fever &   Ague

$ 7.84 to _____ her

in May's death

Loaned to
Bishop Meade
by
Thos H. Meriwether

march 5.
1856

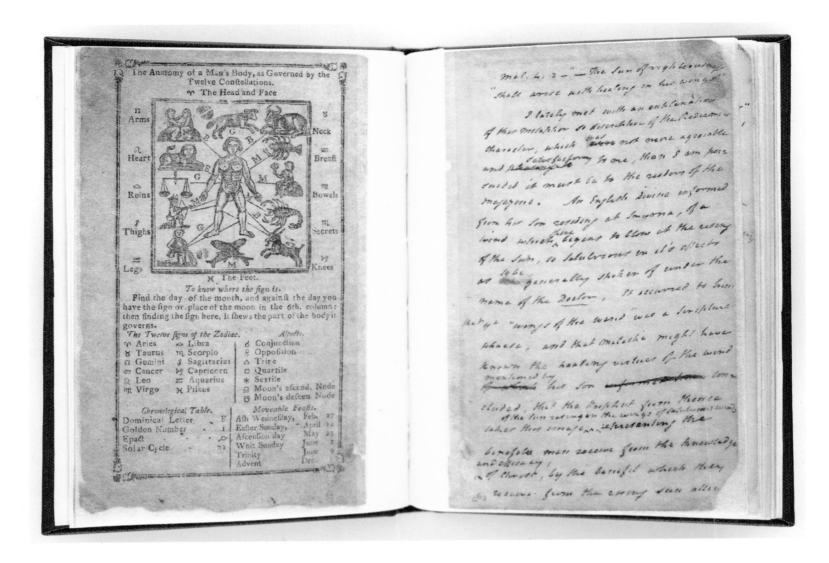

◀ *Virginia Almanack for the Year of Our Lord God 1773.* Williamsburg: Purdie and Dixon, 1773.

Most Revolutionary-era Americans owned few books besides a Bible and perhaps an almanac. Within a single volume, almanacs provided a calendar with weather predictions and astrological information, a gazetteer of general and local information, and some literary selections. The Virginia almanac for 1773 included a calendar and astrological charts calculated for "Virginia, Maryland, N.C. etc.," as well as a list of "representatives for the colony with the number of tithables in each county." The Library of Virginia's copy of the 1773 almanac belonged to William Douglas (1708–1798), an Anglican minister for Saint James Northam Parish in Goochland County from 1750 to 1777. He was

also a minister in King William Parish for nineteen years and in Buckingham County for four years. From 1750 until 1797, he maintained a record of births, marriages, and deaths in Goochland County and surrounding areas; the records were eventually published as *The Douglas Register* (1928). In addition, Douglas was Thomas Jefferson's tutor from 1752 to 1757.

Like many others, Douglas utilized the blank pages of his almanac for a variety of purposes, often as an account book, diary, or notebook. For example, he recorded bits of information in the margins and on the extra leaves in the front of the volume. His notations refer to such things as the number of nails sent to Fork Creek, the date he planted apple trees, and the tithes received from Goochland. NB

▲ *The Town and Country Almanac for the Year of Our Lord, 1805; and the Twenty-ninth of American Independence Calculated for the Meridian of Washington City. The Astronomical Calculations by Abraham Shoemaker of New-York.* Alexandria: Robert and John Gray, 1805.

Abraham Shoemaker, originally from Pennsylvania, provided astrological calculations and weather predictions for a number of regional almanacs published from Georgia to New York. His first Virginia title was the 1805 *Town and Country Almanac.* The Library's copy of the Shoemaker volume belonged to Dr. James Muir (1756–1820). Born in Scotland, Muir was a Presbyterian minister who had served in Bermuda and New Jersey before becoming a pastor in Alexandria, Virginia, in 1789. Muir took his almanac apart, interleaving the printed pages throughout his diary. Portions of the almanac are thus arranged among daily citations for Bible passages, comments on the weather, descriptions of his travels, and quotations from various unnamed sources. The diary also provides information about his church in Alexandria with notations on marriages, deaths, and the sermons preached in his church. NB

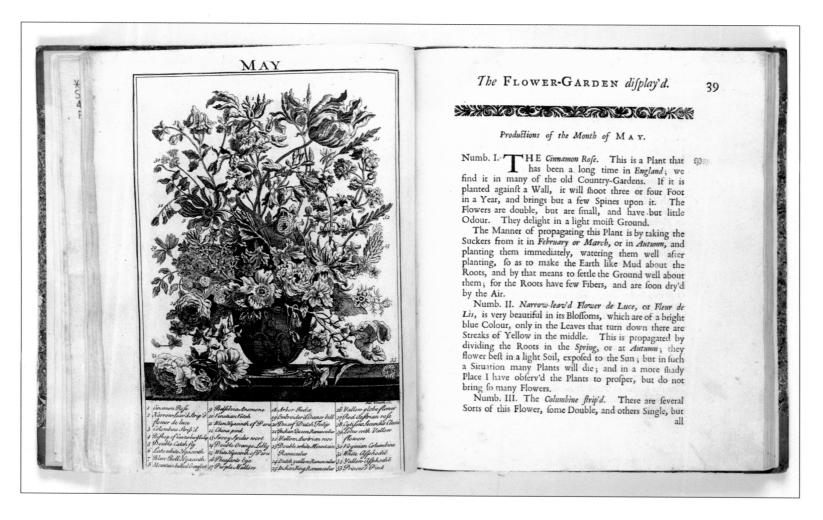

▲ Robert Furber (fl. 1724–1732). *The Flower-Garden Display'd, in Above Four Hundred Curious Representations of the Most Beautiful Flowers.* London: J. Hazard and R. Montagu et al., 1732.

Robert Furber hoped that his *Flower-Garden Display'd* would be a work "very Useful, not only for the *Curious* in Gardening, but the *Prints* likewise for *Painters, Carvers, Japaners,* etc." Indeed, it is the book's artistic rather than practical nature that provides its most immediate appeal. Furber, a Kensington nurseryman, adapted the volume, with its copperplate engravings, from his earlier collection, *Twelve Months of Flowers,* published in 1730. Intended as an elaborate nursery catalog, *Twelve Months of Flowers* was the first of its kind produced in England and was illustrated with a dozen large hand-colored engravings by Henry Fletcher, after paintings by Flemish artist Peter Casteels.

As their titles suggest, both books included plates featuring an arrangement of blooming flowers appropriate for each month of the year. Furber also added a description and history of each plant and its method of cultivation. *The Flower-Garden Display'd* presented a number of American flowers, perhaps for the first time, to English gardeners. The May bouquet included the "Virginian Columbine," no doubt the wild red-and-yellow variety native to Virginia. SM

▶ Jean de La Quintinie (1626–1688). *The Compleat Gard'ner; or, Directions for Cultivating and Right Ordering of Fruit-Gardens, and Kitchen-Gardens.* Translated by John Evelyn (1620–1706). London: Matthew Gillyflower and James Partridge, 1693.

The English translation of Jean de La Quintinie's 1690 French work, *Instruction pour les Jardins, Fruitiers et Potagers,* offered a wider readership the opportunity to learn nearly every aspect of the design and maintenance of late-seventeenth-century gardens. Although English writer and gardener John Evelyn was credited with the translation, he later revealed that "I do not attribute the whole to my self . . . but as a considerable part of it [was], and the rest under my care, the publishers and printers will have it go under my name, altogether against my intentions." Evelyn's name may have been used primarily as a means to promote sales. The English text includes copies of the original plates, some folded, as in the elaborate rendering of "The Kings Kitchen Garden at Versailles." SM

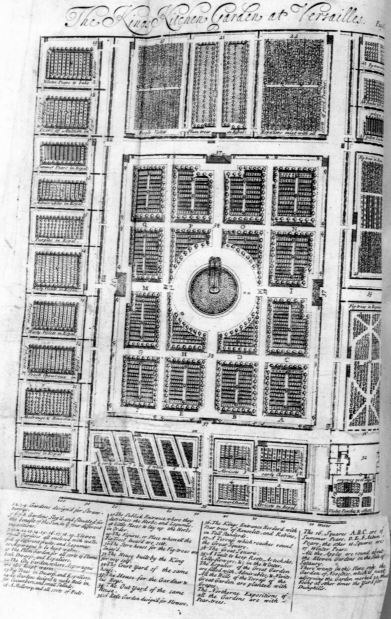

OF
FRUITGARDENS
AND
Kitchen-Gardens.

VOL I. PART I.

CHAP. I.

How Necessary it is for a Gentleman, who designs to have Fruit *and* Kitchen-Gardens, *to be at least reasonably Instructed in what relates to those Kind of Gardens.*

THAT Part of *Gard'ning,* I begin to treat of here, certainly affords a Gentleman who understands and applies himself to it, a great deal of Pleasure ; but that very *Gard'ning* being manag'd by an unskilful lazy *Gard'ner,* is liable to many Inconveniencies, and Vexations. These are Two Noted and undeniable Truths, since nothing in the World requires more Foresight and Activity than those kind of *Fruit* and *Kitchen-Gardens.* They are, as it were, in a perpetual Motion, which inclines them always to Act either for Good or Ill, according to the good or ill Conduct of their Master ; and so largely recompence the Ingenious, as they severely punish the Unskilful.

The Proof of my first Proposition consists in that certainly nothing affords more Delight, first, than to have a *Garden* well seated, of a reasonable largeness, and fine Figure, and that perhaps of our own Contriving or Modelling.

In the second Place, to have that *Garden* at all times not only Neat, for Walking, and to divert the Sight, but likewise abounding in good Things to please the Pallate, as well as for the preservation of Health.

B   Thirdly,

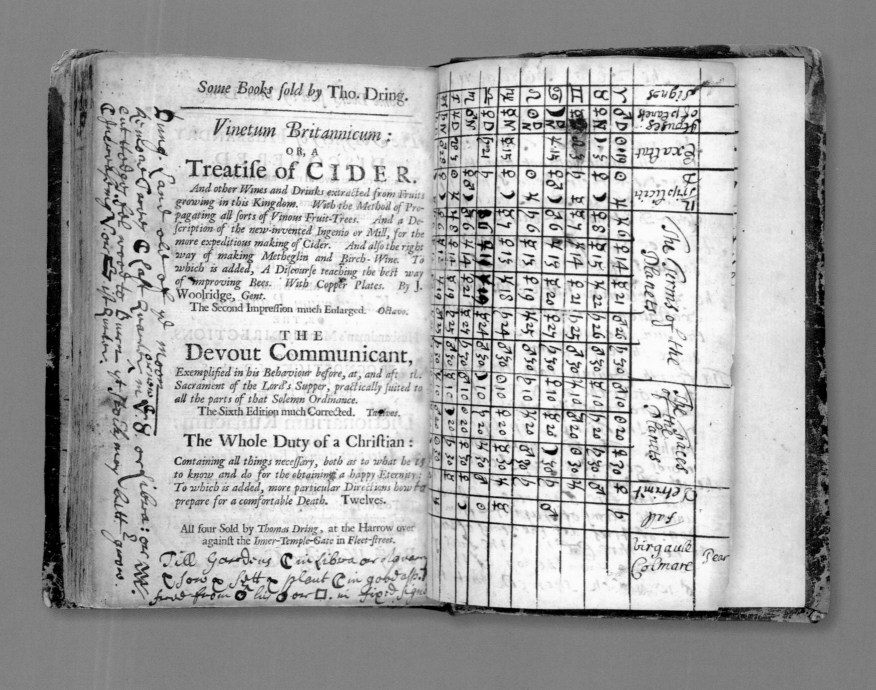

Vinetum Britannicum:
OR, A
Treatise of CIDER.

And other Wines and Drinks extracted from Fruits growing in this Kingdom. With the Method of Propagating all sorts of Vinous Fruit-Trees. And a Description of the new-invented Ingenio or Mill, for the more expeditious making of Cider. And also the right way of making Metheglin and Birch-Wine. To which is added, A Discourse teaching the best way of improving Bees. With Copper Plates. By J. Woolridge, Gent.

The Second Impression much Enlarged. *Octavo.*

THE
Devout Communicant,

Exemplified in his Behaviour before, at, and aft the Sacrament of the Lord's Supper, practically suited to all the parts of that Solemn Ordinance.

The Sixth Edition much Corrected. *Twelves.*

The Whole Duty of a Christian:

Containing all things necessary, both as to what he is to know and do for the obtaining a happy Eternity: To which is added, more particular Directions how to prepare for a comfortable Death. *Twelves.*

All four Sold by *Thomas Dring*, at the *Harrow* over against the *Inner-Temple-Gate* in *Fleet-street.*

▶ William Hanbury (1725–1778). *A Complete Body of Planting and Gardening.* 2 vols. London: Printed for the author, 1770–1771.

William Hanbury, rector of Church Langton in Leicestershire, reportedly possessed "a natural genius for planting and gardening." Hanbury created extensive gardens in Leicestershire and in the neighboring parishes of Gumley and Tur Langton. The estate-gardens became particularly known for their displays of North American plants, at that time still considered exotic for British gardens.

Hanbury's two-volume work included, among other North American species, a description of Calycanthus, accompanied by a fine engraving of the shrub. Referred to as sweet shrub or Carolina allspice, the four varieties of *Calycanthaceae* are deciduous plants with rather large opposite leaves. The plant's rich, reddish-brown, leathery flowers exude an intense fragrance often likened to that of allspice. From each flower a fig-shaped, inedible fruit forms. SM

◀ John Worlidge (fl. 1669–1698). *Systema Horti-Culturæ, or, The Art of Gardening.* 3d ed. London: Printed for Tho[mas] Dring, 1688.

A book sometimes becomes treasured not so much for its rarity, illustrious author, fine engravings, or handsome binding, but rather for how its owner may have used it. Thus, while the Library of Virginia's copy of John Worlidge's *Systema Agriculturæ* (1669) is a far better known treatise, the author's later *Systema Horti-Culturæ* tells a more-interesting story. The 1688 volume is filled with fascinating and copious personal notes on gardening written by the book's first, or at least one of its earliest, owners.

The unknown gardener noted on the inside cover that "Any Corn, Seeds or plant [should] be either set or sown, within 6 hours, before or After ye full moon in Summer or before or after ye new moon in Winter." The scribe also constructed tables and charts of stars and constellations, noting longitude and phases of the moon, by which the writer planned the seasonal work. The writer was knowledgeable on practical matters, such as soil improvement, as well, remarking, for example, "cow dung best for Land if sandy." The notations also include extensive lists of flowers, herbs, vegetables, and other plants. Certainly a reader may glean as much, or more, about horticultural or agricultural practices of seventeenth-century England from the personal jottings and delightful observations so meticulously recorded by a single avid gardener as from the book alone. SM

PLATE V.

Calycanthus.

▶ Mary Randolph (1762–1828). *The Virginia House-wife*. Washington, D.C.: Davis and Force, 1824.

Born at Ampthill near Richmond, Mary Randolph was a cousin of George Washington Parke Custis and reputedly the godmother of his daughter, Mary Anne Randolph Custis, who married Robert E. Lee. More important, however, Mary Randolph was the author of the Old Dominion's first cookbook, *The Virginia House-wife*.

Randolph honed her culinary skills through practical experience. The eldest of thirteen children of Anne Cary and Thomas Mann Randolph, she learned much about domestic management at Tuckahoe, the family's large plantation home in Goochland County. After marriage to David Meade Randolph in 1782, she became known for her lavish hospitality at their Richmond residence. When the family later suffered a financial setback, she opened a boarding house in the city in 1808. In 1819, the Randolphs moved to Washington, D.C., where the author began to gather and record the recipes that would be published in 1824 as *The Virginia House-wife*.

The first regional cookbook published in America, *The Virginia House-wife* was written especially for Virginia cooks. Recipes include many native ingredients, such as corn, squash, and sweet potatoes, as well as foods such as okra, rice, and black-eyed peas that had been introduced from West Africa via the Atlantic slave trade. Randolph's recipe for "Ochra Soup" resembles the stews later called "gumbos," a truly southern culinary specialty. SM

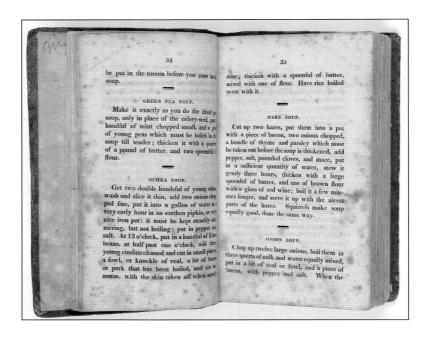

▼ Hannah Glasse (1708–1770). *The Art of Cookery, Made Plain and Easy*. 7th ed. London: A. Millar, 1760.

Undoubtedly the best-known cookery author of the eighteenth century, Hannah Glasse claimed in the first edition of *The Art of Cookery* (1747) that her book "far exceeds any thing of the kind ever yet published." The numerous editions, more than twenty-five, were indeed bestsellers for nearly one hundred years, the last being published in 1843. The seventh edition includes "by way of appendix, one hundred and fifty new and useful receipts."

The *Art of Cookery* was also the most popular cookbook of eighteenth-century Virginia. Although few American cooks owned a cookbook, those who were affluent enough to purchase both the books and the ingredients they demanded relied solely on British editions until the end of the century. Recipes were likely selected or adapted based on the foodstuffs Virginia provided. Pork recipes, for example, were more popular among Virginia cooks than instructions for beef dishes, and pumpkin may have been substituted for turnips in a recipe for pudding or pie.

The author was almost certainly Hannah Allgood, daughter of a prominent London clergyman and the wife of Peter Glasse, a solicitor. She is perhaps best known today as the writer who supposedly instructed her readers to "First, catch your hare," long misinterpreted as a wry comment on the sometimes rudimentary nature of eighteenth-century cooking. However, what she wrote was "Take your Hare when it is cas'd," cased meaning skinned.

It was not until 1796 that the first truly American cookbook was published: *American Cookery* by Amelia Simmons, of Connecticut. And it was not until 1805 that the Alexandria, Virginia, firm of Cottom and Stewart issued the first American printing of Glasse's popular *Art of Cookery*. SM

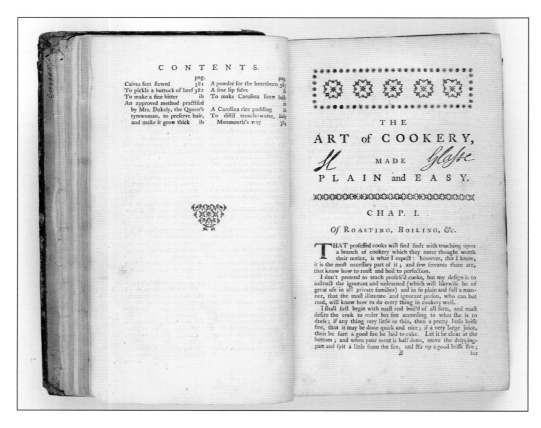

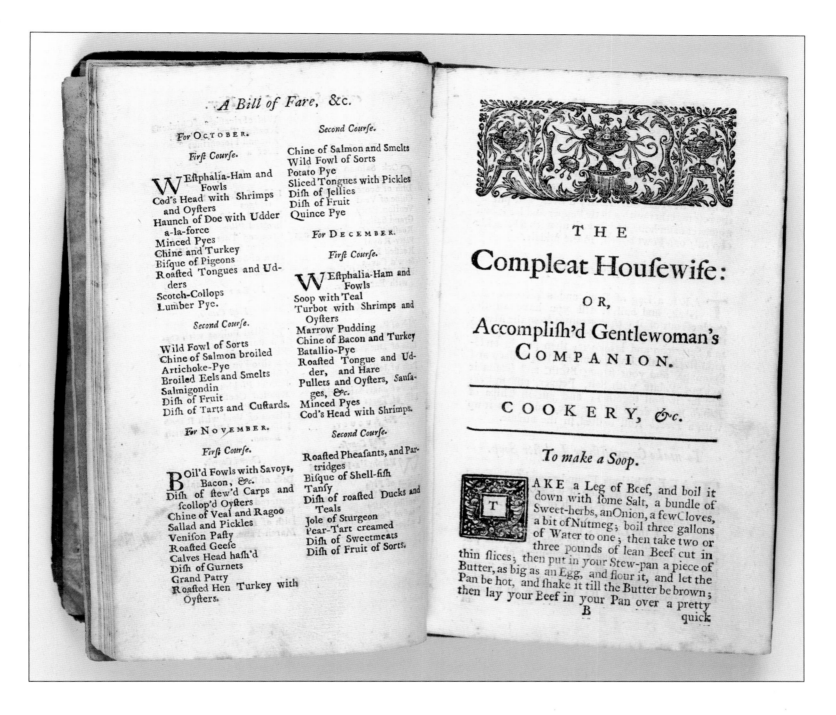

▲ Eliza Smith (fl. 1727–1732). *The Compleat Housewife; or, Accomplish'd Gentlewoman's Companion*. 14th ed. London: R. Ware, 1750.

Eliza Smith is one of the best-known eighteenth-century cookbook authors, perhaps second only to Hannah Glasse. The first edition of her book, *The Compleat Housewife*, was published in London in 1727. The fourteenth edition, "To which is added, a collection of above three hundred family receipts of medicine," appeared twenty-three years later. The eighteenth, and final, edition appeared in 1773. Little is known about the author. The early English editions, in fact, were published with only her initials on the title page.

Smith's work has the special distinction of being the first cookbook printed in America. In 1742, William Parks, of Williamsburg—Virginia's first commercial printer—reprinted a collection of recipes taken from the fifth edition of *The Compleat Housewife*, published in 1732. Known for offering works of a practical nature, in particular demand in a new colony, Parks claimed to have "collected only such [recipes] as are useful and practicable here." The Library of Virginia's collection also includes two other London editions, published in 1729 and 1734, as well as an extremely rare 1752 edition published in Williamsburg. SM

PLATE VIII.

Characterum Musculos in Figuris Indican-   *Explanation of the References that point out*
tium Explicatio.   *the Muscles in the Plates.*

PLATE VI.

Fig. 1.

A. Frontalis.
B. Temporalis.
C. Auris Motores, Ear Movers.
D. Palpebras Moventes, Eyelid Movers.
E. Philtra nominati Narium Motores ⎱ Nose
F. Nares Adducens ⎰ Movers.
G.
H. Longum Par Colli.
I. Scalenus, aut Triangularis.
K. Trigeminus, aut Complexus.
L. Sternoides.
M. Scapularium Musculorum Massa, Mass of
   scapulary Muscles.
N. Pectorales Musculi.

O. Deltoides Scapulæ.
P. Dentatus major Anticus.
Q. Serratus, aut Dentatus Posticus.
R. Cucullaris, aut Trapezius.
S. Sacro-Lumbaris.
Z. Vastus externus.
Δ. Glutæus anterior.
Θ. Glutæus medius.
Γ. Glutæus posterior.
T. Longissimus Dorsi.
U. Semi-Spinatus.
W. Obliquus descendens.
X. Deltoides Femoris.
Y. Rectus.

PLATE VII.

Fig. 2.

A. Frontalis.
B. Temporalis.
C. Mastoides.
D. Palpebrarum Motor.
E. Philtrum Nares movens.
F. Alter Narium Motor.
G. Labia Claudens.
H. Masseter Scalenus.
I. Trigeminus aut Complexus.
K. Trigeminus.
L. Sternoides.
M. Subclavius.
N. Pectorales.
O. Deltoides Scapulæ.
P. Dentatus major Anticus.
Q. Trapezius.
R. Dentatus posticus.
S. Sacro-Lumbaris.
T. Longus Dorsi.
W. Obliquus descendens.
V. Semi-Spinatus.
U. Processus cartilaginosus Scapulæ, The
   cartilaginous Process of the Scapula.
X. Deltoides Femoris.
Y. Rectus.
Z. Vastus externus.
Δ. ⎫ anterior.
Θ. ⎬ Glutæus ⎰ medius.
Γ. ⎭ posterior.
a. Triangularis seu Splenius.
b. Spinatus.
c. Complexi, aut Trigemini Partes.
d. Supra-Spinatus Scapulæ.
e. Spina Scapulæ.
f. Infra-Spinatus Scapulæ

g. Depressor Cubiti.
h. Brachiæus externus.
i. Longus.
k. Biceps.
l. Longi, Bicipitis, & Brachiæ Tendinis In-
   sertio ; Insertion of the Tendon of the
   Longus, Biceps, and Brachiæus.
m. Cubitæus externus.
n. Radiæus externus.
o. Extensor magnus.
p. Radiæus internus.
q. Cubitæus internus.
Λ. Transversalis Abdominis.
Σ. Ventris Rectus.
Ζ. Obliquus descendens.
Π. Biceps Femoris.
r. Gastrocnemius externus.
s. Gastrocnemius internus.
t. Tibius.
u. Flexor Fibulæ.

Fig. 3.

A. Mastoides.
B. Philtrum.
C. Labia Claudens.
D. Cucullaris.
E. Transversalis Colli.
F. Spinatus Colli.
G. Triangularis.
H. Trigeminus, aut Complexus.
I. Sternoides.
K. Subclavius.
L. Deltoides Scapulæ.
M. Processus cartilaginosus Scapulæ.
N. Spina Scapulæ.
O. Supra-Spinatus.
P. Infra-Spinatus.

Q. Biceps.

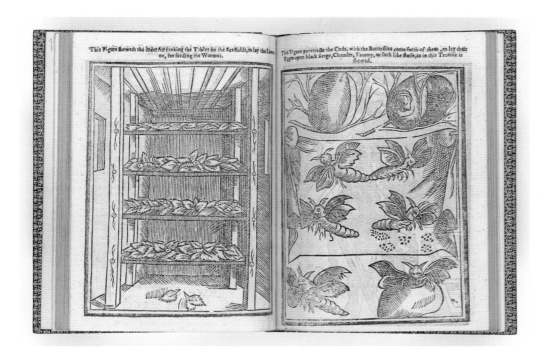

◀ Edward Williams (fl. 1650). *Virginia's Discovery of Silke-Wormes, With Their Benefit. And the Implanting of Mulberry Trees*. London: Printed by T. H. for J. Stephenson, 1650.

In hopes of at last developing a profitable export, Virginia governor Sir William Berkeley (1605–1677) ordered mulberry trees planted along the James River at Jamestown. It was the leaf of the mulberry on which silkworms fed— and it was on the manufacture of silk that Berkeley believed the colony would survive. Berkeley recruited foreign workers to teach silk-making and even established a mulberry-tree nursery at his estate, Green Spring. By 1668 he was able to send a sample of silk to Charles II, but silk manufacturing was never successful in colonial Virginia. The Library of Virginia has two seventeenth-century books in its collection, written and published in England, that served as practical guides for Virginians in the cultivation of mulberry trees and the methods for raising silkworms and making silk. NB

◀ William Cavendish, duke of Newcastle (1592– 1676). *A General System of Horsemanship in All It's Branches*. 2 vols. London: J. Brindley, 1743.

A member of the king's Privy Council, William Cavendish remained a staunch loyalist during the first English Civil War. For his services to Charles I, he was rewarded in 1643 with the rank of marquis. Subsequent disagreements with the royalists over the conduct of the war, however, compelled him to leave England. After three years in Paris, Cavendish settled in Antwerp, where he became famous for his stables and knowledge of horses. In 1657 he published *La Methode et Invention Nouvelle de Dresser les Chevaux*, a theoretical and practical guide to managing and training horses.

After the restoration of the monarchy, Cavendish returned to England, regained his lands confiscated during the war, and in October 1665, by the appointment of Charles II, became

duke of Newcastle. The duke did not return to public life but instead tended his ruined estates and pursued his interests in horses, establishing a racecourse near Wellbeck. In 1667 he published a second book, *A New Method and Extraordinary Invention to Dress Horses, and Work Them, According to Nature*. Reissued in several editions, the book was translated into French in 1671.

Although the duke of Newcastle later wrote numerous plays and poems, he is chiefly remembered for his works on horsemanship. Indeed, it was in 1737, sixty-one years after his death, that a London publisher issued a second edition of his 1657 French-language guide to horsemanship. An English-language translation of the duke's 1657 treatise is included in the first volume of the *General System of Horsemanship*, a beautifully illustrated 1743 compilation of his earlier work published in London. The second volume includes several illustrations of the author training horses at his various estates. DWG

▲ William Tatham (1752–1819). *An Historical and Practical Essay on the Culture and Commerce of Tobacco*. London: Printed for Vernor and Hood, by T. Bensley, 1800.

In 1769, at age seventeen, William Tatham was sent to Virginia to learn the tobacco trade. After five years in Amherst County, Tatham pursued several unsuccessful business interests along the Carolina-Tennessee frontier. He returned to Virginia in 1783 to study law and again in 1789 to organize a geographical department for the state. He had a varied career as a geographer, statesman, soldier, and civil engineer, and as a mapmaker surveyed the Atlantic coast from Cape Fear to Cape Hatteras.

Tatham wrote his *Historical and Practical Essay* to explain how tobacco was grown and to promote better trade relations with England for the tobacco industry. Besides providing detailed descriptions of the tobacco plant and its cultivation, Tatham also explained its commercial aspects, with chapters on public warehouses, inspections, transportation, and British laws. The book includes an appendix with statistics on the import and export trade as well as four copperplate engravings, such as the illustration of the tobacco worm and the moth, or "tobacco hawk," it produces. NB

▼ William Strickland (1787–1854). *Reports on Canals, Railways, Roads, and Other Subjects, Made to "The Pennsylvania Society for the Promotion of Internal Improvement."* Philadelphia: H. C. Carey and I. Lea, 1826.

In 1816, Virginia established the Board of Public Works for the "purpose of rendering navigable, and uniting by canals, the principal rivers, and of more intimately connecting, by public highways, the different parts of this Commonwealth." Virginia clearly considered William Strickland's later *Reports on Canals, Railways, [and] Roads* an important reference work to fulfill the board's mission; the book was listed in the 1828 catalog of the State Library—having been purchased and cataloged within two years of its publication.

Strickland excelled in as many fields as did his famous mentor, Benjamin Henry Latrobe, who trained the younger man in architecture and engineering. Strickland designed and built several Greek Revival buildings in Philadelphia and also became a competent engraver and aquatinter. In 1825, the Pennsylvania Society for the Promotion of Internal Improvement sent Strickland abroad to survey the great railroad, canal, and road projects of Great Britain. Strickland's 1826 report concluded that railroads were destined to outstrip canals as a means of

transportation, a notion thought so radical that the last paragraphs of the book were rewritten before being issued to the society's membership.

In the fine foldout engravings of Strickland's work, Virginians gazed on the most up-to-date technology of the emerging industrial age. The report showed George Stephenson's "patent locomotive engine," only a year after a Stephenson locomotive had run over the pioneering Stockton and Darlington line in England. Stephenson's reputation as the greatest of England's early locomotive builders was forever made with the triumph of his engine, the "Rocket," in a competition near Liverpool in 1829. With the practicality of stream locomotives firmly established, Virginia entered the age of railroading with the construction of the Richmond and Petersburg Railroad, the Louisa Railroad, and the Richmond, Fredericksburg, and Potomac Railroad in the 1830s. GK

◄ John Randall (fl. 1764). *The Construction and Extensive Use of a Newly Invented Universal Seed-Furrow Plough. Also, the Construction of a Draining Plough, upon a very Simple Principle. With the Construction and Use of a Potatoe-drill Machine.* London: J. Wilkie, 1764.

John Randall, a schoolmaster and agriculturalist in York, England, contributed to the development of new agricultural practices by describing several plows of his invention. The first plate in Randall's 1764 book on agricultural implements exhibited his "potatoe-plough," which sowed the potato seeds from a conical hopper as the plow broke the ground. Randall published a second major treatise on farming entitled *The Semi-Virgilian Husbandry, Deduced from Various Experiments: Or, An Essay Towards a New Course of National Farming* (London, 1764), also included in the Library of Virginia's collections.

Virginians, faced with the declining productivity of tobacco fields exhausted by overuse, paid close attention to agricultural innovations in Great Britain, acquiring news of the latest experiments through books, periodicals, and personal contacts. George Washington received two sample plows from the famed English agriculturalist Arthur Young, the great proponent of a system of crop rotation widely practiced in the Norfolk area of England. As Virginia planters increasingly turned to cultivating grains in the late eighteenth and early nineteenth centuries, many adopted and modified the new English agricultural methods, employing deep plowing and crop rotation to improve their lands. Several Virginians as well eventually became leaders in agricultural reform, including John Taylor of Caroline, whose influential book, the *Arator* (1813), appeared in numerous editions, and Edmund Ruffin, founder of the *Farmers' Register* (1833–1843). GK

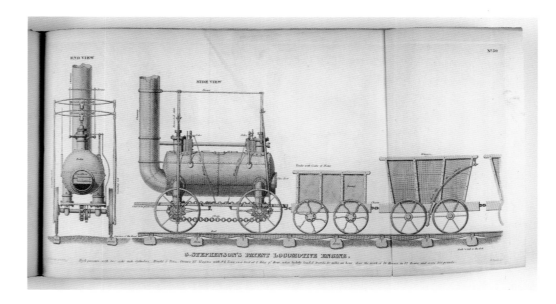

A
PRACTICAL TREATISE
ON
GAS-LIGHT;
EXHIBITING
A SUMMARY DESCRIPTION
OF THE
APPARATUS AND MACHINERY
BEST CALCULATED FOR
ILLUMINATING
STREETS, HOUSES, AND MANUFACTORIES,
WITH
CARBURETTED HYDROGEN, OR COAL-GAS;
WITH REMARKS
ON THE
UTILITY, SAFETY, AND GENERAL NATURE OF THIS NEW BRANCH
OF CIVIL ECONOMY.

BY FREDRICK ACCUM,
OPERATIVE CHEMIST,
LECTURER ON PRACTICAL CHEMISTRY, ON MINERALOGY, AND ON CHEMISTRY
APPLIED TO THE ARTS AND MANUFACTURES; MEMBER OF THE ROYAL
IRISH ACADEMY, FELLOW OF THE LINNEAN SOCIETY, MEMBER
OF THE ROYAL ACADEMY OF SCIENCES OF BERLIN, &c. &c.

WITH SEVEN COLOURED PLATES.

London:
PRINTED BY G. HAYDEN, BRYDGES-STREET, COVENT GARDEN;
FOR R. ACKERMANN, 101, STRAND;
LONGMAN, HURST, REES, ORME, AND BROWN; AND SHERWOOD, NEELY, AND
JONES, PATERNOSTER ROW; AND J. HATCHARD, PICCADILLY.

Price—Twelve Shillings in Boards.

1815.

▲ Friedrich Christian Accum (1769–1838). *A Practical Treatise on Gas-Light*. London: Printed by G. Hayden for R. Ackermann, 1815.

Accum's seminal work on gas lighting was listed in the State Library's 1828 catalog, demonstrating the commonwealth's interest in emerging technologies. A chemist born in the German state of Westphalia, Accum arrived in London in 1793. As an engineer of the London Chartered Gaslight and Coke Company and aided by the art publisher, Rudolph Ackermann (1764–1834), Accum strove to popularize the use of gas lighting. The first edition of his *Practical Treatise on Gas-Light* helped spur the adoption of gas lighting in London and other cities and soon after its publication was translated into German, French, and Italian. Although experiments with gaslights were conducted in Richmond in the early 1800s, the first gasworks did not begin operation in the city until 1851. GK

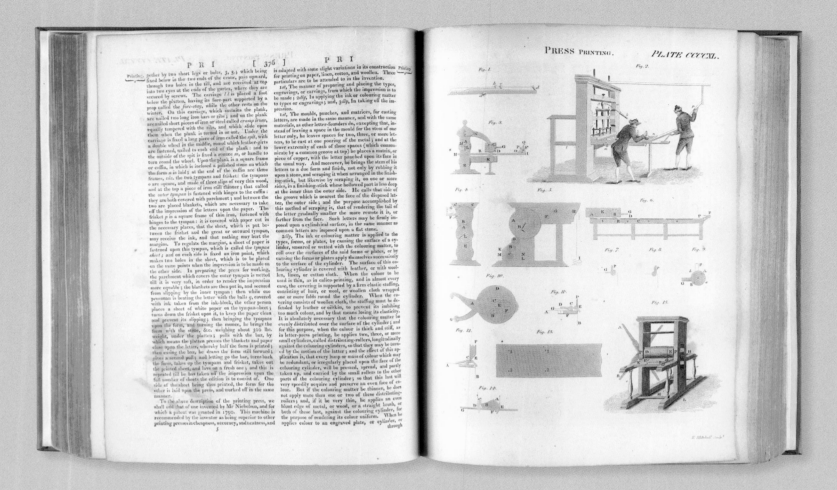

▲ *Encyclopaedia Britannica; or, A Dictionary of Arts, Sciences, and Miscellaneous Literature*. 6th ed. Edinburgh: A. Constable, 1823.

The first edition of the *Encyclopedia Britannica* was published between 1768 and 1771 in three volumes by "a Society of Gentlemen in Scotland." Organized differently than other encyclopedias of the time, the text included lengthy as well as brief articles—many on technical subjects—in a single, alphabetic arrangement. The 1823 "enlarged and improved" twenty-volume sixth edition is listed in the State Library's published catalog for 1828 and is probably the first encyclopedia acquired by the Library of Virginia. In February 1781, Governor Thomas Jefferson and the Council of State had decided to purchase the forthcoming *Encyclopédie Méthodique*, but the title is not listed among the first printed catalog's reference works. The Library of Virginia's collections include more than one hundred encyclopedias dating from the 1700s to the present. NB

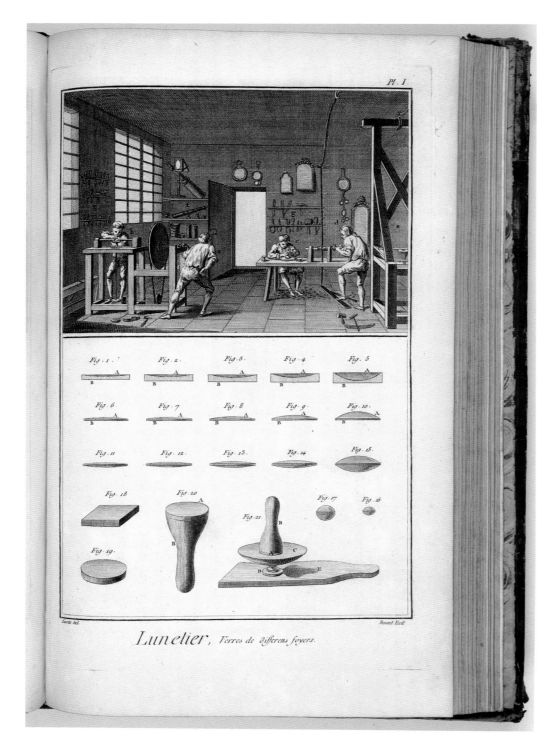

Lunetier, Verres de differens foyers.

◄ Denis Diderot (1713–1784) and Jean Le Rond d'Alembert (1717–1783). *Encyclopédie, ou Dictionnaire Raisonné des Sciences, des Arts et des Métiers, par une Societé de Gens de Lettres.* Paris: Briasson et al., 1751–1765.

The first edition of one of the most important encyclopedias of the eighteenth century remains a monument to the European Enlightenment. Denis Diderot's work emphasized the rigorous and rational study of the natural world, the mechanical as well as fine arts, and the sciences. So revolutionary was its text that the Jesuits in 1751 unsuccessfully attempted to have the initial volume suppressed. When completed in 1765, the encyclopedia included seventeen volumes of essays and eleven volumes of plates. Although Diderot served as editor and as a contributor, much of the text was written by other authors, such as Voltaire, Montesquieu, and Rousseau, all experts in their subject areas. It was the first encyclopedia to include a substantial amount of information on the mechanical arts, highlighted with many detailed plates such as the one depicting the *Lunetiers*, or lens-makers, shown shaping their work on foot-powered treadle lathes. Many contemporaries of Diderot felt the technological articles were unimportant and not appropriate for an encyclopedia. NB

◄ ► Andrea Palladio (1508–1580). *The Architecture of A. Palladio in Four Books, Containing a Short Treatise of the Five Orders, and the Most Necessary Observations Concerning All Sorts of Building.* 2d ed., 2 vols. Revised, designed, and published by Giacomo Leoni (1686–1746). London: Printed by J. Darby for the author, 1721.

Andrea Palladio, described as "probably the most influential figure in the history of Western architecture," was born in Padua, apprenticed to a stonemason in Vicenza, and eventually taken under the care of Count Gian Giorgio Trissino, who sponsored Palladio's education as an architect. Palladio published his first work in 1554, *Le antichità di Roma* ("The Antiquities of Rome"), which for two hundred years remained the essential guide to the grand Italian city. In 1570, at the conclusion of twenty years of intensive building and detailed study of Roman architecture, Palladio published his most famous treatise, *I quattro libri dell'architettura* ("Four Books of Architecture"), an authoritative summary of classical design.

After Palladio's death in 1580, his followers disseminated his ideas throughout the European continent and the English-speaking world. In 1650, Roland Fréart, sieur de Chambray, published a French translation of Palladio's treatise, *Les Qvatre Livres de L'architectvre d'André Palladio.* The first English-language edition of Palladio's work appeared in 1715 when Giacomo Leoni, a self-described Venetian who spent most of his career in England, published *The Architecture of A. Palladio; in Four Books*, which was "improved," revised, and reissued in a second edition in 1721.

Thomas Jefferson, who designed Virginia's State Capitol and the University of Virginia, owned Leoni's 1721 edition and considered Palladio's treatise to be "the Bible." In a copy of that edition, which Thomas Nelson Page presented to the University of Virginia, Page made a manuscript note on the title page that Jefferson had used that edition to make his drawings for the university's Rotunda. Thus Palladio's *Four Books of Architecture*, through Jefferson's interpretation and execution, provided the basis for much of Virginia's Classical Revival architecture and thereby greatly influenced American architectural development. ES

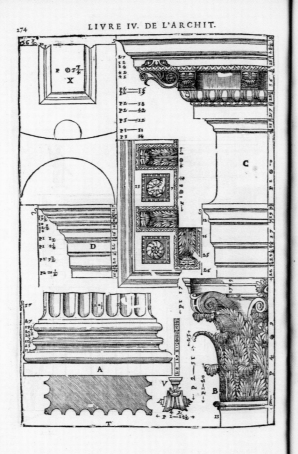

THE MINDE OF
THE FRONTISPEECE,
And Argument of this
WORKE.

FIRE, AIRE, EARTH, WATER, all the Opposites
That stroue in *Chaos*, powrefull LOVE vnites;
And from their Discord drew this Harmonie
That smiles in *Nature*: who, with rauisht eye,
Affects his owne-made *Beauties*. But, our *Will*,
Desire, and *Powres Irascible*, the skill
Of PALLAS orders; who the *Mind* attires
With all *Heroick Vertues*: This aspires
To *Fame* and *Glorie*; by her noble Guide
Eternized, and well-nigh Deifi'd.
But who forsake that faire *Intelligence*,
To follow *Passion*, and voluptuous *Sense*;
That shun the Path and Toyles of HERCVLES:
Such, charm'd by CIRCE's luxurie, and ease,
Themselues deforme: 'twixt whom, so great an ods;
That these are held for Beasts, and those for Gods.

PHŒBVS APOLLO (sacred Poesie)
Thus taught : for in these antient Fables lie
The mysteries of all Philosophie.

Some Natures secrets shew; in some appeare
Distempers staines; some teach vs how to beare
Both Fortunes, bridling Ioy, Griefe, Hope, and Feare.

These Pietie, Deuotion those excite;
These prompt to Vertue, those from Vice affright;
All fitly mingling Profit with Delight.

This Course our Poet steeres: and those that faile,
By wandring Stars, not by his Compasse, saile.

VIRGINIA AUTHORS AND COLLECTORS

The Library of Virginia's collection of books by Virginia authors includes works of fiction, poetry, history, biography, literary criticism, and other areas of nonfiction. During the first half of the twentieth century, the Library compiled and lent boxed sets of these books to counties and communities in Virginia that did not have their own public libraries. Even after the establishment of a statewide public library system, the Library continued to be the central source from which Virginia's citizens obtained copies of books that were unavailable in their local libraries, a role the Library still fulfills.

In order to meet the varied research needs of Virginians and to preserve the cultural heritage of the commonwealth, the Library of Virginia has sought to enlarge and improve the quality of its Virginiana holdings. As a consequence, the Library has an extensive collection of the works of such great American and Virginia writers as Sherwood Anderson, Rita Mae Brown, James Branch Cabell, John Casey, Rita Dove, Douglas Southall Freeman, Nikki Giovanni, Ellen Glasgow, Mary Johnston, and Dumas Malone. The Library regularly sponsors lectures, book signings, teleconferences, and other events promoting Virginia's literary heritage, cosponsoring many of these events with the Virginia Center for the Book.

Since the 1830s, the Library has also been fortunate to have received or acquired books from Virginia bibliophiles, whose private collections of noteworthy volumes have enriched its holdings. The Library owns books that were once in the private libraries of such distinguished figures as Thomas Jefferson, Patrick Henry, Richard Henry Lee, John Stewart Bryan, Douglas Southall Freeman, Thomas Nelson Page, Lila Meade Valentine, and many others.

◀ George Sandys (1578–1644). *Ovid's Metamorphosis Englished, Mythologiz'd, And Represented in Figures. An Essay to the Translation of Virgil's Aeneis.* London, 1626.

This English translation of Ovid's *Metamorphosis* may accurately be described as the first major work of English-language scholarship completed in North America. The translator, who rendered Ovid's Latin verse into excellent English poetry, was George Sandys, who resided in Virginia from 1621 until 1625. Sandys's duties as treasurer of the colony occupied most of his time, but during his leisure hours and at night he completed the translation of the fifteen books of Ovid's poetry that he had begun either before leaving England or while on board ship en route to Virginia. This first edition of Sandys's translation was printed in London in 1626 after his return to England, and was reprinted in 1628 and in 1631.

In 1632 Sandys published a new edition with additional notes, and during the remainder of the seventeenth century that edition was reissued several times. John Dryden and Alexander Pope both praised the poetry of Sandys's translation, and, in his pioneering study of early American literature, Moses Coit Tyler described Sandys's work as "the first utterance of the conscious literary spirit articulated in America." The Library of Virginia also owns a copy of the 1632 edition. BT

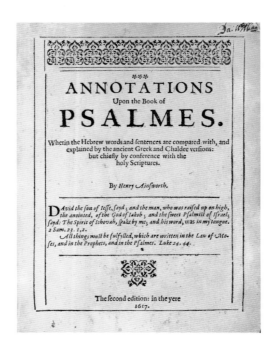

▲ Henry Ainsworth (1571–ca.1623). *Annotations Upon the Book of Psalmes*. Amsterdam ?, 1617.

This copy of Henry Ainsworth's *Annotations Upon the Books of Psalmes*, probably printed in Amsterdam in 1617, made two trips across the Atlantic Ocean on the *Mayflower*. The book's inscription—"This Booke Was given unto me Giles Heale Chirurgion by Isacke Allerton Tailor in Verginia the X of Feburary in the Yeare of Our Lord 1620"—is misleading, however.

Surgeon Giles Heale and tailor Isaac Allerton are recorded among the passengers of the *Mayflower* on its voyage in the autumn of 1620 from the Old World to the New. The Pilgrims onboard the *Mayflower* had intended to sail to the northern portion of the territory included in the charter of the Virginia Company, but they landed instead outside that jurisdiction at a place they called Plymouth in Massachusetts Bay. As they had referred to their destination throughout the voyage as "Virginia," Heale incorrectly used that designation in his inscription. The Pilgrims marked time by the Julian calendar, in which the new year began on 25 March, meaning that the tenth day of February 1620 by the old calendar was 10 February 1621 by the modern calendar.

The name of Mary Heale (spelled Hele) and the Old Style date February 1620 are on the book's flyleaf. Mary, who was a relative of Giles Heale, remained in England. Because she was in possession of the volume twelve months after Heale inscribed it, the recipient must have sent it back to England when the *Mayflower* returned in the spring of 1621.

Sometime during the 1890s this volume was advertised for sale in London. A generous benefactor, whose name is no longer known, saw the advertisement and reference to the inscription and purchased the volume for presentation to the Virginia State Library under the mistaken impression that it had been in Virginia before. BT

► ▼ John Smith (ca. 1580–1631). *The Generall Historie of Virginia, New-England, and the Summer Isles: With the Names of the Adventurers, Planters, and Governours from Their First Beginning, Ano:1584, to This Present 1624*. London: Printed by I. D. and I. H. for Michael Sparkes, 1624.

Captain John Smith published the first edition of his famous history of Virginia in 1624. Smith had previously written short accounts of Virginia's settlement, but his *Generall Historie* provided a lengthy description of the colony's early years, drawing from the recollections of other colonists and including an account of his rescue by Pocahontas.

Since its creation, Smith's sprightly history has been a starting place for writers studying Virginia's earliest days. Robert Beverley, the first native Virginian to write a history of the colony, drew on Smith's *Generall Historie* for his own *History and Present State of Virginia*, published in London in 1705. William Stith used it as the basis for his *History of the First Discovery and Settlement of Virginia*, published in Williamsburg in 1747, the first book-length history printed in Virginia. Doubts about the accuracy of some of Smith's assertions have produced a large scholarly literature. Debate still continues about whether Smith's rescue by Pocahontas actually took place as he described it or whether it was merely a heroic invention.

The Library of Virginia owns many different editions of Smith's *Generall Historie*, including this first edition of 1624 and two copies of the edition of 1632. BT

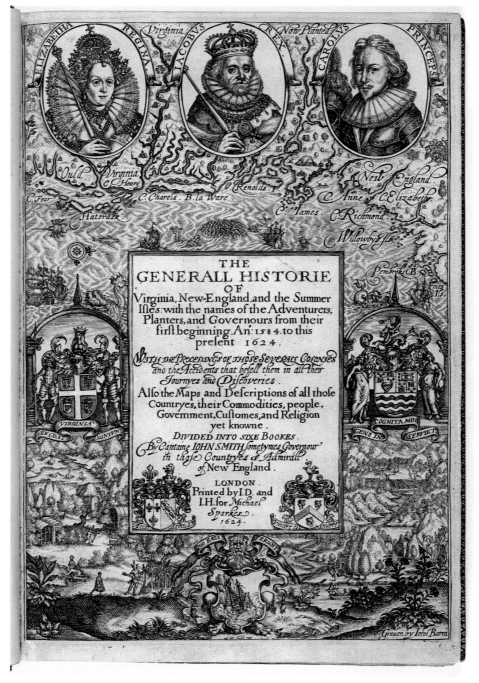

The portraiture of the illustreous Princesse Frances Duchess of Richmond
and Lenox daughter of Thomas Ld Howard of Bindon sonne of Thomas Duke of Norfolk
whose mother was Elisabeth daughter of Edward Duke of Buckingham
Anno 1623. insculptum a Guill: Passeo Londinum.

TO
THE ILLVSTRIOVS
AND MOST NOBLE
PRINCESSE, the Lady FRAN-
CIS, Ducheſſe of RICHMOND
and LENOX.

AY it pleaſe your Grace,
This History, as for the raritie and
varietie of the ſubiect, ſo much more
for the judicious Eyes it is like to vnder-
goe, and moſt of all for that great Name,
whereof it dareth implore Protection,
might and ought to haue beene clad in better robes then my
rude military hand can cut out in Paper Ornaments. But be-
cauſe, of the moſt things therein, I am no Compiler by hear-
ſay, but haue beene a reall Actor; I take my ſelfe to haue a
propertie in them: and therefore haue beene bold to challenge them to come vnder the reach of my owne rough Pen.
That, which hath beene indured and paſſed through with
hardſhip and danger, is thereby ſweetned to the Actor, when
he becometh the Relator. I haue deeply hazarded my ſelfe in
doing and ſuffering, and why ſhould I ſticke to hazard my
reputation in Recording? He that acteth two parts is the
more borne withall if he come ſhort, or fayle in one of
them. Where ſhall we looke to finde a Iulius Cæſar, whoſe at-
chieuments ſhine as cleare in his owne Commentaries, as
they did in the field? I confeſſe, my hand, though able to
weild a weapon among the Barbarous, yet well may trem-

)(ble

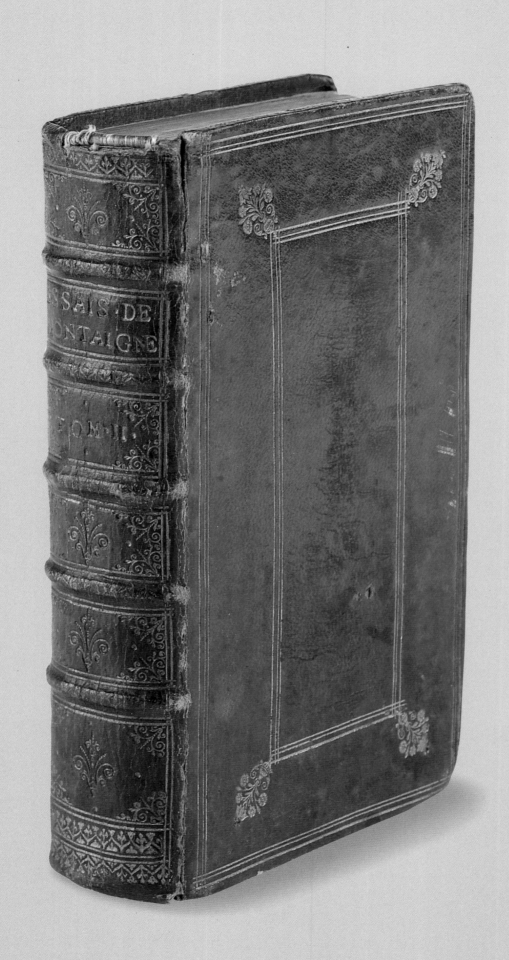

◄ Michel de Montaigne (1533–1592). *Les Essais de Michel, Seigneur de Montaigne.* Vol. 2. Brussels: F. Foppens, 1659.

Michel de Montaigne, an influential French writer who is credited with having established the essay as a unique form of literature, wrote his famous three-volume *Essais* between 1572 and 1587. Born in the Bordeaux region of France in 1533, Montaigne served as a counselor to the Parliament of Bordeaux from 1557 to 1570. A year later, he retired from public life and shortly thereafter began to write his major work. A "vivid and charming" stylist, Montaigne used his own experience, feelings, and philosophy as the basis for his reflections, which ranged from thoughts on sadness, idleness, fear, friendship, and sleep to studies of such classical figures as Cato, Cicero, Caesar, Virgil, and Plutarch. Montaigne's work exerted a great impact on French and English literature for several centuries, as his essays influenced the thought of such noted writers as Descartes, Shakespeare, Webster, Pascal, Rousseau, Emerson, and Gide.

Thomas Jefferson purchased two editions of Montaigne's *Essais*—the 1659 Brussels and the 1669 Amsterdam printings. When he sold his second library in 1815 to the Library of Congress, the 1669 edition was apparently included in the sale. The Library of Virginia obtained volume two of the 1659 Brussels edition in 1953. Entered on a page near the front of the book is the information that the "work was purchased at the sale of Mr. Jefferson's Library," presumably the sale of Jefferson's third library after his death in 1826. The scribe, "L.H.M." recommended that readers "see his initial 'T.' *before* signature 'I,' page 193. Also I after signature 'T' page 433. Every Book in his Library, with few exceptions, was identified in the same manner." ES, ST

▲ *The Proceedings of the Convention of Delegates for the Counties and Corporations in the Colony of Virginia, Held at Richmond Town, in the County of Henrico, on Monday the 17th of July 1775. Reprinted by a Resolution of the House of Delegates, of the 24 February, 1816.* Richmond: Ritchie, Trueheart and Du-val, Printers, 1816.

The Proceedings of the Convention of Delegates, Held at Richmond Town, in the Colony of Virginia, on Friday, the 1st of December, 1775, And Afterwards by Adjournment in the City of Williamsburg. Re-printed by a Resolution of the House of Delegates, of the 24 February, 1816. Richmond: Ritchie, Trueheart and Du-val, Printers, 1816.

In 1816, the House of Delegates authorized reprint editions of the journals of Virginia's four Revolutionary-era conventions that met during 1775 and 1776. Each convention's journal was printed separately, but many sets were bound together in one convenient volume. The Library has several copies of these 1816 reprints, including the bound volume that was presented by the General Assembly to Thomas Jefferson.

Unlike many early American book collectors who affixed elaborate bookplates to their volumes or who signed them conspicuously, Jefferson discreetly marked his books by transforming printer's marks into his own initials. Typesetters in Jefferson's day printed large sheets of paper with the texts for four, eight, or sixteen pages on a side, and then folded the sheets so that only one page of type showed. Binders sewed the folded sheets, or "signatures," together into books. In order to keep the sheets in the proper sequence for binding, printers marked them with letters of the alphabet at the bottom of the first page of a signature. Jefferson identified his books by inking in a small letter *T* before the signature marks *I* or *J*, and he sometimes added a *J* after a signature mark *T*. BT

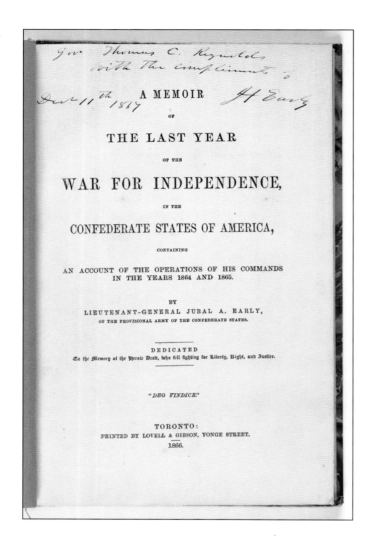

▲ Jubal Anderson Early (1816–1894). *A Memoir of the Last Year of the War for Independence, in the Confederate States of America, Containing an Account of the Operations of His Commands in the Years 1864 and 1865.* Toronto: Lovell and Gibson, 1866.

Jubal Anderson Early, a native of Franklin County, Virginia, graduated from the United States Military Academy at West Point, New York, in 1837. After a year in the army, he resigned his commission and opened a law practice in Rocky Mount, Virginia. Early served in the state convention that debated whether Virginia should join the Confederacy in 1861 and voted against secession, but joined the Confederate army once Virginia's course was set.

He rose steadily in rank, becoming lieutenant general of the Second Corps in 1864. Sent to the Shenandoah Valley where in 1862 Thomas J. "Stonewall" Jackson had won brilliant victories, he suffered a resounding defeat against Union forces led by General Philip H. Sheridan. Many Southerners blamed Early for the loss of the strategically important Valley and raised such an outcry against him that Confederate commander R. E. Lee reluctantly relieved him of command. Early headed west to join Confederate forces fighting in Texas, and then went to Mexico and eventually to Canada, intending never to return to the United States.

While in Canada, Jubal Early published his *Memoir of the Last Year of the War for Independence* (1866), which was attacked by many critics in the United States as "a bitter diatribe" and "a vindictive book bristling with untempered judgments." Early already had a reputation for being rough and outspoken. One contemporary described him as "most emphatic and denunciatory, and startingly profane." In 1869, Early returned to Virginia and settled in Lynchburg. He became the first president of the Southern Historical Society and helped to define the Lost Cause rationale for the South's defeat. By the time of his death in 1894, he had overcome most of the animosity generated by his wartime losses and "enjoyed a reputation as the foremost Southern authority on the war."

In 1946 the Library of Virginia acquired twelve hundred volumes from the library of General John E. Roller (1844–1918), of Harrisonburg. Roller had amassed a large collection of books and manuscripts about Virginia, the South, and the Confederacy, including an autographed copy of Early's 1866 *Memoir*. Early had inscribed the book to Thomas Caute Reynolds, the Confederate governor-in-exile of Missouri, whom he may have met in Mexico. Reynolds died in 1887 and presumably some or all of his library was sold, thereby allowing Early's 1866 *Memoir* to come into the hands of General Roller. ES

▶ Douglas Southall Freeman (1886–1953). *Lee's Dispatches: Unpublished Letters of General Robert E. Lee, C. S. A., to Jefferson Davis and the War Department of the Confederate States of America, 1862–65.* New York and London: G. P. Putnam's Sons, 1915.

Born in Lynchburg in 1886, Douglas Southall Freeman was raised in Richmond and received his bachelor of arts degree from Richmond College in 1904 and his doctorate in history from Johns Hopkins University in 1908. While researching his dissertation at the Virginia State Library in 1906, Freeman worked for reference librarian Kate Pleasants Minor, who was so impressed by his ability that she recommended him for a position at the Confederate Museum. Hired to catalog the museum's papers, Freeman saw his efforts result in his first publication, *A Calendar of Confederate Papers, with a Bibliography of Some Confederate Publications* (1908).

In 1909, following the completion of his studies, Freeman joined the editorial staff of the *Richmond Times-Dispatch*, and in 1915 he became the editor of the city's other major daily, the *Richmond News Leader*, a position he held until his retirement in 1949. In his spare time, Freeman continued to pursue his interest in history. In 1915 he published *Lee's Dispatches*, based on a newly discovered cache of General R. E. Lee's papers. On 29 June 1915, Freeman inscribed a copy of *Lee's Dispatches* to John Stewart Bryan, publisher of the *News Leader*, describing Bryan as "a man who cherished those ideals of courtesy, of constancy and of service our great chieftain incarnated. It is to that man, my friend, I give this book." Bryan died in 1944 and in 1952 his family gave the Virginia State Library several thousand volumes from his library, including this autographed copy of Freeman's *Lee's Dispatches*.

After *Lee's Dispatches*, Freeman spent nineteen years researching and writing a four-volume biography of R. E. Lee for which he was awarded the Pulitzer Prize in 1935. Several years later, he published *Lee's Lieutenants* (1942–1944). He then began what became a seven-volume biography of George Washington. In 1958 he was recognized posthumously with the Pulitzer Prize for *George Washington* (1948–1957), sharing the honor with John Alexander Carroll and Mary Wells Ashworth, who had completed the last volume after Freeman's death on 13 June 1953. ES

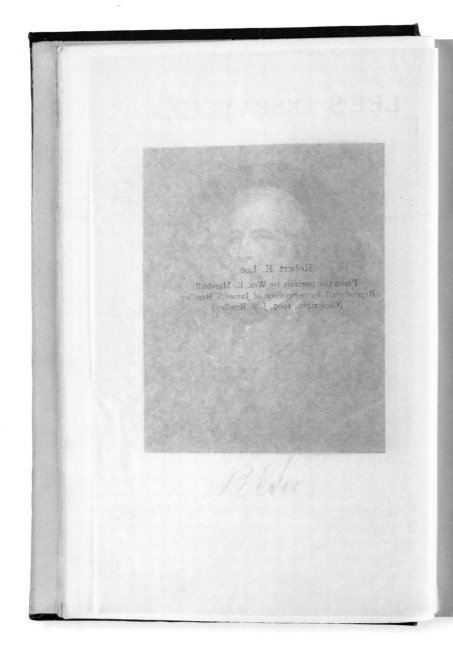

LEE'S DISPATCHES

Unpublished Letters
of
General Robert E. Lee, C.S.A.
to
Jefferson Davis and the War Department of
The Confederate States of America

1862–65

From the Private Collection of
WYMBERLEY JONES DE RENNE
of Wormsloe, Georgia

Edited with an Introduction by
DOUGLAS SOUTHALL FREEMAN

G. P. PUTNAM'S SONS
NEW YORK AND LONDON
The Knickerbocker Press
1915

To John Stewart Bryan:
Would you mind if I tell you
truth: often as, with reverent hands,
I annoted these letters, I rejoiced
to think I knew a man who cherished
those ideals of courtesy, of constancy
and of service our great chieftain
incarnated. It is to that man, my
friend, I give this book.
Douglas Southall Freeman.
June 29, 1915.

THE ROAD TO VIDALIA

CEASE FIRING

BY MARY JOHNSTON

WITH ILLUSTRATIONS
BY N. C. WYETH

HOUGHTON MIFFLIN COMPANY
BOSTON AND NEW YORK :: THE
RIVERSIDE PRESS CAMBRIDGE
1912

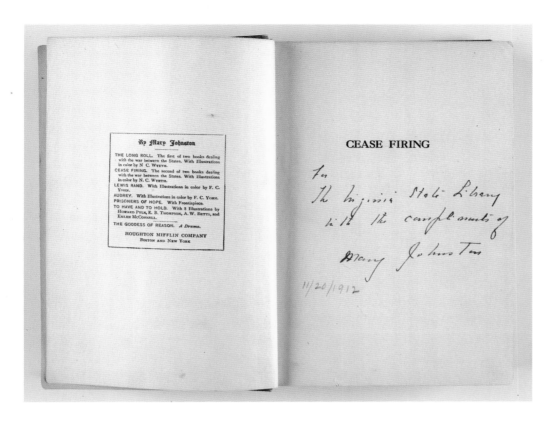

◀ ▲ Mary Johnston (1870–1936). *Cease Firing.* Boston and New York: Houghton Mifflin Company; Cambridge: The Riverside Press, 1912.

At the beginning of the twentieth century, Mary Johnston became one of the country's leading historical novelists. She was born in Buchanan, Virginia, educated at home by tutors, and in 1913 moved with her two sisters to Three Hills near Warm Springs, where she lived the remainder of her life. Her first known published piece, "Royalty on An Outing," appeared in the women's edition of the *Fincastle Herald* on 5 September 1895, when Johnston was twenty-five years old. Three years later she published her first novel, *Prisoners of Hope* (1898). It was an instant success and was followed by her most popular work, *To Have and To Hold* (1900), a fictional account of the women who settled at Jamestown in the early seventeenth century. *To Have and To Hold* was serialized in the *Atlantic Monthly* and twice made into a film. At least fifteen of her twenty-three novels deal wholly or in part with Virginia's history. Johnston's two highly acclaimed Civil War novels, *The Long Roll* (1911) and *Cease Firing* (1912), were written partly as a tribute to her Confederate ancestors. On 20 November 1912 Johnston presented an inscribed copy of *Cease Firing* to the Virginia State Library with her compliments. Mary Johnston is also remembered for her activities on behalf of the cause of woman suffrage. ES

▼ Thomas Nelson Page (1853–1922). *The Old Dominion: Her Making and Her Manners.* New York: Charles Scribner's Sons, 1914.

One of the most popular authors of the Reconstruction South, Thomas Nelson Page was born on his family's estate, Oakland, in Hanover County. A romantic literary spokesman for the bygone days of the Old South, Page was educated as an attorney at the University of Virginia and practiced law for many years in Richmond. Eventually, he abandoned his profession in order to write. His first book, a collection of stories entitled *In Ole Virginia* (1887), is cited as his best work, and "Marse Chan" and "Meh Lady," two stories from this book, have become classics. His numerous other works include *Two Little Confederates* (1888), *Unc' Edinburg* (1889), *Red Rock* (1898), and *The Old Dominion* (1908). President Woodrow Wilson appointed Page U.S. ambassador to Italy in 1913.

The Library of Virginia owns Thomas Nelson Page's personal copy of the 1914 edition of *The Old Dominion*, bearing the author's bookplate. Page evidently gave the volume to his brother Rosewell, a noted Virginia attorney and author to whom the book was dedicated. Page described his brother in the dedication as "a Virginia country gentleman, who by his character, his unselfishness, his devotion to duty and his lifelong habit of spending himself for others, has preserved in the present the best traditions of the Old Dominion's past." Rosewell Page later gave *The Old Dominion* to a friend, W. J. Kingsland Jr. The Library's copy bears Rosewell Page's inscription to Kingsland and Page's signature. SM

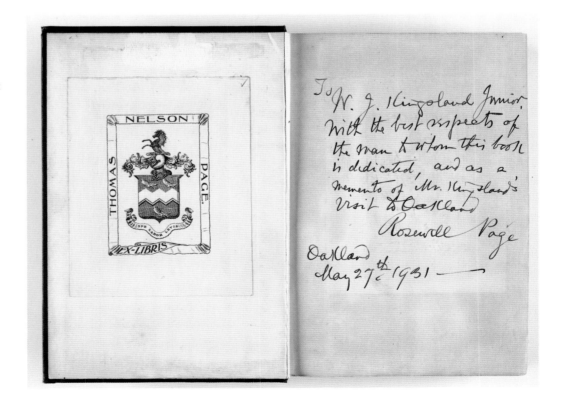

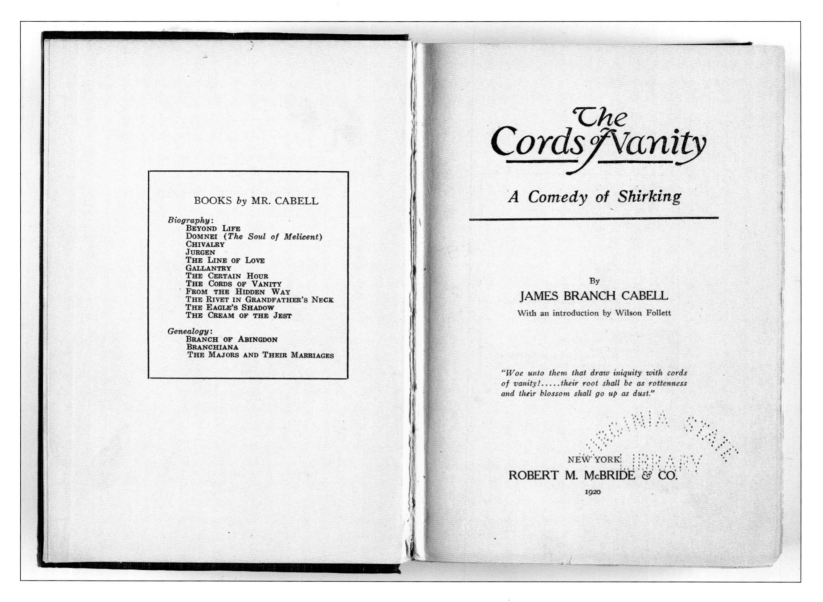

BOOKS *by* MR. CABELL

Biography:
    BEYOND LIFE
    DOMNEI (*The Soul of Melicent*)
    CHIVALRY
    JURGEN
    THE LINE OF LOVE
    GALLANTRY
    THE CERTAIN HOUR
    THE CORDS OF VANITY
    FROM THE HIDDEN WAY
    THE RIVET IN GRANDFATHER'S NECK
    THE EAGLE'S SHADOW
    THE CREAM OF THE JEST

Genealogy:
    BRANCH OF ABINGDON
    BRANCHIANA
    THE MAJORS AND THEIR MARRIAGES

The Cords of Vanity

A Comedy of Shirking

By

JAMES BRANCH CABELL

With an introduction by Wilson Follett

"Woe unto them that draw iniquity with cords of vanity!.....their root shall be as rottenness and their blossom shall go up as dust."

NEW YORK
ROBERT M. McBRIDE & CO.
1920

▲ James Branch Cabell (1879–1958). *The Cords of Vanity: A Comedy of Shirking.* 2d ed. New York: Robert M. McBride and Company, 1920.

A novelist, essayist, historian, and poet, James Branch Cabell was born in Richmond and educated at the College of William and Mary. He served brief stints with the *Richmond Times*, the *New York Herald*, and the *Richmond News*, and spent two years in the coal mines of West Virginia before deciding to make research and writing a full-time occupation. Between 1907 and 1915 his genealogical research led to the publication of three books of family history. Cabell received international fame in 1920 when his controversial novel, *Jurgen*, was declared indecent by the New York Society for the Suppression of Vice. By the time of his death in Richmond in 1958, Cabell had written fifty books.

Cabell presented a signed copy of the second, revised edition of *The Cords of Vanity* to the Library in 1920, the year that it was published. In his introduction to the new edition, critic Wilson Follett wrote that the book, "on its publication eleven years ago, promptly became a book which there were—almost—none to praise and very few to love." Although the main character of the novel, Robert Etheridge Townsend, remained "an example of that special temperament which . . . consistently shirks every responsibility that entails or threatens discomfort," his sarcasm in the 1920 edition assumed a degree of "mellowness" as Cabell attempted to produce "a far less unpleasant book." SM

Inscribed for the Virginia State Library, with the compliments of

James Branch Cabell

2 October 1920

▶ Richard Evelyn Byrd (1888–1957). *Skyward.*
New York and London: G. P. Putnam's Sons, 1928.

Richard Evelyn Byrd was born in Winchester,
Virginia, in 1888. His adventurous spirit was evident by age thirteen when he traveled unat-
tended to the Philippines to visit a family friend
and returned via the Suez Canal and Europe.
Byrd attended the Virginia Military Institute, the
University of Virginia, and the United States
Naval Academy, entering the service after gradu-
ation in 1912. In the navy, Byrd focused his
interest on flying. During World War I, he
received his wings, and, though he never actually
saw combat, he helped the navy plan the first
flight across the Atlantic. After the war, he was
instrumental in developing the navy's aeronauti-
cal programs and was promoted to the rank of
lieutenant commander.

In 1926 Byrd, then a civilian pilot, made what
was believed at the time to be the first flight over
the North Pole, for which he received the Medal
of Honor. He made the journey in the *Josephine
Ford,* named for the daughter of Edsel Ford, a
principal backer of his expedition.

Mounted on the front cover of the Library's
copy of *Skyward,* Byrd's published account of his
legendary flight, are two bits of cloth, beneath
which is inscribed: "A portion of the fabric (showing both sides) which covered the plane Josephine
Ford on her historic flight over the North Pole
on May 9th, 1926, piloted by Commander
Richard E. Byrd." It is one in a series of 500 autographed copies. SM

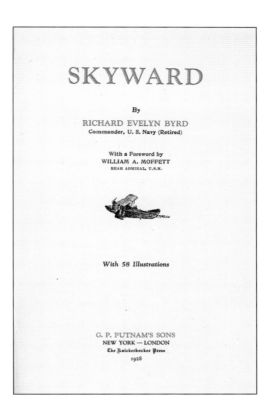

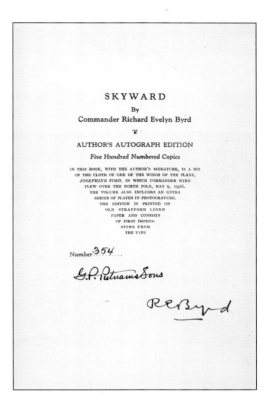

◀ ▶ Sherwood Anderson (1876–1941). *Alice and The Lost Novel*. London: Elkin Mathews and Marrot, 1929.

Late in 1925 *Vanity Fair* praised Sherwood Anderson as the country's most distinctive novelist and quoted H. L. Mencken as describing Anderson's most recent book, *Dark Laughter*, as "profound." A novelist, short story writer, and essayist, as well as the author of the celebrated *Winesburg, Ohio* (1919), Anderson occupied a prominent place among his contemporaries. He was particularly sympathetic to the rising generation of young American writers and helped launch the careers of such celebrated novelists as William Faulkner and Ernest Hemingway.

Despite the acclaim, by the mid-1920s Anderson's artistic powers had begun to fail and his reputation as a writer to decline. He began to withdraw from his old life. In 1926, the same year that Hemingway published a parody of Anderson's style in *The Torrents of Spring*, Anderson spent the summer in the southwestern corner of Virginia. The next year he built a house near Marion, Virginia, dissolved his contract with his publisher, and purchased two weekly newspapers, the *Smyth County News* and the *Marion Democrat*. As editor of the two most influential newspapers in the area, he became absorbed in the culture of Virginia's mountain communities and wrote extensively on the social and economic conditions of the region.

In 1929 Anderson published two works, *Hello Towns!*, a compilation of his columns and editorials, and *Alice and The Lost Novel*, a short volume containing two autobiographical meditations. *Alice and The Lost Novel* appeared in a limited edition of 530 copies. On 15 November 1983 the Library of Virginia purchased one of these autographed copies for its Virginia authors collection. DWG

Five hundred and thirty numbered copies of this story have been set in Monotype Eleven Point Plantin, and printed by Robert MacLehose & Co. Ltd., at the University Press, Glasgow; Nos. 1-500 only are for sale and Nos. 501-530 for presentation.

This is copy No. 81

Sherwood Anderson

ALICE

THERE is a great deal of talk made about beauty but no one defines it. It clings to some people.

Among women now. The figure is something of course, the face, the lips, the eyes.

The way the head sets on the shoulders.

The way a woman walks across the room may mean everything.

I myself have seen beauty in the most unexpected places. What has happened to me must have happened also to a great many other men.

I remember a friend I had formerly in Chicago. He had something like a nervous breakdown and went down into Missouri—to the Ozark mountains I think.

One day he was walking on a mountain road and passed a cabin. It was a poor place with lean dogs in the yard.

There were a great many dirty children, a slovenly woman and one young girl. The young girl had gone

3

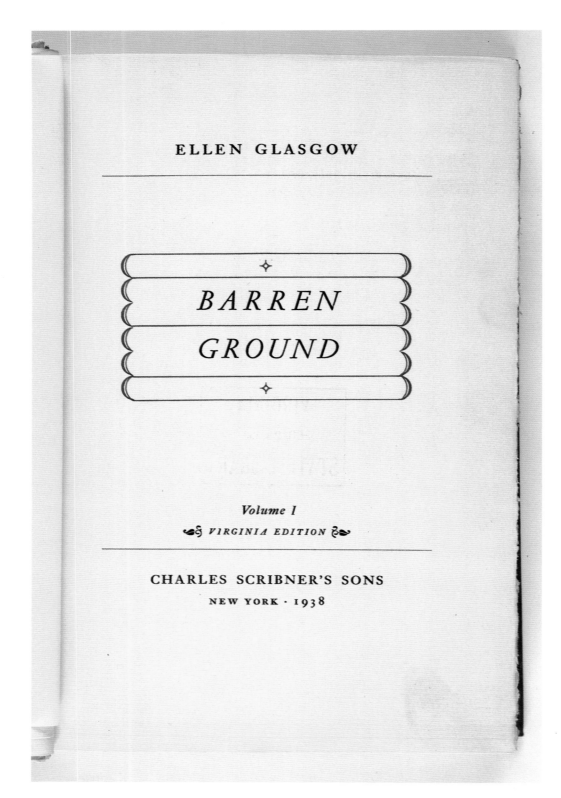

ELLEN GLASGOW

BARREN

GROUND

Volume I

VIRGINIA EDITION

CHARLES SCRIBNER'S SONS
NEW YORK · 1938

◄ ▼ Ellen Anderson Gholson Glasgow (1873–1945). *The Works of Ellen Glasgow*. The Virginia Edition, 12 vols. New York: Charles Scribner's Sons, 1938.

One of Virginia's most-celebrated writers and a winner of the Pulitzer Prize in 1942 for *In This Our Life*, Ellen Glasgow was born in Richmond to a distinguished southern family. She obtained most of her education from her father's extensive library. Although she often traveled abroad, she spent much of her life at her home on West Main Street in Richmond. Glasgow was the logical heir to a tradition in southern writing that owed its literary origins to the romances of Sir Walter Scott, whose influence on the literature of the antebellum and postwar South was pervasive. But while Glasgow dealt with historical themes, she rejected the sentimental idealism of the past and invested her novels with a realism that disclosed a modern, rather than an antiquarian sensibility. This is most evident in her studies of the tradition-bound "southern lady" and in her portrait of the independent woman in her fine novel, *The Sheltered Life* (1932).

When the twelve-volume Virginia edition of *The Works of Ellen Glasgow* appeared in 1938, reviewers seized the opportunity to assess Glasgow's achievement to that point in her career, praising her skill as a novelist of manners and noting her fine sense of irony. A set of this edition, limited to 810 copies, was purchased by the Library in February 1939. *Barren Ground*, Glasgow's personal favorite, is the first volume in the set and contains the author's inscription. DWG

THIS EDITION
PRINTED FROM TYPE
IS LIMITED TO
EIGHT HUNDRED AND TEN COPIES
SIGNED BY THE AUTHOR
TWENTY SETS
ARE FOR PRESENTATION
AND SEVEN HUNDRED AND NINETY
FOR SUBSCRIPTION

The number of this set is
281

Ellen Glasgow

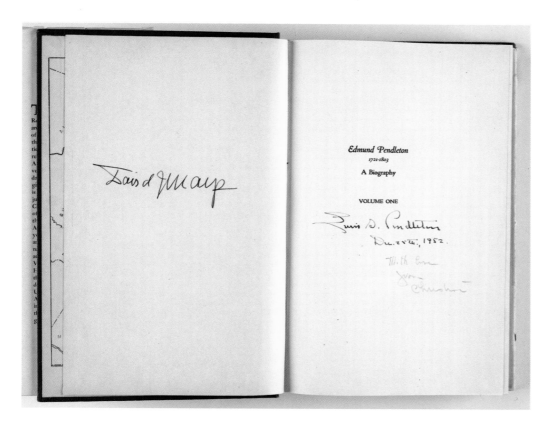

▲ David John Mays (1896–1971). *Edmund Pendleton, 1721–1803: A Biography*. Cambridge: Harvard University Press, 1952.

David John Mays, a lawyer by profession, came to the writing of his two-volume *Edmund Pendleton, 1721–1803: A Biography* as "an unknown man" who undertook to research "the life of a forgotten man." Mays had become interested in the life of Edmund Pendleton while studying for his law degree and over a twenty-eight-year period combed every possible source to assemble almost six hundred document copies as the basis for his study. The result was "a prodigious and masterful biography" of one of Virginia's Revolutionary statesmen, published in 1952 by Harvard University Press, for which Mays won the 1953 Pulitzer Prize for biography.

In addition to being a prominent Richmond attorney and president of the Virginia State Bar Association from 1958 to 1959, David John Mays served on the State Library Board for a decade beginning in 1953 and was president of the Virginia Historical Society from 1963 to 1966. While researching Pendleton's life, Mays discovered an important collection of government papers—United States District Court Ended Causes—documenting a famous mid-eighteenth-century financial scandal that Pendleton was involved in settling. After Mays published his biography, the collection, which now fills more than 450 boxes and volumes, was deposited in the Virginia State Library.

Mays also published a two-volume edition of Edmund Pendleton's letters in 1967. In 1984 the Library reprinted Mays's prizewinning biography. BT

▼ Rita Dove (1952–). *Selected Poems*. New York: Pantheon Books, 1993.

Born in Akron, Ohio, in 1952, Rita Frances Dove became a professor of English at the University of Virginia in 1989 and Commonwealth Professor of English there in 1993. The Library of Congress chose Dove as the poet laureate of the United States in 1993, and she served in that capacity until 1995. When Rita Dove received the honor, she was the youngest poet laureate to that time, the second woman, and the first African American selected for the post after it had been renamed in 1985. Her many other honors include the 1986 Lavan Younger Poet Award of the Academy of American Poets; the 1987 Pulitzer Prize for poetry for *Thomas and Beulah*, the story of her grandparents' lives, which was later made into a movie; and the 1996 Heinz Award and Charles Frankel Prize for humanities.

In September 1993, Dove spoke at the groundbreaking ceremony for the new Library of Virginia building, paying tribute to the Library for providing "services and opportunities vaster than television, headier than a museum, and much more affordable than a night club. . . . Incense should be lit and libations poured, for it represents the essence of civilization, the hope for our human spirit, and the possibility of our youth." In 1994, the Virginia Center for the Book honored Rita Dove by including her on its *Twentieth-Century Virginia Authors* literary map. Rita Dove presented the Library with a signed copy of *Selected Poems* at the gala celebrating publication of the literary map. ES

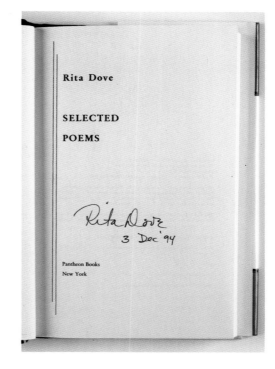

JULY 5. 1776.   THE   NUMBER 79.

VIRGINIA  GAZETTE.

Always for LIBERTY   **AND THE PUBLICK GOOD.**

DON'T TREAD ON ME

High **HEAVEN** *to* GRACIOUS ENDS *directs the* STORM!

IN CONVENTION.
SATURDAY, *March* 25, 1775.

RESOLVED, as the opinion of this Convention, that on account of the unhappy disputes between Great Britain and the colonies, and the unsettled state of this country, the lawyers, suitors, and witnesses, ought not to attend the prosecution or defence of civil suits at the next General Court; and it is recommended to the several courts of justice not to proceed to the hearing or determination of suits on their dockets, except attachments, nor to give judgments but in the case of sheriffs or other collectors for money or tobacco received by them; in other cases, where such judgment shall be voluntarily confessed, or upon such amicable proceedings as may become necessary for the settlement, division, or distribution of estates. And during this suspension of the administration of justice, it is earnestly recommended to the people to observe a peaceable and orderly behaviour, to all creditors to be as indulgent to their debtors as may be, and to all debtors to pay as far as they are able; and where differences may arise which cannot be adjusted between the parties, that they refer the decision thereof to judicious neighbours, and abide by their determination.

In CONVENTION.
WEDNESDAY, *July* 3, 1776.
An ORDINANCE to enable the present magistrates and officers to continue the administration of justice, and for settling the general mode of proceedings in criminal and other cases, till the same can be more amply provided for.

WHEREAS it hath been found indispensably necessary to establish government in this colony, independent of the crown of *Great Britain*, or any authority derived therefrom, and a plan of such government hath been accordingly formed by the General Convention, but it will require some considerable time to compile a body of laws suited to the circumstances of the country, and it is necessary to provide some method of preserving peace and security to the community in the mean time:

Be it therefore ordained, by the representatives of the people now met in General Convention, that the several persons named in the commission of the peace in each county respectively, having in the court of the county taken the following oath, which shall be administered to the first person named who is present by any two of the others, and then by him administered to the others, that is to say: *I* A. B. *do solemnly swear, that I will be faithful and true to the commonwealth of* Virginia; *that I will, to the utmost of my power, support, maintain, and defend, the constitution and government thereof as settled by the General Convention; and that I will faithfully execute the office of*   *for the county of*   *and do equal right and justice to all men, to the best of my judgment, and according to law;* shall each, and every of them, have full

power to execute the office of a justice of peace, as well within his county court as without, in all things, according to law.

And be it farther ordained, that where it shall happen that there is not a sufficient number of magistrates for holding a court in any county already appointed, the Governour may, with the advice of the Privy Council, appoint such and so many magistrates in such county as may be judged proper and necessary.

And whereas courts in the district of *West Augusta* have been hitherto held by writs of adjournment, which writs cannot now be obtained: *Be it therefore ordained,* that the justices residing in the said district, on taking the same oath aforesaid, shall have the power and authority to hold a court within the said district, on the third *Tuesday* in every month, at such place as they may appoint, and shall exercise their office, both in court and without, in the same manner as the justices of the several counties are by this ordinance empowered to do.

Provided always, that upon complaint made to the Governour and Privy Council against any justice of peace, now in commission, of misfeazance in office, or disaffection to the commonwealth, it shall and may be lawful for the Governour, with advice of the Privy Council, on a full and fair hearing of both parties, to remove such justice from his office, if they shall be of opinion that the said complaint is just and well founded.

And be it farther ordained, that the common law of *England,* all statutes or acts of parliament made in aid of the common law prior to the fourth year of the reign of king *James* the first, and which are of a general nature, not local to that kingdom, together with the several acts of the General Assembly of this colony now in force, so far as the same may consist with the several ordinances, declarations, and resolutions of the General Convention, shall be the rule of decision, and shall be considered as in full force, until the same shall be altered by the legislative power of this colony.

Provided always, and be it farther ordained, that all quitrents and arrears thereof, and all duties, aids, penalties, fines, and forfeitures, heretofore made payable to the king, his heirs and successours, shall be and inure to the use of the commonwealth, and all bonds for securing the same shall be made payable to the person or persons having the executive power.

And be it farther ordained, that all bonds to be entered into by sheriffs, or other publick officers, and in all other cases, where the same are required by law, shall be made payable to the justices of the court taking such bond, and, in the names of them or their successours, may be sued and prosecuted at the costs and for the benefit of the publick, or any private person or persons injured by the breach thereof, as often as there may be occasion, until the whole penalty be levied.

And be it farther ordained, that all the present sheriffs now in office under a com-

mission from the late Governour, upon taking the oath before prescribed in the court of their county, shall continue to act, and have all the powers and authorities of sheriff, according to law, until the 25th day of *October* next.

An ORDINANCE to arrange the counties in districts, for electing Senators, and to ascertain their wages.

FOR the regular election of Senators to this Convention, at the time the same shall be adjourned to, and that the people may be more equally represented in that branch of the legislature:

Be it ordained, by the delegates of the counties and corporations of Virginia *now met in Convention, and it is hereby ordained by the authority thereof,* that the counties of *Accomack* and *Northampton* shall be one district; the counties of *Princess Anne, Norfolk,* and *Nansemond,* one other district; the counties of *Isle of Wight, Surry,* and *Prince George,* one other district; the counties of *Dinwiddie, Southampton,* and *Sussex,* one other district; the counties of *Brunswick, Lunenburg,* and *Mecklenburg,* one other district; the counties of *Charlotte, Halifax,* and *Prince Edward,* one other district; the counties of *Chesterfield, Amelia,* and *Cumberland,* one other district; the counties of *Buckingham, Albemarle,* and *Amherst,* one other district; the counties of *Pittsylvania* and *Bedford,* one other district; the counties of *Botetourt* and *Fincastle,* one other district; the counties of *Elizabeth City, Warwick,* and *York,* one other district; the counties of *Charles City, James City,* and *New Kent,* one other district; the counties of *Henrico, Goochland,* and *Louisa,* one other district; the counties of *Hanover* and *Caroline,* one other district; the counties of *East Augusta* and *Dunmore,* one other district; the counties of *Gloucester* and *Middlesex,* one other district; the counties of *Essex, King William,* and *King and Queen,* one other district; the counties of *Lancaster, Richmond,* and *Northumberland,* one other district; the counties of *Westmoreland, Stafford,* and *King George,* one other district; the counties of *Spotsylvania, Orange,* and *Culpeper,* one other district; the counties of *Prince William* and *Fairfax,* one other district; the counties of *Loudoun* and *Fauquier,* one other district; the counties of *Frederick, Berkeley,* and *Hampshire,* one other district; and *West Augusta,* one other district; for every one of which districts one Senator shall be chosen by the persons qualified to vote for delegates, who shall be summoned for that purpose by the sheriffs, or, where there is no such officers, by the clerks of the committees of observation and inspection, to meet at the courthouses of their respective counties, or, where there are no courthouses, at some other convenient places, on the second *Tuesday* in September for the first district, on the 2d *Thursday* in *August* for the 2d and 4th districts, on the 1st *Thursday* in *August* for the 3d, 16th, and 19th districts, on the 1st *Monday* in *August* for the 18th district, on the 5th *Thursday* in

NEWSPAPERS AND PERIODICALS

The Library of Virginia's vast collection of newspapers can probably be dated to 25 March 1783, when the Council of State purchased from Attorney General Edmund Randolph a ten-year run of the *Williamsburg Virginia Gazette* "for public use." Since that time the collection has expanded to include thousands of original copies and millions of microfilm images of newspapers published in Virginia's cities and towns. The Library also has an extensive collection of Civil War–era newspapers and large holdings of Baltimore, New York, Philadelphia, and Washington, D.C., papers that contain significant amounts of Virginia news. Through its participation in the Virginia Newspaper Project, the Library has continued to locate, catalog, and prepare for preservation all the extant copies of newspapers that can be identified as having been published in Virginia.

In addition to newspapers, the Library of Virginia possesses an exceptional collection of periodical literature of several kinds, ranging from popular magazines and historical journals to news magazines and scientific and technical periodicals. Among the most significant holdings are original issues of two of the most influential agricultural publications in the American South—Edmund Ruffin's *Farmers' Register* and the long-running *Southern Planter*, both of which were edited and published in Virginia and widely regarded as among the best and most important journals in their field.

The Library of Virginia also holds a large collection of American and British periodicals of general interest, including a complete set of the famed *Gentleman's Magazine*, which began publication in London in 1731, and valuable copies of such classic American journals as the *Saturday Evening Post*, the *Atlantic Monthly*, and the *Southern Literary Messenger*, which was published in Richmond and edited during its formative years by Edgar Allan Poe.

◀ *Virginia Gazette*, 5 July 1776. Williamsburg: John Dixon and William Hunter Jr.

The 5 July 1776 edition of the *Virginia Gazette* reported the conclusion reached by the delegates to the last of Virginia's revolutionary conventions: that it was "indispensably necessary to establish government in this colony, independent of the crown of Great Britain." After two days of sharp debate in Williamsburg, the members of the convention had unanimously adopted a resolution on 15 May instructing the colony's delegates in Congress to introduce a motion for independence, becoming the first colony to do so. The fifth revolutionary convention subsequently adopted the Declaration of Rights on 12 June and a constitution for the new commonwealth on 29 June before adjourning on 5 July. The following day, Patrick Henry was sworn in as governor. Published the day the convention adjourned, this 5 July issue of the *Gazette* printed an ordinance passed two days earlier designed "to enable the present Magistrates to continue the Administration of Justice." Drafted by Edmund Pendleton and amended by Robert Carter Nicholas, the ordinance was the eighth enacted by the convention.

The masthead of the *Virginia Gazette* declared that it was published "Always for LIBERTY and the PUBLICK GOOD." The paper was the second-oldest in the southern colonies. TR, JM

▲ *Richmond Chronicle*, 18 December 1795.
Richmond: John Dixon.

This issue of the *Richmond Chronicle*, dated 18
December 1795, is the earliest original Richmond
newspaper in the Library of Virginia's collection.
Following eighteenth-century convention,
advertisements were featured prominently on the
front page, while news reports and editorials
were relegated to the second page. The masthead
proclaimed the paper's mission: "The Public Will
Our Guide—The Public Good Our End."

The *Chronicle* was printed on Tuesdays and
Fridays by John Dixon (ca. 1768–1805). On the
front page of this issue, advertisements for land,
books, jewelry, and horses compete with the
announcement of the Richmond Bridge Lottery,
designed to raise enough money to erect a stone
bridge across Shockoe Creek. Also in this issue,
Edmund Randolph announced his intention
to reside in the city of Richmond and practice
law. TR, JM

▼ *Farmers' Register*, 1 March 1838, 31 August
1840. Petersburg: Edmund Ruffin.

Founded by Edmund Ruffin (1794–1865), the
Farmers' Register was "A Monthly Publication,
Devoted to the Improvement of the Practice,
and Support of the Interests of Agriculture." It
was the second agricultural periodical published
in Virginia (the *Virginia Farmer*, begun perhaps
in 1829, being the first). The sixty-four-page,
advertisement-free *Farmers' Register* was founded
at Shellbanks, Ruffin's farm in Prince George
County, where it was originally printed; when
Ruffin moved to Petersburg in 1835, so did the
Register. Ruffin used the *Register* as a means to
advocate agricultural reform, arguing for the benefits of fertilizing "naturally inferior and poor
soils" with marl, a mineral deposit rich in cal-
cium carbonate.

While Ruffin wrote extensively for the journal, he also became an "agricultural traveller,"
making excursions to various Virginia counties
(predominately those in the tidewater) and writing accounts of their farming practices. Before
his tenure as editor was over, he had visited and

reported on twenty counties and written the histories of ninety-two farms, rambling in his travels
from James City (1832) and Charles City (1833)
to Goochland, Chesterfield, and Powhatan
(1837), and finally to Hanover, New Kent, and
King William (1840).

Unable to turn the *Register* into a secure, profitable venture, Ruffin closed his printing shop in
Petersburg in December 1842, a month before his
forty-ninth birthday. Thereafter, Thomas S.
Pleasants (1796–1871) published three more
issues before ending publication with the March
1843 edition. JM

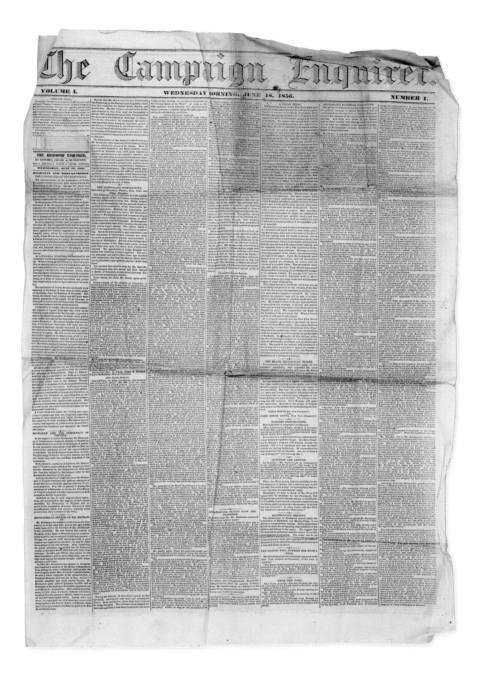

▲ *Campaign Enquirer*, 18 June 1856.
Richmond: Ritchie, Pryor, and Dunnavant.

Nineteenth-century campaign newspapers document the political issues important to voters and candidates in Virginia and provide a means to chart the development of campaigning in the commonwealth. This first issue of the *Campaign Enquirer* announced its intention to appear weekly until 1 December 1856, so that "every fact and principle in issue between the opposing parties, will be thoroughly discussed." The final issue of the paper in the Library of Virginia's collection is dated 12 November. Features in the *Campaign Enquirer* included information of special interest to voters, such as biographical sketches of the candidates and the texts of speeches.

In the election of 1856, Virginia's electoral votes supported the victorious Democratic presidential candidate, James Buchanan, and his running mate, John C. Breckinridge, over Know Nothing candidate Millard Fillmore and Republican candidate John C. Frémont. Frémont's second-place finish in the electoral college, however, signaled the growing strength of the newly formed Republican Party, with its outspoken opposition to slavery in the territories. As a result, the campaign of 1856 sparked a revival of southern efforts to organize a secession movement. With the separation of the slavery and antislavery portions of the Union a distinct possibility, the election of 1856 was "a final warning." The next presidential election would take place amid the ominous rumblings of impending war. TR, JM

▼ *Richmond Enquirer*, Extra Edition, 22 February 1862. Richmond: Tyler, Wise, and Allegre.

Broadside extras were issued by newspaper publishers whenever events occurred to warrant special public notice. These extras were circulated by hand or posted in public places. This rare Civil War example of a *Richmond Enquirer* extra edition contains Jefferson Davis's inaugural address, made on the occasion of the transfer of the Confederate government from provisional to constitutional status.

On the morning of 22 February 1862, rain-drenched Richmonders waited in Capitol Square to see Davis installed as president of the Confederate States of America. At noon, after an opening prayer, Davis delivered his address from a shelter near the Washington monument. Amid cheers and applause, he recounted the events of the past twelve months: "A new government has been established. . . . Our Confederacy has grown from six to thirteen States" and "patriotism, virtue and courage" abounded among the Southern population. "We are in arms," the president reminded the crowd, "to renew such sacrifices as our fathers made to the holy cause of Constitutional liberty." Those who could not attend the inauguration could read Davis's speech the same day on this broadside. TR, JM

DAILY DISPATCH.

Richmond Dispatch.

Richmond Dispatch.

◀ *Daily Dispatch*, 23 December 1862. Richmond: James A. Cowardin and W. H. Davis.

Established in 1850 by James A. Cowardin (1811–1882) and William H. Davis (ca. 1810–1870), the *Richmond Dispatch* was published as both a daily and a weekly, devoting itself to news and eschewing political affiliations. The devastations of the Civil War directly affected the paper's operations. In 1864, one of the *Dispatch*'s owners ran the blockade to purchase a new press in England. The number of columns in the paper was decreased from seven to six because of war conditions; when its employees were pressed into military service, the paper printed only half sheets. The evacuation fire of 2–3 April 1865 during the fall of Richmond destroyed the *Dispatch* office and caused publication to be suspended. The paper resumed operations in December.

This issue of the *Daily Dispatch* was among items traded between Confederate and Union troops during a truce period in Fredericksburg in December 1862. It includes accounts from Northern newspapers of the recent battle, as well as local news: a band of Confederate deserters, captured in Lynchburg, had been sent to Castle Thunder until the men could be returned to their regiments; "an unusual quiet" had descended on Fredericksburg, where it was doubted Union troops would try to cross the Rappahannock again; and a shortage of clothing and shoes among Southern troops was making the winter season especially difficult. In the Richmond mayor's court, justice was dispensed to those drunk in public, runaway slaves, and free blacks in the city without papers; sentences, ranging from twenty-five lashes for stealing wood to a three-dollar fine for "being drunk and lying on the sidewalk," were published for all to see. TR, JM

▲ *Virginia Star*, 11 May 1878. Richmond: Steward, Woolfolk, and Company.

This issue of the *Virginia Star*, dated 11 May 1878, is the earliest copy of an African American newspaper in the Library's collection. The paper was printed weekly by Dr. R. A. Green (fl. 1870s–1880s), Otway M. Steward (1841–1912), and Peter H. Woolfolk (ca. 1820–ca. 1897) from approximately 1877 to 1888. "We Hold these Truths to be Self-Evident," the masthead boldly proclaimed, "That all Men are Created Equal." "Independent in thought, radical in principle, and vocal for the Social, Moral and Educational interests of the colored people," the *Virginia Star* was published every Saturday and could be subscribed to for the fee of two dollars a year.

According to the management, the *Star* was "a necessity in the family of every Colored citizen in Virginia." The paper enjoyed its heyday during the 1878–1882 period, when the talented young lawyer and politician Robert Peel Brooks (1853–1882) edited the paper. Brooks, a Richmond native, was born a slave but went on to graduate from Howard University's law school in 1876. With two classmates, he established the first law firm of African American attorneys in Richmond. Brooks steered the *Virginia Star* from opposition to the Readjuster Party to a highly influential endorsement of it. The Readjusters, who wanted to pay the state's substantial debt at a lower ("readjusted") rate, unified whites and blacks in a third party coalition that triumphed in the gubernatorial election of 1881.

Tragically, Brooks died in September 1882, just prior to his thirtieth birthday. Steward and Woolfolk kept the *Virginia Star* alive for a few years afterward, but the paper's decline coincided with the collapse of the Readjuster movement and the waning of biracial politics in Virginia. Only eleven issues of the *Star* are known to exist; ten are in the Library's collections. TR, JM, JK

▼ *Star*, 24 February 1921. Newport News: Matthew N. Lewis.

Although the *Newport News Star* was published weekly from 1901 through the 1930s, few copies are known to be extant. The masthead of this issue billed it as "the Only Negro Journal on the Peninsula" and urged readers to subscribe if they "Want to Keep in Touch With the Progress of the Race."

The *Star* was owned and edited by Matthew N. Lewis (1859–1926), a Georgia native and graduate of Howard University. Lewis moved to Petersburg, Virginia, in 1882 and began work as agent for the *Lancet*, a local black weekly, and served as campaign secretary for John Mercer Langston in his successful bid to become Virginia's first African American congressman. About that time, Lewis established his own paper, the weekly *Petersburg Herald*, in partnership with another Howard graduate, Scott Wood. The partners had a falling out, and early in the 1890s Lewis moved to Norfolk, where in 1896 he started the *Recorder*, which enthusiastically backed the Republican Party in that year's presidential campaign. The next year, Lewis ambitiously expanded the paper into an afternoon daily, but it proved unprofitable. Lewis then moved to Newport News, where he became a customhouse inspector and launched the weekly *Star*. He edited the paper until his death in 1926. The *Star* continued under the guidance of J. Thomas Newsome (1869–1942) until 1940, when it was absorbed into the *Norfolk Journal and Guide*. TR, JK

▲ ◀ *Camera Work: A Photographic Quarterly* 25 (1909), 22 (1908). New York: Alfred Stieglitz.

The first issue of *Camera Work* was published in January 1903 by photographer Alfred Stieglitz (1864–1946), a leading proponent of the Pictorialist school and a founder of the so-called "Photo-Secession," a group that broke away from what it viewed as a staid and predictable photographic establishment. The journal served as a forum for those who believed in the then-revolutionary concept that photographs were a legitimate means of artistic expression; in its pages photographers, painters, and critics debated the competing aesthetic sensibilities of the early twentieth century.

Under Stieglitz's iron control, *Camera Work* became famous for its technical accomplishments, including the pioneering use of color images and the high quality of its black-and-white gravure illustrations. In fact, the quarterly magazine is notable for being "probably the best-known example of gravure printing." Many of the images were hand-tipped into each copy of the journal, rather than printed directly on the pages. In 1904, thirty of the *Camera Work* prints were used in a show in Brussels and were a great success. In fact, it was not until the show had ended that it became generally known that the prints had been made by the gravure printing-process and were not actually photographs. A 1909 issue of *Camera Work* included this photograph by Ema Spencer (1857–1941). Her work was described in an *International Studio* review as "touchingly appealing." The last issue of *Camera Work* was published in June 1917. JM, ES

▼ *Ye Olde York Times*, 25 April 1936. Yorktown: Civilian Conservation Corps.

The Civilian Conservation Corps was created by act of Congress "for the purpose of providing employment, as well as vocational training, for youthful citizens of the United States . . . through the performance of useful public work in connection with the conservation and development of the natural resources of the United States." In Virginia, restoration and preservation of historic structures as well as archaeological excavations were undertaken in twelve CCC camps located in national parks. At Yorktown, the Civilian Conservation Corps worked at Colonial National Historical Park to restore earthworks, construct gun mounts, and demolish "the unsightly remains of an old hotel." Under the direction of the National Park Service, CCC enrollees restored the site of the 1781 battle that effectively ended the American Revolution.

The CCC camp at Yorktown established a camp newspaper in April 1936 to keep camp residents and the local community informed about the corps's activities. The 25 April 1936 edition of *Ye Olde York Times* features a letter written by B. Floyd Flickinger, superintendent of the Colonial National Monument at Yorktown, praising the paper's first issue and the "splendid work" of the corps. Other news includes reports on the Easter dance (where local girls were guests and the recreation hall was decorated in a "modernistic pattern"), on the third anniversary of the CCC, and on the restoration of redoubts on the Yorktown battlefield. TR, JM

Printed by Jn. Baskett of the Clarendon Printing House in Oxford.

THE
HOLY BIBLE,

CONTAINING THE

Old TESTAMENT and the New:

Newly Translated out of the

ORIGINAL TONGUES:

And with the former TRANSLATIONS

Diligently Compared and Revised.

By His Majesty's Special Command.

Appointed to be Read in CHURCHES.

OXFORD,

Printed by JOHN BASKETT, Printer to the King's most Excellent Majesty, for
GREAT BRITAIN; and to the UNIVERSITY. MDCCXVII.

THE LIBRARY OF THE COUNCIL OF COLONIAL VIRGINIA

The library of the governor's advisory Council was the principal research and reference resource for the colonial government. Its volumes—housed within the Council chamber in the Capitol in Williamsburg—served the needs not only of the royal governor and his Council, but also of the courts, attorneys, and members of the General Assembly. From the very beginning of the colony, government officers perceived the need for and acquired numerous reference books. Thus the collection by the late eighteenth century had reached several hundred volumes and included compilations of English and Virginia statutes, parliamentary debates, reports of the lawcourts of England, volumes on international law and politics, and a large collection of published state papers—all necessary printed documents to guide Virginia's colonial government and ensure that it conformed as closely as possible to the laws and practices of England.

Many of the volumes in the library were destroyed or carried away during the several British incursions late in the American Revolution; others were no doubt lost during the Civil War. Of the entire Council library, only seventy-five volumes are known to have survived. A single book is in the collections of the Virginia Historical Society; a six-volume set is in the Earl Gregg Swem Library at the College of William and Mary. The remaining sixty-eight volumes, representing twenty-five titles, are precious relics of the Library of Virginia's history and are carefully preserved in the Library's Rare Book Collection. Several of the volumes are easily recognizable, featuring a leather rectangle with gold stamping affixed to the front cover, identifying each book as from the "Virginia Council Office 1742." A larger number of volumes are marked with the distinctive and detailed Virginia Council Chamber bookplate, and a few contain handwritten inscriptions identifying them as from the Council library.

◀ *The Holy Bible, Containing the Old Testament and the New: Newly Translated out of the Original Tongues.* Oxford: Printed by John Baskett, 1717.

This magnificent 1717 Bible is from the printing house of John Baskett, identified on the title page as "printer to the King's most Excellent Majesty," and is one of fewer than two dozen copies of the rare and famous edition extant in the United States. The book's numerous and exquisite engravings and large, elegant type make it one of the finest examples of early-eighteenth-century English printing. Unfortunately, the book's typesetters were not so skilled, or as meticulous, as were its engravers and printers. The text includes so many errors that the volume has sometimes been referred to as the "Baskett-full of Errors." The edition is even more familiarly known as "the Vinegar Bible," from the most famous of its several typesetting errors. At the top of the page containing the twentieth chapter of the Book of Luke—with its parable of the vineyard—the typesetter inadvertently set the page-head to read "The parable of the vinegar."

The John Baskett Bible is one of several rare ecclesiastical titles from the Library of Virginia's collection of Council volumes. Among the other religious titles is an elegant 1745 edition of the *Book of Common Prayer* with, like the Vinegar Bible, a Council library bookplate. The prayer book also features the royal coat of arms stamped on the front cover, with "St. James's Chappell 1746" beneath, indicating that the volume once belonged to the household of King George II and was probably first used in the royal chapel at Saint James's Palace, London. As the Church of England was the established church of the colony of Virginia, it is not surprising that an elegant pulpit Bible and *Book of Common Prayer* were in the collections of the official government library of the colony. BT

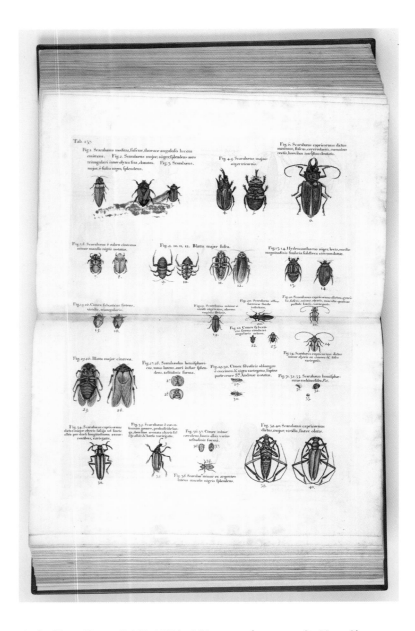

▶ John Harris (ca. 1667–1719). *Navigantium atque Itinerantium Bibliotheca. Or, A Complete Collection of Voyages and Travels. Consisting of Above Six Hundred of the Most Authentic Writers. Originally Published by John Harris. Now Carefully Revised.* 2d ed., 2 vols. London: Printed for T. Woodward et al., 1744–1748.

The government of Virginia probably acquired the two-volume second edition of John Harris's *Navigantium atque Itinerantium Bibliotheca* sometime during the 1750s, in all probability before the editor, John Campbell (1708–1775), published a second revised edition in 1764. Harris, an impecunious clergyman and amateur naturalist, first published the work in London in 1705. Volume two of the first revised edition still wears the distinctive bookplate of the colonial Council. Both volumes were in the library of the governor's Council in the Capitol in Williamsburg until the government moved to Richmond in 1780. They were listed in the first published catalog of the Library, printed in 1828.

The engraving of a right whale, a finback whale, a narwhal, and a walrus, together with a whaling scene, illustrates a lengthy section on the Arctic. During the seventeenth and eighteenth centuries, compilations of accounts of voyages of discovery were often found in learned men's libraries and in the libraries of educational institutions and provided a wide variety of useful information on numerous places, their cultures, and natural resources. BT

▲ Sir Hans Sloane (1660–1753). *A Voyage to the Islands Madera, Barbados, Nieves, S. Christophers and Jamaica, with the Natural History of the Herbs and Trees, Four-footed Beasts, Fishes, Birds, Insects, Reptiles, &c. of the Last of Those Islands.* 2 vols. London: Printed by B. M. for the author, 1707–1725.

Sometime between the mid-1740s and the mid-1770s the government of Virginia acquired Sir Hans Sloane's two handsome reference volumes "illustrated with the figures of the things describ'd." They still bear the bookplate of the colonial Council and were listed in the Library's first printed catalog in 1828 as "Sloane's History of Jamaica, London, 1707." From the early years of the colony, the government's leaders in Virginia had acquired similarly select reference works treating geography, natural history, botany, forestry, and zoology—books that often proved necessary in identifying or evaluating the Old Dominion's native plants and animals.

Sir Hans Sloane was a physician of such note that both Queen Anne and King George II consulted him, and as a collector of plant and animal specimens he was one of the most influential men of his time. In 1687 he traveled to the West Indies, where he lived for fifteen months collecting the specimens used to illustrate his celebrated volumes. The publication of his work won him election to the most prestigious learned societies in Europe. After the death of Sir Isaac Newton in 1727, for example, the members of the Royal Society of London selected Sloane to succeed the noted scientist; Sloane served as the society's secretary and eventually revived the publication of its noteworthy *Philosophical Transactions*. After Sloane's own death, his remarkable assemblage of specimens was carefully kept intact and became the nucleus of the British Museum's renowned collection. BT

them; but when they are attacked, and begin to howl, such as are within hearing run to their Assistance, and the old ones will rather suffer themselves to be killed, than desert their Young. The largest are those which are called Water-Bears, which live upon what they can get at Sea, and have been sometimes found fourteen Miles from Shore. The Skins of those Creatures make very comfortable Cloathing for such as travel in the Winter, and are dressed at *Spitzbergen*, by treading them in hot Sawdust.

The Deer in *Greenland* are grey and shaggy in Spring, afterwards of a dusky Colour, with clest Feet, and Horns like a Hare, or Elk. They have three or four Branches on each Side, about two Inches broad, and a Foot long; their Ears are long, and their Tails short. By feeding upon the yellow Moss, they grow so very fat in three Months, that they eat sometimes four Inches deep on the Ribs, which enables them to hold out during the Winter; and yet many of them are starved, and in the Spring they are all very lean. At the Sight of a Man they fly; but, if he stops, they stop too, and this gives an Opportunity for shooting them. Their Flesh is exceeding good roasted. There are Foxes here of various Colours, and prodigious Numbers of Seals, or Sea-dogs, and Sea-horses, which are the same that, in the *South-Seas*, are called Sea-lions; Animals which we shall hereafter describe. There are very few Land-Fowl, but of Water-Fowl abundance, yet none so curious as to merit a Description here.

18. As for the Fish on this Coast, they deserve Notice, because the taking them is the sole Motive that brings Ships into those Seas, where the Whale-fishing is carried on with great Profit. The true large Whale differs from the rest of the Fish so called by his having no Teeth, instead of which, on each Side of the upper Jaw, grows the Whale-bone, in four or five hundred different Blades, at equal Distances, some exceeding twelve Feet in Length, and a Foot broad at Bottom, growing narrow upwards, like the Sticks of a Fan inverted, the largest of them weighing about twenty Pounds.

He contracts and dilates the Distances of those Blades at the shutting and opening his Mouth, making them serve as Strainers, to separate the Water from the Shrimps, Prawns, and such small Fish as his Food consists of; and, for the same Purpose, on the Inside of the Bone, next the Tongue, grows a Quantity of Hair, to make still a finer Percolation, which is the more necessary, because, notwithstanding the Bulk of a Whale's Body, the Throat of the largest is not above a Foot wide. His Bones are hard, like those of four-footed Beasts; but, instead of having one large Cavity in the Middle, are porous, and full of Marrow. His Eyes measure about six Inches over, with Eye-lids and Hair like a Man's. His Belly and Back are quite red; his Flesh is coarse and hard, like that of a Bull, mixed with many Sinews, and is very dry and lean, because the Fat lies between the Flesh and the Skin. The Fat is mixed with Sinews, which holds the Oil as a Spunge does Water, the other strong Sinews are about the Tail, with which he turns and winds himself, as a Ship is guided by a Rudder.

He swims as swift as a Bird flies, and makes a Track in the Sea like a large Ship under sail. Besides the uppermost thin Skin, there is another almost an Inch thick, but neither of them are very strong, which is believed to be the Reason why the Whale does not exert that mighty Force that might be expected from a Fish of its Size. They are mightily tormented with Lice, which makes them sometimes spring out of the Sea in an Agony. It is also believed they feel great Pains in their Bodies before a Storm, which makes them twist and tumble violently while the Wind blows from the East; but, notwithstanding their violent Agitation, they are naturally very timorous. The middle Sort of them are from fifty to sixty Foot long, and yield from twenty to a hundred Barrels of Blubber, though sometimes they are much larger. *Martens* mentions one that yielded a hundred and thirty Hogsheads. This Blubber lies immediately under the Skin; they cut it into thin Slices, which are put into hot Coppers. The Oil soon melting out, the Skin is thrown away. The Tail

serves for a Chopping-block, upon which they cut the Blubber before it is boiled. The Manner of taking the Whale deserves a particular Description.

19. As soon as the Fishermen hear a Whale blow, they cry out, *Fall, fall!* And then every Ship gets out its Long-boat, in each of which there are six or seven Men; they row till they come pretty near, then the Harpooner strikes him with his Harpoon, which is a sharp Iron, resembling the Head of an Arrow, fixed to a Stick; and this requires great Dexterity. Through the Bone of his Head there is no striking; but, near his Spout, there is a soft Piece of Flesh, into which the Iron sinks with Ease. As soon as he is struck, they take care to give him Rope enough; for otherwise, when he goes down, as he frequently does, he would invariably sink the Boat: and this Rope he draws so quick, that, if it were not well watered, it would set the Boat on fire. The Line fastened to the Harpoon is six or seven Fathom long, and is called the Forerunner. It is made of the finest and the softest Hemp, that it may slip the easier. To this they join a Heap of Lines, of ninety or a hundred Fathom each; and, when there are not enough in one Long-boat, they borrow from another.

The Man at the Helm observes which Way the Rope goes, and steers the Boat accordingly, that it may run exactly out before; for the Whale runs away with the Line as fast as the Wind, and would overturn the Boat if it were not kept strait. When the Whale is struck, the other Long-Boats row before, and observe which Way the Line stands, and sometimes pull it. If they feel it stiff, it is a Sign the Whale still pulls in Strength; but if it hangs loose, and the Boat lies equally high before and behind upon the Water, they pull it in greatly, but take Care to lay it so that the Whale may have it easily again, if he recovers Strength. If he runs out over Level, as he sometimes does, they take Care not to give him too much Line, because he sometimes entangles it about a Rock, and so pulls out the Harpoon. The fat Whales do not sink as soon as dead, but the lean ones do, and come up some Days afterwards. They begin to stink as soon as they expire, and their Flesh ferments, creating such a Steam as inflames weak Eyes. When they see him spout out Blood, they know that he is drawn towards his End, and then prepare for cutting him up. In order to this, they hawl him close to the Ship-side, and with great Knives slice his Sides, cutting the Blubber by a Hook and a Pulley, which they lift up as they cut. Many of these great Flakes they string upon a Rope, and so drag them on Shore, where they are heaved up by a Crane laid upon the Whale's Tail, and chopp'd into small Pieces, afterwards hew'd into Pieces no bigger than Trenchers, and so thrown into Coppers; and as soon as they become brown, are called Fritton, taken out, and cast away.

The Liquor is then laded out into a Boat half full of Water to cool and chuse it; and thence, by long Troughs, that it may be more cool, conveyed into Hogsheads close to the Shore. In the mean time the Head is cut off, and drawn as near as can be to the Shore, and hoisted up by a Crane till the Whale-Bone is cut out, and tied up by Fifties, and then the rest of the Head is boiled for Oil. The Tongue, which in its Figure resembles nearly that of a Wool-Pack, is crammed up with great Care: That of a large Whale will weigh about eight Ton, and will yield from six to eleven Hogsheads of Oil, the' there have been Instances of their yielding twenty-five Hogsheads; but this is look'd upon as a Thing very extraordinary. The Ships that use this Trade carry thirty or forty Men, five or six Sloops, and four or five-hundred to eight-hundred Hogsheads of Blubber. Their Arms consist of sixty Lances, six Sea-Horse Lances, forty Harpoons, ten long Harpoons for striking Whales under Water, fix small Sea-Horse Harpoons, and thirty Lines of ninety or a hundred Fathom each.

20. There are in these Seas several other kind of valuable Fish, many of which are looked upon to be of the Whale-kind, of these the most remarkable is the Fin-Fish, which is full as long, tho' not so thick, as the Whale, by two Thirds: He blows Water higher than a Whale

The WHALE FISHERY and KILLING the BEARS.

The Whale from which the Bone is Taken.

The Whale Louse.

A Spear.

A Harpoon

The Fin Fish.

The Sea Unicorn.

The Morse.

VIRGINIA BEAUTIES

MARCH & TWO STEP

BY
W·C·
POWELL

5

W. C. Polla Co.
PUBLISHERS
CHICAGO U.S.A

MUSIC

Although not as widely known as the Library of Virginia's manuscript, book, and photographic holdings, the collection of original sheet music is noteworthy in its own right and contains many valuable and unusual pieces. Most of the more than 4,500 items are nineteenth-century popular works with Virginia imprints predominating. Much of the sheet music in the collection represents the work of the Old Dominion's composers or the skilled craft of Virginia's printing artists. Others came to the Library as gifts or purchases from Virginia musicians and collectors. Still others—such as the large body of music published in the Southern states during the American Civil War that was acquired by the Library in 1904—complement the strengths of the printed and manuscript holdings, particularly in the area of popular culture.

The Library's collection reflects the explosion of the sheet music industry in the late nineteenth and early twentieth centuries. Local firms continued to churn out compositions even as music publishing increasingly centered on an area of New York known as "Tin Pan Alley" that sold millions of sheets to a mass audience. The popularity of vaudeville, burlesque, and musical theater provided public venues for promoting the songs of the Tin Pan Alley tunesmiths. The piano became a fixture in the parlors of an expanding middle class. Those too skittish to attend the urban haunts of popular music played rags and ballads on their pianos at home, accompanied by the singing of friends and family. Virginia's culture, lore, and natural beauty were popular musical themes among song lyricists, and the Library's holdings testify to the prominent place of the Old Dominion in national song and popular culture.

Besides sheet music, the Library also owns many songbooks, particularly for schools and religious bodies, dating back to the eighteenth century. Among the most significant titles in this group are the songbooks compiled and published by Joseph Funk in the Valley of Virginia in the early nineteenth century. During Funk's long lifetime, the area near his Valley home at Singer's Glen became a focal point for music education and publication, and it continued to be an important center of music publishing for decades after his death in 1862.

◄ W. C. Powell (fl. 1900s). *Virginia Beauties March & Two Step*. Chicago: W. C. Polla and Company, 1903.

This handsome piece of sheet music, written by composer W. C. Powell, is representative of the Library's extensive music collection. Beautifully designed to attract buyers in its day, the piece is a product of the song-publishing industry's heyday at the turn of the twentieth century when sheet music sales reached an all-time high. Unfortunately, little information has survived to reveal much about the composer of *Virginia Beauties* or the popularity of this particular piece. W. C. Powell did write at least one other work, however, *Funny Folks*, a ragtime tune.

The publisher, William C. Polla (1876–1939), owned a music-publishing company based in Chicago early in the twentieth century. A small number of major cities had by that time become centers for the flourishing music business, most notably New York's Tin Pan Alley, but Chicago too emerged as a hub for the bustling new enterprise. During his career, Polla also composed songs, such as his *Dancing Tambourine*, and instrumental music, such as *Pilgrimage to Mecca*. In addition, he arranged and conducted Broadway musicals and radio programs. DSG

▲ Francis Buck (ca. 1821–1848). *Blue Ridge Quick Step*. Richmond: P. H. Taylor, 1847.

Little is known about German-born Francis Buck, although he composed numerous quicksteps and waltzes for the pianoforte between 1844 and 1848 dedicated to Virginians. His *Mediterranean Waltz* (1848) lists him as a professor of music living in Richmond. In all likelihood, Buck taught music privately or at one of the city's academies. He performed at the Exchange Hotel on New Year's Eve in 1847 on a program also featuring publisher and music-store owner Patrick H. Taylor (ca. 1795–1861), playing the flute. Taylor published numerous Buck compositions, including *Le Carnival de Venise; Quick Step* (1847) and *The Jewel Waltz* (1848), copublished with a New York firm. The cover of the *Blue Ridge Quick Step* bears the stamp of William L. Montague's music store, which stood at 158 Main Street, next door to Taylor's establishment. James A. Cowardin (1811–1882), to whom the *Blue Ridge Quick Step* was dedicated, was a prominent newspaper editor and publisher in antebellum Virginia.

Buck died suddenly in 1848 at the age of twenty-seven. The *Richmond Enquirer* eulogized him "as a musician of high order," and lamented that "the beauty of his compositions was just gaining throughout the United States that praise which he justly merited."

The popularity of martial music grew during the Mexican War. Francis Buck composed several paeans to the victorious American forces, including *The Vera Cruz Grand March* (1847)—"respectfully dedicated to Majr. Genl. Winfield Scott, commanding the forces of the U.S. at the surrender of the city & castle of Vera Cruz"—one of more than fifty arrangements and compositions by Buck found in the Library's holdings. GK

▼ Philip H. Masi (ca. 1808–1890). *The Norfolk Female Institute Polka & Schottisch*. Baltimore: Miller and Beacham, 1853.

Philip H. Masi, a native of Massachusetts, moved to Norfolk in 1831 from Washington, D.C., where he had been the organist for Saint Patrick's Catholic Church. Bringing with him years of experience and musical knowledge, Masi taught private lessons in piano, violin, and flute and also composed musical scores. In 1853, he became the organist at Norfolk's Christ Episcopal Church, where he stayed for thirty-one years. Considered Norfolk's leading musician of his era, Masi introduced Gioacchino Rossini's *Stabat Mater* (1842) to the city with a handpicked choir and group of soloists at the recently completed Saint Mary's Catholic Church in 1858.

The Norfolk Female Institute Polka & Schottisch actually consists of two works—*The Norfolk Female Institute Polka* and *The Norfolk Female Institute Schottisch*—but the cover of each piece combines the titles. Published in 1853, Masi's composition honored the Norfolk Female Institute, a private girls' school established in July 1849, where Masi served as professor of music.

He wrote at least one other work in honor of the school, his 1855 *Norfolk Female Institute Quadrilles*. The school lasted at least until the Civil War.

The polka originated in Bohemia as a round dance perhaps as early as 1800 and, with the waltz, became one of the most popular ballroom dances of the nineteenth century. It was introduced in Prague in 1837 and reached the United States in May 1844, where it inspired a number of jokes about presidential candidate James K. Polk. With a 2/4 meter and its characteristic short heel-and-toe half-steps, the polka emerged as a staple of military bands and mid-nineteenth-century sheet music.

The schottische, a slower version of the polka, was another form of round dance introduced to American ballrooms in the late 1840s. Although its origins are unknown, nineteenth-century dance-masters considered the schottische to be German and called the dance a German polka. Written in either 4/4 or 2/4 meter, the rhythm of the schottische is more pronounced than that of the polka. The dance movement consists of a step, a leap, and a hop with a pivot—this last motion resulted in frequent collisions between the dancing couples and became one of the identifying characteristics of the schottische. DSG

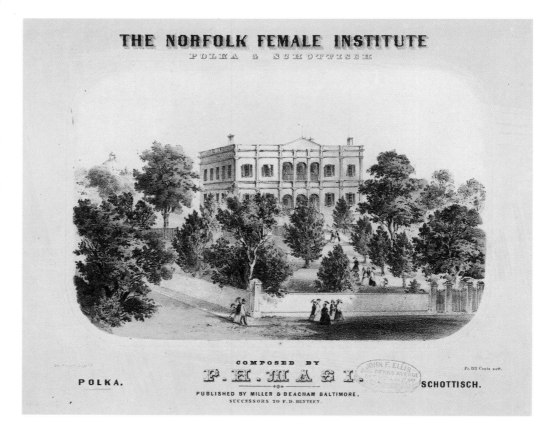

▲ Joseph Funk (1777–1862). *Die Allgemein Nützliche Choral-Music. Enthaltend: Auserlesene Melodien, Welche Bey Allen Religions Verfassungen Gebräuchlich Sind. . . . Verfasset von Joseph Funk* (*The Universally Useful Choral-Music Book. Containing Melodies Which Are Used in All Denominations. . . . Written by Joseph Funk*). Harrisonburg: Laurentz Wartmann, 1816.

Joseph Funk was the best known of several publishers of sacred music residing in the Valley of Virginia in the early nineteenth century. A year before Funk's *Die Allgemein Nützliche Choral-Music* appeared, Rockingham County printer Ananias Davisson had issued a hymnal entitled *Kentucky Harmony*, which introduced to a southern audience a new musical notation called the "shape-note." This notation gave different shapes to notes of different pitch, making it possible for untrained singers to read the music. Davisson's successful hymnal inspired Joseph Funk, a Mennonite teacher and farmer of German descent who lived in the Rockingham County community of Mountain Valley (later Singer's Glen), to embark on his publishing endeavors. His first venture into the shape-note field, depicted here, was printed in Funk's ancestral tongue at Harrisonburg by Laurentz Wartmann, who probably also printed Davisson's *Kentucky Harmony*. Funk's later work, *A Compilation of Genuine Church Music, Comprising a Variety of Metres, All Harmonized for Three Voices*, published in 1832 at Winchester, appeared in English, as did all subsequent editions of the work.

Funk's songbooks were printed by others until 1847 when Funk established his own press in his home community near Harrisonburg, becoming the first Mennonite publisher in the United States. His hymnal, issued from 1851 onward as *Harmonia Sacra*, has been through no less than twenty-five editions (the latest in 1993 published by Eastern Mennonite University in Harrisonburg), with more than 80,000 copies sold. Following Funk's death in 1862, a grandson formed a partnership, called the Ruebush-Kieffer Company, which continued publishing the *Harmonia Sacra* well into the twentieth century. JK

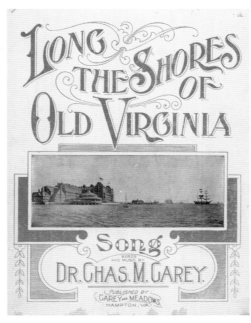

▲ Charles M. Carey (fl. 1890s–1920s). *Long the Shores of Old Virginia*. Hampton: Carey and Meadows, 1905.

Among the amateur songwriters who joined the tide of sheet-music producers at the turn of the twentieth century was Dr. Charles M. Carey, a Hampton optician and jeweler. Born in New York in June 1849, Carey moved his family to the Hampton Roads, Virginia, area about 1896. In his spare time, Charles Carey composed music, writing several pieces with Virginia history themes and publishing them himself. By 1907 he had written *Virginia, My Southland Home*; *There's So Many Want My Money*; *Reba Waltz*; and *Baby's High Chair*.

In 1907 Virginia celebrated the 300th anniversary of the English landing at Jamestown with the grand Jamestown Ter-Centennial Exposition that opened on 26 April 1907 and closed in November. In honor of the event various tunesmiths composed sheet music that could be bought as souvenirs. Charles M. Carey proved no exception and wrote at least two pieces for the exposition: the *Salute to Jamestown March*, and the *Return of Capt. John Smith*, which he described as a comedy song. In the latter Carey wrote, "I am Captain John Smith of old Jamestown / I came in my automobile / Pocahontas she was coming with me / But nervous she thought she would feel." Revisiting an attraction close to his own home, Carey had Smith describe his accommodations: "I am having such pleasure at Old Point / At Chamberlin Hotel so grand / While eating fresh fish, clams and oysters / By electric machine I am fanned."

Two years earlier, Carey had published his *Long the Shores of Old Virginia*, which featured a photograph of the Hotel Chamberlin on the cover. Describing his supposed boyhood along Virginia's shores, Carey remembered "Bathing in the rolling billows / And sailing on her bays," and promised "'Long the shores of old Virginia will I stay / Where the ships are sailing and at anchor lay / Whether seeking work or wealth / Yes, real pleasure, play or health / I would stay in old Virginia till I'm gray." DSG

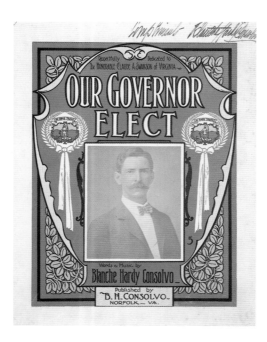

▲ Blanche Hardy Consolvo (1880–1961). *Our Governor Elect*. Norfolk: B. H. Consolvo, 1905.

This piece, autographed by the composer, was written to commemorate the election of Claude Augustus Swanson (1862–1939) as governor of Virginia in November 1905. A Democrat from Pittsylvania County, Swanson had served seven terms, from 1893 to 1906, in the United States House of Representatives. As governor, he worked especially for educational reform and better roads for the commonwealth. After his gubernatorial term, Swanson returned to the U.S. Congress as a member of the Senate from 1910 to 1933.

Composer Blanche Hardy Hecht Consolvo was born in Norfolk on 28 December 1880, the daughter of Jacob Hecht, a local merchant, and Sanna Moritz Hecht. Jacob Hecht was an accomplished musical scholar, an active member of the Norfolk Symphony Society, and choirmaster of Ohef Sholom Temple. In 1901, Blanche Hecht married businessman and entrepreneur Charles H. Consolvo. A singer as well as a composer, Blanche Consolvo was elected the first president of the Norfolk Opera Company, formed in 1914 "to promote local interest in musical affairs." Consolvo later divorced her husband and married Count Auguste Manfredi Carlaggi in New York City in 1922. Her admiration for Claude Augustus Swanson inspired the name of her only child, Charles Swanson Consolvo. DSG

▼ Max F. Brownold (1855–1925). *La Debutant*. Washington, D.C.: John F. Ellis, 1891. Overprinted by Brownold and Allemong, Music Dealers and Publishers, Roanoke, Va.

By the 1880s, many Virginia communities included at least one store selling sheet music. Some local businesses also doubled as publishers, pushing their own titles along with those of other composers. One such business was conducted by Max F. Brownold, born in Kentucky in 1856, and his father, Emanuel Brownold, a watchmaker, who opened E. Brownold and Son for the "Watch, Jewelry and Music Business" on Main Street in Berryville in Clarke County, Virginia, in May 1883.

Recent arrivals in town, the Brownolds were a musical family. Max's German-born father played several instruments, and his mother, Margaret, also an emigrant from the German states, taught music. The younger Brownold directed concerts, performing on the piano while his father played the guitar or violin. A reviewer commented that Max Brownold "evidenced superior talents as a musician." Within a year of opening E. Brownold and Son, however, the Brownolds sold the business and another they owned in Charles Town, West Virginia, to settle their debts with creditors in New York, Boston, Philadelphia, and

Staunton. The younger Brownold then taught music from his home on Main Street and composed pieces such as *La Debutant*, written in 1891 and dedicated to Berryville debutante Sarah "Sadie" Grimshaw Deahl, the daughter of cabinetmaker Horace Peake Deahl and Mary Elizabeth Deahl.

Max Brownold and his wife, Agnes, eventually settled in Roanoke, where he formed a sheet music and musical instrument company with J. Edwin Allemong, a local lawyer. By 1912 the company was known as Brownold and Allemong and Edwin Allemong's wife Nettie had joined the firm. Among the pieces of sheet music they offered for sale was Max Brownold's 1891 *La Debutant*, which they had overprinted with the new Brownold and Allemong logo. The owners also tempted local musicians with the assurance that they were "prepared to correct amateurs' manuscripts and publish same." And even if the customer could only hum the tune and not write it down, Brownold and the Allemongs could "take down amateurs' compositions at reasonable rates." The collaboration lasted only a few years, however, as Max Brownold had joined forces with Edward D. Naff, selling musical merchandise and codirecting the new Roanoke School of Music by 1914. Within four years, Brownold was on his own, teaching music at his studio on Campbell Avenue until his death in 1925. DSG

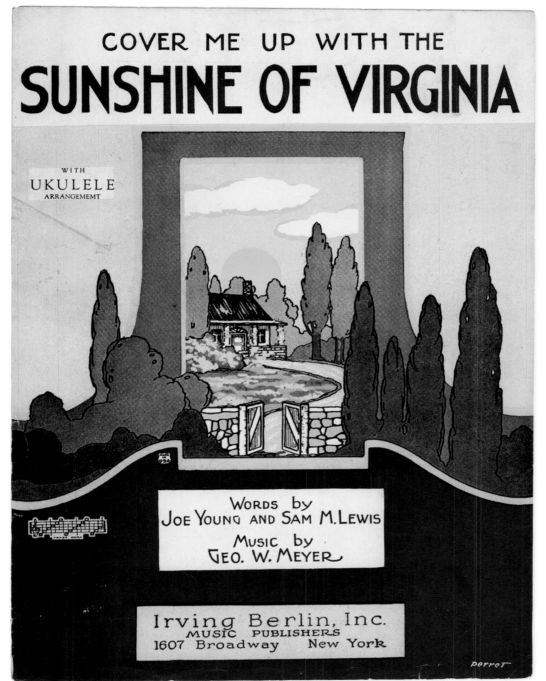

◀ *Cover Me Up With the Sunshine of Virginia.* With ukulele accompaniment. Words by Joe Young and Sam M. Lewis, music by George W. Meyer. New York: Irving Berlin, Inc., 1923.

New York's Tin Pan Alley tradition attracted numerous songwriters, among them the prolific team of Joe Young (1889–1939) and Sam M. Lewis (1885–1959), who collaborated with various composers between 1916 and 1930 to create such standards as *Rock-A-Bye Your Baby With A Dixie Melody, Dinah, I'm Sitting On Top of the World, In a Little Spanish Town, How Ya Gonna Keep 'Em Down on the Farm?,* and *Five Foot Two, Eyes of Blue.* At least three of Young and Lewis's songs had a Virginia theme, *I'm Gonna Make Hay While the Sun Shines in Virginia* (1916), *Who Played Poker With Pocahontas, When John Smith Went Away* (1919), and *Cover Me Up With the Sunshine of Virginia* (1923), the last written with George W. Meyer (1884–1959), who composed the music. Meyer, Young, and Lewis began their musical careers at about the same time in the early 1910s. Meyer was a self-taught pianist who worked in department stores in Boston and New York before becoming a song plugger for a firm of music publishers. Young started as a singer and song plugger, like Meyer, before embarking on a stint entertaining the troops in the First World War. Like Young, Sam Lewis was a vocalist and began his career singing in cafes.

Cover Me Up With the Sunshine of Virginia, popular in 1924, was published by the music company founded in 1919 by Irving Berlin (1888–1989), and was included in Berlin's sixty-page *Universal Dance Folio for Piano Selected from the Most Popular Song Hits of the Season, No. 8* (1924). One of the most influential figures in the history of American popular music, Berlin published his first piece of music in 1907 at age nineteen. He quickly became a leading composer and publisher, writing more than eight hundred songs—the best-known perhaps being the "second US National Anthem," *God Bless America*—and publishing millions of pieces of sheet music for an expanding American middle class with a seemingly insatiable thirst for the latest popular songs and dances. DSG

Land Office Military WARRANT, No. 795

To the principal SURVEYOR of the Lands set apart for the Officers and Soldiers of the Commonwealth of VIRGINIA.

THIS shall be your WARRANT to survey and lay off in one or more Surveys, for *Moses Wade* his Heirs or Assigns, the Quantity of *One Hundred* Acres of Land, due unto the said *Moses Wade*

In consideration of his services for *three* years as *a Soldier in the Virginia Continental Line*

agreeable to a Certificate from the Governour and Council received into the Land Office. GIVEN under my Hand, and the Seal of the said Office, this *12th* Day of *June* in the Year One Thousand Seven Hundred and *83*

John Harvie L. Off.

PERSONAL PAPERS AND ORGANIZATIONAL RECORDS

In addition to the official government documents that form the heart of the Library of Virginia's collections of original manuscripts, there is also a substantial body of important papers of Virginia families and individuals as well as the records of private organizations that have influenced the growth and development of the commonwealth. These extensive files cover a wide range of Virginians' activities, from personal correspondence and diaries, even research notes and drafts of poetry, to records of political, professional, and educational organizations. Among the largest and most important collections of family manuscripts are the voluminous papers of the politically prominent Tazewell family from Norfolk, of the Gravely family from Southside Virginia, whose records cover two centuries, and of the Bryan family of Richmond, well-known industrialists, writers, editors, and educators for several generations. The Personal Papers Collection also includes an exceptionally valuable and important collection of Robert E. Lee's wartime letters to Jefferson Davis, a gift to the Library from the wealthy financier Bernard Baruch.

The Library of Virginia's collection of manuscript and printed organizational records includes some of the Library's most interesting items, such as the papers of the Equal Suffrage League of Virginia, among the best organizational archives of its kind in the United States. The Library's first formally accessioned collection of unofficial archival materials (accepted 26 March 1912) is the Charles M. Wallace collection of African American melodies, compiled in and around Richmond during the years 1896–1912. The Library of Virginia also preserves the archive of the Virginia Library Association, founded at the State Library. Among the papers is a minute book for the first meeting in December 1905, when John Pendleton Kennedy, the first state librarian appointed under the authority of the State Library Board, was elected the association's first president.

◀ Land Office Military Warrant, No. 795, issued to Moses Wade, 12 June 1783. Printed form with manuscript notations. Richard Clough Anderson–Allen Latham Collection, 1771–1887, Box 11, Folder 1, Acc. 23634d.

To encourage its soldiers to enlist for longer terms of military service during the American Revolution, Virginia offered a reward, or bounty, to all who agreed to serve for three years, or "for the war," in either the new nation's Continental Line or in one of the state's own regiments. Here the Virginia Land Office issued Moses Wade a warrant for 100 acres for serving in the "Virginia Continental line." A veteran or his heirs received land based on his rank and length of service: 100 acres to a private with three years' service increasing to 10,000 acres for a ranking officer with similar service. The warrants could be, and often were, assigned or sold to others before being redeemed, as was Moses Wade's warrant.

To obtain his land, a veteran sent the state authorities his proof of service, and the register of the Land Office issued a bounty warrant. The applicant, or his heirs or assignees, then took the bounty warrant to the district surveyor who located the bounty land and recorded it. Since most bounty land was in the present-day states of Ohio and Kentucky, the record of the disposition of the warrants will be found in those states. Those men who had served in the Northwest Territory with George Rogers Clark received land in what is now the state of Indiana.

The Moses Wade warrant is in the Anderson-Latham Collection, purchased in two lots in 1912 and 1950 to augment the Land Office records. Anderson served as principal surveyor of bounty lands in Kentucky and Ohio until 1819, and his son-in-law Allen Latham established a land-claim agency in Ohio about 1816. The collection of almost 2,500 items includes about 140 warrants, as well as correspondence, court records, and surveys. RC, DSG, LH

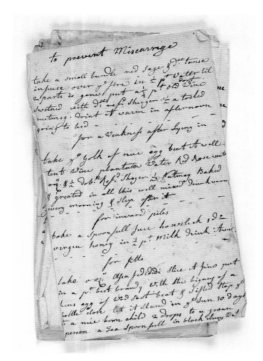

◀ "Receipt to Prevent Miscarriage," ca. 1810. Gibson Family Papers, 1775–1864 (1919), Box 6, Acc. 25342.

Tucked among the papers of the Gibson family, of Richmond and Petersburg, is a circa 1810 recipe for preventing miscarriage. If ailing during the early months of pregnancy, the recipe advised, a woman should infuse an herbal mixture of red sage and tansy with water. Long used for its therapeutic benefits, sage tea was thought to cool fevers, purify the blood, and calm the stomach and nervous system (something especially useful to pregnant women). Once reduced, the herbal drink was laced with "old Port Wine," sweetened with refined sugar, and spiced with nutmeg. "Drink it warm," the recipe's author advised, before "going to bed." Copied in after this potion was another, containing egg yolks, sugar, and spices, that attempted to ease "Weakness after Lying in."

Pregnant women faced a multitude of life-threatening risks. Giving birth was a fearsome ordeal, with the results largely beyond a woman's control. "I am now Every Day Expecting," wrote one Virginia woman in the 1750s, "Either to give life or lose it—Whichsoever it pleases heaven." Pregnancy threatened death as much as it promised life. Death from complications of childbirth was so common that an early-nineteenth-century medical manual, *The Married Lady's Companion*, listed "Fear of Death" along with "Various swellings of the legs," "Cramp," and "want of Sleep" as normal symptoms of pregnancy.

The "Receipt to Prevent Miscarriage" reflects the healing traditions of folk medicine. Herbal infusions and home remedies, when shared among the community of women, continued the established practice of English botanic medicine. Herbs were administered internally as teas, as well as in syrups, pills, and vapors; they were likewise applied externally by way of poultices, plasters, baths, and salves. Midwives often kept herb gardens where sage and other plants were tended in preparation for expectant women's ills. By brewing a cup of sage tea, the gap between the Old World and the New was narrowed, offering familiar comfort during the trying times of pregnancy. The Library of Virginia received the Gibson Family Papers from Alice D. Chamberlayne in 1961. JM

▶ Joseph Bryan (1845–1908), Eagle Point, Gloucester County, to Pat and Ran Bryan, 11 June 1856. Bryan Family Papers, 1679–1943, Box 4, Acc. 24882.

Letters written by children of any era are infrequently found in manuscript collections. Ten-year-old Joe Bryan penned this letter to his brothers "Pat" (presumably St. George Tucker Coalter Bryan, generally called Saint) and "Ran" (John Randolph Bryan) from the family home in Gloucester County, reporting his activities. He proudly told of catching a muskrat, "the largest I ever saw," and informed his brothers that he could now "swim quite well." Despite these diversions, Joe missed his brothers and felt isolated in the country. A rare visit from a young friend gave him "a fine time as you may imagine for I have been so lonesome anybody would suit me." Joseph Bryan later attended the University of Virginia and served with Mosby's Rangers during the Civil War. After 1865, he became a Richmond newspaper publisher, influential in Virginia's civic and political affairs.

The Library acquired the Bryan Family Papers in 1952; the collection includes correspondence, genealogical materials, business and legal papers, diaries, and ephemera related to the Bryan family of Virginia and Georgia. Represented in the papers are John Randolph of Roanoke (1773–1833), Joseph Bryan (1773–1812), John Randolph Bryan (1806–1887), Joseph Bryan (1845–1908), and John Stewart Bryan (1871–1944). MW

Eagle Point June 11th 1856

My dear Pat And Ran

I want to see you more and more every day. I caught a muskrat and he was the largest I ever saw. Little Fee Taylor came to see me the other day and we had a fine time as you may imagine for I have been so lonesome any body would suit me! Dr Gordon came down to see us the other day and stayed some time and then went away and left his gloves & umbrella. I have been bathing some time and can swim quite well. Uncle Joe came to see us on his way back from the North last week. Pa has finished the new boat and she is launched the first day we went to the skool neck to see boys colt was which is hurt. Carys back now.

Uncle Eliza Jn has come down from the Brook and says Pa has exchanged old John for Mr Morris's colt and sendt down to Richmond for a very good mare to work in his place. Good bye may God bless you, your affee brother — Joe Bryan

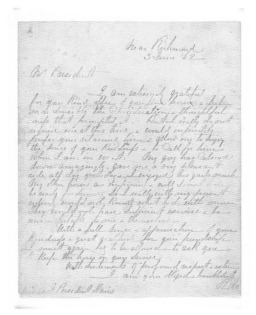

▲ Robert Edward Lee (1807–1870), "Near Richmond," to Jefferson Davis, Richmond, Va., 3 June 1862. Robert E. Lee–Jefferson Davis Correspondence, 1862–1865, Box 345–346, Acc. 23458.

The letter dated 3 June 1862 is the first in a collection of confidential dispatches between General R. E. Lee and Confederate president Jefferson Davis. Assigned to replace the wounded Joseph E. Johnston during the vital, swirling Seven Days' campaign outside Richmond, Lee confronted a force far larger than anything he could muster. Davis was especially eager to demonstrate confidence in his former military

aide and, as a special gift, sent General Lee a horse. In his reply, penned only a day after he had accepted command of what would become known as the Army of Northern Virginia, Lee took the time to express his gratitude—and politely to decline Davis's present. Lee did not need a mount: "My grey," he remarked, "has calmed down amazingly." The horse was Traveller. Lee had purchased him in western Virginia only a few months before and already placed great confidence in him. Lee also admitted that his "other horses are improving & will soon I hope be ready for service." Strenuous campaigning forced Lee eventually to rely on six different mounts; besides Traveller, the general also rode Grace Darling, Richmond, Brown Roan, Ajax, and Lucy Long. His gray, however, would always remain his—and the army's—favorite.

The Lee-Davis letters, totaling 152 items, followed a long and sometimes mysterious path to the Library's collections. They were apparently removed from President Davis's office when Richmond was evacuated in April 1865 and then sent to Davis's private secretary, Burton Harrison, in Washington, Georgia. Harrison carried the letters with him when he moved to New York City. By 1914, Wymberley Jones De Renne owned the dispatches. The collection next belonged to Bernard Baruch, the financier and advisor to Presidents Woodrow Wilson, Franklin D. Roosevelt, and Harry Truman. Baruch presented the collection to the Library of Virginia on 3 October 1949. Baruch's father, a doctor, had attended the Medical College of Virginia, and Baruch had already further established his ties to the commonwealth by donating funds to restore the college's nineteenth-century Egyptian Building and to establish the Baruch Center of Physical Medicine. DR

▲ Charles Montriou Wallace Jr. (1866–1957). Memoranda of Negro Melodies. Charles M. Wallace Jr. Collection of Negro Melodies, 1896–1912, Acc. 1.

Charles M. Wallace Jr., a Richmond lawyer and member of the Virginia General Assembly's House of Delegates (1897–1898, 1901–1904), collected a remarkable sampling of the music and verse of the commonwealth's African American population. In a number of instances, Wallace noted when and where he heard the music and identified the singer. He also included a few melodies from other southern states.

Beginning his work about 1896 and finishing in 1912, Wallace made a fair copy of his notes, which he then sent to the Royal Anthropological Institute of Great Britain and Ireland. That same year, the State Library received the remaining rough notes and drafts—the first formal accession of unofficial manuscript material. To date the Library has acquired more than thirty-five thousand additional accessions of personal papers.

Wallace published other works on Richmond history and culture, including *The History of the Capitol of Virginia* (1936), no doubt partially drawn from his long service in Democratic Party politics, and *The Boy Gangs of Richmond* (1938), based on his childhood memories. MW, GK

VOTES FOR WOMEN

Mrs. C. E. Townsend
E. S. League of Virginia

DELEGATE

NASHVILLE
1914

VOTES
FOR
WOMEN

VOTES FOR WOMEN

Mrs. C. E. Townsend

NATIONAL LEAGUE
OF
WOMEN VOTERS
BALTIMORE, MD.
APRIL 20-30, 1922

ALTERNATE

VOTES
FOR
WOMEN

I
Take
Her
Paper

Mrs. C. E. Townsend

NATIONAL
SUFFRAGE
CONVENTION

Delegate

Atlantic City
1916

◀ Equal Suffrage League of Virginia. Buttons, ribbons, and name badges, 1909–1922. Equal Suffrage League of Virginia Papers, ca. 1909–1935, Box 22, Acc. 22002.

The Equal Suffrage League of Virginia was formed in 1909 by a small group of Richmond activists. The league elected reformer Lila Meade Valentine as its president and included writers Ellen Glasgow and Mary Johnston, artists Adèle Clark and Nora Houston, and physician Kate Waller Barrett among its members. Within its first few months, the league joined with the National American Woman Suffrage Association and began a campaign to inform the citizens of the commonwealth about the suffrage issue. Virginia suffragists employed a variety of campaign techniques to enlist women to their cause: making speeches across the state (often from decorated automobiles), renting booths at fairs, and distributing "Votes for Women" buttons. By 1919, the league claimed twenty thousand members.

The Equal Suffrage League of Virginia Papers were donated to the Library of Virginia in 1942 by Ida Mae Thompson, a Charlotte County native who had served as the office secretary at the Equal Suffrage League headquarters in Richmond. Thompson had brought her skills as a typist, manager, and tireless organizer to the league in 1913. After the organization disbanded, she continued her secretarial duties with the new League of Women Voters of Virginia. Later, as clerk for the Work Projects Administration's Virginia Historical Records Survey, Thompson gathered information on Equal Suffrage League chapters across the state. The assembled questionnaires, correspondence, membership lists, publications, buttons, ribbons, and badges comprise the Equal Suffrage League collection. JM

▼ Equal Suffrage League of Virginia. Suffrage Calendar, 1912. Equal Suffrage League of Virginia Papers, ca. 1909–1935, Box 7, Folder 421, Acc. 22002.

The 1912 calendar, drawn by cartoonist Josephine W. Neall and published in Philadelphia, features a cover illustration of a suffragist speaking to a crowd. Women often prepared for such activities in special suffrage schools, where they were educated about political issues and trained as debaters and speakers. The Lynchburg branch of the Equal Suffrage League, for example, cooperated with the Randolph-Macon Woman's College League to present a series of classes for suffrage workers in 1915, charging 25¢ a lesson, $1.50 for the entire course. Directed jointly by Elizabeth L. Lewis (president of the Lynchburg league) and Nellie V. Powell (a Randolph-Macon instructor), classes were intended to cover "the questions of the day, political, social, legal, and historical," as well as public speaking.

Other pages of the calendar include quotes from suffrage literature supporting the claim that women, while homemakers, had a responsibility to be politically active. "Home is not contained within the four walls of an individual home," suffragists argued; instead, "home is the community." Suffragists staunchly maintained that women, in order to be good mothers, needed to be good citizens. When antisuffragists argued that men were the commonwealth's natural-born leaders, intellectually and physically superior to their female helpmates, suffragists countered that women could add valuable insight and energy to solving a number of problems largely ignored by politicians, including education, health reform, and child labor. A map on the calendar's last page shows Virginia with "man suffrage only." JM

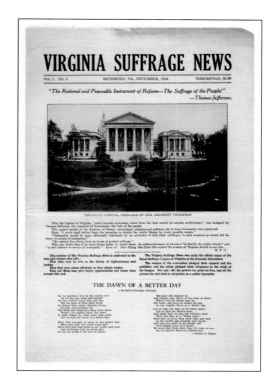

▲ Equal Suffrage League of Virginia. *Virginia Suffrage News*, vol. 1, no. 3. Richmond, December 1914. Equal Suffrage League of Virginia Papers, ca. 1909–1935, Box 12, Folder 748, Acc. 22002.

The *Virginia Suffrage News* became the official organ of the Equal Suffrage League of Virginia at the group's Roanoke convention in November 1914. Published monthly by managing editor Alice Overby Taylor, the paper included articles on such social issues as working conditions and child labor, as well as on the political fight for the vote at the local, state, and national levels. The December issue challenged Virginia women to work for laws benefiting the "exploited immature toilers" in the state's seafood factories. "Crab salad and deviled crabs may not appeal so alluringly to gustatory delight," the paper warned, when it became apparent that children as young as six were employed to clean them.

On the front page of the newspaper's third issue, an image of the Capitol illustrated a persuasive article by editor-in-chief Mary Pollard Clarke arguing that if Thomas Jefferson, Virginia's "greatest democrat," were alive in 1914, he would have favored the vote for women. Inside, advertisements for official suffrage "sashes, badges, pins, medals," and banners appeared with those for curtains, carpet, hats, and suits. Local leagues reported their activities to the paper: Randolph-Macon members posted cartoons on the college bulletin board; Alexandria members planned a meeting with the Virginia Anti-Tuberculosis Association to stress the need for in-home nurses; and Richmond members held a bake sale to benefit the league and the American Red Cross. The Equal Suffrage League collection contains three issues of the Virginia Suffrage News, including the first, published in October 1914. JM

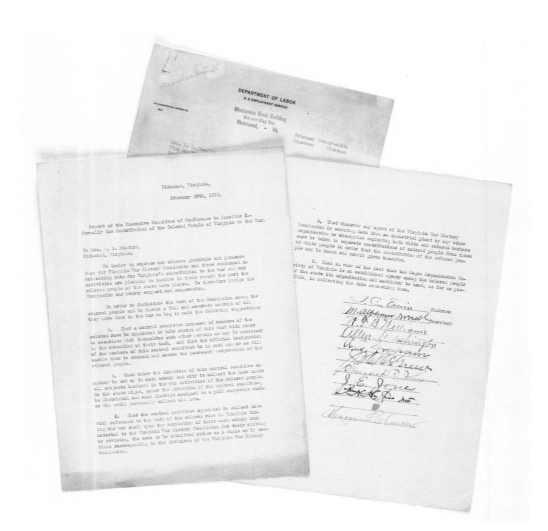

▶ Virginia Library Association Minute Book, 1905–1924. Bound Manuscript. Virginia Library Association Records, 1905–1985, Box 1, Folder 1, Acc. 32434.

Among the collections preserved in the Library of Virginia are those of various organizations that have directly influenced the lives of the commonwealth's citizens. A notable example is the papers of the Virginia Library Association, organized in the first State Library building on Capitol Square on 6 December 1905. The association elected John Pendleton Kennedy, then state librarian, as its first president. Several other members of the State Library staff were also elected officers. The membership immediately went on record in support of the American Library Association's movement to generate interest in libraries throughout the United States. Now an affiliated chapter of the American Library Association, the Virginia organization has for ninety-one years fostered an exchange of information among librarians and promoted library interests across the Old Dominion. The Virginia Library Association donated these records to the Library of Virginia in June 1985. DR

▲ "Report of the Executive Committee of [the] Conference to Consider Informally the Contribution of the Colored People of Virginia to the War," 25 February 1919. Mary-Cooke Branch Munford Collection, 1905–1930, Box 2, Acc. 28142.

On 7 January 1919, Governor Westmoreland Davis formed the Virginia War History Commission to collect, edit, and publish source material concerning the commonwealth's participation in the Great War. Under the direction of editor Arthur Kyle Davis, the sixteen-member commission devised a topical approach to documenting the Old Dominion's role in the conflict, recruiting Mary-Cooke Branch Munford (head of the Women's Committee of the Council of National Defense during the war) as an associate for the project's segment on war work and relief organizations. Mary Munford's assigned portion

was also to include "the story of the Virginia negro in war time." To assist her, a board of thirty African American Virginians collected local information, and a board-appointed African American field agent traveled the state "to stir the colored people to active work, both in securing war records of the soldiers and in gathering the facts of negro civilian activities in war time."

In February 1919, shortly after the War History Commission was formed, Mary Munford received the "Report of the Executive Committee of [the] Conference to Consider Informally the Contribution of the Colored People of Virginia to the War." The committee's proposal included the signatures of banker Maggie L. Walker and the chairwoman of the Working Force of Negro Women, Margaret R. Johnson. Arthur Kyle Davis predicted in August 1920 that "Virginia will have reason to be proud of the story of the negroes in war time as told by their own writers." JM

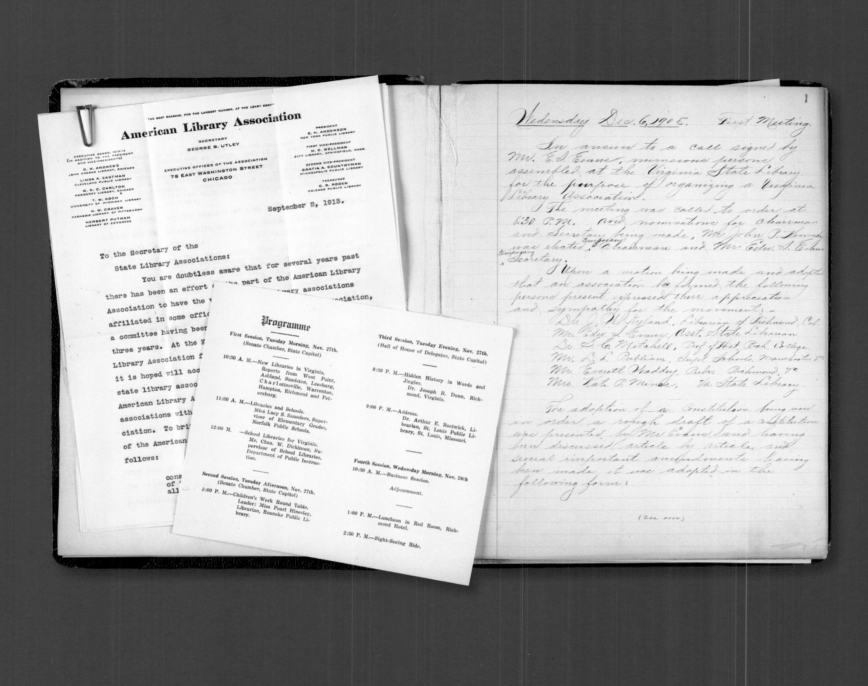

American Library Association

"THE BEST READING, FOR THE LARGEST NUMBER, AT THE LEAST COST"

SECRETARY
GEORGE B. UTLEY

PRESIDENT
E. H. ANDERSON
NEW YORK PUBLIC LIBRARY

FIRST VICE-PRESIDENT
H. C. WELLMAN
CITY LIBRARY, SPRINGFIELD, MASS.

SECOND VICE-PRESIDENT
GRATIA A. COUNTRYMAN
MINNEAPOLIS PUBLIC LIBRARY

TREASURER
C. B. RODEN
CHICAGO PUBLIC LIBRARY

EXECUTIVE BOARD, 1913/14
(IN ADDITION TO THE PRESIDENT AND VICE-PRESIDENTS)
E. W. ANDREWS
CLEVELAND PUBLIC LIBRARY
LINDA A. EASTMAN
CLEVELAND PUBLIC LIBRARY
W. N. C. CARLTON
NEWBERRY LIBRARY, CHICAGO
T. W. KOCH
UNIVERSITY OF MICHIGAN LIBRARY
H. W. CRAVER
CARNEGIE LIBRARY OF PITTSBURGH
HERBERT PUTNAM
LIBRARY OF CONGRESS

EXECUTIVE OFFICES OF THE ASSOCIATION
78 EAST WASHINGTON STREET
CHICAGO

September 2, 1913.

To the Secretary of the
State Library Associations:

You are doubtless aware that for several years past there has been an effort on the part of the American Library Association to have the various library associations affiliated in some official... a committee having been... three years. At the...
Library Association...
it is hoped will acc...
state library assoc...
American Library A...
associations with...
ciation. To bri...
of the American...
follows:

Programme

First Session, Tuesday Morning, Nov. 27th.
(Senate Chamber, State Capitol)

10:30 A. M.—New Libraries in Virginia. Reports from West Point, Ashland, Sandston, Leesburg, Charlottesville, Warrenton, Hampton, Richmond and Petersburg.

11:30 A. M.—Libraries and Schools. Miss Lucy S. Saunders, Supervisor of Elementary Grades, Norfolk Public Schools.

12:00 M.—School Libraries for Virginia. Mr. Chas. W. Dickinson, Supervisor of School Libraries, Department of Public Instruction.

Second Session, Tuesday Afternoon, Nov. 27th
(Senate Chamber, State Capitol)

2:00 P. M.—Children's Work Round Table. Leader: Miss Pearl Hinesley, Librarian, Roanoke Public Library.

Third Session, Tuesday Evening, Nov. 27th.
(Hall of House of Delegates, State Capitol)

8:30 P. M.—Hidden History in Words and Jingles. Dr. Joseph B. Dunn, Richmond, Virginia.

9:00 P. M.—Address. Dr. Arthur E. Bostwick, Librarian, St. Louis Public Library, St. Louis, Missouri.

Fourth Session, Wednesday Morning, Nov. 28th
10:30 A. M.—Business Session.
Adjournment.

1:00 P. M.—Luncheon in Red Room, Richmond Hotel.

2:30 P. M.—Sight-Seeing Ride.

1

Wednesday Dec. 6, 1905. First Meeting.

In answer to a call signed by Mr. E. S. Evans, numerous persons assembled at the Virginia State Library for the purpose of organizing a Virginia Library Association.

The meeting was called to order at 8:30 P.M. and nominations for Chairman and Secretary being made, Mr. John P. Kennedy was elected temporary Chairman and Mr. Edw. S. Evans temporary Secretary.

Upon a motion being made and adopted that an association be formed, the following persons present expressed their appreciation and sympathy for the movement:—

Dr. J. W. Ryland, Librarian of Richmond, Va.
Mr. Edw. S. Evans, Asst. State Librarian
Dr. S. C. Mitchell, Prof of West Rich. College
Mr. D. L. Pulliam, Supt. Schools Manchester, Va
Mr. Ernest Maddey, Pub. Richmond, Va
Mrs. Kate P. Minor, Va. State Library.

The adoption of a Constitution being now in order a rough draft of a Constitution was presented by Mr. Evans, and having been discussed article by article, and several important amendments having been made it was adopted in the following form:

(see over)

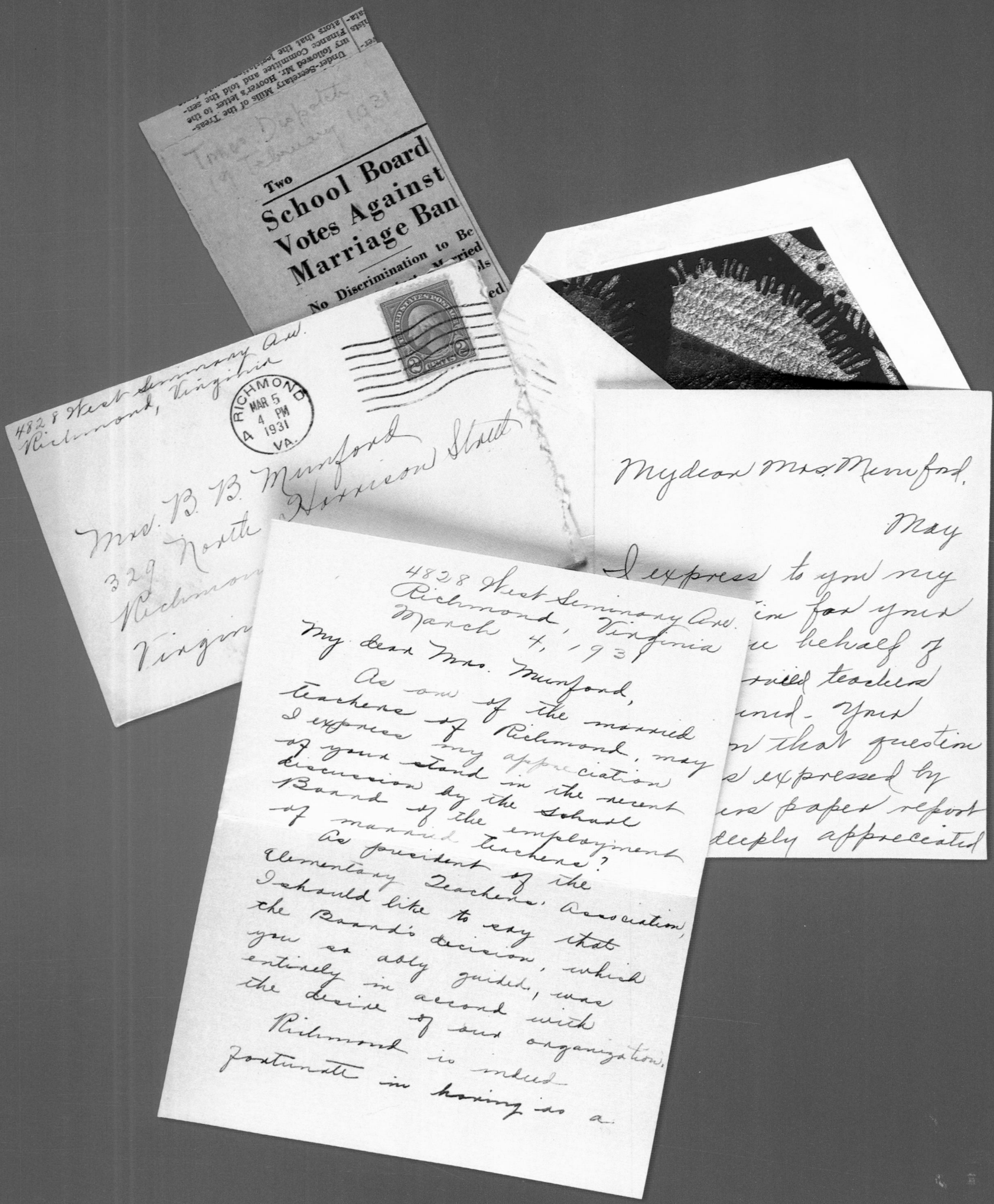

Two

School Board Votes Against Marriage Ban

No Discrimination to Be

4828 West Seminary Ave.
Richmond, Virginia

Mrs. B. B. Munford
329 North Harrison Street
Richmond, Virginia

RICHMOND
MAR 5
4 PM
1931
VA.

4828 West Seminary Ave.
Richmond, Virginia
March 4, 1931

My dear Mrs. Munford,

As one of the married teachers of Richmond, may I express my appreciation of your stand in the recent discussion by the School Board of the employment of married teachers?

As president of the Elementary Teachers' Association, I should like to say that the Board's decision, which you so ably guided, was entirely in accord with the desire of our organization.

Richmond is indeed fortunate in having as a

My dear Mrs. Munford,

May I express to you my ... for your ... behalf of ...ried teachers ...und. Your ...w that question ...s expressed by ...er paper report ...deeply appreciated

◄ Margaret H. Forbes, Richmond, and Eleanor P. Rowlett, Richmond, to Mary-Cooke Branch Munford (1865–1938), Richmond, March 1931. Mary-Cooke Branch Munford Collection, 1905–1930, Box 3, Acc. 28142.

On 18 February 1931, the Richmond City School Board voted to end its discrimination against married teachers. Several weeks later, board member Mary Munford received letters of appreciation from two Richmond teachers, Margaret H. Forbes and Eleanor P. Rowlett, for her efforts in opposing the ban against having married women employed in the classroom. Before the Richmond school board's ruling, a female teacher after her marriage could be reemployed only with an outstanding endorsement from a principal willing to ignore the common perception that a wedded woman's place was in the home rather than in the classroom. As a result, women were routinely forced to choose between marriage and a teaching career. "That is ridiculous!" argued Mary Munford, the only woman member of the school board. "Women with the experience of marriage," she pointed out, "are better qualified as teachers by this experience, and I object strenuously to penalizing a woman for being married." Despite the stance taken by Munford and others, a study published three years later, *The Status of the Married Woman Teacher*, still reported that "women teachers must foreswear marriage and family life in order to make of teaching a life's work."

Mary Munford's fight against such discrimination reflected her longstanding belief in the importance of education for women. In 1910, Munford had founded the Co-Ordinate College League for the establishment of a college for women at the University of Virginia. At the time, the commonwealth supported four degree-granting colleges for men, but none for women. While there were four normal, or teachers' education, schools for female students, none gave regular diplomas or was accredited. Faced with the staunch opposition of University of Virginia alumni, bills to establish a coordinate college failed in every legislative session between 1910 and 1918. On the other hand, without well-organized alumni to object and perhaps at the request of college president Lyon G. Tyler who wanted to reverse declining enrollments, a bill to admit women to the College of William and Mary passed in 1918. At that same session, however, the House of Delegates defeated three bills that would have allowed women to attend the University of Virginia as full-time students. Two years later, however, women were finally admitted to the University of Virginia's graduate and professional programs. That same year, Munford was appointed the first woman member of the board of visitors at the College of William and Mary. In 1926 she became a member of the board of visitors at the University of Virginia as well. JM

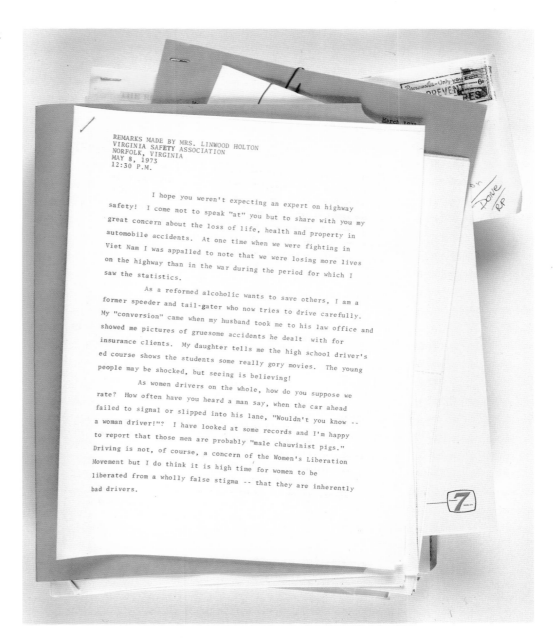

▲ Virginia Harrison Holton (1925–). Speech to the Virginia Safety Association, Norfolk, 8 May 1973. Mrs. Linwood Holton Personal Papers, 1970–1974, in A. Linwood Holton Personal Papers, 1969–1974, Box 58, Acc. 28253.

Speaking before the Virginia Safety Association in 1973, Virginia Harrison "Jinks" Holton argued that women were better drivers than men. In 1971, she reported, twice as many men as women were involved in accidents in Virginia. Women were undeserving of the "wholly false stigma" of being inherently bad drivers; men who argued that they were, she remarked, were probably just "male chauvinist pigs." Holton concluded her remarks by offering tips for driving safely, urging women to "learn how to drive on the modern highways" and to change their own flat tires.

Her husband, Abner Linwood Holton Jr. (1923–), served as governor of Virginia from 17 January 1970 to 12 January 1974. Governor Holton's personal papers along with those of his wife were donated to the Library of Virginia after his term of office ended and include about 30,000 items. During the same period, the Library also received more than 230,000 pieces of the governor's official correspondence—documents that are state records and, by law, part of the commonwealth's archival collection. JM

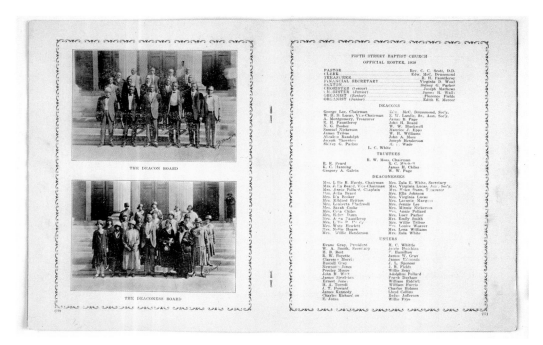

▲ Fifth Street Baptist Church, Richmond. *Programme of the 50th Anniversary of the Fifth Street Baptist Church, October 5 to 19, 1930, Richmond, Virginia.* Richmond: Printed by Service Print Shop, Edw. McC. Drummond, 1930.

Many churches recorded their activities and accomplishments in bulletins, brochures, and other printed materials that have fortuitously found their way into the Library of Virginia's collections of local and community history. The fiftieth anniversary program of Richmond's Fifth Street Baptist Church is a prime example of the literature.

According to the program, the church was founded in July 1880 by members of the First African Baptist Church and met in the Odd Fellows Hall at 1417 East Franklin Street under the leadership of its first pastor, the Reverend Henry H. Mitchell. Soon thereafter the congregation moved to a building at Fifth and Jackson Streets and in 1886 financed a new church building at 629 North Fifth Street. The church remained at that location until the congregation dedicated a new Classical Revival structure on 4 July 1926 at 705 North Fifth Street, where in 1930 it celebrated its golden jubilee. The congregation moved once more, in October 1975, to a new church building in the Highland Park neighborhood of Richmond.

The program for the golden jubilee includes a brief sketch of each of the pastors who had served the church, making it an important resource for researchers interested in Richmond's religious history. Perhaps of greater historical significance are the many photographs of the men and women who made the church such a vital and vibrant institution within its extended African American neighborhood. Because so many similar institutional publications have been discarded or otherwise lost through time, those that survive in repositories such as the Library of Virginia provide uniquely localized glimpses into the past. ST

▼ J. H. Bradley, compiler. *Official History of the Norfolk Fire Department, From 1740 to the Present Day.* Norfolk: W. T. Barron and Company, Printers, 1898.

In 1897, when the Norfolk Fire Department decided to publish a small volume celebrating its history as well as its modern-day accomplishments, it was engaging in an activity that has been popular with civic and community organizations throughout the nineteenth and twentieth centuries. The Library of Virginia's printed collections abound with similar historical accounts compiled by churches, schools, hospitals, banks, neighborhood associations, benevolent societies, fraternal orders, and municipal institutions across the Old Dominion. Over time, these books and booklets have become invaluable research sources as the information they contain is often unavailable elsewhere.

The story of the Norfolk Fire Department was written not only to provide a historical record, but also to raise money for the city's Fireman's Relief Fund. The volume includes an account of Norfolk's efforts in the eighteenth and nineteenth centuries to protect citizens from fire hazards, tracing the city's involvement back to 1740, with its use of a drum to sound the alarm. In the 1750s, the city purchased its first fire engine and water buckets. For many years, the book's compiler noted, the Norfolk Fire Department was enmeshed in local politics, but by the 1890s its officers won selection on the basis of merit, not political patronage. The volume also contains biographical sketches of several leading fire officials, the location of every fire-alarm box then in the city, and a number of attractive advertisements that give modern researchers a sense of the vitality of Norfolk's turn-of-the-century commercial life. ST

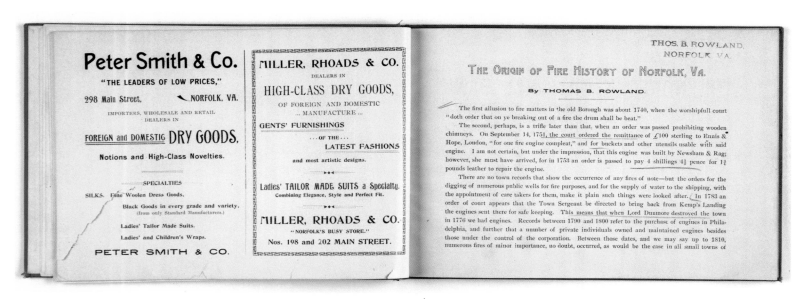

Charles M. Robinson
Johnson Architect
Richmond, Va.

Bird's-eye View of Complete Plant.

VOL. I. NO. 1.   FEBRUARY, 1909.

THE NORMAL BULLETIN

State Normal and Industrial School for Women

HARRISONBURG, VIRGINIA

PROSPECTUS

"That our daughters may be as corner-stones, polished after the similitude of a palace."

First Year Begins September 28, 1909

Published by the State Normal and Industrial School for Women, at Harrisonburg, Virginia. Issued quarterly. Application has been made at the post-office at Harrisonburg, Virginia, for admission as second-class matter.

▲ State Normal and Industrial School for Women. *The Normal Bulletin*. Harrisonburg: State Normal and Industrial School for Women. Printed by Daily News Print, 1909.

The Library of Virginia has an extensive collection of bulletins, catalogs, yearbooks, reports, and other material published by private academies, secondary schools, colleges, and universities across the commonwealth. The size of each institution's holdings varies from school to school, ranging from a ten-page list of students attending a seminary for young ladies in the 1860s to extensive volumes of catalogs and yearbooks for several state universities.

The prospectus for the State Normal and Industrial School for Women at Harrisonburg, founded in 1908, is typical of such items in the Library's collection. Published in February 1909 to entice students to enroll for classes in the fall,

the 106-page publication provides a wealth of information about the school's mission, objectives, courses of study, physical plant, faculty, and student life. The publication fulfilled its purpose and, as the institution continued to grow, the school's name changed four times: to the State Normal School for Women at Harrisonburg in 1914, the State Teachers College at Harrisonburg in 1924, Madison College in 1938, and James Madison University in 1977. The school admitted men to summer sessions in 1910 and to regular sessions in 1946. Madison College became coeducational in 1966.

By itself, the 1909 document is important in tracing the story of a single educational institution. When combined with similar material in the Library's extensive collections, it takes on added meaning as an indispensable resource for documenting the broad, rich history of education in Virginia. ST

BOOKS

ROMANCE
HISTORY TRAVEL

N.C.W.

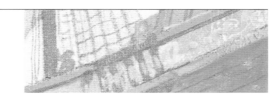

BROADSIDES AND POSTERS

In addition to books, newspapers, magazines, journals, pamphlets, and other printed items with multiple pages, the Library of Virginia's collections also include a large and important variety of broadsides and posters. They range in size from very small, pocket-size items to quite large poster art. Bibliographically, broadsides and posters are defined as items printed on one side of a single sheet of paper. The Library also has a representative collection of handbills, items printed on both sides of a single sheet.

The Library of Virginia has for many years been particularly interested in the collection and study of broadsides. In 1971 and 1975, for example, Assistant State Librarian Ray O. Hummel Jr. completed two bibliographies of broadsides printed within the southeastern United States before 1877. Hummel's compilations included thirty-four hundred broadsides printed in Virginia, more than for any other southern state. Of those, the Library has so far assembled a remarkable collection of approximately eighteen hundred.

One of the Library's oldest and most valuable broadsides is a 1630 proclamation by King Charles I imposing regulations on the cultivation and trade of tobacco. Other broadsides in the Library's collections cover a wide variety of subjects, from political campaigns to World War II propaganda, and from announcements of theatrical programs to advertisements for the sale of land or books or racehorses.

The Library has also assembled a remarkable collection of posters. As the commonwealth's research and reference institution, it received many of them as a participant in federal, state, or national library programs. An art form dating back to the late 1700s, posters were at first used primarily as political statements. By the nineteenth century, posters were increasingly manifestations of national pride, industrial progress, even class consciousness. More and more, they also served as commercial advertisements—for manufactured products, the performing and studio arts, or for gala expositions of industrial development. By the 1900s, many, commissioned by various agencies of the federal government, were intended to raise morale and instill patriotism during the First and Second World Wars. Printed in vibrant full-color designs, the posters encouraged men and women to join the armed services, civilians to invest their time and resources in numerous national defense efforts, and everyone to strive toward the shared goal. Other government-sponsored posters helped many Americans face the harsh realities of the Great Depression. Numerous other posters were meant to encourage reading and were especially popular during the 1920s and 1930s. And still others were published to introduce commercial programs, products, or services. Skillfully designed and meticulously printed, the posters offer researchers an aesthetic glimpse into a remarkable facet of popular culture.

◄ N. C. Wyeth (1882–1945). *Books: Romance, History, Travel.* New York: National Association of Book Publishers, 1928. 21 ⅛ x 13 ⅝ inches.

As a striking advertising ploy, the National Association of Book Publishers in 1928 commissioned the artist N. C. Wyeth to develop a single image evoking the romance and sense of discovery to be found in books. Well known as the illustrator for new editions of such classics as *Treasure Island* (1911), *Kidnapped* (1913), *The Last of the Mohicans* (1919), and *The Oregon Trail* (1925), Wyeth created an enticing scene with a seventeenth-century adventurer on the deck of a galleon in heavy seas. Such fanciful images by Wyeth and other popular artists in the 1920s and 1930s proved particularly effective in fostering reading—and the sale of books. EC

▲ Jon O. Brubaker (b. 1875). *After all—there is nothing like A Good Book!* N.p., n.d. 20 ½ x 13½ inches.

▶ *Public Libraries: An American Contribution to Civilization.* Chicago: American Library Association, 1926. 29 x 22 inches.

▶ Magnus Norstad (b. 1884). *Back to Nature Books.* New York: n.p., n.d. 21 x 13½ inches.

Throughout the 1920s and the Great Depression little public funding existed in Virginia for local library service. The Old Dominion was, in fact, among the last states in the country to promote the establishment of public libraries. According to a 1936 study by the American Library Association, nearly 70 percent of the commonwealth's citizens were without any form of public library resources, a situation at the time evident in only nine other states. Fifty-six Virginia counties, for example, had no public libraries in 1935, and those that did provided an average of barely eight cents per capita for their community libraries—or less than one book per citizen. Recognizing a dire need, the General Assembly in 1936 enacted Virginia's first comprehensive general library law, intended to "promote the establishment and development of public library service" throughout the state.

Among the collections of the Library of Virginia are handsome posters from the 1920s and 1930s designed to encourage reading and, by implication, legislative and community support for public libraries. Printed in vibrant, colorful designs, the posters enticed potential library patrons to books on varied subjects—from nature and the great outdoors to tales of adventure, or to fanciful poetry and books "of imagination." Commissioned and distributed by organizations such as the American Library Association and the United States Department of the Interior's Bureau of Education, posters went to bookdealers, to schools, and especially to community libraries.

Two of the posters have particular appeal to young readers, featuring children enjoying books, whether alone or shared with others. Jon O. Brubaker's *After all—there is nothing like A Good Book!* conveys the magic and sense of wonder a good story can impart. And Magnus Norstad, of Norway, illustrated how educational books—in this case "Back to Nature" books—could also enrich a child's world.

The American Library Association chose a patriotic theme to celebrate its fiftieth anniversary in 1926 with a reading poster that emphasized the democratic nature of public libraries, "an American contribution to civilization." The organization estimated that in 1925 more than 25 million people across the nation had borrowed approximately 250 million books from their local libraries. EC, SM

Back to Nature BOOKS

M. NORSTAD

◄ *By the King. A Proclamation concerning Tobacco*. London: Printed by Robert Barker et al., 1630. 15 ½ x 12 inches. Acc. 1631 E58.

Printed by Robert Barker, "Printer to the Kings most Excellent Maiestie," and issued at Whitehall on 6 January 1630 (or 1631, by the New Style calendar), the proclamation by King Charles I is the oldest document of its kind in the Library of Virginia. The particular black-letter print and the use of the Old Style, elongated letter *s*, which superficially resembles the letter *f*, as well as the use of the letter *u* in place of a *v* and of the letter *i* instead of the letter *j*, reflect the antiquity of the text and of the imprint.

Charles I sought to prohibit the cultivation of tobacco except in particular regions of his several dominions and to regulate its trade so that it benefited the overall economy of the realm. The proclamation forbade the cultivation of tobacco in England, Ireland, Wales, and on the islands of Jersey and Guernsey, "the same being utterly unwholesome to bee taken." It also prohibited the importation of tobacco from the colonies of other European countries. And it provided for the regulation of the quality of any tobacco imported from the king's American colonies through the port of London, "that Our Subjects be not abused by corrupt Tobacco."

The early broadside proclamation is very unlike the famous pamphlet, *A Counter-Blaste to Tobacco*, published by the king's father in 1604. James I vigorously campaigned against the use of tobacco, particularly because he hated the "perpetuall stinking torment" created by the "filthie smoake." King James I concluded his exhortation with a memorable sentence, describing the use of tobacco as a "custome lothsome to the eye, hatefull to the Nose, harmefull to the braine, dangerous to the Lungs, and in the blacke stinking fume thereof, neerest resembling the horrible Stigian smoke of the pit that is bottomlesse"—in other words, an awful stench much like the vapors of Hell. BT

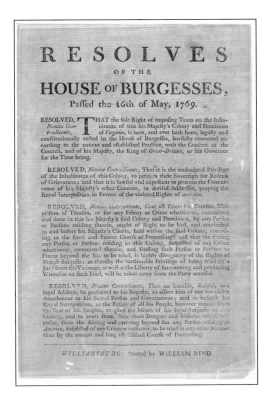

▲ *Resolves of the House of Burgesses, Passed the 16th of May, 1769.* Williamsburg: Printed by William Rind, 1769. 11 ¾ x 7 inches. Acc. 1769 VB.

Meeting in secret session on 16 May 1769, the colonial House of Burgesses directly denied the asserted right of Parliament to tax the people of Virginia. The burgesses' resolutions thus formed the colony's most direct challenge to Parliament made between the Stamp Act of 1765 and the Coercive Acts of 1774 and 1775.

When the royal governor, Norborne Berkeley, baron de Botetourt, learned of the substance of the resolutions, he summoned the entire House of Burgesses to appear before him in the Council chamber. In a memorable scene, Lord Botetourt addressed the members of the assembly: "Mr. Speaker, and Gentlemen of the House of Burgesses, I have heard of your Resolves, and augur ill of their Effect: You have made it my Duty to dissolve you; and you are dissolved accordingly." The governor thus legally terminated the May 1769 General Assembly of Virginia.

Before the governor dissolved the General Assembly, however, the House of Burgesses had ordered that its resolves of 16 May be published and immediately sent "to the Speakers of the several Houses of Assembly, on this continent." Williamsburg printer William Rind produced the broadside for distribution throughout the colony and beyond. BT

▼ *Ten Dollars. The above reward will be given to any one who, within thirty days from this time, shall give certain information of the person or persons who lately set fire to that part of the Blue Ridge which was the property of the late George William Fairfax.* Winchester: Printed by Richard Bowen, 1793. 7 ¾ x 6 ½ inches. Acc. 1793 T289.

The extremely rare 1793 broadside advertisement is one of the earliest imprints by a pioneer printer in the lower Shenandoah Valley, Richard Bowen. An English immigrant, Bowen in 1787 opened a printing office in Winchester and in April 1788 began the publication of a weekly newspaper, the *Virginia Centinel.* Bowen continued to work in Winchester as a printer and newspaper publisher until his death in 1808.

George William Fairfax (1724–1787) had been one of the most prominent men in northern Virginia and the owner of thousands of acres of land in several counties. He had also served in the House of Burgesses from 1748 to 1758 and as a member of the governor's Council from 1768 to 1773 before he returned to Great Britain. His agent, Bataille Muse (1750–1803), had been left in charge of several of his properties in the northern portion of the Potomac Valley, including Shannon Hall, purchased by one of Fairfax's relatives, Ferdinando Fairfax (1769–1820), in 1780. Shannon Hall was in that portion of Berkeley County that in 1801 became Jefferson County, now part of West Virginia.

So well known were the Fairfax family and its extensive landholdings that by identifying a particular part of the "Blue Ridge" as that "which was the property of the late George William Fairfax," Ferdinando Fairfax's printed offer of a reward was specific enough for any reader. Bataille Muse apparently dated several copies of the broadside and added a second message that "Those indebted to Mr. Fairfax are desired to Pay by the 10th of June & oblige B Muse." BT

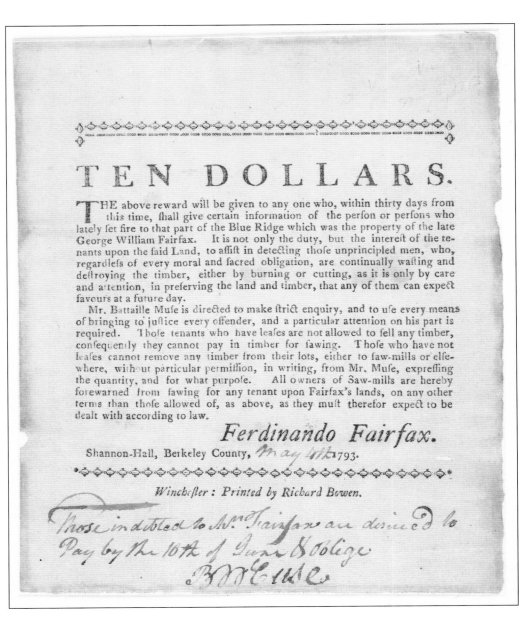

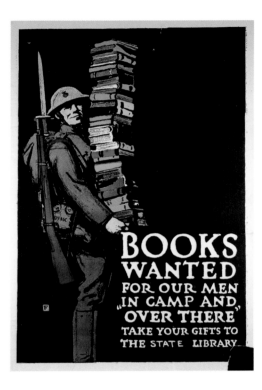

◀ Herbert Andrew Paus (1880–1946). *Save your Child from Autocracy and Poverty: Buy War Savings Stamps.* Washington, D.C.: United States Treasury Department, ca. 1917. 30 x 20 inches.

◀ Charles Buckles Falls (1874–1960). *Books Wanted for Our Men in Camp and "Over There": Take Your Gifts to the State Library.* N.p., ca. 1917. 42 x 28 inches.

▼ *Food is Ammunition—Don't waste it.* United States Food Administration Poster, No. 5. New York: Heywood, Strasser and Voight Lithography Company, ca. 1917. 29 x 21 inches.

Within weeks after the United States entered the Great War in 1917, the Society of Illustrators met in New York City to find a way that artists might assist the war effort. Under the leadership of Charles Dana Gibson (1867–1944), its members launched what became the Division of Pictorial Publicity, part of the Committee on Public Information. Believing that "posters must play a great part in the fight for public opinion," the division required artwork that encouraged patriotism and sacrifice on the home front. More than three hundred of America's foremost cartoonists, designers, illustrators, and painters worked for the division. Within twenty months, from its organization in April 1917 to the war's end in November of the following year, the division submitted at least seven hundred poster designs to various agencies.

Throughout the war, the Old Dominion sported posters of all types, samples of which are among the collections of the Library of Virginia. Many posters reminded those at home of measures they could take to help the war effort. One poster, *Food is Ammunition*, warned civilians not to waste valuable food supplies. Others stressed the importance of the war in the fight for liberty for future generations. Wartime posters also advertised programs designed to raise morale, as well as funds. Local libraries and the American Library Association, for example, coordinated a campaign to collect reading materials for military libraries and for distribution to individual soldiers and sailors. The program's artwork—*Books Wanted for Our Men in Camp and "Over There"* by Charles Buckles Falls—was easily adapted to any community. The Virginia State Library simply printed over the original instruction to "take your gifts to the public library," changing it to read "the State Library." JM

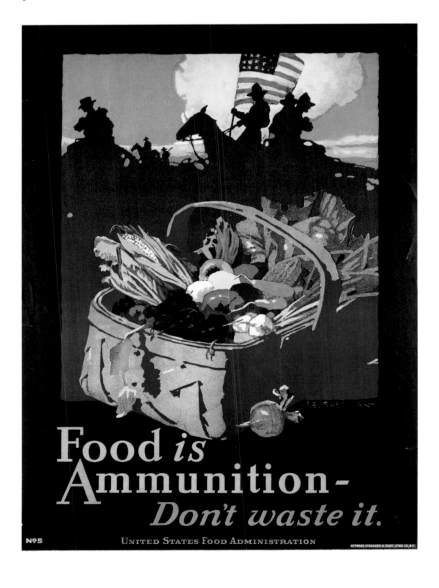

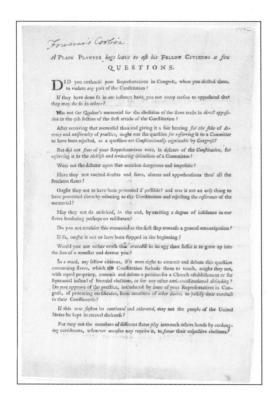

◀ *A Plain Planter begs leave to ask his Fellow Citizens a few Questions.* N.p., ca. 1790. 12 ½ x 7 ¾ inches. Acc. 1790 P698.

The Library of Virginia's unique copy of an undated political broadside includes the autograph signature of Francis Corbin (1759–1821). Corbin represented Middlesex County in the House of Delegates from 1784 through 1794 and was a member of the Virginia Ratification Convention of 1788, during which he voted in favor of the federal Constitution. He campaigned for the United States House of Representatives at least three times but was never elected despite, according to a 1790 account, distributing among the electors "strong grogg & roasted piggs."

The undated petition from "a plain planter" may have been in Corbin's possession during the highly partisan 1790 congressional campaign. During the early months of that year the House of Representatives debated the constitutionality and propriety of receiving and acting on petitions from Quakers in the middle Atlantic states (including some from Virginia) who wanted Congress to take steps to curtail the importation of slaves from foreign countries. The Constitution, ratified two years before, restricted Congress from closing the foreign slave trade until 1808. It did, however, allow Congress to levy a tax on the importation of slaves.

Both the slave trade and the petitions both provoked heated debate in Congress and also, as the existence of the broadside suggests, during several subsequent political campaigns. James Madison, who took part in the debates in the House of Representatives, regretted that the issue had arisen at all: he described the discourse as "shamefully indecent as the matter was evidently misjudged." Some people believed that it was unconstitutional even for members of Congress to receive or consider petitions critical of the slave trade.

Whether the issue played a significant part in Corbin's unsuccessful 1790 congressional campaign is not known, nor is it known for certain when he wrote his name on the broadside. Considering the volatile nature of the debate, the broadside may have circulated anonymously in his district and perhaps been signed only after the election. BT

▶ *Grand Rally of the Whigs of Augusta, on Wednesday & Thursday Next.* [Augusta County], 1844. 12 x 17 ½ inches. Acc. 1844 W57.

With the 1828–1836 presidency of Democrat Andrew Jackson, an Indian fighter and planter of humble origins, a new era of mass politics emerged. Fiery stump speeches, boisterous and large barbecues, and spirited torchlight parades replaced the more sedate campaigns of the early Republic. Although it was slow to respond, the Whig Party finally grasped the realities of the new popular politics, especially the importance of establishing the supposedly egalitarian origins of any candidate. In 1840, for example, Whig campaign literature emphasized William Henry Harrison's reputation as a western Indian fighter, ignoring his lineage as the scion of an important Virginia family.

The printed announcement of the summertime "Grand Rally" in Augusta County was part of the presidential contest of 1844 between the Whig candidate Henry Clay, of Kentucky, a Virginian by birth, and the Democrat James K. Polk. The broadside concluded with a particular invitation to "the *Ladies*, from every part of the county, . . . to grace the occasion with their presence." Although women could not vote, they had by the 1840s become increasingly important in political campaigning and public discourse. Virginia's Whig women, for example, worked in the symbolic rustic "log cabins" commonly put up for party rallies, participated in political discussions, and eventually funded and erected a statue of Henry Clay in Richmond's Capitol Square. GK

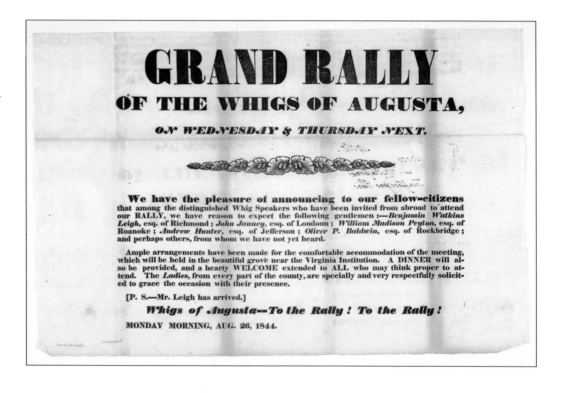

◀ *Virginia Springs. Richmond & Danville, South-side and Virginia and Tennessee Railroads! Summer Arrangement!* Richmond: Dispatch Steam Presses, 1855. 21 ¼ x 8 ¼ inches. Acc. 1855 V8.

Western Virginia's mineral-spring resorts were extremely popular in the nineteenth century. Travelers from throughout the United States, but especially the South, visited the resorts, taking the "cure" and enjoying the bucolic rural landscapes and restorative mountain air. On their way to the springs, tourists also sought the sublime and picturesque beauty of the state's natural wonders such as the Peaks of Otter and Natural Bridge. Virginia's gentry in particular frequented the springs, where the nightly dances and other entertainments made them a favorite place for courting a prospective wife or husband.

The expansion of the Old Dominion's railroad network during the 1850s made the long trip to western Virginia's resorts far easier. Broadside advertisements urged urban dwellers from Richmond and Petersburg to escape the humid, unhealthy summers by riding the train. Travelers could complete in one day—getting "through by day-light"—what had formerly taken several days over bumpy, dusty roads through the mountains. In 1855, Virginians visiting the springs could experience the state's newest railroad, the Virginia and Tennessee. The route linked several other rail lines and greatly accelerated the population growth and economic development of much of southwestern Virginia and eastern Tennessee. GK

WADE HAMPTON!

My Thoroughbred Stallion will stand the present season, commencing 1st April and ending 30th June, 1876, on my farm in Spotsylvania county, and also in Fredericksburg, Va., upon the following terms:

By the season, $15, to be discharged by the payment of $12, if paid on or before the 30th June, 1876.

The Groom is not authorized to make any deviation from the above terms without my written approval.

PEDIGREE:

WADE HAMPTON, a Blood Bay Horse, was foaled on the 17th day of April, 1869; is by Cohee, and grandson of Imported Skylark, dam Pad, by Wilton Brown; g. dam, Pad, by Walnut; gg. dam by Champion; ggg. dam by Gallatin; gggg. dam, Peggy, by Gallatin; ggggg. dam, Trumpetta, by Hephestion; gggggg. Peggy, by Bedford. Cohee, the sire of Hampton, was by Imported Skylark; his dam Agnes, by Imported Luzborough; his g. dam, Matilda (alias the old Cropp mare) was by Sir Archy; his gg. dam, Noli me Tangere, was by Colonel Tayloe's Topgallant, out of Castianira, the dam of Sir Archy.

C. B. MORTON.

March 22d, 1876.

[News Job Office print, Fredericksburg.]

◀ *Wade Hampton! My Thoroughbred Stallion will stand the present season, commencing 1st April and ending 30th June, 1876, on my farm in Spotsylvania county, and also in Fredericksburg, Va.* Fredericksburg: News Job Office Printers, 1876. 21 ¾ x 8 ¼ inches. Acc. 1876 M88.

On 22 March 1876, Spotsylvania County farmer and horse breeder Charles B. Morton (1835–1928) advertised that his seven-year-old bay stallion, Wade Hampton, a thoroughbred named after the famous Confederate cavalry officer, would stand for stud for $15.00 a season. Following the usual practice in such a business, Morton included the horse's pedigree. Traditionally printed on only one side of an unfolded, sometimes large, single sheet of paper and displayed "broadside" to the general public, imprints such as Morton's were a common medium for advertising items or services for sale.

Horse breeding and racing had enjoyed great popularity among Virginians during the colonial era and by the early nineteenth century elite jockey clubs in the major urban centers ran racetracks in the surrounding countryside, such as the Tree Hill and Fairfield grounds near Richmond. While wealthier Virginians funded and organized the courses, all classes of Virginia society attended race days. Eventually, widespread gambling, drinking, and other disorders at the tracks diminished the respectability of horse racing. Trotting matches, held at the state fairgrounds, became the province of less affluent Virginians, while those who could afford a fine racing steed might compete in steeplechases and foxhunts at exclusive clubs. DWG

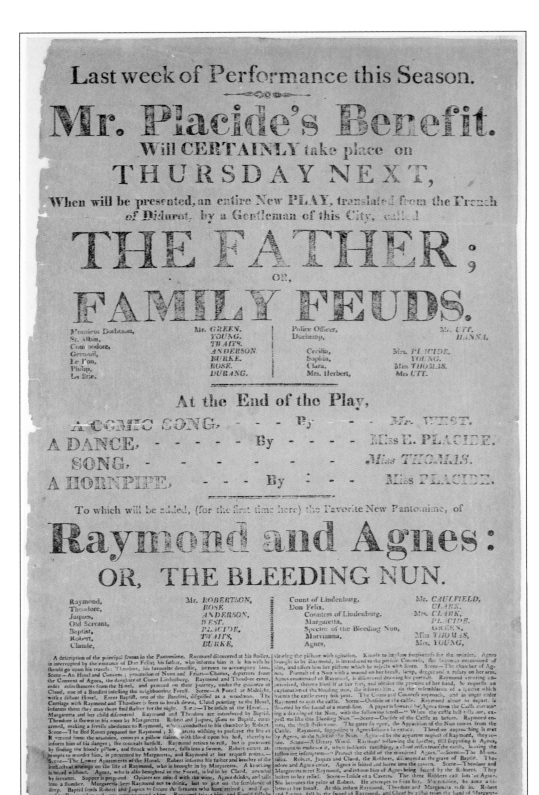

On the night of 26 December 1811 a crowd of more than six hundred holiday revelers packed the Richmond Theatre to attend a performance of *The Father; or Family Feuds* and a pantomime, *Raymond and Agnes: or the Bleeding Nun.* The Placide Stock Company was concluding its season at the new brick theater on Academy Square, across Broad Street from the Capitol grounds. During the opening of the pantomime's second act, however, frightened cries of "fire" erupted as a blaze suddenly spread from the stage scenery. Before the conflagration ended, seventy-two men, women, and children had lost their lives or were mortally injured, including Governor George W. Smith.

News of the disaster quickly reached other East Coast cities, many of which responded with great sympathy. The Library's collections include more than twenty discourses, sermons, accounts, and memorials from Boston, Baltimore, New York, and Philadelphia. The news affected so many in part because of an evangelical sentiment that viewed the fire as God's judgment on earthly amusements. James Muir, the minister of a Presbyterian church in Alexandria, for example, published *Repentance, or Richmond in Tears*, soon after the disaster.

Virginians, led by John Marshall, a Richmond resident and chief justice of the United States Supreme Court, raised money for a church to be erected on the theater site to commemorate the dead. Designed by noted architect Robert Mills, it was dedicated in 1814 as Monumental Church. A memorial in the portico lists the names of the fire's victims, buried beneath the church in a common crypt, and a bronze plaque near the church's entrance pays homage to the bravery of Gilbert Hunt, a slave blacksmith, who saved many from the flames with the aid of Dr. James D. McCaw.

In a compilation of accounts of the disaster printed in 1879, George D. Fisher remarked that the broadside for the evening's performance had been found in the papers of printer John Warrock and was at that time exhibited "hanging in a plain frame, on the south side of the State Library room, in the Capitol." GK

◀ *Keep us flying! Buy War Bonds.* United States Treasury Poster. Washington, D.C.: United States Government Printing Office, 1943. 28 x 20 ¼ inches.

▼ *Don't Shiver next Winter . . . Order Coal Now!* Solid Fuels Administration for War Poster. Washington, D.C.: United States Government Printing Office, 1944. 26 x 18½ inches.

▶ Dan V. Smith. *WAAC: This Is My War Too! Women's Army Auxiliary Corps. United States Army.* N.p., 1943. 38 x 25 inches.

More than three hundred thousand Virginians served in the armed forces or the merchant marine during World War II. Many others worked in civilian jobs directly supporting the war effort. With so many army and navy installations, essential ports, and defense industries in the state, Virginians fought the war both at home and abroad. Hundreds of posters issued by the United States Office of War Information and other government agencies between 1941 and 1945 reflected and encouraged such participation, bolstering morale, informing the public, soliciting donations, and urging further involvement in the war effort.

Posters were an especially effective and succinct means of communication on the home front. They appeared on store windows, in train stations, tacked to library bulletin boards, and pinned to post office walls across the commonwealth. At the war's end, most of them were discarded or forgotten. The Library of Virginia, however, received many of them as examples of federal or state publications, and thus preserved them as part of its extensive government documents collection.

Among the items in the Library's remarkable collection is one issued by the federal government's Solid Fuels Administration for War to remind citizens of the importance of ordering coal early to ward off the winter cold. Another, by Dan V. Smith, celebrated the Women's Auxiliary Army Corps, formed in 1942 and soon thereafter renamed the Women's Army Corps; by war's end, more than ninety-nine thousand American women had served in the corps. In a Treasury Department poster, a black airman urged Americans to "keep us flying" by buying war bonds. "Every single man, woman, and child," Franklin D. Roosevelt proclaimed on the eve of the war, "is a partner in the most tremendous undertaking in American history." Tacked up in a school cafeteria or corner grocery, wartime posters were vivid invitations to accept the president's call to action. JM

WAAC

THIS IS MY WAR TOO!
WOMEN'S ARMY AUXILIARY CORPS
UNITED · STATES · ARMY

DAN·V·SMITH

FINE ARTS

The Library of Virginia's extensive collection of paintings and statuary probably dates from 1872 or 1873 when the Library acquired a portrait of William Branch Giles and a bust of Robert E. Lee. It was then, too, that the General Assembly's Joint Committee on the Library authorized the fifty-year-old institution to begin collecting portraits of governors and of other notable Virginians. By 1904, nearly ten years after it had moved into its first permanent building, the State Library was exhibiting eighty-four portraits in its art gallery. Two years later, when the Library published its first catalog of artwork, the number had risen to ninety-six portraits and six pieces of statuary, some of which had been in other collections assembled by the commonwealth before the 1870s.

Most of the Library's works of art feature notable Virginians, but some are equally as important as examples of the work of particular artists, many of them Virginians. Among the best-known and most accomplished painters represented in the collection are Julien Binford (who completed the mural in the lobby of the second State Library Building), William Garl Brown, John A. Elder, Flavius J. Fisher, James Westhall Ford, Louis M. D. Guillaume, George P. A. Healy, William J. Hubard, George Bagby Matthews, Edward F. Peticolas, William Ludwell Sheppard, Charles Balthazar Julien Fevret de Saint-Mémin, and Thomas Sully.

The Library's sculpture collection contains two busts by Virginia sculptor Edward Virginius Valentine—Scottish poet Robert Burns, completed in 1870, and Virginia historian William Wirt Henry, finished in 1901. Valentine is further represented by the portrait busts of Confederate generals Albert Sidney Johnston, Robert E. Lee, and J. E. B. Stuart. The collection also contains examples of work by Caspar Buberl and Virginia sculptors Alexander Galt and Moses Ezekiel. Much of the Library's collection of portraits and statuary is exhibited in the Capitol of Virginia.

◀ Robert Stephenson Smyth Baden-Powell, first baron Baden-Powell of Gilwell (1857–1941). *John Smith* (ca. 1580–1631). Bronze, ca. 1905. Height 23 inches.

Robert S. S. Baden-Powell is best known as the founder of the Boy Scout movement of the early twentieth century. Born in London, Baden-Powell was the son of the Reverend H. G. Baden-Powell, a professor at Oxford, and Henrietta Grace Smyth. His mother's family claimed descent from Captain John Smith, whom Baden-Powell greatly admired.

Baden-Powell and his subject John Smith had much in common. Both were military men, authors, and key figures in British colonial affairs. John Smith actively promoted the London Company's colonization plans and in 1606 set sail for North America. As a member of the governing council at Jamestown, Smith explored the region and, in an episode later embellished by legend, was captured and held prisoner by Indian chief Powhatan. In 1608, Smith published his *True Relation of such Occurrences and accidents of noate as hath hapned in Virginia since the first planting of that Collony*, detailing his experiences in the new land. After venturing to New England in 1614, Smith returned to England where he remained, promoting English colonization until his death seventeen years later.

Baden-Powell began his military career as a junior officer in India and won rapid promotion and fame in colonial Africa. His resourceful defense of Mafeking, South Africa, in 1899–1900 against a much larger force during the Boer War brought him accolades and promotion to general. During his years as a British soldier, Baden-Powell published accounts of colonial Africa and *Aids to Scouting for NCOs and Men* (1905), a guide for training soldiers in military reconnaissance that presaged his work with the Boy Scouts.

After his heroism at Mafeking, Baden-Powell remained in South Africa as a military administrator, sculpting in clay as a release from the increasing burdens of bureaucratic paperwork. In 1903 Baden-Powell returned to England where he executed his bust of John Smith. Several collectors offered Baden-Powell large sums for the completed work, but at a private showing late in 1905, New York judge Charles Mayer, the son of a Virginian, claimed that "the only place for [Baden-Powell's] work was the newly remodeled state capitol at Richmond." The artist agreed, and in March 1906 Governor Claude A. Swanson reported to the General Assembly that he had received the bust, which was then in the State Library. In a joint resolution, the House and Senate proposed that Smith's likeness "be suitably mounted in the rotunda of the capitol as a memorial to the founder of the Colony of Virginia." The bust was later exhibited at the Jamestown Festival Park and then returned to the Library of Virginia. GK, EC

▲ Edward Virginius Valentine (1838–1930). *James Ewell Brown Stuart* (1833–1864). Marble, 1866. Height 30 inches.

The bust of famed Confederate cavalry leader J. E. B. Stuart is one of several works by Richmond sculptor Edward Virginius Valentine in the collections of the Library. Valentine studied in Europe from 1859 through the Civil War years before returning to Richmond in September 1865. In 1870, he received the commission for a sarcophagus for the tomb of Robert E. Lee in Lexington, Virginia. The resulting *Recumbent Lee* made Valentine's reputation and remains his best-known work. Valentine sculpted portrait busts of writers, politicians, and Confederate leaders; he also completed several genre studies of African Americans. Despite his obvious talent, Valentine refused to enter competitions, which he considered insulting to artists. To generate commissions, he instead opened his studio to visitors and marketed his work by placing photographs and casts of his various sculptures in store display windows in Baltimore, Boston, Cincinnati, New York, and Washington, D.C. By advertising and by personal recommendations, Valentine steadily built a reputation as a major southern artist.

In March 1866, a reporter for the *Richmond Whig* visited Valentine's studio and published a glowing report of the artist's work on busts of Thomas J. "Stonewall" Jackson and Stuart, noting that "Mrs. Jackson and Mrs. Stuart both visited the studio and assured Mr. Valentine that the works were perfect." Valentine soon thereafter cast the clay bust of Stuart in plaster. The Hollywood Memorial Association of the Ladies of Richmond exhibited the likeness at Stuart's grave in Richmond's Hollywood Cemetery on 31 May 1866 during ceremonies in honor of the Confederate dead. The *New York Daily News* reported that the bust "stood in front of a floral alcove, about eight feet high, formed of flowers and evergreens culled from the choicest collections." Lumpkin and Company, a Richmond photographic studio, sold a carte de visite of the display "for the benefit of the Hollywood Memorial Association."

William Alexander Stuart, the fallen cavalryman's brother, commissioned a marble bust from Valentine in 1869. In October, Valentine shipped his plaster bust to Jonathan Scott Hartley in New York, who carved the work with the artist's close guidance. Valentine showed a concern for detail that marked his entire career. At Valentine's request, Flora Stuart, the Confederate hero's widow, loaned buttons from Stuart's jacket and vest to assist the carver. The completed work arrived in Richmond early in 1870 and was displayed in a local store. The bust was still on public display, at the firm of Spades and Gibson, commission merchants, when Alexander Stuart in 1872 decided to donate the work to the commonwealth. Valentine wrote Stuart that "My mother informs me that you spoke of having it placed in the Library at the Capitol, but I think that in the Rotunda a more favorable light would be on it." Despite Valentine's comments, Stuart explicitly stated that "as long as the memory of my brother shall be dear to the people of Virginia, his native State, so long will it be the pleasure of myself and my posterity to allow his bust to remain in the library." The donation came at a time when the State Library had taken a renewed interest in expanding the scope of its collections. Governor Gilbert C. Walker, in accepting the gift for the Library, hoped that "its presence there will serve as an incentive to other public-spirited citizens to make similar contributions of busts, portraits, or relics of Virginians eminent in war and peace." GK

▶ Henry Inman (1801–1846). *John Marshall* (1755–1835). Oil on canvas, ca. 1832. 36 x 28 inches.

Henry Inman's portrait of John Marshall is renowned both as one of the artist's strongest works and as the best of the many artistic representations of the man who served as chief justice of the United States Supreme Court from 1801 to 1835. The Library's copy, painted by Inman soon after he had completed the original, captures the sagacity and wisdom of the aged jurist. Marshall posed for the original portrait in Philadelphia under inauspicious circumstances. He had traveled to consult with the distinguished physician and "father of American surgery" Philip Syng Physick regarding a gallstone. The Law Association of Philadelphia (now the Philadelphia Bar Association) commissioned Inman to capture Marshall's likeness while he was visiting the city. Only a day or so after sitting for the artist, Marshall underwent a successful operation for his condition.

Born in Utica, New York, Inman had moved his studio to Philadelphia after a distinguished career in New York City as a miniaturist, portraitist, and illustrator, as well as cofounder and officer of the National Academy of Design. His interests in Philadelphia included a partnership in a lithography firm, which almost immediately issued a print of the Marshall portrait. Asher Brown Durand (1796–1886) requested a copy of the painting from Inman in 1832 in order to make an engraving for publication in his *National Portrait Gallery of Distinguished Americans* (1837). Inman complied, and Marshall later purchased the second oil-on-canvas portrait for his daughter Mary who lived in Richmond and was married to Jacquelin Burwell Harvie. Two of her daughters, Ann F. and Emily Harvie, inherited the painting and lent it to the Virginia State Library. Beginning in the 1880s, the Library for many years exhibited the portrait in the Capitol among the likenesses of other notable Virginians. Emily Harvie bequeathed the painting to the Library of Virginia on her death in 1920. GK

▲ Howard W. Montague (1810–1876), attributed. *Virginia State Capitol*. Oil on canvas, ca.
1860. 17 ½ x 21 ½ inches.

The work of an untrained artist, the painting
is attributed to Howard W. Montague, a Baptist
minister from Essex County, and is believed to
have been completed in approximately 1860.
Although little is known of the view's origins, it
is nevertheless important as a historical source
for at least two reasons.

First, Montague included in the left-hand
portion of his painting of the Capitol a partial
view of Richmond's city hall, an intriguing
example of architecture in its own right. The
well-known southern architect Robert Mills—
designer of Richmond's Monumental Church
and the District of Columbia's Washington
Monument—completed a design for "a new
courthouse and town hall" in March 1816.
Mills's design, captured in Montague's painting,
was widely admired. One observer went so far as
to declare its architecture "the most perfect in
the city; even more so than the capitol." The
building with its two impressive four-column por-
ticos and large, central interior space was razed
in 1873 and a new city hall later erected on the
same site.

Second, while the painting's handsome colors
may be only a clever device by a self-taught
artist to infuse his rather flat building with some
semblance of three-dimensional depth, the hues
might also convey an idea of the Capitol's general appearance at the time. Period black-and-
white photographs suggest that the Capitol was
painted with successive schemes of contrasting
colors but of course do not reveal specific col-
orations. Perhaps the unassuming painting captured a detail otherwise lost. Moreover, the
artist's use of color reflects a common architectural technique of the period. For years, the
Capitol's exterior brickwork remained exposed,
although by at least 1796, "to make them appear
like stone," the brick walls and columns had
been "partially whitened with common white-
wash." Later, workers further refined the structure's appearance, covering the red brick with
stucco, which was then scored and painted to
resemble more expensive and more substantial
stonework. EC

▲ Artist unknown. *Simón Bolívar* (1783–1830). Egg tempera on wood panel, ca. 1827. 13 x 11 inches.

The son of a wealthy Venezuelan aristocrat of Spanish descent, Simón Bolívar was educated in Europe, where he was greatly influenced by the revolutionary writing of Jacques Rousseau and of Voltaire. Fired by the vision of an independent Hispanic America, he returned to Venezuela in 1807 determined to free his homeland from Spanish rule. For twenty-three years he struggled against the Spanish, political rivals, royalists, and others to achieve independence for much of northern South America. In time, however, Bolívar realized that his dreams of an independent, unified hemispheric organization were threatened by civil war. Perceiving that his very presence posed a threat to the peace of several newly independent nations, Bolívar retired to Colombia, where he died of tuberculosis in 1830.

Often compared to George Washington, Bolívar had already achieved a revered place in the history of Latin America—and in the imaginations of North Americans and Europeans as well. It was not unusual for merchants, ship's captains, diplomats, and other visitors to South America to explore the sites of Bolívar's greatest triumphs and most desperate setbacks—and to seek small tokens associated with his fight for independence. For citizens of the United States in particular, the exploits of "El Liberator" reconfirmed the sanctity of the revolutionary spirit. The small portrait of "the South American Washington," painted by an unknown artist, was brought to the United States from Peru in 1827 by Captain William R. Smith. In 1875 Benjamin H. Smith presented it to the State Library. DWG

▼ James Westhall Ford (1806–1868). *The Prophet Wabokieskiek, Black Hawk, and Nasheaskuk.* Oil on canvas, 1833. 30 x 35 inches.

In the spring of 1832, a band of Fox, Sauk, and Winnebago Indians under the leadership of the famed warrior Black Hawk attempted to halt the wave of white settlement in the upper Mississippi Valley. After nearly four months, however, Black Hawk and several of his advisors were at last captured and for nearly a year held hostage, eventually at Fort Monroe, Virginia.

En route to Hampton Roads under army escort, Black Hawk and several companions arrived in Richmond on 28 April 1833 where they spent two and a half days at the Eagle Hotel on Main Street. Although he was undoubtedly rushed, the artist James Westhall Ford managed to paint a group portrait of Black Hawk flanked on the right by his son, Nasheaskuk, and on the left by the medicine man Wabokieskiek (also known as the Prophet). In accordance with earlier orders issued by President Andrew Jackson, Black Hawk wore a double-breasted coat instead of his native garb. Ford advertised the painting in the 17 May edition of the *Richmond Whig and Public Advertiser,* inviting the public to visit his studio where, for a fee of twenty-five cents, they could view the triple portrait as well as a full-length study of Black Hawk alone. The artist also completed a dual painting of Black Hawk and the Prophet. A Pennsylvanian, Ford had come to Virginia in 1823 to paint a portrait of Martha Jefferson Randolph for Thomas Jefferson. Ford continued to work in Virginia until 1859. ST, DWG

◀ John Adams Elder (1833–1895). *Appomattox.*
Oil on canvas, ca. 1888. 29 x 23 inches.

After five years of study in Germany, the
artist John Elder worked in New York City until
he established a studio in his hometown of
Fredericksburg, Virginia, on the eve of the Civil
War. Elder enlisted in the Confederate army and
during the war was frequently detailed to Richmond
to make drawings for the Ordnance Department.
In the postwar years he became known for his
finely rendered genre scenes of southern life, but
gained particular fame for his paintings of former
Confederate generals and of wartime scenes, such
as his oversize depiction of the Confederate coun-
terattack at the Battle of the Crater during the
defense of Petersburg.

Like so many of his works, Elder's several variant paintings entitled *Appomattox* emphasized the
ruin of war as well as the spirit of the Southern
soldier. Elder adapted the figure from one of his
larger works, a painting of Robert E. Lee deliver-
ing his farewell to the soldiers of the Army of
Northern Virginia, and completed both full- and
three-quarter-length views of the contemplative
Confederate veteran. In 1888, the artist used the
same figure for a bronze statue commissioned by
the R. E. Lee Camp, No. 2, United Confederate
Veterans, of Alexandria. That same year,
Secretary of the Commonwealth Henry W.
Flournoy, as ex officio state librarian, reported the
purchase of one of the three-quarter-length studies of the soldier and announced its installation in
the State Library. DWG

◄ George Peter Alexander Healy (1813–1894). *William Segar Archer* (1789–1885). Oil on canvas, 1846. 30 x 25 inches.

William Segar Archer was a native of Amelia County, where he practiced law after graduating from the College of William and Mary. Following two terms in the General Assembly, he was elected to Congress in 1819. There he served sixteen years, eventually as a supporter of President Andrew Jackson and from 1829 to 1835 as chairman of the House Committee on Foreign Affairs. He broke with Jackson during the president's second term, allied with the new Whig Party, and lost his seat in Congress in 1835. Six years later, a small Whig majority in the General Assembly, which then selected Virginia's United States senators, chose Archer to replace the Democratic incumbent for a six-year term. Archer's Senate service plunged him into controversies over slavery, territorial expansion, the annexation of Texas, and the disruption of the Whig Party during the administration of his college classmate President John Tyler. By the end of Archer's term, the Democrats had regained control of the General Assembly and refused to return him to the Senate. He retired to Amelia County, where he died in 1855. Archer never married, and his will left his extensive properties to his three sisters, one of whom, Martha J. Archer, presented his portrait to the State Library in 1881.

A highly successful portraitist, George P. A. Healy painted his likeness of Senator Archer in 1846, probably in Washington, D.C., following a year of travel throughout the United States painting portraits of such prominent Americans as Andrew Jackson, Henry Clay, and John Quincy Adams for King Louis Philippe of France. Archer impressed the personable Healy as "the Virginian, tall, dark, refined in appearance and manner." A native of Boston, Healy was largely self-taught as a painter, although he eagerly sought out the leading artists of his era and closely studied their works. Healy had visited Paris in 1834 and had soon thereafter received commissions for portraits in both France and England. In 1842 he returned to the United States, traveled often to France, settled in Chicago in 1855, then returned again to Europe in 1866. He continued to cross the Atlantic regularly and died in Chicago in 1894. Healy was as prolific as he was popular, and his work won considerable prestige for American art at home and abroad. JK

◄ W. H. M. Cox (fl. 1870–1890). *Fitzhugh Lee* (1835–1905). Oil on canvas, 1890. 33 x 28 inches.

W. H. M. Cox was a portrait artist who worked in Richmond about 1890 and whose likeness of Rosa Wood Flournoy, in colonial costume for a ball, had been exhibited to local acclaim. Shortly before Governor Fitzhugh Lee left office in 1890, Cox received the commission to paint his official portrait. Lee's successor, Governor Philip Watkins McKinney (1832–1899), so admired the painting that he secured Cox's services for his own portrait. Both paintings hang in the Capitol. Cox had worked as a painter in Colorado Springs, Colorado, during the 1870s and 1880s and exhibited works in Denver in 1883. He had moved to Texas about 1886 and sometime afterward arrived in Virginia. His work and whereabouts after 1890 are unknown.

His subject, Fitzhugh Lee, was born in Fairfax County and graduated from the United States Military Academy at West Point in 1856. In 1861, he resigned his commission to enter the Confederate army. Lee served with distinction, first as the colonel of the 1st Virginia Cavalry, then as a brigadier general and later as a major general. He was severely wounded at Winchester in 1864. After his term as governor of Virginia from 1886 to 1890, Lee served as U.S. consul in Cuba from 1896 to 1898, during which time diplomatic relations with Spain deteriorated. When the Spanish-American War began, Lee received an appointment as a major general of volunteers and later, following Spain's quick surrender, as the military governor in Havana, serving through 1900. Lee died in Washington, D.C., in 1905, while serving as president of the Jamestown Ter-Centennial Exposition. JK

▶ John Adams Elder (1833–1895). *Jubal Anderson Early* (1816–1894). Oil on canvas, ca. 1869. 29 x 25 inches.

John Elder painted Jubal Early's portrait sometime after the Confederate general's return to his home in Virginia from a four-year exile. Early's tribulations began in the closing months of the Civil War, when his defeat in the Shenandoah Valley in March 1865 prompted a public outcry against him and caused his removal from command by Robert E. Lee. Early returned to his home in Rocky Mount, Virginia, suffering from pneumonia and the rheumatism he had contracted during the Mexican War. After Lee's surrender and the dissolution of the Army of Northern Virginia, Early decided to start southward on 21 May 1865 to join General Edmund Kirby-Smith in Texas and continue the struggle. He arrived too late, however, and learned that the forces in Texas had already capitulated.

Early did not believe that he had been covered by the terms of Lee's surrender and he refused to request a parole. From Texas he went on to Cuba, then into Mexico, and from there finally to Canada, intending never to return to the United States. His continued refusal to ask for a pardon kept him in Canada for three years until the lame-duck president Andrew Johnson issued a blanket unconditional amnesty for combatants against the United States in December 1868. While the amnesty technically did not cover high-ranking officers, Early interpreted it as the government's acknowledgment that it could not hold former Confederate officers responsible for resisting Union "usurpations and encroachments." In January 1869 Early notified his niece Ruth Hairston Early that he was headed home by way of Missouri. He arrived in May and sometime thereafter sat for the portrait by John Elder.

Over time Early became the spokesman for the veneration of the Confederacy and its heroes and thereby redeemed his reputation. While he was never personally popular, Early's "patriarchal beard gave distinction to his appearance" and he became widely admired throughout the South. Elder caught some of that patriarchial aura in his portrait. The painting was presented to the State Library by Jubal Early's niece Ruth H. Early in 1914.

John Elder at age seventeen had studied with Daniel Huntington (1816–1906) in New York City and for the ensuing five years with Emanuel Leutze (1816–1868) in Düsseldorf, Germany. After the Civil War, Elder worked in Richmond, painting southern and wartime scenes as well as portraits, including several of Robert E. Lee. While in Biloxi, Mississippi, working on a portrait of Jefferson Davis, Elder contracted malaria. The disease, combined with the artist's weakness for alcohol, contributed to his slow decline during the last five years of his life. DWG

Elevation of the South Front of that part of the Building which is proposed to be first erected, as shewn in N.º II.

Elevation of the South Front as it will appear on completion of the Whole Design, as shewn in the plan N.º I.

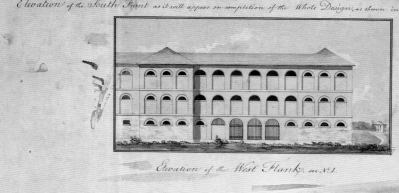

Elevation of the West Flank, as N.º I.

◀ ▼ Benjamin Henry Latrobe (1764–1820). *Elevations and Drawings for the Virginia "Penitentiary House."* Ink and watercolor on paper, 1797. "Elevation of the South Front, . . . " 19 ⅞ x 14 ¾ inches; and "View in Perspective of the Gate," 19 ⅞ x 14 ⅛ inches (*detail below*). Department of Corrections, Drawings and Plans, 1797, Record Group 42.

Benjamin Henry Latrobe remains one of America's most significant architects and engineers: the Bank of Pennsylvania, the Philadelphia Waterworks, the United States Capitol, and the Roman Catholic Cathedral of Baltimore stand as the most prominent examples of his genius. Born in Fulneck, near Leeds in Yorkshire, England, Latrobe worked for John Smeaton, Britain's most-accomplished engineer, and then for the noted architect Samuel Pepys Cockerell. Latrobe arrived in the United States early in 1796 and spent the next several years in Virginia.

The Virginia State Penitentiary, since demolished, was Latrobe's first major public commission in America and a monument to the era's penal reform movement. The General Assembly had already, in 1796, agreed to restrict the death sentence to cases of first-degree murder. The legislature had also instituted a revised system of labor and confinement, a reform that was to be implemented within a new penitentiary. Latrobe's elevations of the south front of the proposed prison building show an entryway and a "keeper's house" at the center of the ranges of cells.

The plan reflects the Enlightenment's reliance on solitary confinement and surveillance as a means to reform prisoners. The very term *penitentiary* suggested a new way of dealing with criminals. Throughout most of the eighteenth century, the reform of criminals had been thought impossible, and thus public ostracism and severe punishment—including execution—were routine. In contrast, later reformers emphasized that criminality was a product of environment and that individuals could redeem themselves through "penitence"—pondering their sins in solitary reflection. Latrobe's plan also called for the separation of male and female prisoners, a practice seldom followed in earlier jails. In completing his "View in Perspective" of the prison's solemn and imposing main entrance, Latrobe adapted elements from English architect George Dance's design for Newgate Prison, especially the stark festoons of chains bracketing the inscription over the passageway. The design detail, however, was not included in the construction of the building, completed by Major John Clarke after Latrobe left Virginia in 1798. Only seven sheets of Latrobe's design for the Virginia prison survive. GK

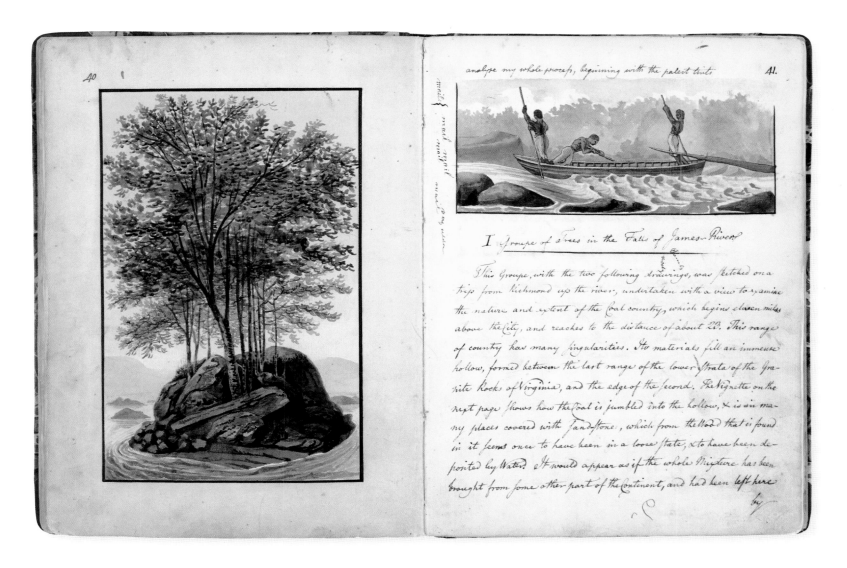

▲ Benjamin Henry Latrobe (1764–1820). *Groupe of Trees in the Falls of James River*, from "An Essay on Landscape, explained in tinted Drawings." Watercolor, ink, and pencil on paper, 1798–1799. Acc. 25060.

Architect, naturalist, and traveler, Benjamin Henry Latrobe compiled a two-volume sketchbook, entitled "An Essay on Landscape," in 1798–1799. A portion of the drawings and notes chronicle a trip from Richmond to Cumberland County on behalf of the Appomattox Navigation Company, which sought his suggestions on how to improve navigation along the Appomattox River. Latrobe prepared the two books for the great-granddaughter of Governor Alexander Spotswood, Susan Catharine Spotswood (1774–1853), who was studying drawing and watercolor painting with Latrobe.

In a note appended to the second volume, Latrobe explained that some of the drawings were made in Richmond in September and October 1798 while he was supervising construction of the state penitentiary, which he had designed. Although he complained about "defects in the drawings," Latrobe was fond of the two sketchbooks, commenting that the second one had "travelled with me in all my excursions . . . & has been my favorite, & consoling companion in solitude, to the injury of its external appearance."

The Library of Virginia received the volumes from the estate of John Stewart Bryan about 1952. Two sketches, together titled *Groupe of Trees in the Falls of James River,* reflect Latrobe's affection for Virginia's riverways. The artist commented that the "Banks of the Virginia rivers at their Falls are inexhaustible in beautiful groupes, and perhaps of none more than of James river."

His views of the James and Appomattox Rivers also depict landscape features of "many singularities," features that in fact were often obstructions to river traffic, even hampering the progress of the shallow-draft, elongated wooden craft known as the "batteau." However, whenever "the Water in the river is moderately high," Latrobe commented, "a batteau will carry 12 Hogsheads of Tobacco, or from 200 to 300 Bushels of Coal." Of his small sketch of three African American rivermen poling their boat upstream, Latrobe wrote that his illustration was inaccurate: his "batteau" was far "too short: they are from 60 to 75 feet long, & from 5 to 6 feet broad." He added, too, that "Each of them is managed by 3 Men, who with great dexterity often carry them 30 Miles against the stream in one day." JM, EC

◀ David Hunter Strother (1816–1888). *Contrabands in Virginia.* Pen-and-ink sketches, July 1862. Pierre Morand Memorial Collection. Rare Book Collection.

The three sketches of Virginia slaves who had escaped to Union lines are from a series of approximately three dozen drawings by David Hunter Strother assembled in the postwar years by a Philadelphia collector, Pierre Morand (fl. 1890s). In 1896, Morand sold the collection to John Codman Ropes (1836–1899), a prominent Boston lawyer and ardent collector of Civil War materials. Ropes had donated his own library to the Military Historical Society of Massachusetts and purchased the Morand collection of drawings in order to augment his already generous contribution. The correspondence between Ropes, Morand, and the society's librarian concerning the purchases, along with forty-six drawings by Strother and several lesser-known artists, were bound into a single volume entitled "The Pierre Morand Memorial Album of Original Drawings." At some later date, the society's library was sold, and the volume passed into the possession of a private collector. The Library of Virginia purchased the bound collection in 1984.

The artist David Hunter Strother was born in Martinsburg in what is now West Virginia, first studied art in Philadelphia, and later continued his studies in France and Italy in 1840–1843. On his return to the United States in 1844, Strother began publishing his illustrations in magazines and books. In December 1853, under the pseudonym "Porte Crayon," he contributed an illustrated account of a trip into Randolph County, Virginia, to *Harper's New Monthly Magazine.* It was Strother's first essay in what became an enormously popular and extensive series of articles about life in Virginia and the South that appeared in *Harper's* throughout the 1850s. He became one of the magazine's highest-paid contributors and in 1857 gathered some of his articles into a volume entitled *Virginia Illustrated . . . , by Porte Crayon,* with 138 of his pen-and-ink drawings.

A Unionist, Strother at the outbreak of war volunteered his services to the North. He entered the army as a captain and in June 1862 won a promotion to lieutenant colonel of the 3d West Virginia Volunteers. His knowledge of western Virginia and his skill as an artist made him a valuable aide on the staffs of Generals George B. McClellan, Nathaniel Banks, John Pope, and David Hunter. The artist, however, resigned his commission in September 1864, pleading poor health. Although Strother hoped to resume his former career, literary tastes had changed, and his writings and sketches never regained their prewar popularity. From 1879 to 1885 he served as consul general in Mexico City, then retired to Charleston, West Virginia, where he died in 1888. JK

▶ William Ludwell Sheppard (1833–1912). *Sharp-shooter.* Pen and ink, ca. 1882. Bound in the special first edition of Carlton McCarthy (1847–1936), *Detailed Minutiae of Soldier Life in the Army of Northern Virginia, 1861–1865.* Richmond: C. McCarthy and Company, 1882.

Born in Richmond, William Ludwell Sheppard attended the Richmond Academy, where he studied under Claudius Crozet, the famed engineer, draftsman, and veteran of the Napoleonic Wars. After a further period of study in New York in the late 1850s, the young artist traveled abroad, visiting European museums and galleries. With the outbreak of the Civil War, Sheppard returned home and enlisted as a private in the Richmond Howitzers. Later promoted to second lieutenant and assigned to the Army of Northern Virginia's Topographical Department, he worked as an assistant engineer and draftsman. After the war, Sheppard returned to painting, specializing in nostalgic southern genre scenes and romanticized depictions of Confederate army life. He won a national reputation for his illustrations in the most popular magazines of the day, including *Harper's Weekly, Frank Leslie's Illustrated Newspaper,* and *St. Nicholas: An Illustrated Magazine for Young Folks.* Sheppard also completed much of the artwork for the *Century Magazine's* four-volume *Battles and Leaders of the Civil War* and illustrated books by several fellow southerners, including the Virginia novelists John Esten Cooke and Thomas Nelson Page.

Among Sheppard's best-known work is a collection of pen-and-ink drawings completed for Carlton McCarthy's *Detailed Minutiae of Soldier Life in the Army of Northern Virginia, 1861–1865,* published in Richmond in 1882 and compiled from a series of vignettes of military life first published in the *Southern Historical Society Papers* between 1876 and 1879. The Library's leatherbound first edition of the McCarthy volume includes Sheppard's original thirty-one drawings, such as the *Sharp-shooter,* commissioned for the project. DWG

FRONT ELEVATION.

▲ First Battalion Virginia Volunteers Armory, 1895. City Hall Collection, City of Richmond, Local Records Collection. 22 ¾ x 24 inches. Acc. 34886.

In 1993, Richmond city employees discovered a collection of architectural drawings thought to be primarily from the 1870–1910 files of the city engineer. The drawings have since been deposited as part of the Library's Local Records Collection and have already yielded fascinating details about Gilded Age Richmond.

The front elevation of the armory planned for the First Battalion Virginia Volunteers on Richmond's West Leigh Street is from one of two designs proposed for the building. The second, a less-expensive plan for a single-story structure, was never adopted. With its elaborate crenelated towers and terra-cotta decoration, the armory was one of three built in the city in the 1890s. Together, they accommodated local military units and served as social centers, secure storage for arms, drill facilities, and meeting halls. The Leigh Street armory housed the four companies of the famous First Battalion Virginia Volunteers, drawn from Jackson Ward, the city's foremost African American community. Such was the immense pride in the new facility that the neighborhood held a weeklong "Military Bazaar" to mark the armory's 12 October 1895 opening, complete with a series of banquets, drill exhibitions, and elaborate receptions.

The battalion's use of the armory was unfortunately brief. After the Spanish-American War, the Richmond City Council voted in March 1899 to convert the "Colored armory" for use as the Monroe School. Following long service to the city in various ways, the former armory was declared surplus in 1988. It is the oldest armory building now standing in Virginia. SR

▼ Robert Mills (1781–1855). Plan of Richmond City Hall, 1816. City Hall Collection, City of Richmond, Local Records Collection. 10 x 14 inches Acc. 34886. .

The most significant drawing in the City Hall Collection, and one far older than the others, is an 1816 plan by Robert Mills for the first Richmond city hall. Mills, the architect for the Washington Monument in the nation's capital and Richmond's Monumental Church, is considered the first American-born professional architect. Mills came to Richmond in 1816 and immediately began working on a drawing for the "Courthouse," noting in his journal on 18 March that he had "Met the Commissioners of Court H. who approved of plan & met the Town Hall who confirmed it." The first sessions of the city council and courts were held in the building in December 1818.

Mills's building stood in the area between Capitol Square and Broad Street and remained the center of local government for more than fifty years, housing courts, offices, and the city's archives. Despite its long history, relatively little is known about the building. Hysteria over the structural integrity of older public buildings in the wake of the collapse of a courtroom gallery in the Capitol in April 1870 prompted the demolition of the city hall in 1873. It was replaced by the High Victorian Gothic gray-stone hall built on the site between 1887 and 1894.

Besides providing one of the few images of Richmond's first city hall, the drawing also presents an excellent example of the draftsman's craft in the nineteenth century. Mills plotted the finely detailed intersections of lines by "pricking" tiny holes through the paper. Practically invisible to the unaided eye, the prick-marks aid in the identification of Mills as the author of the important document. SR

▶ Ernest Gilbert. *Proposed Layout of Approach to Virginia War Memorial in Byrd Park.* Watercolor on paperboard, 1932. Bureau of Surveys and Design, Department of Public Works, Richmond. City Hall Collection, City of Richmond, Local Records Collection. 24 x 31 inches. Acc. 34886.

The Virginia War Memorial Commission was created by an act of the General Assembly on 20 March 1924 to erect a memorial honoring those Virginians who had served in the World War. Although it was agreed that the monument should be located in Richmond, once the commission had selected a site in William Byrd Park at the head of Blanton Avenue, "there arose a great hue and cry." After several hearings, the commission's decision was upheld, in part because the city had contributed the land and agreed to provide "adequate landscape treatment" and wider roads "approaching and adjacent to the memorial." The commission unanimously selected a design proposed by architects Paul Cret, of Philadelphia, and Marcellus E. Wright, of Richmond. Work began in January 1926 but three months later ceased in the face of renewed public agitation. In response, the General Assembly ruled that the memorial should be a carillon, "or singing tower." The commission then hired the Richmond firm of Carneal, Johnston, and Wright (in association with Cram and Ferguson, of Boston) to design the tower. The Carillon was dedicated on 15 October 1932.

This proposed plan met Richmond's promise to address the "beautification of the grounds and approaches to" the carillon. A slightly revised version was approved by the City Planning Commission on 18 July 1932. The monument, casting its slender silhouette eastward, overlooks an expansive lawn, which was created by clearing trees along four blocks of Blanton Avenue. SM

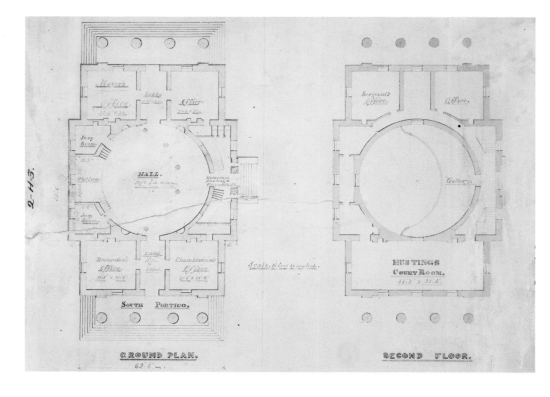

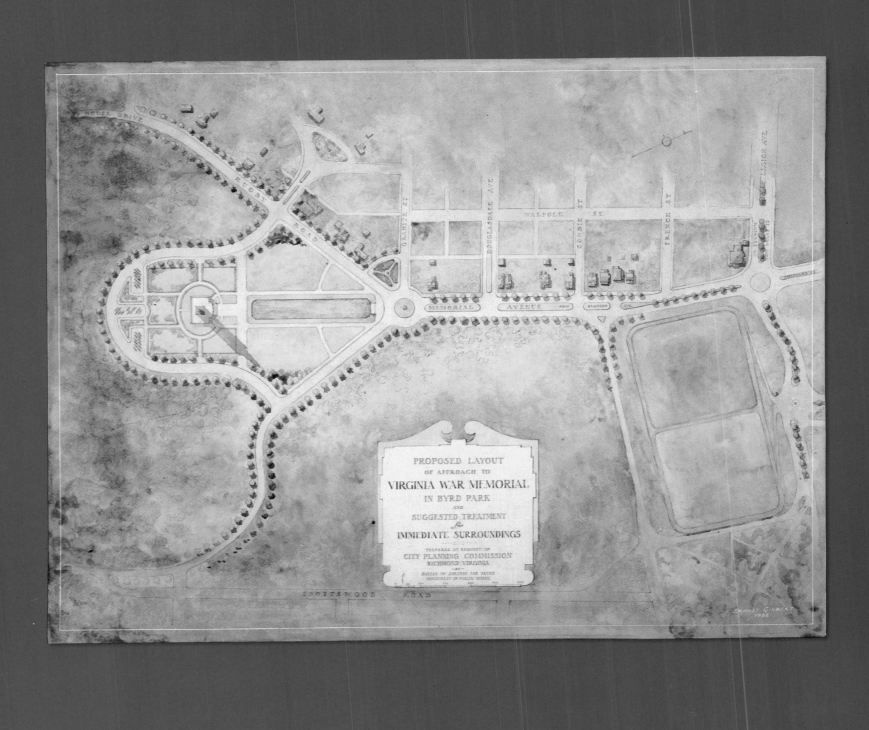

PROPOSED LAYOUT
OF APPROACH TO
VIRGINIA WAR MEMORIAL
IN BYRD PARK
AND
SUGGESTED TREATMENT
for
IMMEDIATE SURROUNDINGS

PREPARED AT REQUEST OF
CITY PLANNING COMMISSION
RICHMOND VIRGINIA

BUREAU OF STREETS AND DRAINS
DEPARTMENT OF PUBLIC WORKS

FURTHER EXPLORE VIRGINIA'S TREASURES

The rare and important items highlighted in this book are only a tiny fraction of the treasures held by the Library of Virginia. We invite you to visit the Library to consult our collections in person. You may also wish to visit our home page on the World Wide Web at http://leo.vsla.edu. The Library's home page provides access to our on-line catalogs for books, periodicals, and other printed materials; electronic card indexes to numerous archival collections; and images of manuscripts, records, and photographs from selected collections. You can also reach Virginia-wide projects such as the Virginia Newspaper Project and the Virginia Colonial Records Project. In addition, the following printed bibliographies, abstracts, archival guides, and inventories provide access to many of our most important collections. Researchers should consult the Library's Publications and Educational Services Division for further information on the Library's resources in print, especially printed editions of state documents, church records, and personal papers. A complete list of in-print titles is also accessible through the Library's home page.

Auditor of Public Accounts Inventory, compiled by John S. Salmon and J. Christian Kolbe (1992).

Board of Public Works Inventory, compiled by John S. Salmon (2d ed., rev., 1996).

Bacon's Rebellion: Abstracts of Materials in the Colonial Records Project, compiled by John Davenport Neville (1976).

Cavaliers and Pioneers: Abstracts of Virginia Land Patents and Grants, 1623–1732, abstracted by Nell Marion Nugent, volumes 1–3 (1934, 1977, 1979; reprint, 1992).

A Guide to Bible Records in the Archives Branch, Virginia State Library, compiled by Lyndon H. Hart III (1985).

A Guide to Business Records in the Virginia State Library and Archives, compiled by Conley L. Edwards III, Gwendolyn D. Clark, and Jennifer D. McDaid (rev. ed., 1994).

A Guide to Church Records in the Archives Branch, Virginia State Library and Archives, compiled by Jewell T. Clark and Elizabeth Terry Long (1981; reprint, 1988).

A Guide to Genealogical Notes and Charts in the Archives Branch, Virginia State Library, compiled by Lyndon H. Hart III (1983; reprint, 1988).

A Guide to State Records in the Archives Branch, Virginia State Library, compiled by John S. Salmon (1985; reprint, 1988).

Maps Relating to Virginia, compiled by Earl G. Swem (1914; reprint, 1989).

More Virginia Broadsides Before 1877, by Ray O. Hummel, Jr. (1975).

Office of the Second Auditor Inventory, compiled by Emily J. Salmon and John S. Salmon (1981).

Portraits and Statuary of Virginians Owned by the Virginia State Library, the Medical College of Virginia, the Virginia Museum of Fine Arts and Other State Agencies: An Illustrated Catalog, by Ray O. Hummel, Jr., and Katherine M. Smith (1977).

A Preliminary Guide to Pre-1904 County Records in the Virginia State Library and Archives, compiled by Suzanne Smith Ray, Lyndon H. Hart III, and J. Christian Kolbe (1987; reprint, 1994).

A Preliminary Guide to Pre-1904 Municipal Records in the Archives Branch, Virginia State Library and Archives, compiled by Lyndon H. Hart III and J. Christian Kolbe (1987).

Southeastern Broadsides Before 1877: A Bibliography, edited by Ray O. Hummel, Jr. (1971).

Treasurer's Office Inventory, compiled by Emily J. Salmon, revised by John S. Salmon (2d ed., 1981).

Virginia Land Office Inventory, compiled by Daphne S. Gentry, revised by John S. Salmon (3d ed., reprint, 1988).

Virginia Legislative Petitions: Bibliography, Calendar, Abstracts from Original Sources, 6 May 1776–21 June 1782, edited by Randolph W. Church (1984).

Virginiana in the Printed Book Collections of the Virginia State Library, edited by Donald Haynes (1975).

KEY TO CONTRIBUTORS

BB   Barbara Batson

NB   Nancy S. Brantley

EC   Edward D. C. Campbell, Jr.

RC   Robert Young Clay

MF   Mark Fagerburg

DSG   Daphne S. Gentry

HG   Henry D. Grunder

DWG   Donald Wilson Gunter

LH   Lyndon H. Hart III

KH   Kelly Henderson Hayes

GK   Gregg D. Kimball

JK   John T. Kneebone

WL   William E. Lange

JM   Jennifer Davis McDaid

MM   Marianne M. McKee

SM   Stacy Gibbons Moore

TR   Tom H. Ray

DR   W. Donald Rhinesmith

SR   Selden Richardson

ES   Emily Jones Salmon

BT   Brent Tarter

ST   Sandra Gioia Treadway

MW   Minor T. Weisiger

INDEX

The Common Wealth: Treasures from the Collections of the Library of Virginia was designed by Paris Ashton-Bressler of the Virginia Department of General Services, Office of Graphic Communications. Page layout was produced by Paris Ashton-Bressler using Apple Power Macintosh 7600/120 and QuarkXPress 3.32. Text was composed in Goudy Roman and Italic. Printed on acid-free Productolith dull-coated paper, 100-lb. text by Carter Printing Company, Richmond, Virginia.